STUDIES IN
ANTHROPOLOGICAL METHOD

General Editors

GEORGE AND LOUISE SPINDLER
Stanford University

STUDYING THE YĄNOMAMÖ

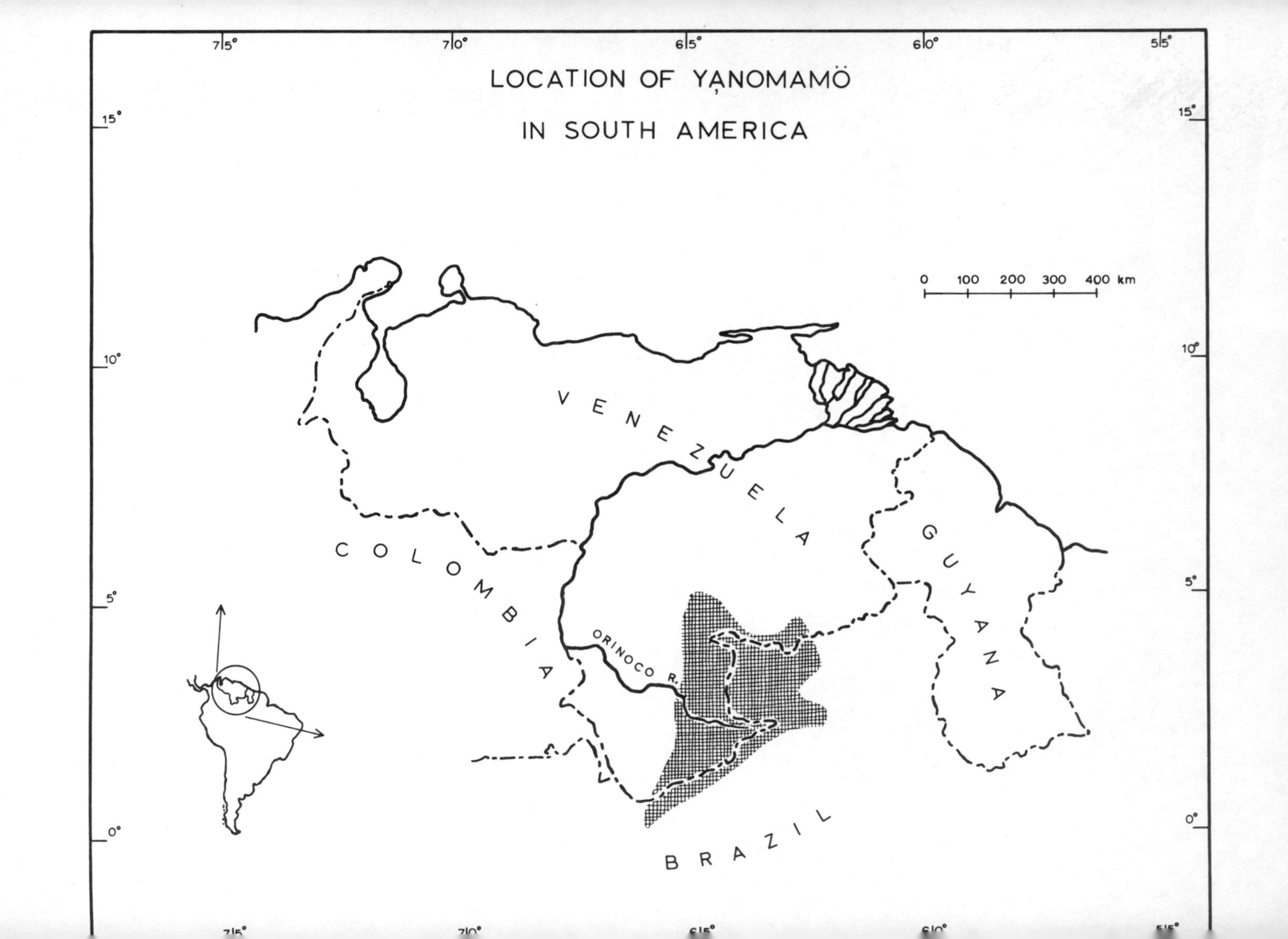
LOCATION OF YĄNOMAMÖ
IN SOUTH AMERICA
75°
70°
65°
60°
55°
15°
10°
5°
0°
0
100
200
300
400 km
VENEZUELA
COLOMBIA
GUYANA
BRAZIL
ORINOCO R.

STUDYING THE YĄNOMAMÖ

NAPOLEON A. CHAGNON
Pennsylvania State University

HOLT, RINEHART AND WINSTON, INC.
New York Chicago San Francisco Atlanta
Dallas Montreal Toronto London Sydney

For Carlene, Darius, and Lisa

with love and gratitude for your patience
while I lived so long away from you

and for Leslie A. White

teacher and friend, a scholar whose words
all students of anthropology should read

Library of Congress Cataloging in Publication Data

Chagnon, Napoleon A. 1938-
Studying the Yąnomamö

(Studies in anthropological method)
1. Anthropology—Field work. 2. Yanomama
Indians. I. Title. II. Series.
GN345.C45 918.7'6 73-14731
ISBN 0-03-081244-5

Printed in the United States of America
3 4 5 6 7 059 9 8 7 6 5 4 3 2 1

FOREWORD

ABOUT THE SERIES

Anthropology has been, since the turn of the century, a significant influence shaping Western thought. It has brought into proper perspective the position of our culture as one of many and has challenged universalistic and absolutistic assumptions and beliefs about the proper condition of man. Anthropology has been able to make this contribution mainly through its descriptive analyses of non-Western ways of life. Only in the last decades of its comparatively short existence as a science have anthropologists developed systematic theories about human behavior in its transcultural dimensions, and only very recently have anthropological techniques of data collection and analysis become explicit and in some instances replicable.

Teachers of anthropology have been handicapped by the lack of clear, authoritative statements of how anthropologists collect and analyze relevant data. The results of fieldwork are available in the ethnographies and they can be used to demonstrate cultural diversity and integration, social control, religious behavior, marriage customs, and the like, but clear, systematic statements about how the facts are gathered and interpreted are rare in the literature readily available to students. Without this information the alert reader of anthropological literature is left uninformed about the process of our science, knowing only the results. This is an unsatisfying state of affairs for both the student and the instructor.

This series is designed to help solve this problem. Each study in the series focuses upon manageable dimensions of modern anthropological methodology. Each one demonstrates significant aspects of the processes of gathering, ordering, and interpreting data. Some are highly selected dimensions of methodology. Others are concerned with the whole range of experience involved in studying a total society. These studies are written by professional anthropologists who have done fieldwork and have made significant contributions to the science of man and his works. In them the authors explain how they go about this work and to what end. We think they will be helpful to students who want to know what processes of inquiry and ordering stand behind the formal, published results of anthropology.

ABOUT THE AUTHOR

Napoleon A. Chagnon was born the second of twelve children in Port Austin, Michigan, in 1938. He is married and has two children. At present he is an Associate Professor of Anthropology at the Pennsylvania State University.

Dr. Chagnon began his academic training in the physics curriculum at the Michigan College of Mining and Technology at Sault Ste. Marie, Michigan (now Lake Superior State College). He transferred to the University of Michigan in his second year of undergraduate training to continue his program in physics.

However, at the University of Michigan, physics is within the College of Literature, Science, and the Arts, and Chagnon was required to take a number of liberal arts courses that radically affected his later training and, ultimately, his career choice. In particular, he elected anthropology courses from Professors Elman R. Service and Leslie A. White, whose incisive and eloquent lectures, Chagnon says, revealed to him a perspective and method for looking at human behavior that no other discipline was capable of offering. He switched from physics to anthropology and ultimately earned his B.A. (1961), M.A. (1963), and Ph.D. (1966) degrees in anthropology at the University of Michigan.

On completing his Ph.D., Chagnon joined the Department of Human Genetics at the University of Michigan's Medical School to participate in a multidisciplinary study of the Yąnomamö Indians, a study under the direction of that department's chairman, Dr. James V. Neel. This collaboration grew out of a joint field study they made in 1966, at the end of Chagnon's first field trip. In conjunction with the multidisciplinary study Chagnon ultimately spent a total of three years living among the Yąnomamö Indians in Venezuela and Brazil, visiting over fifty villages and meeting more than 3000 Yąnomamö. He has returned to the Yąnomamö for eight consecutive years, his most recent trip being in 1972.

Chagnon also held a joint appointment in the Department of Anthropology at the University of Michigan from 1967 to 1972, when he accepted an Associate Professorship in Anthropology at the Pennsylvania State University, from which department he will enter into the second phase of his long-range research interests in the Yąnomamö: intensive analysis of his accumulated field data and an extensive field study of several Yąnomamö subpopulations by his students and himself.

Dr. Chagnon has thus far published some forty articles, two books, and three educational films, and plans, in conjunction with Timothy Asch of Brandeis University, to produce approximately fifty ethnographic films on the Yąnomamö from film they shot in 1968 and 1971. He is also writing, with William G. Irons of Pennsylvania State University, an introductory textbook on anthropology.

ABOUT THE BOOK

Napoleon Chagnon's well-known case study, *Yąnomamö: The Fierce People,* begins with a first chapter on doing fieldwork among them. It is one of the features of this case study that makes it one of the most widely used in this series. Ever since *The Fierce People* appeared in 1968 readers have expressed their strong interest in a more complete account of Chagnon's experiences and methods of research with the Yąnomamö. The present study is a response to this wish, and as the reader will discover, a very satisfying one. *Studying the Yąnomamö* is satisfying because in it Chagnon explains not only how he went about the collection of data, why he considered it important, and how he organized it analytically, but also because his personal experience is described in vivid detail. Much of what he describes is pure adventure of the kind that most field anthropologists encounter in some degree, but rarely in quite this dramatic a context, for there are few people remaining in this world like the Yąnomamö. Once one is started with this methods study it is hard to stop until one has read it all the way through: a compelling and exciting adventure is described on these pages. It is the honest and very frank report of how one man became so much a part of the Yąnomamö way of doing things that he could not extricate himself from this relationship excepting on Yąnomamö terms.

Some readers will feel that Chagnon went too far, that he allowed his "objectivity" to be reduced by overengagement. This is not the way we see it, for as the fieldwork we ourselves have done and that of others reported in *Being an Anthropologist* leads us to conclude, a deep personal involvement is necessary in order to achieve the most meaningful goals in field research. Obviously Chagnon was not allowing his feelings full expression for the three years of time that he spent (over a period of eight years) in Yąnomamö villages. His personal space, his possessions, his body, his image of himself, to say nothing of his personal values and tastes, were handled roughly many times. His response was usually calculated, with the objectives of his fieldwork uppermost in mind. But in the end he revealed his humanness in typical Yąnomamö terms, with something added because he was not Yąnomamö but both an anthropologist and a North American. He will probably return to the Yąnomamö many times. How will his relationship change over time? Perhaps he will find that nothing has changed despite the rumors and legends that have grown up about his encounters with powerful figures, or perhaps he will be so thoroughly ensconced within the Yąnomanö system that he will have less freedom of movement than he had before.

The reader will find *Studying the Yąnomamö* compelling, instructive, and unique. There may never be another account in such close range written about one's anthropological fieldwork with a people still sovereign, a people whose cultural tradition and origins are totally separate from Western culture.

Stanford, California
September 1973

GEORGE AND LOUISE SPINDLER
General Editors

PREFACE

"L'exotique est quotidien." The ethnographer Georges Condominas gave that title to one of his books about the Mnong Gar of the central highlands of Vietnam. It is a formidable phrase, "the exotic is everyday." What kind of world can it be where the strange is commonplace, and the unusual a matter of daily occurrence? It cannot be the humdrum world encountered by you or me, for we got used to the exotic in our own culture when we were children; we grew up to accept its marvels and enormities, its fascinations, quirks, and horrors, almost without question and with only an occasional bellow of pain or rage, almost never one of wonder.

Napoleon Chagnon knows how it feels to be in a place where the exotic is part of everyday experience. Where the assumptions that govern your daily life and mine may not be valid. Where the casual utterance of a personal name may set off a dangerous storm of wrath. Where ball-point pens may write so poorly as to seem forever under water. Where a borrowed loincloth may be alive with a tormenting fungus. Where the tourist must be able, not merely to paddle his own canoe, but fashion it from scratch and keep it afloat. Where every approach to a new village is a complete mystery. Where the mystery is whether you will be hospitably received or killed on the spot.

Those of us who have already met the Yąnomamö, most likely through something written by Chagnon, know that we will embark in this book on a trip through a culture quite different from our own. In a sense, then, the reader of this book can be invited to share, however vicariously, in genuine adventures. Yet, for all its intrinsic excitement and even occasional melodrama, the book is much more than an account of the thrills of first contact between a scientist/anthropologist and what the mass media like to call "a tribe of stone-age men."

Why would anyone take the chances described by Chagnon in the first chapter? Even other Yąnomamö were forthright in advising him against attempting a first contact with the remote village of Mishimishimaböwei-teri. The trip alone was hazardous. As the Yąnomamö viewed it, the way was menaced by fantastic hordes of ferociously evil spirits. Through poorly mapped or unknown country, the trip required days in a canoe and an uncertain period of time on foot, cutting through the jungle, to reach that place. Most sensible people, most sensible Yąnomamö, would not have gone on that journey. Why Chagnon did, and why he decided he could, and how he did is just part of what is to come.

One of Chagnon's main motivations for living among the Yąnomamö, for returning several times, for risking first contact, must be that he wishes to render the exotic commonplace. He is committed to understand Yąnomamö behavior; he wants to explain Yąnomamö culture. Do the Yąnomamö prepare treacherous feasts to which they invite their enemies, only to fall upon them in the midst of festivities? Do they prize warfare and relish combat? Do they beat and exploit those among them who are women? Do they kill many of their babies, mainly females? Are they nonetheless an expanding population, spreading into new areas?

How are we to understand these and other things about the Yąnomamö? What are the facts, and how have they been gathered and tested? How are different sectors of their culture, different aspects of their behavior, related? How do any of the foregoing peculiarities depend upon the way the Yąnomamö obtain their living, or the way they are socially organized? In attempting to answer such questions, particularly the first, pertaining to our knowledge about the Yąnomamö, Chagnon has once again bypassed the literary task of giving us the classic of adventure I still expect one day to get from him. Instead, he whets our interest with a rousing first chapter and then produces an utterly serious, scrupulous book about anthropological method and theory.

It blows the mind, mine at least, to know that Chag does not live among the Yąnomamö merely with canoes and outboard motors and Coleman lamps and boxes of soft pencils and specially selected notepaper, but with reams of IBM computer printouts! A significant portion of the total Yąnonamö is in his data bank, and it goes with him through the jungle, to be checked again and again against local reality. Equally shaking is the knowledge of the miles of movie film that now exist, complementing Chagnon's written record of Yąnomamö culture. Almost everything to be found in this book, including most of the named characters, can be seen by student readers in their classrooms, through the use of those films. This combination of coverage places the Yąnomamö virtually in a class by themselves in the didactic literature of ethnography.

It may be asked if the Yąnomamö want such a role. After all, we are deep into the time when many victimized peoples are asserting rights to a say in their own destiny. Yet, to a remarkable degree considering the century, the Yąnomamö are an autonomous and sovereign people, encysted within states of whose existence many of them are unaware. As yet, many Yąnomamö villages are essentially independent of the economic and political forces that may ultimately bind and alter them. They are also substantially beyond the range of the state monopoly on killing, so they run their own wars, vendettas, and murders, without Venezuelan or Brazilian interference. They may not long continue thus. The outside is breaking in. Metal tools and pots are ubiquitous. Missionaries have been active in the region for some time. Even the population of anthropologists is growing. Alterations of the culture are likely. But thanks to work such as this, the Yąnomamö and we will have a permanent record, unusually detailed, of their way of life before the heaviest vectors of change broke in.

If the Yąnomamö did not originally invite Chagnon, neither did they repel him, and it is absolutely clear that they could have done so, had they wished, with minimal consequences. The happy conjunction of this people and this anthropologist is a boon for all those who cherish some notion that the proper study of mankind is humanity itself. So many of us deplore the lost opportunities of past centuries and mourn the vanished opportunities to do scientific ethnography on cultures largely untouched by elements and pressures emanating from metropolitan powers or other highly organized sociopolitical states. But Chagnon has done just this; he has brought the tools of modern anthropology to the intensive study of a remarkable society. Welcome, then, to this account by Chagnon which, while highlighting the methodological, does so in a remarkable frame in which the exotic, even if a daily phenomenon, is nonetheless accounted for and explained, as befits a contribution to the science of culture.

May 1973 MORTON H. FRIED

AUTHOR'S PREFACE

I had several objectives in writing this book the way I did.

First, I have attempted to preserve what I consider to be an intimate relationship between ethnography, methodology, and theory. In pursuit of this objective, I have included substantial quantities of incompletely analyzed data in the hope that students can appreciate the stickiness of the operation most anthropologists call "analysis," an operation we never discuss very much. Perhaps it would have been more prudent to wait until I had completed this phase of my work and present the "final product" as if that product were arrived at in a straightforward, mechanical, predictable way. However, I feel that more should be said about this phase of the profession, and the examples I provide should contain lessons of their own. Data analysis often involves a good many false starts and blind alleys; the examples discussed in this book may eventually prove to be such, and, if so, I think that is worth demonstrating.

Second, I aim this book at students who have read my first monograph, *Yąnomamö: The Fierce People*, and who might wish to know more about this fascinating Indian tribe. Ideally this book should be used in introductory courses in anthropology, in conjunction with *The Fierce People.* One of the chapters (Chapter 4) might, however, be reserved for a thorough discussion and consideration in a more advanced course in cultural anthropology. The appendices, which provide a good deal of new data, are primarily intended for use with the numerous films that will be produced as a supplement to this book and the earlier monograph. Data knows no course level, and I expect that both serious students and colleagues alike will make use of it for their respective purposes. A word of caution is in order about the statistical data discussed and summarized in several of the chapters in this book: I have not yet finished the enormous task of systematically checking all the information, so the material that is presented, while being close to the final product, is still provisional.

Third, I am interested in experimenting with the teaching of anthropology. In particular, I am convinced that there is an important place for ethnographic film in the teaching of anthropology, and I have designed this book in such a way that maximum advantage can be taken of the some 30 or 40 films that I will be producing with my colleague, Timothy Asch, over the next several years. Some of these are listed in Appendix G. Nearly all of the films were taken in the village of Mishimishimaböwei-teri, the Yąnomamö village that constitutes the main focus of this book. Each film will be accompanied by a published study guide that describes the content of the film and the individuals in it; the individuals will be identified by number in the study guides, and these numbers can be found in Appendix A of this book. In addition, the study guides will occasionally contain suggestions about the theoretical significance of the event filmed or suggestions about how the film might be used in classes.

Some instructors will continue to schedule films for their classes and merely take the day off. I hope that by providing a more integrated set of resources—

monographs, journal publications, study guides, and films—I can contribute something to the teaching of anthropology. The films, just as assigned readings, contain important information that not only can, but should be integrated into anthropology courses.

Anthropology can be an exciting craft. In this connection I have attempted to convey a representative range of personal reactions that characterized portions of my field experience—the excitement of contacting unknown peoples, the frustrations of checking and cross-checking information, anger and resentment at being intimidated constantly, the danger and threats to my life, the fun, the happiness, the personal friendships and enmities, and the pleasure of finally being in a position to sit down and begin to put it systematically together in the way I think it fits. It is an unconventional mixture—an experiment in teaching of another kind—but I am convinced that at the end of this book the reader will remember much of it for a longer time.

Fourth, I touch on a number of theoretical issues in the several chapters and provide enough data so that the student can evaluate the issues in full view of the relevant facts. One such issue is the relationship between warfare and cultural ecology. Some of my colleagues hold the view that tribal warfare is largely a kind of mechanical response to population pressure, crowding, shortages of strategic resources, or particular kinds of dietary deficiencies. I call that position into question with respect to Yąnomamö warfare and provide enough data so that the reader can make a decision on his own. To be sure, in the *general* evolution of culture the relationship between demographic factors and resources has been such that warfare can legitimately be interpreted as an expected outcome of crowding and competition. However, in specific cases, such as the Yąnomamö, the Jívaro, the Tupinamba, and many other Tropical Forest tribes, it is necessary to look at other factors, in particular, the nature of tribal political organization. The point I wish to make is that we cannot assume that tribal warfare everywhere is a direct response to population density and resource shortages, but it has everywhere political dimensions and attributes that can be related to the very nature of the tribal social design. Tribal warfare is, in many cases, the extension of politics in the absence of other means. Those other means are organizational features, and tribal culture as I use the term lacks those organizational features. (See Sahlins, 1968, and Fried, 1967, for discussions of tribal and egalitarian societies respectively.)

Finally, a note about the organization of the book. I have followed a case study approach for the most part, focusing on one particular village, Mishimishimaböwei-teri. Chapter 1 deals with my attempt to make contact with this group, a people who had never seen foreigners prior to my going there. Thus, the book begins with a fairly detailed, if not exciting, account of what it was like to contact a hitherto unknown group. Chapter 2 describes how I collected the data that were necessary to establish the position of this village in the context of its political past and its pattern of community fissioning and relocation. That is, Chapter 2 documents the process of population expansion and movement that describes how Mishimishimaböwei-teri came to be located where it is. Chapter 3 deals with the techniques I employed to collect the genealogical information and constitutes the basis of many of my conclusions about demography, political organization, and population expansion. Chapter 4 outlines the present state of my study and describes some of the analytical techniques and directions I will be exploring to understand the dynamic process of population growth and its effects on the stability and composition of Yąnomamö villages. This is the most exploratory and theoretical chapter of the book. Chapter 5 recounts some of the more personal aspects of my fieldwork. It is a partial account of how my relationship to one headman in particular came to dominate my work and ultimately became a serious obstacle to continued fieldwork in Mishimishimaböwei-teri. More importantly, it deals with the nature of political leadership and draws attention to the personal characteristics of a very successful and very competent headman. There is also a methodological lesson in this chapter. Not all field experiences are idyllic and pleasant at all times. Mine had its share of personal joys *and* difficulties, and for what educational value they may have, I pass them on to others, who, in planning their own field research, might consider them in terms of their expectations of the field situation. Thus, the book ends where it began, in Mishimishimaböwei-teri. Everything in between is directed toward establishing the position of the village in its historical, demographic, and political context. The several appendices give specific material about the residents of Mishimishimaböwei-teri that will enable the reader to take a more detailed look if he so chooses.

It goes without saying that each Yąnomamö village is in some respects very different from other villages. And, each cluster of related villages has characteristics that distinguish it from other, similar clusters. I have drawn attention to the demographic properties of villages and village clusters to underscore this point, and to show how political and social behavior are affected by those properties. Indeed, I regard the demonstration of this as one of the primary accomplishments of my work to date: no village can be meaningfully understood apart from the complex historical and demographic processes that led to its emergence from a larger whole. Few tribal populations remain in the world where these important processes can be documented in aboriginal circumstances, and what we can learn from the Yąnomamö will put us in a better position to understand the rise and extension of the tribal mode of life elsewhere in time and space. The specific configurations I describe can not be expected to exist all over Yąnomamö land, for the variations I describe in two subpopulations must be assumed to exist elsewhere as well. My several colleagues who are studying different groups of Yąnomamö can well appreciate this from their own research, and hopefully will provide us with a more complete range of facts that speak to this social and demographic variability. And the students I train to continue this aspect of my own work will likewise contribute to a more precise understanding of this important phenomenon. It will disappear forever in a decade. We shall all be poorer when it does. It has been a unique privilege to live among the Yąnomamö, to glance fleetingly at a time and a style that lie only dimly in our own past, and it has been frustrating to feel inadequate to capture its quality in the written word, the diagram, the moving image.

ACKNOWLEDGMENTS

I would like to express my gratitude to colleagues, friends, and students who generously contributed their time to critically read the manuscript of this book during various stages of its preparation, and to offer many helpful suggestions. I exonerate all of them for any of the deficiencies that remain herein, and thank them for having drawn my attention to those that I corrected according to their sympathetic and informed opinions.

In particular, I express my gratitude to a number of professional colleagues and friends: Profs. Warren T. Morrill (Pennsylvania State University), William G. Irons (Pennsylvania State University), Eric R. Wolf (City University of New York, Lehman College), Conrad P. Kottak (University of Michigan), Mervyn J. Meggitt (City University of New York, Queens), Morton H. Fried (Columbia University), and Robert L. Carneiro (American Museum of Natural History). Two of my colleagues in human biology disciplines also read and criticized portions of the text that were within their special domain, and I thank them for their suggestions: Dr. Jean MacCluer (Pennsylvania State University) and Dr. Richard Spielman (University of Michigan).

Many of the computer summaries and a good portion of the card punching that lay behind the analysis were the work of Michael J. Levin, a Michigan graduate student, who worked indefatigably on my data for two years. I thank him for his enormous effort and for allowing me to utilize a number of his excellent programs. My initial interest in computerization of the data developed out of conversations with and suggestions made by Profs. Bennett Dyke and Jean MacCluer of Pennsylvania State University, who also helped me make the initial steps in that direction. David Penkala (Pennsylvania State University) provided, often on very short notice, some of the printout summaries that are included in this book.

Several graduate students at Pennsylvania State University assisted me with proofreading, data compilation, and photographic work, and I am grateful to them, especially Luis Hurtado, John Jacoby, Donald Rice, and James Dutt.

I am also indebted to Mary Ann Harrell, editor, Special Publications Division of the National Geographic Society, for her painstaking effort at reading the manuscript and commenting on matters of style and form. I have incorporated a good many of her astute suggestions, and the text reads much better for it.

Finally, I should like to thank my many friends in Venezuela for their patient encouragement and support during the eight years that I was their guest. In particular, I am deeply indebted to Dr. Miguel Layrisse and Dr. Zulay Layrisse, who, in addition to their unflinching professional support, frequently invited me into their home and gave me much personal encouragement. Others were no less gracious and sympathetic in their support, and I am deeply indebted to them as well: Prof. J. M. Cruxent, Dr. María Matilde Suarez de Azuaje, Dr. Erika Wagner, Dr. Nelly Arvelo de Jiménez, Dr. Marcel Roche, Dr. Alberta Zucchi de Romero, and the administration of Instituto Venezolano de Investigaciones Científicas (I.V.I.C.).

While I was in the field I had numerous occasions to call upon many missionaries and residents of Amazonas for favors and material support. In particular, I am indebted to Padre Luis Cocco, Salesian, James P. Barker of the New Tribes Mission, and Juan Eduardo Noguera, a long-time resident of the area. Despite the fact that many of the missionaries were aware of my disagreements with some of their policies, most of them were very hospitable and sympathetic to my scientific objectives. In particular, I wish to thank Padre Luis Cocco, one of the great human beings of all time, and the Sisters at his mission for the unflinching support and kindness they demonstrated during the eight years I descended on their mission and used it as a jumping-off point, storage depot, and communications center.

This book is based on fieldwork that was supported by the National Institute of Mental Health, the United States Atomic Energy Commission, the Wenner-Gren Foundation for Anthropological Research, and the National Science Foundation (International Biological Program Funds). I am also indebted to the Venezuelan Air Force and CODESUR for transporting me and my equipment into the field on various occasions. Finally, I thank Thomas Magner, Associate Dean of Research at Pennsylvania State University, for grants that covered computer time and wages to programmers and typists.

N.A.C.

CONTENTS

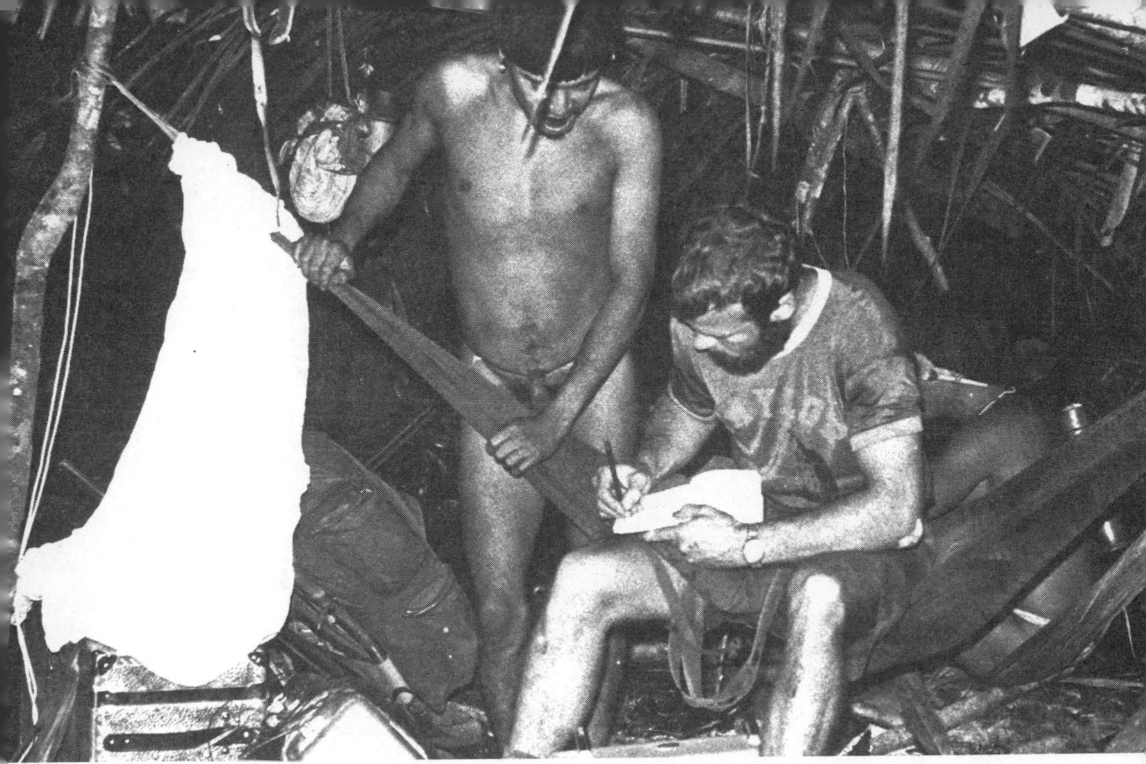

The author traveling between Bisaasi-teri and Reyaboböwei-teri. Rerebawä looks on as I record some of his observations. (Photograph by Timothy Asch.)

Kạobawä chanting with a Shamatari. He warned me about them.

Möawä and his father-in-law, Dedeheiwä—the secular and spiritual authorities of Mishimishimaböwei-teri.

Mishimishimaböwei-teri raiders preparing to depart from Kaobawä's village.

1 / First contact with the Mishimishimaböwei-teri

A thousand previous days concluded with the same melodic incantations, pierced irregularly by a half-scream, half-growl as the shaman struck a powerful blow with his arm or arrow at one of a multitude of humanoid spirits (*hekura*) radiant in their fiery halos, bearing incandescent names, and partaking of the substance of human souls. I did not have to look up to know that the score of glistening men, streaked with green, *ebene*-ladened nasal mucus, were growing more aggressive and violent as the effect of the magical powder hit them, and their foreboding preoccupation with sickness and death became more complete. They were growing surly, and I made a mental note to avoid that area as I methodically went through my IBM printout of village residents and photographed people, moving unobtrusively from house to house. I had run out of film and returned to my house—a section of the roof I shared with the headman and his family—to fumble another roll of Tri-x into my Pentax, attempting to keep my sweaty hands from fouling the pressure plate and focal plane. Droplets formed on my forehead, tickling as they coalesced and ran down my nose, stinging as they seeped into the corners of my eyes.

Dedeheiwä, the accomplished shaman, and Möawä, his son-in-law and the man whose house I shared, were leading the afternoon session in front of Yoinakuwä's place, some 40 yards off to my left. I could recognize their somber droning above the voices of the others, for I had gotten to know these two men quite well over the past three years. The village *waiteri*—"fierce ones"—were assembled to drive out the perceived, but mostly imagined, sickness that Dedeheiwä diagnosed as the effects of *hekura* sent by his enemies in Yeisikorowä-teri, a village far to the south. Dedeheiwä, as was his style, led the attack—very vigorously for a man his age. I remember taking periodic glances in their direction, unconsciously aware that the mood was volatile and a few of the men were becoming uncontrollable. I was concerned about what the headman's younger brother, Yahohoiwä, might do. Living in the shadow of the headman's renown, he had every reason to be concerned about his status and ferocity. He was, however, an unpredictable character and quite capable of violent expressions. Earlier in the day he expounded about his ferocity to me at considerable length and named the men he had killed on various raids—just before demanding a machete. He was piqued when I didn't give it to him, annoyed because I was seemingly oblivious to the status he had and had developed so carefully in his exposition. Later, he openly insulted me as I passed before his house taking identification photographs and making sketches of the hammock positions and sleeping arrangements there. When I paid his remark no attention and passed his hammock in silence, he became more irate. I didn't see him coming and realized the degree of his anger only when I felt the sharp blow of his clenched fist on my chest. I could let his verbal insult bounce off unattended, but I could not take a smart thump on my pectoral that lightly. Why? Two reasons. First, it invites more of the same—or escalation. Second, after three years of that kind of thing I was reaching a saturation point and beginning to despise the pecking system within which I had to conduct my fieldwork. In this particular case, I retained enough of my wits and cultural relativism to measure my response. He was an edgy, unpredictable, and boisterous man, and very concerned about his personal status. Yąnomamö men do not tell you how fierce they are unless there seems to be some question about the validity of their claims.

I dropped my field books and pencils when he hit me, and pretentiously mimed, in the most grotesque manner, the kinesthetic prancings of Yąnomamö ferocity incarnate. The observing women and children giggled and squirmed, as I expected they would. The scene, potentially explosive, was now one of the sub-human buffoon fieldworker exhibiting agonistic stances of the least convincing kind; clearly aware that the provocation called for a reaction, but seemingly incapable of pulling it off in the appropriate fashion. But, the reaction was recognizably Yąnomamö for all its ribaldry. In the midst of the chuckles I smacked him

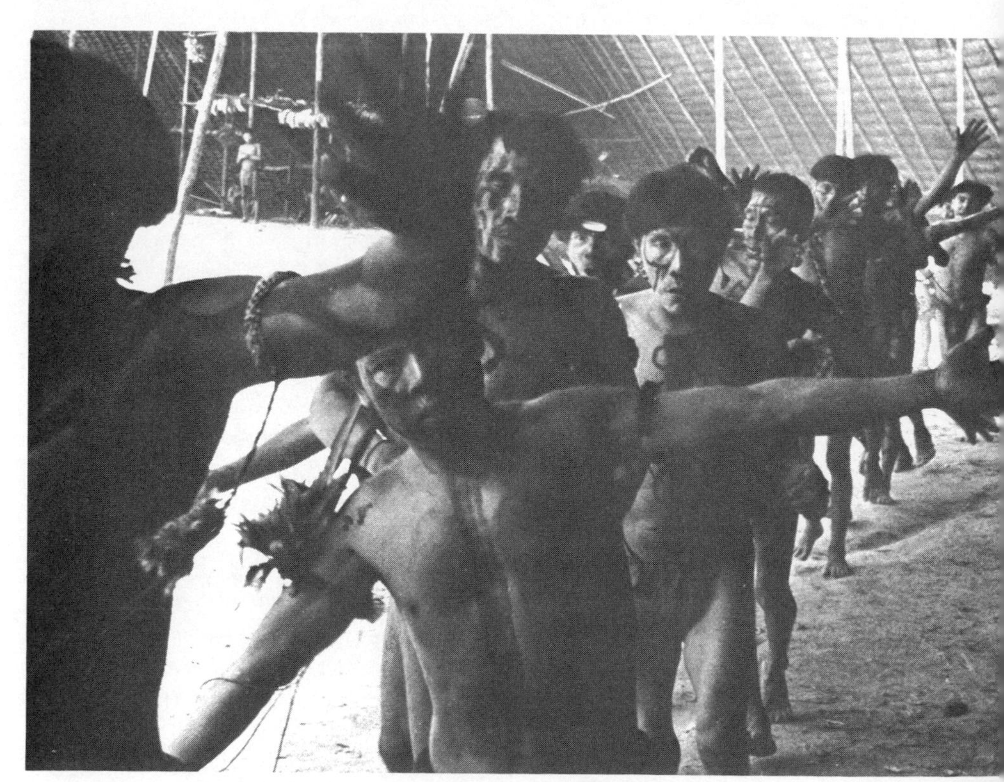

Figure 1.1—Some of the shamans were growing surly.

Figure 1-2—High on drugs, a Shamatari shaman is "cooled" by his more sober peers.

back on the chest. To the observer, it was one of those slow-motion, fake blows. But I put a little "English" on the tail of it and I knew from his surprised look that it stung, just enough to communicate to him that I might not be teasing as much as my antics implied. It was a joke with a grain of kinetic truth.

For the time being I had made a public farce out of something that I knew was gnawing at him, and went about my work as if there were nothing amiss. I knew him well enough to avoid him for the time being, and when he and the others assembled for their daily *ebene* party, I was well advised to stay at a distance.

I closed my camera and began putting my notebooks and tape measure back into my side pack to resume my work. The din of the chanters suddenly gave way to the alarmed screams of women and children who scrambled in terror for the safety of the backside of the *shabono* roof. Men shouted and tried to disarm Yahohoiwä, who had, in the ecstacy of his high, taken up his bow and arrows and was now running back and forth, eluding his pursuers and intimidating the women and children. I watched briefly as the men approached him cautiously and attempted to disarm him. They stayed at a comfortable distance, and he kept them at bay by ominously pointing his arrow at them. I had seen this, too, on many other occasions. The rules of the "game" are to permit the man to display his ferocity (chasing women and children), even to the point of letting him discharge an arrow or two wildly into the roof. The general panic he creates strokes his ego, and the concern that the men show for him, their attempts—often very delicate, flattering entreaties to disarm—reinforce the feeling that *here is a man to be feared and respected.* They usually succeed in taking the weapons away and then devote their attention to the man to "cool" him down. Rarely do these displays lead to actual violence, although I recorded a few incidents that did. My reaction was: they are 40 yards from me and the men are already attempting to disarm him, so I can ignore it.

I congratulated myself at the wisdom of having decided to avoid that area of the village and continued putting my cameras and notebooks into my side pack. Then the women and children in the house next to me shrieked in unison and scattered. Most of them escaped by diving out the back of the house. I looked up to see Yahohoiwä staggering toward me with a wild, glazed look on his face. His nocked arrow was aimed right at my chest. Yąnomamö, like most people, resent being stared at. I looked into his eyes and knew that the glint was not altogether chemically induced. I decided I was not going to play this stupid game with him and do what he obviously wanted me to do: turn tail and dive out the back of the house as the women and children had done. I also suspected that if I *did* play the game he might not be compelled, because of the earlier incident, to play the game according to the rules and shoot to miss. The thought of his barbed arrow in my retreating rear did not appeal to me, and quite frankly, I was getting angry. I decided to make a stand and stare him down. He was about to shoot when he realized that I was not going to run, and this startled him enough that he temporarily "lost" the nock in his arrow. I could tell he was annoyed, but by the time he had recovered his nock he was at a poor angle to get a good shot at me: he had run almost past me and had to turn slightly to shoot. His arrow whizzed past my ear and imbedded itself in the roof behind me. The men caught up to him and dragged him back to the chanting arena in front of Yoinakuwä's house and soothed him. I went about my work, but with diminished enthusiasm.

He came over to visit with me that evening and sat silently, watching me prepare my supper. When he decided to speak, it was in a low, carefully chosen, apologetic tone. "Older brother!" he began. "I was very frightened of you today when you stared into my eyes. I fear you now because you do not run from danger." I listened to his explanation and told him that I, too, was frightened of him and thought, when I saw his face, of all the men he said he killed. I told him that I knew him to be fierce and that others, even in distant villages, knew of him and his reputation. He seemed relieved at this and quite pleased. His mood changed immediately, and he began to chatter inquisitively about my work. Order was established again. We both knew what to expect from each other in the future, more or less.

I was always on less certain terms with Möawä, his brother, the headman of Mishimishimaböwei-teri. He was the toughest, most successful headman I ever met. The kind of relationship was essentially the same: peck a little, create a crisis, then back off at stalemate—and begin again. Unlike Yahohoiwä, Möawä was confident of his reputation and status. He did not have to resort to displays only while on *ebene*. There was no mistaking that Möawä was a man of his word, someone who commanded awe and respect. He was formidable; it showed in many ways—his tone of voice, his bearing, the way others jumped at his suggestions, or fled from his presence when he was angry and hurled insults and threats at the world at large. He was a true *waiteri*, a true leader, and a true Shamatari. As the Yạnomamö say, he was a *rä bäröwei*—the one who *really* lived there. We ultimately came to irreconcilable differences in 1972 and parted on strained, if not hostile, terms.

Kạobawä and Rerebawä (discussed in Chapter I of *The Fierce People*) had been accurate in their predictions of what my experience among the Shamatari, the collection of some dozen villages to the south of their village, would be like. These were the people against whom Kạobawä and his ancestors had waged ceaseless war for half a century, war that continues to this very day. They had warned me about the treachery of the Shamatari and I ignored their counsel. This was unwise in some respects. In 1971 I made an error in judgment that very nearly cost me my life. I made a similar error in 1972. These specfic incidents ultimately led me to decide to terminate particular aspects of my field research. But before I get into these incidents, personality conflicts, and the

Figure 1.3—Yahohoiwä—he was at a poor angle and his arrow missed me.

coercive power of gifts and gift-giving, let me begin with the history of my interest in the Shamatari population and how I made first contact with Möawä's village.

It is increasingly improbable that anthropologists will have the opportunity to be the first representatives of their culture to make contacts with peoples who have never seen outsiders before. There are few descriptions of what this is like, so I recite in considerable detail what my own experiences were. The methodological lesson has to do with the wisdom and necessity of visiting large numbers of villages in order to make censuses and check on the accuracy of genealogies, because a settlement pattern study by design and nature requires this kind of data. My own reasons, after a number of unusual setbacks and obstacles, became quite irrational in spite of the scientific merit that the objectives had.

Actually, my intent from the very beginning of the fieldwork was to study the Shamatari groups to the south of the Bisaasi-teri. Although most of the Shamatari were totally uncontacted by the outside world, members of two of their villages—

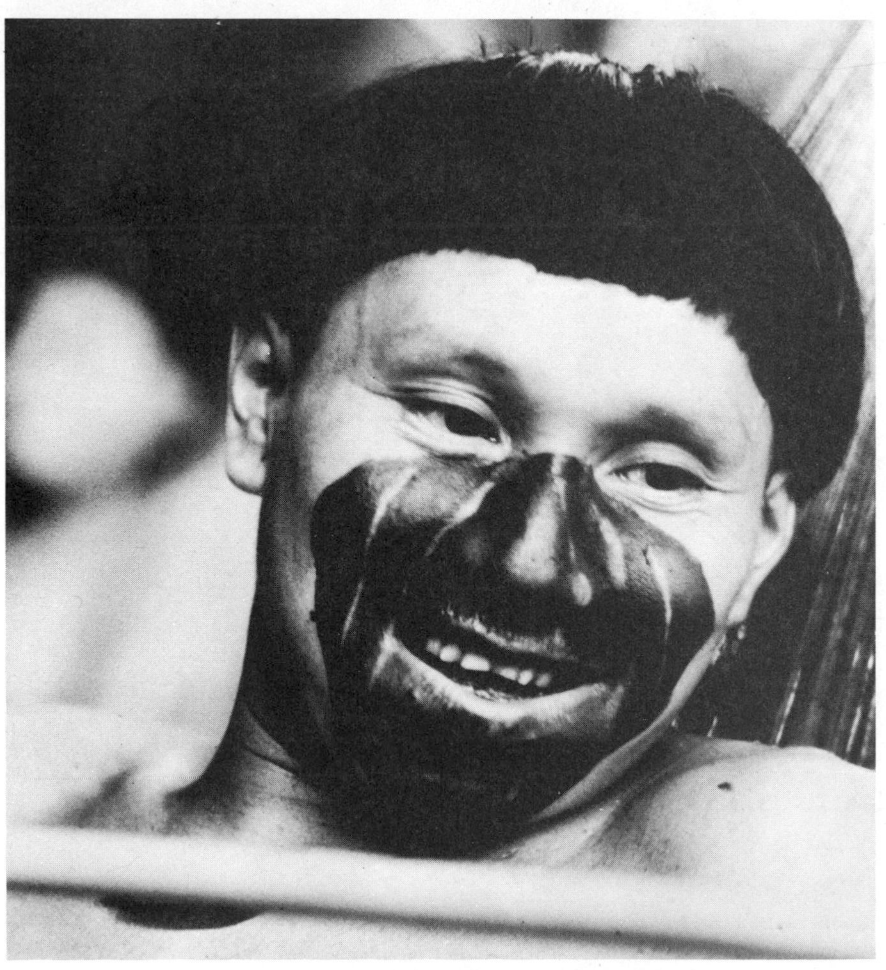

Figure 1.4—Möawä, headman of great renown.

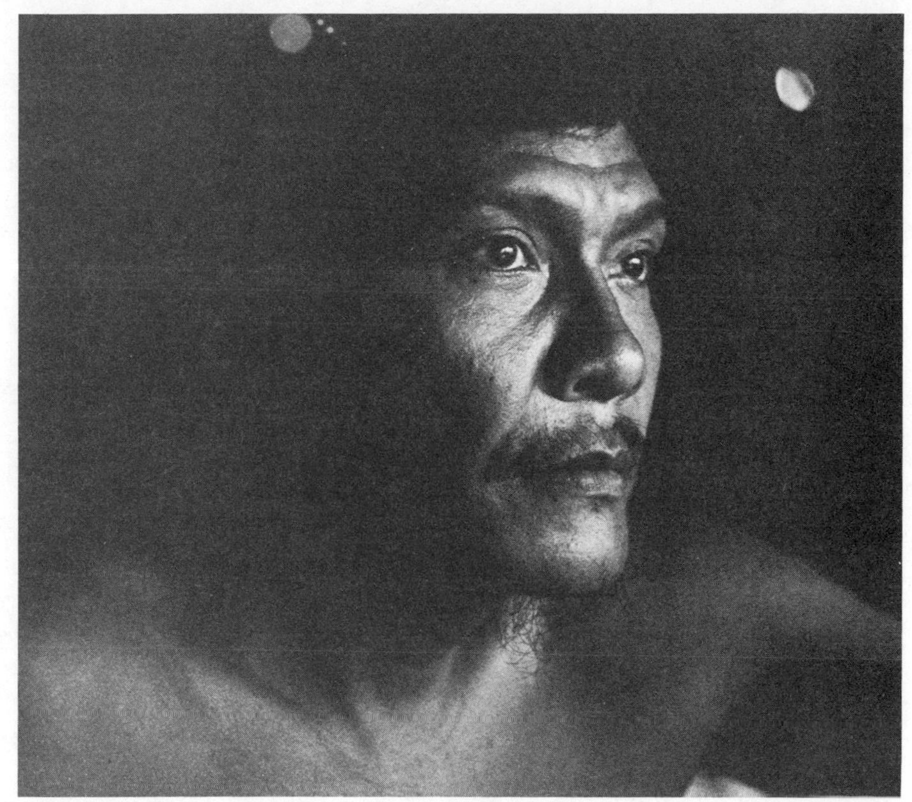

Figure 1.5—Ką̧obawä, leader of great poise and dignity. He knew the treachery of the Shamatari first-hand and advised me not to go there.

Mǫmariböwei-teri and Reyaboböwei-teri—regularly visited the Bisaasi-teri to trade and feast (see Figure 1.7). My plan was to spend enough time in Bisaasi-teri to learn Yąnomamö and then initiate work among the two Shamatari villages to the south. I made no attempt to conceal my interest in the Shamatari, and this, I later came to realize, annoyed the Bisaasi-teri. It was clear to them that I was to be merely a temporary guest in their village.

I actively sought out Shamatari informants who had moved into Bisaasi-teri from one of the two villages, or who had been captured by the Bisaasi-teri in past raids. They earned many of the trade goods (*madohe*) that I initially gave out in Bisaasi-teri. Rules of etiquette are such in Yąnomamö culture that visitors like myself should not display a lack of interest in the hosts, and it goes without saying that the visitor should generously give his *madohe* to his hosts. The Bisaasi-teri were justifiably aggrieved that my objectives to live with the Shamatari would ultimately lead to a lack of supply of steel tools, so they incessantly advised me *not* to go to the Shamatari villages.

It took longer to learn Yąnomamö than I expected, and before long I was deeply involved in the study of the Bisaasi-teri and related groups. As I planned to return to the field the following year, I elected to spend the remainder of my

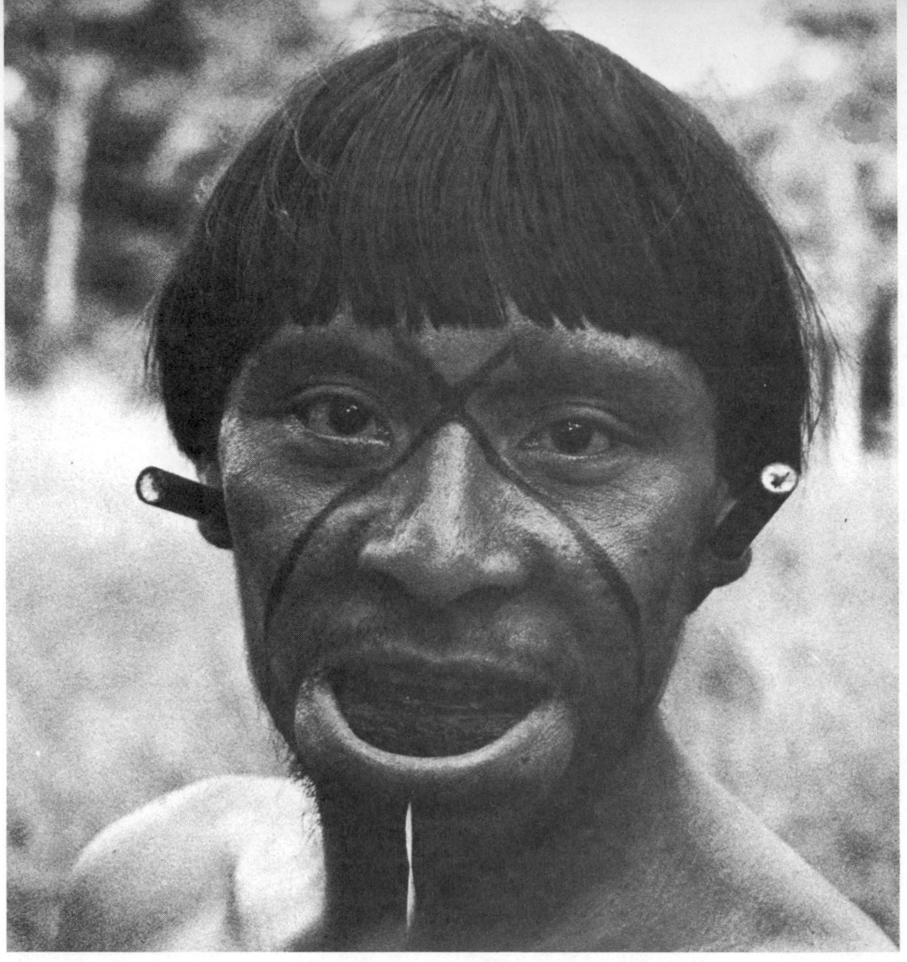

Figure 1.6—Rerebawä, frequent companion on my trips to the Shamatari.

first field trip rounding out my data on the Bisaasi-teri and scale down my project on the Shamatari to more modest proportions. I decided that I would make a more elaborate study of the Shamatari on the next field trip.

But even a *small* study of the Shamatari was not to the liking of the Bisaasi-teri, who actively attempted to keep me in their own village. It soon became known to the members of the two Shamatari villages that I was interested in living with them, and, furthermore, intended to visit other villages to their south, especially a village that everybody referred to as "Sibarariwä's village" (Möawä's village—Mishimishimaböwei-teri). Sibarariwä was the acknowledged headman of the Mishimishimaböwei-teri group, a man with a reputation for treachery and ferocity. He was deeply involved in the treacherous feast of 1950 which claimed the lives of so many Bisaasi-teri men, and the Bisaasi-teri despised him. The two closest Shamatari groups also despised Sibarariwä, for he and his people raided them constantly, even though they were closely related to each other. While members of the first two Shamatari villages were anxious to have me visit them, they were not enthusiastic about the possibility of my visiting Sibarariwä. They, too, wanted a monopoly on my steel tools. Despite the fact that they were at war with Sibarariwä's village, a few individuals from these two villages continued to visit

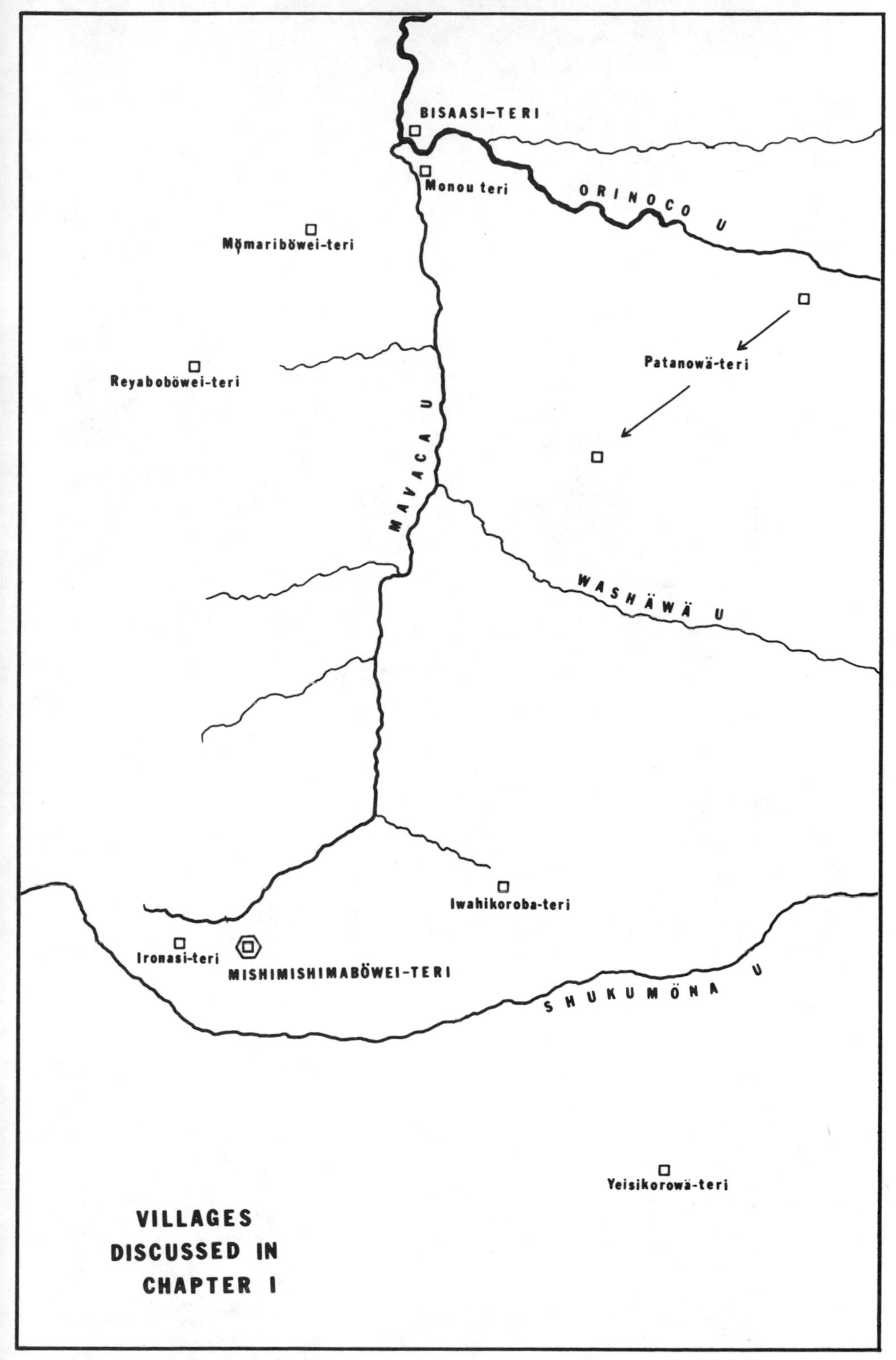

Figure 1.7—Villages discussed in Chapter 1.

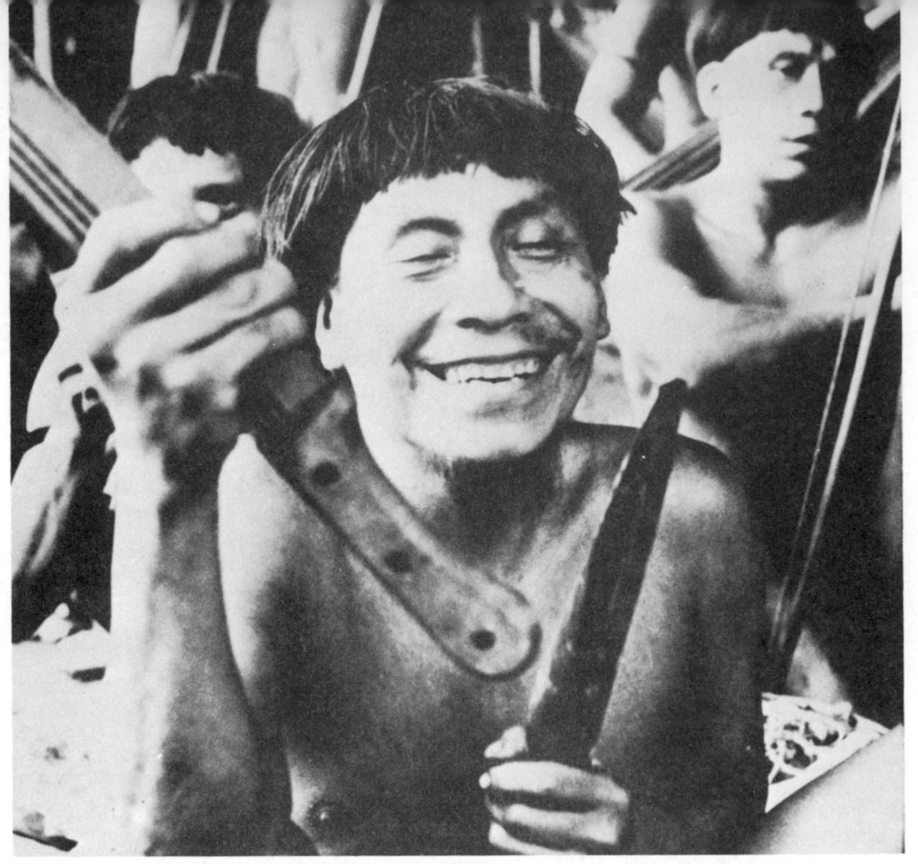

Figure 1.8—Sibarariwä, the fabled headman of Mishimishimaböwei-teri.

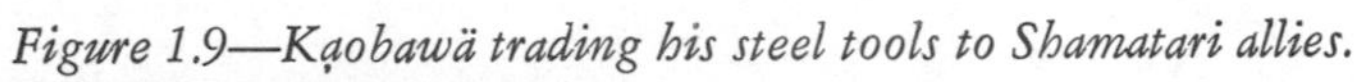

Figure 1.9—Kąobawä trading his steel tools to Shamatari allies.

their kinsmen in Mishimishimaböwei-teri, and this visiting kept a small, but constant trickle of badly-worn steel tools going to Sibarariwä's village. The Bisaasi-teri would obtain machetes from foreigners like me or the missionaries. When these were worn out, they would pass them on to the first Shamatari group, the Mọmariböwei-teri, who would wear them down even more before passing them on to their neighbors, the Reyaboböwei-teri. By the time the tools reached Sibarariwä's village, they were usually unrecognizable as machetes. Most of them were broken into two or more pieces, and none of them had handles. The Bisaasi-teri did not want me to give my tools directly to the Mọmariböwei-teri when I went there to visit, and the Mọmariböwei-teri did not want me to take my tools past them to the Reyaboböwei-teri. Each group wanted a monopoly.

It was not difficult for me to get guides to take me to the first village (Mọmariböwei-teri) in the trading network, since a considerable number of young men from that village were living in Bisaasi-teri as sons-in-law while they were doing bride service. They were more than willing to take me to their village if the pay were a machete. I usually brought a few extra machetes with me to their village (Mọmariböwei-teri) for trading purposes. Once I reached the village (a 10-hour walk), my guides would be coerced by their elders to terminate the trip there. They did not want me to continue on to the Reyaboböwei-teri, suspecting that I might give valuable machetes to them. They usually told me that the village was very far away, the trails were terrible, the jungle was flooded and, besides, nobody was home: "they all went on a long trip far, far away" was a common story, and it usually worked. The thought of walking two more days to find an empty village is not an exciting prospect.

Still, I managed to accumulate a rather large body of demographic, historic, and genealogical information on the two closest Shamatari groups, and it soon became clear from these data that I had to visit Sibarariwä's village to fill in many gaps. The genealogies clearly showed that the residents of Sibarariwä's group were agnatically related to the residents of Reyaboböwei-teri and Mọmariböwei-teri, and the historical data[1] showed that the three groups had a common origin: they had once been a single village.

The Bisaasi-teri and the two closest Shamatari groups used a different strategy to prevent me from visiting Sibarariwä's village, which was said to be located somewhere on the Shukumöna River, not far beyond the headwaters of the Mavaca River. They recited to me the gruesome tales of treachery and violence that characterized their own dealings with Sibarariwä's people, and assured me that Sibarariwä would kill me and my guides if I ever went there. At first these stories impressed me enough to cause me to question my plans to contact Sibarariwä's group. It was clear from the demographic data I collected on "cause of death"[2] that Sibarariwä's village had a well-deserved reputation for fierceness, for many Bisaasi-teri, Mọmariböwei-teri, and Reyaboböwei-teri had died at the hands of Mishimishimaböwei-teri archers.

[1] By "historical data" I mean *informants'* verbal accounts of the past history of villages—the migrations, fissions, wars, and consequences for group dispersal.

[2] See Chapter 4.

As the months wore on and I became better acquainted with the nature of Yąnomamö trade, and, as trade principles applied to me, their desires for monopoly, I began to suspect that much of the information I had been given about Sibarariwä's group might have been exaggerated. I also became better at identifying the circumstances in which informants would most likely lie, and the informants who would most likely lie under *any* circumstances. By carefully selecting the informants and the circumstances, I began broaching the question from a less direct angle. I cannot describe all of the factors that went into identifying the truthful informants—much of it has to do with judgment and subjectivity that can best be described as intuition. To be sure, I could make objective determinations on the accuracy of statements about genealogical relationships, and so forth, but to evaluate the accuracy of an informant's statement about the probability of an event happening is quite another matter. The question, essentially, was: would the Mishimishimaböwei-teri kill me if I went there to visit them? The answer that the Yąnomamö had uniformly given me until then was a unanimous *Yes*, but the circumstances were always the same: the answer was always given in public by the older men who were concerned about the possibility that I would give machetes to the Mishimishimaböwei-teri, machetes that they might otherwise claim for them-

Figure 1.10—Shamatari archer from Mishimishimaböwei-teri.

selves. The Mishimishimaböwei-teri, of course, were their enemies, and even if I refused to heed their advice, it was unlikely that I would be able to recruit guides from among the Bisaasi-teri.

I decided to approach this question differently: I would only inquire about the matter *in private* from younger men who were keen on adventure and most likely able, for kinship reasons, to visit Sibarariwä's village with little chance of personal danger to themselves. I never broached the subject unless I was working privately with an informant whose word I had learned to trust on other matters. My first encouraging answer came from a young man named Wakarabewä, who had married into Biaasi-teri. His father lived in Mǫmariböwei-teri and was a brother to Sibarariwä. Wakarabewä said his father occasionally visited Sibarariwä, and he felt that I might be able to go along on such a visit also.

Let me describe, to the extent that it is possible, some of the factors that I weighed in making a subjective conclusion that I might visit Sibarariwä's group and come back unscathed. Wakarabewä was a stranger in Bisaasi-teri and quick to point out the lies and deceptions that the Bisaasi-teri fed me. He had married into Bisaasi-teri and was doing bride service to his father-in-law, the headman of the lower group of Bisaasi-teri, whose *shabono* (village) was some two hundred

Figure 1.11—Wakarabewä, my first Shamatari guide. He feared neither the notorious residents of Sibarariwä's village nor the Raharas.

yards downstream from Kąobawä's. As a son-in-law he was expected to do all manner of onerous tasks for his father-in-law, and as a Shamatari was subject to a considerable amount of ridicule and harsh treatment. Like many other people, the Yąnomamö tend to be bigoted and seize upon any opportunity to make invidious distinctions between themselves and anybody else who is slightly different: the Bisaasi-teri in general, have a low opinion of the Shamatari—and vice versa. I discussed this in *The Fierce People* when I described the relationship of Rerebawä to the Bisaasi-teri—he, too, had married into Bisaasi-teri from a different group and experienced the same kind of treatment.

Wakarabewä's father-in-law was particularly unpleasant to him. He denied Wakarabewä sexual access to the girl while at the same time he allowed the young men of the natal village to enjoy these privileges. Wakarabewä was bound by the taboos associated with the in-law relationship and could not complain about it, but he privately related his bitterness to me. He was not related by blood to anyone important in the village and, out of his bitterness, freely told me about lies that had been given to me by the Bisaasi-teri. When he told me in private that he didn't think Sibarariwä would kill me if I went to his village, provided I was with Wakarabewä or his father, I concluded that a trip there was not entirely out of the question. But, I had an uneasy feeling about accepting the word of a seventeen-year-old youth when the consensus of the adults was precisely the opposite. Still, other young Shamatari informants, under similar circumstances, concurred in Wakarabewä's predictions to varying degrees. I was careful not to let them know what Wakarabewä told me, so as to have independent opinions. As I became better acquainted with some of the older men in Bisaasi-teri, men like Kąobawä, I was able to create circumstances during informant sessions in private that led to important modifications of their public positions. None of these men ever said that I would be perfectly safe if I should visit Sibarariwä's village, but some of them suggested that the possibility existed. This was qualitatively a different kind of story than the official position that a trip there would lead to certain death.

About ten months after I had been in the field a group of young men from Reyaboböwei-teri visited the Bisaasi-teri. They also visited me to ask for steel tools when the Bisaasi-teri were not in my hut. They mentioned that a group of men from Sibarariwä's village had recently visited Reyaboböwei-teri. They told me that Sibarariwä's group had recently moved away from the Shukumöna River and was now living very close to the headwaters of the Mavaca River. After careful, devious questioning, I concluded that it was possible to ascend the Mavaca River in my dugout canoe to a point very close to the putative new location of Sibarariwä's village. The rivers were quite high because of recent rains, so I decided to make an attempt to contact Sibarariwä's village.

Wakarabewä, in a matter-of-fact way, agreed to come with me and suggested the names of a few more young Shamatari men who might be amicably received by the Mishimishimaböwei-teri. I talked with these young men and secured their promises to come with me.

Word soon spread through Bisaasi-teri that I was, at last, planning to go up the Mavaca to try to find Sibarariwä's village. My hut was visited by party after party of Bisaasi-teri who strongly advised me against such a foolish thing. When their stories of treachery and murder failed to frighten me into canceling my plans, they began a new tactic: *Raharas.*

Raharas were created when Man was in his infancy. They were associated with the Great Flood and deep water. When the flood receded, the *Raharas*—awesome serpents—took up residence in the Orinoco River, somewhere near its head-waters. They have never been seen in the Orinoco, so the presumption is that they migrated to other rivers after the Flood and now live there.

While no one had ever seen *Raharas*, their behavior was well known to the Yąnomamö. They rise up out of the water and devour those who are foolish enough to attempt to cross the rivers, especially rivers that are unfamiliar to the Yąnomamö. Furthermore, it is alleged that an underground river connects the Orinoco with the upper Mavaca, and that the *Raharas* took this course and migrated to the Mavaca.

Raharas almost resulted in the cancellation of my planned trip up the Mavaca. Since none of the Bisaasi-teri or Shamatari had ever ascended the Mavaca very far, they were unable to discount the assertion that it teemed with *Raharas.* Kąobawä and Shararaiwä, his youngest brother, took it upon themselves to apprise me of the dangers. Shararaiwä told me and my Shamatari guides that the *Raharas* would surely rise up and devour us—canoe, motor, gasoline, and paddles. The others nodded and clicked their tongues to indicate their subscription to Shararaiwä's claim.

My guides, who were by this time being badgered by the Bisaasi-teri to withdraw from the trip, looked gloomily at the ground and remained silent. I could see that the *Rahara* story was frightening them, and I was worried that they would refuse to come. I was also growing very annoyed with the Bisaasi-teri for going to such ludicrous ends to prevent me from reaching Sibarariwä's village. I had a long, heated argument with Kąobawä and Shararaiwä on the existence of *Raharas*, but concluded that any further discussion along this line would be fruitless. Just as you don't argue with the missionaries about the existence of God and angels, you don't argue with the Yąnomamö about the existence of *Raharas.*

I changed tactics and conceded that perhaps there *were Raharas* after all. Yea, I knew there were *Raharas* and had, in my youth and in my native jungles of Michigan-urihi-teri, slain many of them.

Yąnomamö logic, fortunately, permits of such inconsistencies: it is not so much a matter of *what* you assert, as of *how* you assert it and the kinds of details you give to support your argument.

Yes. I knew *Raharas* very well indeed. I was a good shot when it came to *Raharas* and most certainly would be able to apply my skills should we run into any *Raharas* on the Mavaca. I would keep my double-barreled shotgun loaded at all times with *Rahara* shot to be ready for them.

My young guides listened attentively and seemed less gloomy as I continued my argument.

I knew from my vast experience at *Rahara*-hunting precisely where one had to hit a *Rahara* in order to kill it in one shot, and I gave an anatomical demonstration: "Right here! In the neck! Just below the head!" I also had a very special kind of cartridge called *Rahara Brahaishaömodimö* ("something made for killing *Raharas* at a distance") and showed them several cartridges with rifled slugs protruding from the plastic jackets. Back in 1965 it was possible to make such an argument, since none of the Yąnomamö had yet been given shotguns. Now it is impossible: I know of at least forty Yąnomamö in various villages along the Orinoco, including the Bisaasi-teri, who have shotguns.

Shararaiwä flushed with anger when I shifted my argument and asserted that I had special knowledge about the fabulous beasts. He and Kąobawä held the advantage only so long as they had a monopoly on knowledge, and since neither of them had ever seen a *Rahara*, let alone killed one, I immediately gained the upper hand. Shararaiwä stalked off in a huff, muttering that he was sure the *Raharas* on the Mavaca were bigger and fiercer than those in Michigan-urihiteri. In quitting the argument he lost it.

At least I thought he lost it: one of my four guides backed out the next morning and another asked me if it wouldn't be wiser for him to come on my second trip, after I exterminated the *Raharas.* My canoe was loaded for the trip and I knew I had to get under way immediately, since the risk of losing all my guides increased by leaps and bounds the longer I remained in Bisaasi-teri. I managed to talk the guide into making the trip by doubling the previously agreed-upon pay but I was unable to recruit one more guide to replace the one who backed out. We left Bisaasi-teri with my dugout canoe heavily loaded with provisions, the roar of my outboard motor drowning out the screams and rejoinders of the adult men who were still attempting to prevent me from finding the Mishimishimaböwei-teri. They were angry with me and with my guides: "You'll see! They'll kill you all! They will pretend friendship at first, and when you are off your guard they will fall on you with bow staves!"

The trip was unsuccessful. We ascended the Mavaca River for two full days, chopping our way through logs and deadfalls for much of the second day. When we pulled up along the bank to make camp for the second night, the river was so narrow that it was difficult to negotiate the hairpin curves in the current without touching the river bank on one side or the other.

When my guides set about collecting vines, leaves, and poles for our temporary hut, they returned hastily to the canoe where I was cleaning game, their faces ashen with fear. They had found a fresh, recently-traveled trail a few yards away from the river. I was happy about the discovery and went to investigate. As we examined the trail and speculated about its origin and terminus, two of my three guides demanded that we leave for home immediately: they were sure we were very close to the village and they were not going to go any further. Only Wakarabewä indicated that he was willing to go on. Since you do not abandon your guides in the middle of enemy territory, there was no choice but to turn back. I was furious with them and asked why they decided to come in the first place. Their answer: "For a machete, an axe, and a large cooking pot!"

They had been so certain that we would never get close to the village that they came along for the ride and the pay! They also knew that on such trips I always shot a great deal of game and gave it away to the families of my guides. For them, the trip was just going to be a hunting trip with high pay, and they

Figure 1.12—The upper Mavaca River—Bahana-u. A vast and nearly unoccupied expanse between the Namowei-teri and the Shamatari villages. It is said that this river abounds with Raharas.

had no intention of reaching the village. Needless to say, I turned the canoe around and we went home. I was so furious that I refused to let any of them have any of the game that I shot, which was considerable, since nobody had hunted in that region for years.

I made a large smokerack outside my hut when we returned and put the meat on it to cure. Most of it was stolen during the night by the Bisaasi-teri. The next day, Torokoiwä, one of Kąobawä's older brothers, visited me to tell me the following story. It was good, he argued, that I did not actually reach the village. Some years ago a group of foreigners like myself ascended the Shukumöna River and met a hunting party from Sibarariwä's village. The foreigners had guns and machetes. The Shamatari hunters acted friendly and gained the confidence of the foreigners. They asked them if they could examine their strange possessions. When the foreigners gave them the shotguns and machetes to examine, the Shamatari fell on them with the machetes and hacked them to pieces.[3]

Perhaps I was foolish and perhaps it was fortunate that I did not make it to the village. Perhaps the Shamatari were every bit as treacherous as the Bisaasi-teri made them out to be and I was not experienced enough to predict their behavior. I decided to put Sibarariwä's village out of my mind for the remainder of

[3] Torokoiwä, I later learned, had gotten the story confused. Foreigners were not involved, nor were shotguns. A group of Yąnomamö from several mission villages ascended the Shukumöna River to raid Sibarariwä. They killed one man from Sibarariwä's village, not vice versa.

my field trip and concentrate on improving what data I had on the Bisaasi-teri and the two closest Shamatari groups.

Just before I left for home at the end of my first fifteen months of fieldwork I was again visited by young men from Reyaboböwei-teri. They told me that a group of men from Sibarariwä's village had visited them shortly after my abortive trip, and that they informed them of the trip. I asked them what the reaction was among them, and their reply was, in effect, that Sibarariwä's group wanted me to come and visit them. The visitors had asked the Reyaboböwei-teri to pass this information on to me. The Reyaboböwei-teri, of course, passed it on only when they were certain that I was leaving for home and would not have an opportunity to act on it! I had seen numerous Reyaboböwei-teri since they had been informed of the invitation, but none of them mentioned it to me until I was already packed for my trip home.

My fieldwork the following year, 1967, took me to Brazil. On my way home I stopped in Venezuela to again make an attempt to contact Sibarariwä's village. I intended to have Wakarabewä's father guide me, but as luck would have it, he had been bitten by a snake and could not walk.

I returned to Venezuela again in 1968 for more fieldwork among the Yąnomamö. I was determined to contact the village during this trip, for it had now become an obsession. Most of my first month of the 1968 field trip was committed to participation in a medical-anthropological and ethonongraphic film study of the Yąnomamö (see Preface and Appendix G). When my medical and film-making colleagues left for home, I turned my attention to Sibarariwä's village once again. My guide problems seemed less severe because I had the good fortune of meeting Karina, a young boy about twelve years old who had lived all of his life in Sibarariwä's village. He was actually from Mǫmariböwei-teri, but he and his mother were abducted when he was an infant and he had returned to his natal village only within the past year. I had met him briefly in 1967, shortly after he had returned to Mǫmariböwei-teri, but since he had never seen a foreigner before, he was then very frightened of me and avoided me all the time I was in Mǫmariböwei-teri.

Like many of my best informants, Karina was something of an outcast. The Yąnomamö are very strange in their treatment of people like Karina. His father was the headman of Mǫmariböwei-teri, a man who had sired at least a dozen children. Many of this man's sons were adults and very prominent in the political affairs of the village. Yet Karina, because of his long residence in Sibarariwä's village, was rather badly treated by his kinsmen when he returned home—almost as though he were a complete stranger from an enemy village. For example, they knew he was petrified at the very thought of being near me—a foreigner—when I visited them in 1967, so they kept dragging him—kicking, weeping and terrified—over to me so I could frighten him even more. The boys of his age also teased him mercilessly, and the adults ordered him around as if he were a recently captured enemy child.

I met him again in 1968, after he had visited the mission at Mavaca and had lost most of his fear of foreigners. When I asked him if he would take me to Sibarariwä's village, I was giving him an opportunity to show the others that he was important, an opportunity that he enthusiastically accepted. He was almost at that age when Yąnomamö boys like to show their elders that they are fearless and responsible, but because of his constant mistreatment in Mọmariböwei-teri during the year, he was even more anxious to make this kind of demonstration.

He was very willing to tell me the names of everybody in Sibarariwä's village and how they were related to each other, a tremendously important addition to the genealogies I had at that point.

I worked with Karina for about a week on genealogies and census data before we made our first attempt to contact Sibarariwä's village. One of the members of the medical group, a young geneticist, remained with me after the others had gone home. He wanted to collect blood samples from the members of Sibarariwä's village should I ultimately reach the group and find them favorably disposed toward the blood sampling. The decision would rest on me and my interpretation of their probable reaction. I mention this only because the presence of the geneticist created a schedule that had to be met. We had arranged at a considerable expense for a bush pilot to come in and pick up the geneticist and blood samples on a specific date. The pilot would land at one of the recently cleared airstrips down the Orinoco, and we had to be there at that date, with or without the samples. The geneticist had to catch that flight, whether or not we had blood samples from the Shamatari.

We made several attempts in rapid succession to ascend the Mavaca. On the first two trips we were forced to turn back after getting only about a half-day upstream. The first time one of my barrels of gasoline turned out to be diesel fuel, and the motor would not run on that. The second time we had an electrical failure in the ignition system of the motor and had to return for repairs.

On the third trip, with our schedule now very tight, we made it two full days upstream before another electrical failure in the ignition system occurred. Under normal circumstances—that is, when I am working alone with no definite schedule to meet—I would have continued on in spite of the motor trouble, even if it meant paddling back for three or four days. But the geneticist faced the risk of waiting another month at a desolate airstrip for another flight to come in. The failing motor slowed our speed down to almost nothing, since it was running on only one cylinder. It showed every indication of getting worse, so I reluctantly turned back when it became apparent that we could not reach the village with sufficient time to get to know the people well enough to set upon them with needles and test tubes, and still get back to the airstrip on schedule.

My two guides—Karina and another man—were growing very disgusted by this time. We had made three abortive attempts to reach the village in a single week, and turned back just when it seemed that we were very close to our objective. They do not understand about things like airplane schedules and being at a specific place at a specific date. I got the geneticist to the airstrip in time and then spent the entire night tearing down the motor. The problem was a faulty coil, which I repaired by cannibalizing one from another motor I kept as a spare. By the time I had reassembled the motor, it was four o'clock in the morning. I had not unloaded my canoe, so I had to be up before six to make sure that the Bisaasi-teri did not unload certain portions of it for me.

I learned at dawn that Karina was sick and that the other guide was not going to come with me. He was disgusted and decided to go on a long fishing and hunting trip; he had left during the night so as to prevent me from tempting him into going by increasing the pay.

Karina was reacting to a measles inoculation I had given him. Measles had hit the Yąnomamö for the first time in their biological history. It entered the tribe at a number of missions. (See Neil, Centerwall, Chagnon, and Casey, 1970.) There are very few human populations in the world that are virgin for measles, a fact that attests to the long isolation of the Yąnomamö population. The vaccination causes a mild case of measles—a high fever for two days or so. I knew that Karina would be a little weak from the vaccination, but I knew that he would be back to normal in two days. We had vaccinated 2,000 Yąnomanö during the previous six weeks, and I knew what the reaction would be.

After some considerable persuasion, I managed to talk Karina into coming along one final time. I was obsessed with determination to reach Sibarariwä's group. I coaxed him from the village into the dugout canoe, covered him with my clothing, and set a small aluminum boat over the top of the larger canoe to protect him from the rain and the sun.

There I was, with a twelve-year-old guide, so feverish that he could barely walk, about to set off again for the almost legendary village of Mishimishimaböwei-teri, tired and disgusted. I was also feeling a little phlegmatic myself from a severe fungus infection. Some three weeks earlier I had visited the Patanowä-teri and, as is customary, entered the village as a Yąnomamö visitor, resplendent with feathers, red paint, and a scarlet loincloth. [Documented in Neel, Asch, and Chagnon, 1971, *Yanomamo: A Multidisciplinary Study*.] Unfortunately, I did not have my own loincloth with me, so I borrowed one from a Yąnomamö. He happened to have a rather contagious and virulent fungus infection of his groin. Soon afterwards I didn't need a loincloth: I was naturally scarlet from my knees to my navel, itching and burning like crazy. The condition was aggravated by sitting in the rain in wet clothing for days on end, and the only remedy I had was a can of foot powder. You can't imagine the mirth provoked among the Yąnomamö by watching the resident fieldworker in a most indescribable position sprinkling foot powder on his groin. By now I was down to the last of my gasoline supplies and I was worn to a frazzle—no sleep, countless hours of running an outboard motor, disappointed in my luck. This would be my last try at reaching the village. If I did not make it this time, I decided I would give up. I had wasted altogether too much time chasing a phantom.

I did not know if I would encounter rapids and new deadfalls on the trip and I needed another guide. Karina was too small, even assuming that he recovered in two days, to help heave the bulky, heavy dugout canoe over logs and rapids. A few young men appeared at the canoe to see us off for the umpteenth time. I asked one of them, Bäkotawä, a youth of some eighteen years, if he would be interested in coming along with us. He said he would like to, provided I would pay him an axe, machete, and cooking pot. I agreed to his price and asked, "Will you be afraid like my guides were before and want to turn back when we get close to the village?" He scoffed and said that he didn't "know how to be afraid"

. . . he was already a man, and fierce. He added that he would tell the Mishimishi-maböwei-teri that he was from Patanowä-teri, not from Bisaasi-teri. I asked Karina if he would support Bäkotawä's story when we reached the village. He whimpered an affirmative, so Bäkotawä quickly got his weapons and hammock and joined us. He also brought the few missionary rags he called clothing—to show the Shamatari he was no mere savage, but cosmopolitan.

We traveled eight hours the first day. Karina was feeling much better that evening, and his fever had broken.

The second day brought an unexpected and unwelcomed surprise. We had gone only about two hours when we ran into two huge, partially submerged trees that blocked our passage. The river had dropped enough during the week to expose about a foot of the immense logs above the water, far too much to get over with the dugout. The trees were submerged too deeply in the river to try to cut through them with axes, so we had to leave the big canoe behind at this point and transfer the supplies to the small, aluminum canoe. I had a small, brand-new outboard motor with me for the aluminum canoe, but my luck was consistent: it wouldn't run. (I learned later that the gasoline lines were plugged with dirt.) We had no choice but to use the much larger motor, or paddle. I had made it at least one full day beyond this point on previous trips and I knew we had a long way to go, so I elected to use the large motor. We set off with a giant motor on a tiny canoe. We couldn't go as fast as we had been going in the dugout, but we were going much faster than we could paddle, so it was a reasonable choice.

We traveled nine and a half hours the second day. The river had dropped at least five feet since my trip of a week earlier, but we had fewer problems with deadfalls. The small canoe was light enough so that we could easily drag it through or over any obstacles.

On the third day, about eleven o'clock, Karina suddenly motioned me over to the right bank: "There! Over there! I know this place!" He jumped out of the canoe and disappeared into the jungle. Bäkotawä and I followed quickly behind him. There was a large trail a few yards from the river. Karina said that we were within a day's walk of Sibarariwä's village, and that this was a trail they used when they visited the Iwahikoroba-teri, who lived due east of this spot.

Karina also said that the river turned west from here (see Figure 1.7) and that it would be quicker to walk to the village, which lay somewhere to the south of us. Karina and I were very excited and pleased about reaching this familiar point. Bäkotawä became very moody and said nothing.

The riverbank was steep and high. I was afraid that if we left the canoe in the river, a sudden rain would swell the river enough to wash it away. I insisted that we put the boat and motor up on the bank, knowing that we would have been in serious trouble if our boat got away.

Our load had been reduced considerably by this time. We had used up much of the gasoline and had dropped off most of the remaining fuel along the way for the trip home. We were down to our food, hammocks, my trade goods for Sibarariwä's people, my cameras, tape recorder, notebooks, film, two shotguns, and a transistor radio. Everything but the trade goods fitted comfortably into the two packs. Since we were within a day's walk from the village, we decided to leave everything except a few trade goods behind and later send the Shamatari down to the boat to get them. We also decided to cache food here for the trip home, since it would be silly to carry it into the village and then back.

In making an inventory at this point, I was surprised to discover how little food we had with us. I had been so preoccupied with motor problems, gasoline, and guides that I had paid too little attention to our food. The box was the same one I had packed for the first trip, and I had not added anything to it. Our food consisted of about three pounds of rice, two pounds of manioc flour, one pound of sugar, several cans of sardines, two chocolate bars, three cups of powdered milk, a quarter-pound of salt, and one pound of coffee. It was not anything to worry about if Sibarariwä's village was just a day away, since we could expect to be fed by our hosts. And as long as we had cartridges, meat would be no problem. I still had *all* of my *Rahara* cartridges. We left the sugar, milk, manioc, coffee, and half of the sardine supply at the river for the trip home, bringing the rice, chocolate, and the remaining sardines with us, plus a small cooking pot for the rice.

It took us about an hour to store our supplies, make sure they would keep dry, and load the packs. We started off shortly after midday. Although it had not rained much downstream for the past week, the trail here was unusually slippery and wet. We followed the base of a large hill most of the time, gradually getting higher and higher. I was surprised to find swamps and potholes so high above the river elevation. About three o'clock a terrific storm broke, and we huddled together under a small plastic tarp for almost an hour trying to keep the packs from getting soaked. We continued after the rain stopped, reaching a Yanomamö "resting" stop on the trail.

Well-traveled trails have these spots every three hours or so. They are usually flat places where the trees are thin and widely scattered and the sky can be seen. The Yanomamö stop to rest on long trips, and usually fall into the habit of using the same place over and over. Some even have names. As they sit around and chat, their hands are always busy, breaking branches, chopping on logs with machetes or axes (if they have any), repacking their loads in their baskets. The resting stops soon take on the aspects of junkyards, battered trees and discarded debris lying around. One often hears about the putative "conservation" concerns of primitive peoples for their environment. My experience has been that if the Yanomamö had our technical skills and their "conservation" attitudes, Amazonas would be a cesspool in no time.

Karina told us about the last time he was at this spot, on a trip from Iwahikoroba-teri. He showed us the log that Börösöwä, the Iwahikoroba-teri headman, sat on, where the others sat, what they talked about, who threw away the pack basket that was lying there rotting, and so on. For the first time since I had been trying to contact these Shamatari groups they seemed real; they were no longer just names in a genealogy. I was certain for the first time that I was going to reach their village.

Karina told us that there was a large camp ahead of us and, a few hours beyond that, the village. It was four o'clock by the time we reached the camping site. It had not been used for at least a year. Karina said that Sibarariwä made this camp after a fight in the village with Möawä. Afterwards part of the group moved here temporarily until tempers cooled off. It was fairly large, large enough for over a hundred people. The things that impressed me most were the mildew and dampness of the area, and the thousands of termite grubs that were hatching out in the dilapidated huts.

We decided to sleep there for the night, since by going on we would arrive at the village after dark. I preferred to have as much daylight as possible during my first day's visit, a Yąnomamö trait that I think is functionally useful. I made the mistake of not hanging my shoes or the packs up over the fire that night, and they were covered with termite grubs inside and out the next morning.

We were famished. The only meal that day had been some dry, smoked alligator left over from the day before. We decided to eat a big meal before pushing on, knowing that our visit would cause such a sensation in the village that we were not likely to have much time for cooking or eating. We boiled enough rice for both supper and breakfast and stuffed ourselves with it.

That night Karina was in a mischievous mood and began teasing Bäkotawä. He recounted the treacherous feast that Sibarariwä had staged for the Bisaasi-teri and the revenge feast that the Bisaasi-teri held in return. He told him of their anger over the deaths that resulted, and implied that he *might* tell Sibarariwä that Bäkotawä was actually from Bisaasi-teri, not from Patanowä-teri. He talked about how fierce the people in this village were, and how many raids they had gone on, who they killed, and how much they hated the Bisaasi-teri. I finally had to shut him up. I knew that Bäkotawä was getting frightened.

The next morning Bäkotawä announced that he was too frightened to go on and said he wanted to go back to the canoe. I was angry, mostly about Karina's mischief, but I was determined not to turn back this time. Silently, so as to not expose my anger, I unpacked the food and gave him his share of the rice. There were matches and cooking pots at the canoe, and he knew where to find them. I had two shotguns, although neither Bäkotawä nor Karina knew how to use them; I brought the extra one along to make them feel more secure. I gave one of them to Bäkotawä, along with a dozen or so cartridges and a quick lesson in how to load and shoot a gun. There were also fishhooks at the canoe, so he would be able to keep himself fed while Karina and I pushed on. I sternly warned him not to put the canoe in the water for *any* reason. He argued that although he was frightened now because we were so close to the village, he would not be frightened at the canoe. He said he would make a camp there and wait for us to return. I told him we would be gone about three or four sleeps, and he agreed that he would be quite content to wait for us there.

Karina and I left about 7:00 A.M. and before long began running into fresh signs of Yąnomamö. We saw footprints in the mud that were made during or after yesterday's rain, and we found several *rasha* fruits on the trail. Someone had passed through the area yesterday, and was carrying *rasha*. About an hour after we left our camp we came upon an abandoned garden and an old village site, one that had been deserted for many months. Someone had been foraging in the garden and had cut the *rasha* from the still-producing trees. My skin began to tingle; we were very close.

At 9:30 we crossed a small stream at the base of a hill. Karina said it was the one that the people bathed in and got their water from, but since there were very few footprints in the sand he was sure the village was deserted. A few minutes later we crossed over the peak of the hill and found ourselves in a modestly large Yąnomamö garden. We stopped and listened, but heard only sounds of the birds and insects. Karina pointed out the top of the *shabono* over the tops of the banana plants. We continued down the trail and walked into the village. It was deserted and all but one small section had been burned down. We walked over to this section and put our packs down in the shade. Karina was more disappointed than I was. We sat there, discussing the possible location of the group. Karina pessimistically suggested that they had gone to one of their several camping areas on the Shukumöna-u but hesitated to guess which one.

He wanted to turn back and go home. I suggested that we look around in the garden to see if anyone had returned to it recently. We soon found many signs of life; the people could not be very far away, for they were returning to the garden to fetch food. We found a stalk of ripe plantains and ate several of them.

We decided to follow their trail along the Mavaca River to the southwest, toward a camping area Karina said they preferred to others. We left everything behind except our hammocks and our weapons and traveled quickly. It was soon apparent that we were on the right trail, for their signs became fresher and more numerous as we went along. We had followed the trail for about an hour and a half when Karina suddenly stopped and motioned for me to be quiet. Ahead of us we could hear people talking! We had found them!

I suddenly felt very limp and worried. What had I gotten myself into? This was it, buddy. Perhaps all those earlier troubles were Fate's way of telling you to stay home and mind your own business.

Karina told me to stay where I was and let him go in first; they would be very frightened if I walked in with absolutely no warning, and might shoot me. I gave him my shotgun and took his bow and arrows. He disappeared down the trail, entered the temporary camp, announcing himself with a series of short, high-pitched whistles. The voices stopped for a second and the jungle was quiet. They then cheered when they recognized who it was. They stopped again and all was quiet for several minutes. Then there was a moment of excited buzzing. I knew they had been informed of my presence. I wiped the mud off my legs and straightened my loincloth. Karina soon reappeared and beckoned me to come in. I stalked into the clearing in proper Yąnomamö fashion and stood there in the middle while the men ran screaming about me, waving their bows and arrows and pointing them at me. My head was whirling with excitement, and my mouth was dry. Out of the corner of my eye I could see women and children running from the houses, making for the woods and safety. It was too much for them. Finally, one of the old men grabbed me by the arm and led me to a hut, motioning me to lie down in the empty hammock. They were as nervous as I was. Each time I moved, they jumped away from me. I lay in the hammock as a visitor should, one hand behind my head and one hand over my mouth, with my legs crossed and eyes fixed on some invisible object above the heads of everyone.

In the hammock next to me lay a young, muscular, handsome man of obvious importance, a man whom I recognized as a leader. He was too young to be Sibarariwä, or else Sibarariwä had preserved his age well. I managed to attract Karina over to my hammock and ask him if he were Sibarariwä. He answered: "No! He is someone else. He is big!"

I later learned that his name was Möawä. A year later I learned that he was *the* headman, and his renown had eclipsed that of Sibarariwä—his classificatory father. Indeed, they had fought, and Sibarariwä left with the largest faction of the village with him. Möawä, because of the force of his character, was beginning to lure them back into his fold, and by 1970 he had most of Sibarariwä's earlier followers in his village. Thus, the old leader, whose name and reputation had been indelibly fixed in the minds of his mortal enemies, the Bisaasi-teri, was replaced and driven out by a younger, fiercer man. That must have been an accomplishment of great moment, for Sibarariwä was by no means old, decrepit, or senile.

Karina told them that we left the packs at the *shabono* and two men were sent to get them.

It is impossible to describe the noises they made on seeing me for the first time.

Figure 1.13—We were disappointed to find their village deserted.

Figure 1.14—Mishimishimaböwei-teri camp, where I first made contact with them.

The Yąnomamö are noisy people to begin with, but when they are excited, they are even noisier. They hissed, clucked, and hooted, and screamed. The adult men shooed the younger ones away and crowded around the hammock, each trying to elbow his way closer for a better look. Soon they were all around me. They

Figure 1.15—Möawä—meaner than Sibarariwä, his predecessor.

are not supposed to approach the visitor for several minutes, and should not stand upright over the hammock. The etiquette system fell to pieces that day. Only Möawä remained aloof, eying us all with an expressionless, cold glint. Finally one of them touched my leg and pulled his hand back as if he had burned it. He clicked his tongue excitedly. Another tried it, and another. They grunted and clicked some more. One thing they kept exclaiming effervescently, over and over again, was: "Whaaa! Look how hairy he is! He is covered with hair!" They gradually got bolder, and soon there were dozens of hands being rubbed up and down my arms, legs, and chest. Finally, one of the older men in the front row screamed at one of the younger men in back to go out into the woods and fetch his father and the others who were camped there. He bolted away and ran out of the village, reappeared a second later with a sheepish look to fetch his weapons, and zipped off again. He was so excited that he almost left his bow and arrows behind, which is pretty excited for a Yąnomamö.

The examination went on for over an hour. They observed the etiquette rules in that they did no ask me any questions at first, but finally they began directing their comments to me. The first thing that they wanted to know was why I took so long to visit them. They claimed that they had repeatedly sent messages out to me by the way of the Mǫmariböwei-teri and Reyaboböwei-teri, asking me to come and visit, but I never came. They told me many things about myself that surprised me. They quoted things I had said to other Yąnomamö, and related in considerable detail how I recently fell off a rock on a trip to Reyaboböwei-teri and hurt my arm. They wanted to see the scar. They rubbed it gently and told me they knew how much it hurt me at the time of the accident. I was flabbergasted. They scolded the women for running away in fear and ordered them back into the village. I was a friend. Finally Karina, who had been fed but largely ignored up till now, suggested to them that I was weary from my trip and probably hungry. Some of them leapt to their feet and dashed home, returning with ripe plantains, bananas, and whatever other morsel of food they had around, offering it to me. I had hardly gotten a mouthful down when I heard the shouts of the others returning from the jungle. A dozen more men ran into the village shouting: "Where is he?" "Where is he?" The examination process was repeated again. Others straggled in and joined the crowd. I was covered with red pigment from head to foot. It was getting dark and the crowd began thinning out, but the village was a din of excited conversations. The people of Mishimishimaböwei-teri had seen their first foreigner. He was larger and fuzzier than they had imagined.

It started to rain hard and people frantically began hauling leaves in from the jungle to patch up the holes in their roofs. I was relieved that they left, and strung my own hammock. This caused another minor sensation, as they had never seen a hammock like mine. It was made of nylon, and was three times the size of theirs. Things quieted down again for a while, but the chatter was very lively.

By and by a distinguished looking older man walked silently out of the rain into the village clearing, carrying a long pole. He was using it as a walking stick, although he was not hobbling. He headed straight for the hut I was in and, as he approached, a man in one of the hammocks next to me got up quickly and re-

Figure 1.16—Sibarariwä. His entry into camp cast a shadow of gloom over everything.

treated to the hut next door. The older man leaned his club on the front pole of the house, wiped the rain from his face and got into the hammock that had just been vacated. A woman in the hut next to us immediately brought him some roasted plantains and retired nervously. The village had become strangely quiet after the older man come in. I knew I was in the presence of Sibarariwä.

Karina had told me that I should address him as either *shoriwä* (brother-in-law) or *shoabe* (father-in-law, grandfather, or mother's brother). This would relate us to each other in the best possible way according to the Yąnomamö kinship practices. It would automatically create between us a kinship bond that implied certain modes of behavior and mutual obligations that other kinship terms did not convey. I decided that I would call him *shoabe*, since it implied more obligations on my part, and thus put him in a somewhat superordinate position, something that I felt would be appropriate. He certainly commanded the awe of the others; the village was no longer the same after Sibarariwä entered. It was tense and strained. I did not like it.

The few stragglers who were sitting around my hammock at the time got up and left, saying nothing, leaving the two of us lying in adjacent hammocks trying to ignore each other, each waiting for the other to make the first gesture. Since I was the visitor, I expected him to break the ice. He was silent and poker-faced, and pretended not to know I was there. I was afraid that the tensions building up because of our silence would lead to bad feelings, so I called to him: "Father-in-law! I have come to your village to visit you and bring *madohe.* Is it true that your people are poor and in need of machetes?" I could hear the whispers of excitement around us after I spoke. "Yes! We are poor in machetes," he said cynically, implying that I ought to know better than to ask stupid questions when I could plainly see that they were poor. His tone of voice did not inspire any warm feelings in me.

We chatted half-heartedly for a while. I could tell that things were not going too well and that this old goat was not going to be overly friendly with me. I concluded by telling him that I would give him the cooking pot I had with me and one of the knives in the morning, and that I would bring him a *big* gift on my next visit. This visit was primarily to discover if they were friendly and if they were in need of steel tools, as the rumors said—a story I always tell when I visit a village for the first time. One must always imply that he has many more possessions *back home* and intends to bring them on his next visit, provided the people are friendly. It is like the relationship between the goose and golden eggs. If you want more eggs, be nice to the goose.

Sibarariwä's solemn arrival and demeanor threw a cloud of uncertainty over an otherwise enthusiastic welcome. I decided to ignore him and struck up conversations with people in the other huts. Both he and Möawä ignored each other conspicuously. Soon a modestly large crowd of men were around my hammock again, and the mood reverted to the excitement of midafternoon. I explained to them that I came to see how many people there were and told them I already had their true names memorized. They were surprised, and moderately annoyed, and wanted to know who told me. I said it was "someone from Mǫmariböwei-teri," thereby keeping Karina out of trouble. I would speak to each one in the morning and find out what kind of item he would like me to bring him on my next visit. They were enthusiastic about this and agreed to cooperate with me and point everyone out when I mentioned their names. So long as I already knew their names there was no point in lying to me about them. I showed them my field ledger and where their names were written. They would point to a name and ask me who that was. I would whisper the name into the ear of one of them and he would relate it to the others by some teknonymous or kinship reference, and they would roar with laughter, amazed that the magical scribbles actually meant something.

That night I dug my transistor radio out of my pack and tuned in a news broadcast. They were amazed again at the strange contraption, but were able to recognize male and female voices. They insisted on my tuning in a station with a female speaker, and crowded around to listen attentively to a language they did not understand. (As I recall, it was in Dutch, and I didn't get much out of it either!) Every once in a while I would try to find a station more to *my* liking, but they insisted on hearing a female voice. Most of them went home when I turned the radio off, but a few of them hung around to stare at me—and periodically ask me if I were sleeping yet.

I fell asleep worrying about Bäkotawä. More precisely, I began worrying about what he would do. What if he got so frightened that he could no longer bear to wait for us to come back? What if he took the canoe and left us? I decided that I would go to the river soon and check on him. The Mishimishimaböwei-teri, thanks to Karina, knew he was there and insisted on inviting him to the village.

The next morning I began the delicate task of identifying everyone by name and numbering them with indelible ink to make sure each person had only one name and identity. I estimated their ages and noted their spouses if my information was incomplete in this respect. I had 270 names in my field ledger, but the village contained no more than 80 people at the time. There had been a recent fight over a woman and the village was split into two parts. As luck would have it, I had found only the smallest part. The others were across the mountains on the Shukumöna-u living near another garden. My present hosts were mad at them and did not want to take me there. They felt sure that they would reunite again, probably before my next visit. I methodically identified everyone, whispering the names into Karina's ear, who then translated them into kinship circumlocutions. By ten o'clock I had numbered everyone in the group and the census was as complete as I could make it for the time being. I had noted after each name the item he or she wanted me to bring on my next visit, and they were surprised at the total recall I had when they decided to check me. All I did was look at the number I had written on their arm, look the number up in my field book and tell the person precisely what he requested me to bring him. They enjoyed this, and pressed me to mention the names of particular (unimportant) people in the village, laughing hysterically when I would whisper his name into someone's ear. The others would ask if I got it right, and the informant would give an affirmative quick raise of the eyebrows, causing everyone else to laugh.

After this task was over, I had essentially completed the major objective of the trip and passed the time with my hosts, doing what they wanted me to do. They wanted me to shoot my gun, as they had never seen one before. I had them fill a gourd with water and blew it to pieces at 15 yards, spattering water and debris all over. This impressed them. They wanted to see how strong I was and we lifted each other, bent arms to show our muscles, and other silly displays. They wanted to show me how close the Mavaca River was to their camp site and we went for a walk to the river. There was a small waterfall they wanted me to see. It had no name, and when I indicated my surprise, they decided to name it for me. It is now *Shaki tä bora*, at least to the people who really know. ("*Shaki*" for Chagnon, *bora* for falls, and *tä* is the classifier.) By midafternoon we were back at the camp, and it was raining hard. They knew I had trade goods at the boat and were anxious to have them. They badgered me constantly until I agreed to go to the canoe to check on the trade goods. Most of the adult men decided to come along to see my canoe, but Sibarariwä was not among them. He had left at dawn and returned to a small camp he and a few others had made away from the others, taking the cooking pot and knife I had given him.

We left for the canoe about three o'clock, using a much better trail than the one Karina and I had followed. It rained hard all the way and we traveled at a very fast pace, knowing that we would not make it by dark. We intercepted the original trail about an hour before reaching the river. We found spent cartridges every few hundred yards: Bäkotawä had been playing around with the shotgun, probably shooting at everything from parakeets to spiders. There was no telling how many cartridges he had shot before he got to this point, but at the rate we were finding the empties on this stretch of the trail he probably was out of ammunition by the time he reached the canoe.

Figure 1.17—The author and the Mishimishimaböwei-teri at Shaki Tä Bora. (Photograph by Karina. The scratches are because the film got wet.)

None of the men brought food or hammocks with them. They planned to take me to the canoe, trade bows and arrows for the machetes I had cached there, and return home early the following morning. They would be hungry, but they were too excited to think about food. They could make hammocks from bark in a few minutes and would sleep in these makeshift contraptions for the night.

Karina was in the lead, followed by several men and myself. The main body followed behind me. About 6:30 P.M. as dusk settled and walking became difficult, we reached the spot where we left the canoe. Needless to say, my greatest fears had been realized. Bäkotawä had taken the canoe, motor, trade goods, food—everything. I refused to believe my eyes at first. He did not know how to run the motor, so why would he want to take that? Why the trade goods? He knew that the Shamatari would be furious when I promised them fifteen machetes, six axes and twelve cooking pots and then was unable to deliver them. It was as if he were trying to get me into the most unpleasant of all possible jams.

He had not even spent the night there: there was no sign of a house, no fire, nothing. At first I thought we were at the wrong place, but on close inspection and after Karina insisted, I was convinced we weren't. The river had come up several feet since we had left the spot two and a half days ago and it did not look the same. But our tracks were there. My first suspicion was that he had moved everything across the river and downstream a little, to get off the main trail and conceal himself. I fired my shotgun two times, but no reply came. Perhaps he knew I had Shamatari with me and was too afraid to return my signal.

We made camp in complete darkness. I had a piece of plastic tarpaulin with me, and when the rain came all my twenty companions huddled together around my hammock and spent the night shivering. It had been too dark to make adequate shelters, and the driest spot was under my tarp, so none of us got much sleep.

At dawn I gave Karina my shotgun and two cartridges and a quick lesson in how to fire both chambers. He was to walk along the river until midday and fire the cartridges when he turned back, waiting to see if Bäkotawä would reply. Meanwhile, some of the young men were sent back to the garden, which was four hours behind us, to fetch food. I spent the morning contemplating my plight and trying to weigh the alternatives in the event that Bäkotawä could not be found. I was almost out of food and had only five or six cartridges left. I could get vegetable food from the Yąnomamö in case I had to walk back, but I would have to have them carry it. Our packs already contained just about as much as two men would want to transport over that distance.

There were two possible ways to walk out. The trail to the northeast would take us to Iwahikoroba-teri, two or three days' walk from our camp. The Iwahikoroba-teri were uncontacted, and my companions were not anxious to have me find out where they lived, probably because they suspected that I would visit only them in the future and bring my steel tools there. From Iwahikoroba-teri it was four or five days' walk to a new garden made by the Patanowä-teri, a group I knew well. I had spent two weeks with them a month earlier, but at their old garden. I knew that if I reached their village, I could get some of them to guide me to Bisaasi-teri, a further three- or four-day trip.

The arguments against this plan, besides the reluctance of my potential guides to consider going this way, were several. First, the rainy season had started and most of the jungle before us was inundated. Many detours would be required and walking would be slow through the swamps. If it were eight or ten days' walk in the dry season, it could easily become fifteen or more days' walk in the wet season. Second, my shoes would not last that long, and my feet were in no condition to make such a trip barefooted. Third, if anyone heard about my plight and tried to find me, I would be too far away from the river to hear them and an embarrassingly large "rescue" operation might develop unnecessarily.

The alternative trail was to the northwest, to Reyaboböwei-teri. It was at least a week's walk to that village according to my companions, and two or three days from there to Bisaasi-teri, depending on how fast you walked (I did it in two and a half difficult days earlier in 1968). All of the above arguments applied against this alternative, in addition to two further disadvantages. The distance between provisions was greater, and there was a war developing between my present hosts and the Reyaboböwei-teri. Wadoshewä, a prominent local man, told me that he had recently visited the Reyaboböwei-teri and was chased out of the village by their headman, Idahiwä, who threatened to kill anyone who visited there in the future. The possibilities of walking out seemed remote at best, and I decided to consider doing so only as a last resort. I could, after all, live indefinitely with the Mishimishimaböwei-teri if I had to, and I was certain that someone would sooner or later come up looking for me. It might be weeks or months, but they would come.

The thought of living for weeks with the Mishimishimaböwei-teri on the occasion of my first contact did not appeal to me, and my mind turned to other possibilities.

While waiting for Karina to return, and already convinced that Bäkotawä was gone for good, I decided to make a bark canoe with the help of the Shamatari. Whenever the Yąnomamö have feasts they make troughs to contain the gallons of soup consumed at the feasts. The troughs are similar to crude canoes, and are occasionally used as such. They are so heavy and poorly made that they are usually discarded after the maiden voyage, usually a downstream trip. The bark deteriorates rapidly and loses its resiliency after a few days. It then collapses like a post-Halloween jack-o-lantern, and rots quickly. When I asked my companions to help me find an *arapuri* tree, the tree whose bark is used for the trough, they insisted that none could be found in the area. My spirits sank again. Making the bark canoe and going downstream in it would have been merely an inconvenience and I was largely viewing my plight as exactly that. Now that I learned that the bark canoe idea was out of the question, I began worrying that perhaps my situation was more serious.

Figure 1.18—The type of bark canoe I had hoped to build to descend the Mavaca.

Next, I decided to make a log raft. The Yąnomamö groups near the Orinoco all know how to make them. The Shamatari knew what I meant when I asked about log rafts, but confessed that they had never made one. I was amazed at this information, since I thought this was a universal cultural trait among them. And since they had at one time lived on the Shukumöna-u, I was doubly amazed at their ignorance of this craft. They explained that they only cross the Shukumöna-u in low water, and make bridges for that purpose.

Log rafts are simple to make, and I knew that they could do it with a little help. Their palisades are essentially upright log rafts, so they had the basic skills to execute the task. We had my single machete to work with and spent most of the morning cutting logs and collecting lianas with which to lash them. I was not happy about this alternative, since rafts are very clumsy, and Karina was by no means an accomplished seaman. We would have great problems guiding a log raft through the snags and curves in the river, but it was still a much better option than walking.

Figure 1.19—My spirits sank when the log raft did. They turned to hide smiles.

I instructed them to cut only light, pithy trees. I helped pick out the trees, measuring the proper length, and hauled them to the river when they were felled. My companions took turns chopping with the machete. By mid-day we had assembled the materials at the river's edge and were ready to lash the logs together. My spirits picked up as we tied the logs together with vines. By early afternoon it was as wide as I dare let it get and still be controllable: I called the work to a halt.

The Shamatari gathered at the bank for the test run. I stepped onto the crude craft and it promptly sank, and with it, my spirits. My companions tried hard to look concerned and worried, but many of them turned their faces so I could not see their grins. They laugh at the most unusual things.

I slunk back to my hammock to wait for Karina to return and thought once again about walking out. Perhaps we could make it back to the spot where we had left the large canoe, which I calculated to be about halfway between our camp and Bisaasi-teri. But we would have to follow the river for the greater part of the way in order to be sure that we did not pass the canoe. And, the river naturally flows through the lowest area and, therefore, would bring difficult walking. The major argument against this alternative was that I could not predict Bäkotawä's behavior. Since he took with him virtually everything I left at the river, there was little reason to expect that he would pass the big canoe by without adding that to his list.

I moped in my hammock for the remainder of the afternoon, and took notes on the events of the past few days. Later in the afternoon Karina and his companions returned silently to the camp and flopped into their hammocks. They had walked all day, reaching the spot where Karina, Bäkotawä, and I had made our last camp. Karina reported that not only was Bäkotawä not there, he had even stopped to collect the empty gasoline tank we left behind! Karina had fired the shotgun twice, but Bäkotawä had not responded.

The rest of the village learned of the situation and people were streaming into our camp all day long, bringing food and hammocks. A more substanial camp was ultimately constructed, and all the huts were covered with *kedeba* leaves to keep the rain out. At least we would be dry, fed, and rested.

While I was lying in my hammock contemplating my situation, one of the men confronted me with the following argument. Since I was a foreigner and since foreigners knew about canoes, I ought to know how canoes were made. I told him that I knew how to make them (which was not exactly true) but I did not have the appropriate tools with which to do it. It would take axes, and Bäkotawä had taken all my axes. He then said that they had two old axes in the village.

With this my spirits lifted once again. I told him that if he would send for the axes and help me hollow out a tree, we would make a canoe. I was the best damned canoe-making foreigner they would ever meet. Two young men were immediately dispatched to the village to fetch the axes. They must have run all the way to the village and back, for they returned a few hours later, after dark. They covered the round-trip distance in about six hours, the time that it took Karina and me to walk it just one way!

Meanwhile, we went looking for an appropriate tree. I did not know what trees the Makiritare Indians used for their canoes. I told my companions that I needed a large tree that was pithy on the inside, and they presently found one that they claimed met these requirements.

We all retired in much better spirits that evening, listening to female voices on the transisitor radio and munching on roasted plantains and *rasha* fruits that the women had brought to us.

The 6:30 A.M. broadcast the following morning from the Catholic Mission had no news about airplanes, and the seven o'clock broadcast from the Protestant

Mission said nothing about Bäkotawä coming back yet. The Protestants did advise me, knowing that I had my transistor, that the plane scheduled to pick me up had been moved ahead from the fifteenth of April to the sixth, which gave me three days' notice! Even if I had been at Bisaasi-teri this would have been inconvenient. From where I was, it was impossible to make it back to Bisaasi-teri in three days. And, I feared, in three weeks.

We began working on the tree about 8:30 in the morning. The axes were so badly worn down and dull from use that progress was quite slow. The axes had been traded inland to the Shamatari after having been used by previous owners until they were nearly worn out.

The tree indeed was pithy in the center, a factor that contributed to our progress as the dull axes detracted. I measured off the length I thought would be sufficient to carry Karina and me—about 12 feet—and we cut off the trunk at that point. The tree was about 24 inches in diameter. Next, I scratched an outline of the area we were to hollow and we set about removing the interior of the tree. It was hot and humid and we soon were puffing and sweating profusely. The men were in excellent spirits and cooperated happily, making a game out of the project. I, delighted with their cooperation, had to watch them like a hawk, since in their enthusiasm they chopped recklessly, getting the canoe too thin at spots. By early afternoon it was taking shape. It looked like a cigar with a gouge cut out of it, but it looked suspiciously seaworthy. By that I mean that it looked as though it would float. I decided that I did not know enough about canoe making to attempt to spread it open with heat, which would have made it flatter on the bottom and therefore less likely to roll over, but would risk splitting the log in half. I decided to lash an outrigger on it. At about 2:00 P.M. I felt any further effort to get it thinner with the axes and machete would risk splitting the log in two. There were already several serious cracks appearing in the bottom, and we had to wrap vines around the ends of the log to prevent it from splitting further. We dragged it to the river, some 100 yards away, where we planned to test its seaworthiness. I was a little anxious that the canoe would be like the raft—buoyant enough to float by itself, but not buoyant enough to hold two men.

We had gotten almost to the river when the lead man spotted a tree with honey in it and the work came to an immediate halt. There is nothing that will excite the Yąnomamö like a cache of honey, and they immediately set about smoking the bees out of the nest and digging the sweet liquid out of it with leaves. A crude basket was made from another kind of leaf, and the honey was put into it with water. The Yąnomamö are not what we would consider sanitary chefs. They end up with a brew that is about 5 percent honey, 80 percent water, and 15 percent debris consisting of half-dead bees, wiggling larvae, leaves, honeycomb, and dirt. It is all consumed with great gusto, the container being passed from hand to hand, each man taking a deep draught before having it snatched by the next. They usually blow the most obnoxious debris off the surface and drink under it, but I was never thirsty enough to drink very much of the beverage.

As luck would have it, the honey tree was right at the spot where we planned to launch the canoe. Most honeybees in this area are stingless, but these were an exception. Soon the water and the bank were covered with groggy insects that attacked furiously, but the men didn't seem to mind. They just swatted their ankles and dipped the larva-filled honeycombs into the mead and munched on them, clucking with gastronomic pleasure. The bees were too much of a nuisance to let us do much more work on the canoe that afternoon, and besides, it was getting late.

Still, we had to see if it would float and cautiously put it into the river. To everyone's delight, especially mine, it stayed on top of the water. However, like any log, despite every improvement, it promptly rolled over. We even tested it with one man inside while the others prevented it from rolling. I breathed easily for the first time: it still floated. I managed to talk a few of the more enthusiastic workers into cutting the poles for an outrigger, and to find one of the "buoyant" trees we used for the raft. I cut two pairs of notches on each gunwale and tightly lashed in the outrigger poles with vines. Then we lashed the outrigger log to the end of this and tried the canoe again. This time it remained afloat without rolling, but the outrigger log was not very buoyant, and would sink if too much weight was put on that side of the canoe. I called for a volunteer to find a more buoyant log. By this time my companions were understandably tired of raft and canoe manufacturing and insisted that there was not a more buoyant log in the jungle. They wanted to go home.

I had difficulty talking them into helping make canoe paddles, but Möawä volunteered to help me and ordered a few more young men to join in. That night we whittled three crude paddles by the dancing firelight, one being a reject that had been thinned too much on the handle to make it very useful. I decided to take it along as a spare.

We listened to the radio again that night, stations with female vocalists and newscasters. The people of Holland will be pleased to know that their relay station at Bonnaire in the West Indies passed on a lesson on the Dutch language that was attentively heard by some 35 Yąnomamö. We slept well, satisfied that the crisis was over and I could get back downstream. We were proud of our labors.

I listened to the mission broadcasts again in the morning, but still no word about Bäkotawä, who had been on the river four days at that point.

We walked to the canoe, which was moored with vines a few hundred feet below our camp. We carried the packs and their contents to it, including a number of *toras*, bamboo containers that I bartered for with small knives. The *toras* all contained large numbers of curare arrow points that were made in the village while I was visiting.

The bees had regained their strength and inflicted revenge on us for robbing the honey, so we worked quickly. Karina wanted to be the first to try the canoe, an honor I conceded to him without argument. One of the men swam across the Mavaca with the long vine that was tied to the canoe. Karina jumped in with one of the paddles, and the man pulled him out into the river and across. Trying desperately to look like an expert boatman, he paddled the clumsy log with his equally clumsy paddle. From the difficulty he had keeping his balance in the canoe I could tell that it was going to be an interesting trip. Karina weighed all of 75 pounds and the canoe was just barely afloat. I weighed twice as much, and our gear, despite its small volume, probably accounted for another 40 pounds. With some difficulty he managed to maneuver the canoe back to port and we carefully loaded the equipment in, tying everything down with vines, including the shotgun.

The cracks that I noticed yesterday were worse, and my friends tried to plug them with mud. I managed to convince them that it would wash out and gave them one of my shirts to tear up and use as caulking. The repairs took just a few minutes and seemed to be adequate.

The moment of truth having arrived, I bade my companions goodbye and told them I would be back in the following dry season with many trade goods to repay their kindness. They assured me that they would reunite with the others who had separated from them and rebuild the *shabano* at the spot where the old one was burned down, urging me to return as soon as possible. I instructed Karina to sit in front and to exercise great caution when paddling, for the canoe was very tippy. I climbed in the back.

Much to my horror I discovered that the water came to within a half-inch of the gunwales. We were floating, but just barely. Then Karina took one small dip with his paddle, shifting his weight ever so slightly from center, and the left gunwale dropped below water level. We sank instantly, not having gotten one foot offshore. Everything got soaked except the few items—cameras, lenses, and field notes—that I had put into a waterproof rubber bag. We frantically tried to grab the packs before they went under, but it was too late. Only our heads were above water, and we looked very stupid indeed. Our friends turned their faces to conceal their grins. It *was* funny, and I had to turn my face also.

We dragged the canoe out into the bank again, unpacked everything, and re-sorted it. The *toras* full of curare arrow points were the first to go. Möawä, who had helped me whittle the paddles, ordered a number of young men to make a small hut across the river in which I could store the items I would leave behind. He then told me he would make sure that nobody stole anything, since he was well aware of the fact that I disliked theft and might not return if they stole anything from me. I normally would have been enchanted by such a friendly gesture, but at this point I was feeling pretty low. It really did not matter very much if they did steal everything, did it? I humored them by pretending I was still concerned about my worldly possessions. I took only those items that were absolutely essential for survival, and those that had some scientific value, keeping my field notes and leaving behind things like antivenin for snake bites. The Shamatari transported the excess equipment to the other side of the river, using the canoe as a ferry. They were perceptive enough to swim *alongside* the canoe rather than ride *in* it. One of the biggest losses when we capsized was my remaining package of cigarettes, and I desperately needed one then.

After reloading the canoe, we went through the motions of farewell, but only halfheartedly. We all expected that the canoe would capsize as soon as we got into the current, and that I would be returning to the village with them.

Karina and I climbed into the canoe for the second time. The water came to within two inches of the gunwales; my hopes revived slightly.

The canoe was in a shallow backwater adjacent to a sharp bend in the river. There were several large logs blocking the way, but we pushed off into the current anyway—and promptly got hung up in the snags and sank instantly. Fortunately, we were able to stand on a sunken log and refloat the canoe while the others chopped the logs out of our way. I could tell that paddling was going to be almost out of the question: Karina was too clumsy. Each time he took a stroke, he leaned over, and the water rushed into the canoe. While we were waiting for the Shamatari to clear this deadfall, I asked one of them to cut us two long poles.

I tied the paddles down with vines and bailed the canoe out with a gourd, which its friendly owner suggested I might find useful for this purpose and presented to me as a farewell token.

We climbed into the canoe again and were immediately caught up in the current. We were so precariously balanced that we couldn't turn around to wave to our companions. I was very grateful for their help and encouragement.

I do not know how many times we swamped that first day. I had no idea that a boy so small could be so inept and so clumsy. Each time he moved, he immediately caused the canoe to ship water. Instead of jumping out when he saw that we were sinking, he hung on for dear life and sank with the canoe. Had he jumped over the side, as I did, the canoe would have continued to remain afloat and we could have bailed it out with no problem. Still, he did not seem to catch on, and we ended up dragging the swamped canoe and contents to shallow water, bailing it out, and starting over again.

There was a logical reason for Karina's reluctance to jump out of the canoe into the river. He explained that he was afraid of *yahedibä* (electric eels). I assured him that there were none and urged him, whenever the canoe started to swamp, to jump out—the consequences would have been the same for him whether or not he jumped out. In both cases he had to get into the water. Still, he was frightened of eels. With good reason. About midday, as we were bailing out after one of our mishaps I stepped on a log beneath which lived an electric eel. I didn't know what hit me, but I felt a sharp pain in my leg and was knocked flat from the jolt. I saw the eel swim into deeper water as I got to my feet.

The outrigger was a bright idea, but had one built-in disadvantage: it acted as a snag-catcher and caused us many problems. We invariably capsized when it got caught on a snag: the current was strong enough to turn us sideways in the river, and since we were held fast by the outrigger, the water would rush over the edge and swamp us.

Sharp bends were a problem also. Unless we managed to keep to the inside of the bend, the current would force us against the bank on the opposite side and when the outrigger touched the bank we would go under again in the deepest water. It is a hopeless feeling to see a sharp bend ahead of you and try to delicately pole such a clumsy canoe to the inside of the curve. The immediate reaction is to pole harder, but when you do, your weight shifts just enough to cause you to ship water. Once it starts coming over the edge, you're done.

The natural hazards were not nearly so frustrating as the one sitting in the canoe with me. Yąnomamö are not river people, and if Karina may be taken as a typical example, they have good reason not to be. By the end of the first day of travel he still did not know which side he had to pole on to make the canoe go to the left or right. There were times that first day when I could not really decide whom I wanted to choke the most, Bäkotawä for abandoning me up the

Mavaca, or Karina for being so incompetent. By the time it was dark I was so hoarse from screaming "to the left," "to the right," and so on, that I could barely talk. He would sulk conspicuously, and turn away as an uncontrollable smile lit his face, a pedestrian imp dwarfed by my undershirt. I had to choke down an occasional smile myself.

Although it rained most of the day, compounding our discomfort, and the river was coming up quickly, we managed to find a sandy spit on which to make camp. We were in a very swampy area and exhausted from the day's work, so we did not look very hard for leaves to cover our shelter.

When it came time to cook our rice for supper, another discovery capped our comic tragedy. I had been conserving the rice for the trip home and had not eaten any since the evening before contacting the village. I had given my *only* cooking pot to Sibarariwä! There we were—no pot to cook our only food in. I had luckily stored the rice in a tin can, and we were obliged to use that as our cooking pot. It was a stroke of luck that I had given Bäkotawä his share of the rice in the plastic container. We would have gotten pretty hungry had I kept the plastic container and given Bäkotawä the tin.

Our hammocks and clothing were soaked, and it was uncomfortable to be in them. But the fire warmed us up and the hot rice tasted good. The thing that really picked up our spirits was the evening broadcast from the Protestant Mission that Bäkotawä had arrived in Bisaasi-teri late that afternoon. The broadcast was full of static, but I managed to hear several things. The missionary could not do anything to help. The measles epidemic had spread to another village and the only available motor and canoe were being used by those who went there to help. He did not know if they had a transistor radio, or when they were coming back.

I learned also that Bäkotawä had tipped my canoe over a few times and had lost much of my equipment. He did manage to save the motor and drag it out

Figure 1.20—Karina and my hand-hewn dugout canoe.

of the river onto a bank somewhere, but only he knew the precise place. When he got to about an hour above Bisaasi-teri, he unloaded the axes, machetes and cooking pots "because they were heavy" and he was "tired of paddling" their dead weight. He had paddled them four and a half days and decided, one hour away from his destination, that they were too heavy! Why did he take them in the first place?

I decided that it was best to push on the next day. It might be some time before help came and we were getting low on food. Our fire went out during the night and at dawn we woke up shivering, cold, and damp. We ate the leftover rice, packed the radio and hammocks, and pushed off once again.

The river was broader and deeper now, and our poles were only marginally useful. It was not long before we had to abandon them entirely and revert to the paddles. When we did, we had a rapid series of misfortunes. We had gotten fairly efficient with the poles and could keep from tipping the canoe after some practice, but the paddles required more exertion and we capsized several times before we could get the hang of it. We lost our spare paddle on one sinking. Later in the day we got snagged in an overhanging tree and capsized again, losing another paddle. At about three o'clock that afternoon, shortly after losing the second paddle, we reached the big canoe. We were both surprised that it was still there, but were very happy that it was. Even the nest of cooking pots I had left in the canoe was still there!

I had hoped that Bäkotawä would have put the motor in the big canoe as he went by, but he had discarded it somewhere upstream, before reaching the big canoe. We transferred our equipment to the big canoe and cut more poles for pushing. The river was now quite deep, but the poles enabled us to keep away from the banks and overhanging brush, keeping the bugs from falling onto us as they had been doing for the past two days. Our single paddle was too short and too small to be of much help in the big canoe. We were largely at the mercy of the current.

I remembered that our original first camp was only about two hours downstream by motor from the big canoe. I had hoped we could reach it, for if help did come, they would probably camp there at the end of their first day. It was one of those inviting camping places—high, and with a sandbar.

Now that we were in the big canoe, we could stand up, walk around, and in general, revert to our old, clumsy ways. More important, we could unlash the shotgun and shoot game for supper. I had not looked at the shotgun for two days. It was a mess. I had tied it under my seat and it had spent much of the past two days under water. The barrels were badly rusted, and the breech opened with considerable difficulty. I loaded it and kept it handy. Before long we glided past a large alligator, which I killed on the first shot. We dragged him into the canoe after severing his spinal cord with the machete.

Alligator meat is pretty grim fare. It looks tasty, white, and firm like a boiled lobster. It even resembles lobster in flavor. But it is as tough as shoe leather, no matter how you cook it. But I was pretty hungry for meat at that point, and even the thought of alligator made my mouth water.

By dark we decided that we could not reach the earlier campsite, so we made camp at the mouth of a small creek. I shot another alligator at this spot, so we had plenty of meat for the remainder of the trip. The last few hours with the big canoe convinced me that we would have to make another paddle before going on in the morning. The canoe was just too heavy to control with our single, crude paddle.

We were now at a point on the Mavaca where we could make it all the way back to Bisaasi-teri in about 24 hours of continuous travel. From here the river was broad, and all we had to do was keep the canoe in the middle of the stream. The current would do the rest.

We boiled more rice and roasted some of the alligator for supper. We were both dog-tired and fell asleep as soon as we finished eating.

The next morning I learned by radio that the other missionary and his Makiritare Indian companion had returned to Bisaasi-teri. They were planning to come up to look for me immediately. The radio message also gave the approximate location of the spot where Bäkotawä had put my motor. We had already gone past it, and would have to go back upstream to get it when the missionary got here. We decided that it was better to remain in camp all day, since we had to go back to get the motor anyway. Thus, we spent the day lying in our hammocks, chatting, and wishing we had some tobacco. I was not feeling very well and needed the rest. My numerous scratches and insect bites were infected and the fungus on my groin was flaring. The combination of poor food, tropical bacteria, and work was wearing on me. I thought about my tins of powdered milk and powdered chocolate, and how good the combination would taste.

We came to life when we heard the soft humming of wild turkeys in the jungle behind us. Karina went ahead of me and quickly pointed one out. I shot it and ran on to see if there were more. Karina was ahead of me, excitedly pointing out another bird. I was down to my last cartridge. When I closed the badly-rusted breach the chamber fired accidentally: the firing pin had rusted so badly that it did not retract when I opened the breech after the previous shot. Karina stood there gaping at me as a three-inch sapling toppled over just a few feet from his head. I had almost shot him, and I was very badly rattled from this experience.

By late afternoon we had forgotten about the close call and were waiting for the turkey and rice to get done. We dined in great comfort and style that evening, although we were both disappointed that the boat had not reached us. Perhaps we were further upstream from my old campsite than I thought.

By nine o'clock that night we were convinced that the boat would not reach us until the next day, so we went to sleep. A shotgun blast just a few feet from our hammocks got us to our feet in a second: it was Antonio, a Makiritare Indian, and Rerebawä, my fierce friend. They had made it to my old camp and were out hunting for their supper. They were unaware that Karina and I were sleeping just a few feet above the alligator they had just shot, and our shouts to them were as startling as their shotgun blast was for us. They paddled to shore and Rerebawä and I hugged each other happily. He was nearly convinced that the Shamatari had killed me and was relieved to see me alive and well. He told me that he would never let me go on another trip without him, despite the

Figure 1.21—Antonio, expert Makiritare canoe-builder, simply had to try my canoe.

dangers to which he might be exposed. Karina begged half of his wad of chewing tobacco and collapsed back into his hammock, contented. "I nearly died of poverty!"[4] he exclaimed as he lay in his hammock, contentedly sucking on the used wad. I myself was having such a nicotine fit that I considered asking for a share in the wad. Knowing the missionary attitude about tobacco, I didn't really expect to be able to bum a cigarette from the rescue team.

I was so delighted to see the "rescue" team that I presented Antonio and Rerebawä with the cooking pot of boiled turkey and rice. They took it back to their own camp, a few minutes downstream, to share with the missionary. As it turned out, I had as much food as they! They had left in such a hurry that they brought only enough manioc flour to last them one day, plus the shotgun I had loaned to Bäkotawä. It was amusing to me to ponder the question of who was rescuing whom. Had I remained upstream, they would have gotten pretty hungry within the next day, especially if I had remained in the village. They could have eaten alligator or turkeys for a long time, but meat without vegetable food is not very satisfying. I fell asleep thinking about the Yąnomamö verbs that describe eating. Particularly the verb *dehiaö*: "to eat a bite of meat and then a bite of vegetable food and chew both together." Their language captures so many important sensations.

The next morning at dawn they returned the empty cooking pot and we left to collect the equipment I left behind, and to look for the motor. Another missionary, who remained downstream, had questioned Bäkotawä for hours and had drawn a

[4] Their word for "being without tobacco" is best translated as "poor" or "poverty."

crude sketch map with the approximate location of the motor. It made very little sense to anybody except Bäkotawä, Karina, and me, since it was full of references to things like "where Shaki shot two turkeys," "where we left the empty gasoline can after our second sleep," and so on. Still, it was meaningful enough that I knew approximately where we had to begin looking for the motor, which we found late that morning. It was in poor condition, to say the least. Both cylinders were full of water, and we worked for about an hour before we got it all out. In attempting to start it we accidentally set it on fire, but we acted quickly and got it out before too much damage was done to the wiring. It finally started, and we were on our way again.

The river had come up four or five feet; it had been raining almost constantly since we left in our makeshift canoe. All of the deadfalls that caused us so much grief as we gingerly tried to prevent a capsize were now covered with water. We were able to travel at full throttle most of the way up to the cache of equipment, since I had chopped out those impediments that were above water level. By dusk we had found the cache and were on our way back home. Nothing was missing, so Möawä had kept his word.

The next morning we reached the spot where I had abandoned the makeshift canoe. Antonio, an expert boat maker, was enchanted with my first canoe and simply had to try it. He got in, paddled it around, inspected the outrigger, and then began laughing and shaking his head. He was surprised at my resourcefulness, but apparently not at all satisfied with the technical execution, for he kept pointing out various other species of trees that would have made a much better craft.

When we reached the spot where we first met the rescue team, Karina and I transferred over to my large dugout and we came the rest of the way down by ourselves.

Thus began my work among the Mishimishimaböwei-teri, the village that had, in my mind, become almost a fable because of the numerous setbacks I had sustained in previous attempts to reach it. The several and confusing village names reduced to just one: it was no longer "Sibarariwä's village" nor Möwaraoba-teri, nor Dạadaamöböwei-teri, nor any of the other names that it used to go by. It was now Mishimishimaböwei-teri, and the man who now "really lived there" was Möawä, who was younger than Sibarariwä and presumably more competent politically. He was competent enough to cause Sibarariwä to move off and form his own small village, a new group called Ironasi-teri, which lay a half day's walk to the southwest of Möawä's group.

I was now in a position to initiate the more tedious work of checking all the information I had accumulated up to that point and expanding on it. The friendly first contact led to reciprocal obligations between me and the Mishimishi-maböwei-teri, verbal promises that would effect the transfer of my *madohe* to them, moving against continued cooperation and friendship. Past experience taught me that their expectations would increase with time, and I worried, as usual, whether my fieldbooks would become justifiably enriched with the esoterica of my craft. I also knew that they were very many, and knew that large villages contained correspondingly large egos in the persons of their leaders. The Bisaasi-teri had, for years, related to me the renown of Sibarariwä. I had just met the man who succeeded him, and he communicated authority and competence in a most unmistakable way. It concerned me. I had not previously studied a village as large as this one, and I suspected that it remained large because of the skill and authority of Möawä's presence. I knew that life there would not be as tranquil as it had been in the smaller villages to which I had grown accustomed.

2/Settlement pattern and village interrelationships

Some definitions emphasize that anthropology is the intensive study of single, isolated communities—as if this were not merely the traditional approach, but a methodology of preference. Had I followed this procedure in my fieldwork and study of the Yąnomamö I would have a very misrepresentative picture of their culture. If I learned anything from my initial (1964–1966) fieldwork, it was that the individual village often deviated from the pattern implied by the whole. There was enormous variability in size, composition, and political status. I could not, for example, hope to understand the contemporary political stance of a particular village without knowing how that village was related to neighbors in its lineage composition, its history, and its *past* political dealings with them.

It was my growing awareness (from field experience) of how the whole affected the part—how the cluster of historically related villages formed a more intricate pattern that none of its constituent villages exhibited—that led to my interest in the process of village fissioning, settlement pattern, and political relationships of the particular villages to their neighbors.

This chapter deals with the historical and political relationships of the people of Mishimishimaböwei-teri and how I collected the various kinds of data to document these relationships. Briefly, the important ties between villages can be most revealingly shown by (a) demonstrating the population fissions and settlement movements through time, (b) collecting native accounts of past historical events, and (c) documenting how the individuals in the interrelated villages are genealogically descended from the same ancestors. This chapter deals only with settlement pattern and (native) historical accounts; Chapter 3 discusses the genealogical aspects of my study. That Mishimishimaböwei-teri cannot be meaningfully described as an isolated or isolable village will become apparent as its political past and genealogical ties to other groups emerge in the next two chapters. This raises an important methodological point. A multivillage tribe is the culmination of a pattern of population growth and fissioning, and its constituent parts—the villages—must at some point be examined from the perspective of what influence the whole has exercised on the parts, in particular, what light the process of growth and fissioning sheds on the specific nature of the villages of the tribe. In some ethnographic cases multivillage tribes have experienced generalized depopulation, and the composition of villages often reflects a pattern of aggregation of once-separate groups that are coalescing to maintain a modicum of their former social patterns. Many of the Gê-speaking tribes of central Brazil owe some of their characteristics to the process of depopulation and agglutination of formerly separate entities (Nimuendaju, 1939, 1942, 1946; Lévi-Strauss, 1963).

In other tribes, such as the Yąnomamö, population growth and fissioning continuously lead to the formation of new villages, and the rate of this growth process exercises an important influence on the political characteristics of the recently formed villages. To be sure, the complementary process—agglomeration by fusion—also takes place, but it is much less significant than the fissioning when the general character of the village is considered. Within-group fighting, not depopulation, leads to fusion and agglomeration among the Yąnomamö, and, in a sense, the process is in reality only a component of the fission process: fusions in this tribe result from fissions, *not* from depopulation. The rate of population growth and fissioning among the Yąnomamö would probably be quite high if it could be compared with rates for other, similar tribes.

A methodological consequence of this kind of growth rate is that the fieldworker can often find in several widely-scattered villages adults who all lived together in an earlier, common village—people whose verbal accounts can be utilized to reconstruct the immediate past history of a whole series of interrelated villages. The theoretical implications of this kind of growth rate are intriguing. The conditions under which the fissions take place are often violent and lead to bitter warfare between the recently separated groups. This gives a peculiar character to the warfare pattern, in that much of the fighting is between villages that are closely related by common descent, a characteristic that is disturbing to those who regard tribal warfare as a contest between enemy aliens. How much of this can be attributed to the *rate* of population growth, if any, and how much to the conditions of fissioning also becomes a fascinating problem, the answer to which has an important bearing on the ethnohistory of all parts of the world where agriculturally-based tribal populations radiated into unoccupied niches and spread over the landscape—vast areas like the Tropical Forest of South America or the Eastern Woodlands of North America. This theoretical problem is beyond the scope of this book and I will address the data to it elsewhere.

One of the isolable issues becomes a question of whether there is an intrinsic relationship between *rate* of growth and warfare intensity, and whether population density and warfare among all swidden cultivators are closely correlated, as has often been assumed. Before becoming too enmeshed in this important issue, let me describe the process of village growth and settlement dispersal through time and the methods I developed in the field to collect the requisite data. Then we will return to some of the theoretical issues that the data raise.

NEW PROBLEMS IN SETTLEMENT PATTERNS

Shamatari settlement pattern is rather more complex than that characterizing the Namowei-teri populations described in *The Fierce People.* Several factors are involved that were not characteristic of the Namowei-teri. First, there are many more villages in the Shamatari population. Second, some of the ancient garden sites were once occupied by other Yąnomamö groups whose relationships to Shamatari I have not worked out, and may never be able to work out unless I conduct several additional months of fieldwork in northern Brazil in the headwaters of several large affluents of the Rio Negro. Third, there seems to have been much more fissioning and subsequent recombining of groups or portions of groups, which confuses the pattern. Fourth, the Yąnomamö groups that migrated through the Mavaca River basin before the arrival of the Shamatari used names for their gardens that were later used by specific Shamatari groups for gardens in the same areas, or, even more confusing, gardens in different areas. Fifth, some of the Shamatari groups, after splitting away from each other, adopted identical names for distinct gardens. Thus, I had to devise different field techniques to unravel the somewhat more complex fabric of interrelationships among the Shamatari villages than I used in my initial study of the Namowei-teri populations.

In addition to describing these techniques and their results in this chapter, I also provide the reader translations of tape recordings taken from my original data. These translated texts are "historical" accounts from old informants about the political incidents—fights, wars, fissions—that guided my reconstruction of the history of the Shamatari villages. They contain the incidents that the informants felt were important in accounting for the fissioning and present distribution of the several villages most closely related to his or her own. There are two reasons for giving lengthy texts. First, it will provide the reader an indelible example of the field technique itself. Second, and perhaps equally important, it projects a more personal and more intimate characterization of Yąnomamö culture as its spokesmen relate it in the context of interviews. The selections from my tapes are made primarily to illustrate field problems and field techniques, but the content of the transcription is often informative and amusing in its own right, and conveys, far better than I can, a kind of "feeling" for their culture. The transcripts contain many place names; it is not necessary to remember them as you read, since the objective of the exercise does not hinge on knowing and remembering them. One thing that comes out is the rather casual and constant reference to violence and warfare in the history of the Shamatari. If the experience I had among the Namowei-teri villages stimulated me to describe the Yąnomamö as "the Fierce People," my subsequent work among the Shamatari would lead me to describe them as the "Fiercer" people. This will be documented later in the material dealing with genealogies and demography.

BACKGROUND

Before I made contact with the Mishimishimaböwei-teri in 1968 I already had accumulated a rather large amount of data on them and on their history. This information came from three sources. One source was the contact I had with people in the villages of Mǫmariböwei-teri and Reyaboböwei-teri, located some 10 hours' and 25 hours' walk to the southwest of Kąobawä's village respectively. I had complete genealogies and census data on both of these groups before ever meeting the Mishimishimaböwei-teri, data that clearly showed that all *three* groups had common ancestors.

Another source of information was several old women in Kạobawä's village, women abducted from the Shamatari population when they were very young. They gave me information on history and genealogical ties that reflected the days when they were young and lived with the Shamatari.

Finally, Kạobawä and a number of the older men in his village were familiar with the broader interrelationships among the Shamatari villages. Some of them, as young men, had regularly visited Shamatari villages, and at least one of my informants had done bride service among the Shamatari some 35 years earlier.

With these three sources of information, along with the information given to me by Karina, and what I had learned on my first visit to Mishimimishimoböwei-teri, I began to piece together the settlement pattern. My initial attempt was discouraging, for the complexities mentioned above soon emerged. The pattern was obviously different from the pattern I was able to determine for Kạobawä's group: the Shamatari population was very much larger, there were more villages and more complex kinds of interrelationships stemming from recurrent fissioning and subsequent recombinations. The Shamatari also penetrated an area that was occupied by other populations, living in some cases in the same areas, reclaiming garden areas that were once cleared by other Yạnomamö groups, and assuming the same names for the gardens. I was attempting to describe a complex sequence of village fissions and migrations that took place during a hundred years, but I had only three "windows" through which I could peek: that early portion of the history given to me by the old women; that portion—more recent history—known to Kạobawä; and finally, the most recent portion related to me by informants from the two closest Shamatari villages.

Perhaps one of the most serious obstacles to my initial attempts to make sense out of the settlement pattern was the fact that all published maps of the area turned out to be completely wrong. They showed the Mavaca River flowing from east to west in its headwaters, which were also erroneously shown to be exceedingly long, originating near the headwaters of the Orinoco. The information given to me by the Yạnomamö was inconsistent with this geographical fact, and I foolishly questioned the Yạnomamö information rather than the cartographic "facts." It took a trip to Mishimishimaböwei-teri to convince me that the Mavaca River headwaters flowed from west to east and were comparatively short. I also learned to put more credence in what the Yạnomamö said about geography, and less in what the United States Air Force Navigation Charts or the National Geographic Society said.

Before I could describe the settlement pattern, I first had to make my own crude map of the area. The maps given in this chapter, particularly for the Mavaca River and its affluents, do not correspond to published maps but are based on my own exploration of the river.[1]

After I began traveling to Mishimishimaböwei-teri in my dugout canoe, I

[1] In 1972 the government of Venezuela began mapping the area from the air with the side beam radar techniques. Detailed and precise maps will soon be available.

began mapping the Mavaca and its tributaries, getting the Yąnomamö name for each stream, no matter how insignificant its size. Each time I ascended the Mavaca River I would note the exact time I left and the exact time I passed particular rivers, mountains, and other geographical features. For most of the first day of travel I could operate the outboard motor *and* write the information directly into my field book as I traveled. Thereafter, the river became very narrow, choked with deadfalls, sunken logs, and areas characterized by incessant sharp bends with swift current. Thus, on the second and third days I recorded the information on a small cassette tape recorder, for it was dangerous to attempt to maneuver the boat and take notes at the same time. The tape-recorded entries would be something like this:

> 9:37 A.M.: A small stream coming in from the west smaller than the Kedebaböwei-u. About two hours above the camp I made last year when Waroiwä was with me. Dedeheiwä says it is called Mayebö̜ökōbö-u and that there are no abandoned gardens on it. Dugout canoe, 18 h.p. motor, two Yąnomamö with me, plus a light load.

The information about the type of motor, boat, and load would enable me to correct for speed when I compared the map made on this trip with similar maps made on other trips when I used a different boat and motor. These maps and notes would also help me plan subsequent trips, for I could estimate my gasoline requirements more accurately and not bring any more weight with me than absolutely necessary. I always kept track of the time I spent eating, filling gas tanks, and chopping through logs so I could correct the time spent to reach each particular stream.

After several trips I had a fairly detailed map of the streams that drained into the Mavaca River, and the relative distances between their mouths. Figure 2.1 is a photograph of one of my field books with the map I made on one such trip. I then drew a large-scale map shown in Figure 2.2 based on the information I collected on numerous trips. With the major streams roughly located, I began putting the gardens and villages on the map as accurately as I could, relating them both to the rivers and to several widely-spaced locations from which I took magnetic compass bearings to all the gardens and villages.

I used the magnetic compass to obtain bearings in the following way. I listed all the gardens I had learned about, putting them in alphabetical order. Then I would ask an older, and therefore knowledgeable, man, such as Dedeheiwä, to point to the abandoned garden. I would then record the bearing and note that all bearings from that informant were taken from a particular spot, such as the "mouth of Washäwä River" or "the village of Bisaasi-teri," and so on. These points were far from each other, and where the several bearings to each garden intersected—lines drawn from the particular known points to the particular unknown gardens—I put a dot on my map to represent the garden. Then I would take clusters of gardens and try to determine how far apart in "sleeps" they were from each other, what rivers or streams they were on, and whether my informant had ever been there. (A sample of these map notes is given in Figure 2.5.)

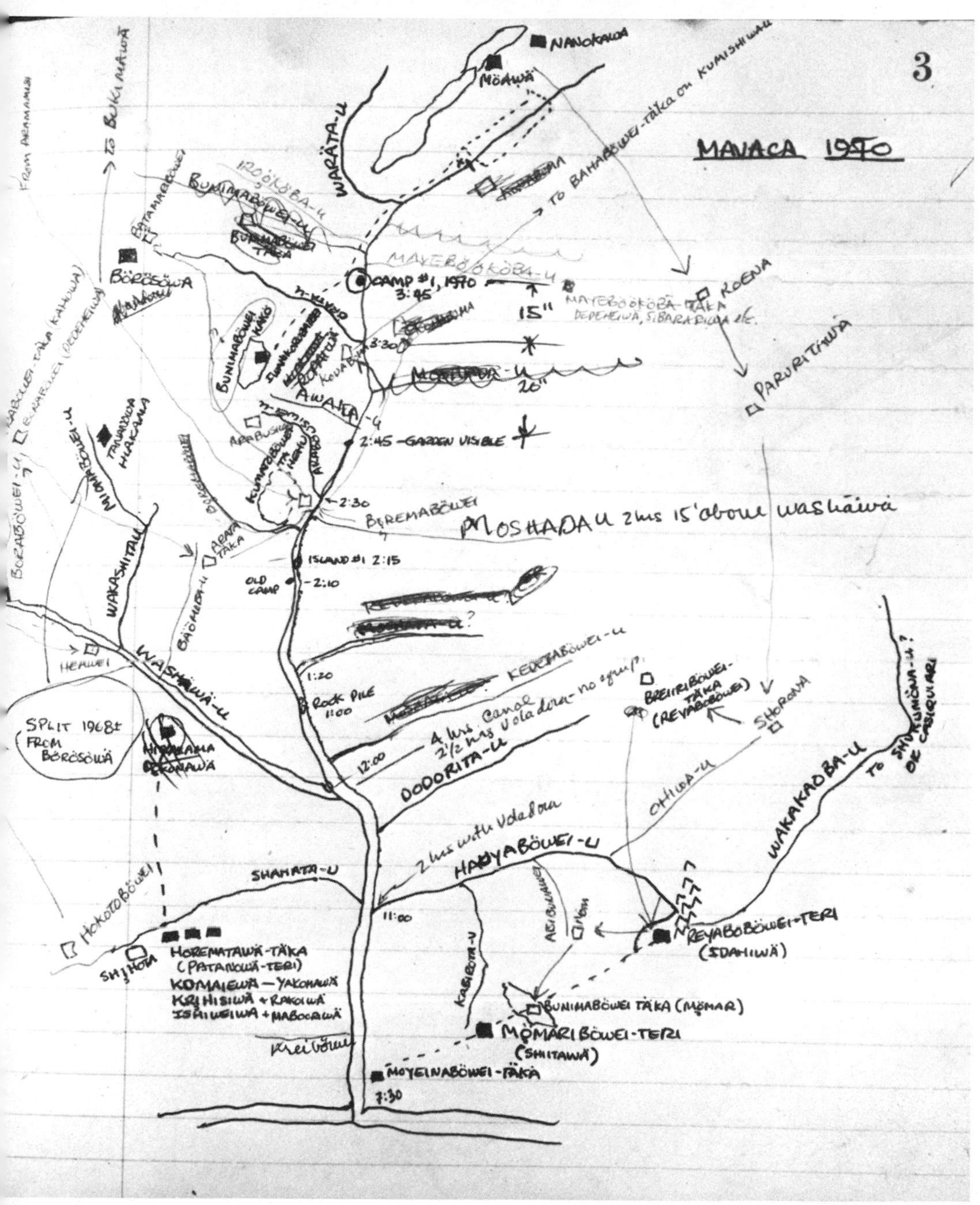

Figure 2.1—Photograph from field book of crude map of Mavaca region.

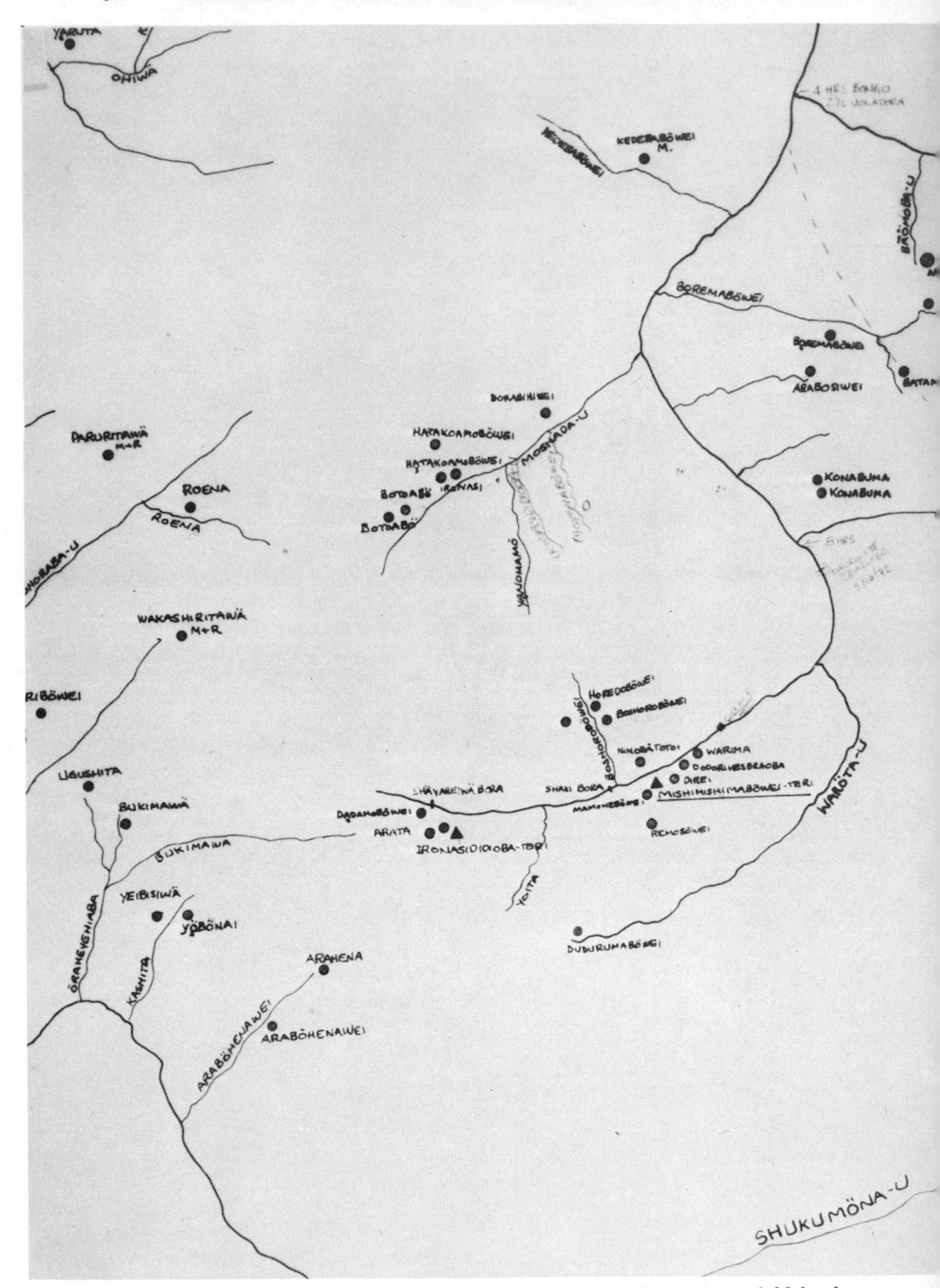

Figure 2.2—Photograph of neat, redrawn version of map from field book.

One problem with this approach was that some of my "known" or fixed points, such as the "mouth of Washäwä River," were not, in fact, known points in a cartographic sense. None of the maps were accurate. Therefore, in 1972 I brought a theodolite into the field with me and fixed the position of some of these points by taking star shots.

DIRECT APPROACH TO SETTLEMENT PATTERN

I developed several methods for obtaining data on village histories and migration patterns, some direct and others indirect. My first attempt at deciphering the Shamatari settlement pattern followed the techniques I used to collect similar information about Namowei-teri history: I would ask the informant to tell me about the places, names of gardens, on what rivers they were located, why they were abandoned, where the group moved to next, and whether or not a village split had taken place at that location. I began this work long before I had ever made contact with the Mishimishimaböwei-teri, so the plethora of names of villages, people, rivers, and mountains was very confusing: I had never seen these places and had never met any of the individuals. Because of multiple names for identical places, identical names for different places, and my general ignorance of the geography of the region, my initial attempts were not very successful.

As in the past, I used a tape recorder and large pad of lined yellow notebook paper to record the information. I wrote the names of the rivers and gardens on the paper, constructing a crude, schematic map as I went along, simultaneously recording everything that was said so that I could later check back and verify my informant's story and compare it with other informants' accounts.

The following text is a transcription of a tape recording I made in 1965 concerning the history and settlement pattern of the Shamatari. Although I did not actually reach Mishimishimaböwei-teri until 1968, I had taken one trip up the Mavaca headwaters, coming very close to reaching the area they occupy (see Chapter 1). My informants were Kạobawä and Yanayanarima, an old woman of some seventy years who had been abducted as a young girl from the Shamatari region. Yanayanarima is one of Dedeheiwä's sisters, that is, sister of the old shaman and one of the prominent leaders in Mishimishimaböwei-teri (see Chagnon, 1973, film *Magical Death*). I often asked Kạobawä to be present when I interviewed the old Shamatari women, for he was well aware of my objectives and encouraged the women to relate the more important details without spending too much time discussing peripheral incidents. Yanayanarima was given to daydreaming, and my command of the language in 1965 was not good enough to be able to distinguish the important incidents from the insignificant ones. Kạobawä's knowledge of Shamatari history was sufficiently good so that he could summarize the important information for me after the old woman left.

The informant session of which this transcript is just a small part lasted several days, up to five hours each day. The entire recording is exceedingly monotonous and repetitious. The old woman is not very enthusiastic, is slightly senile, and has difficulty keeping her attention fixed on the work. This section of the tape

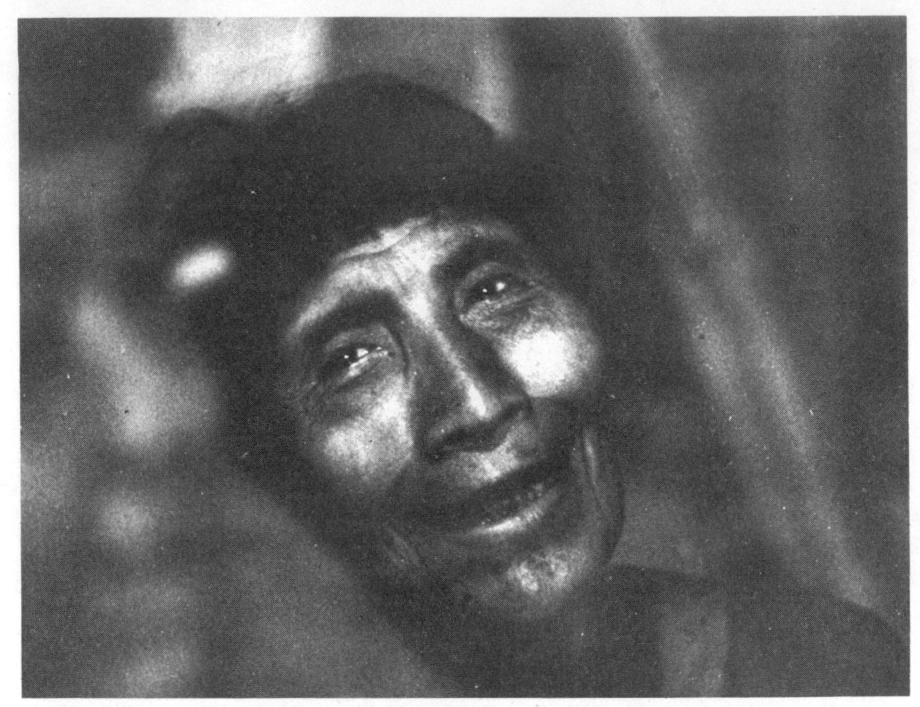

Figure 2.3—Yanayanarima, the old woman.

deals with an important group known in the past as "the Konabuma-teri," a village that I had heard about from Kąobawä, who visited there often as a young man when his group was living at Patanowä-teri. He told me that the Konabuma-teri lived on the upper Shanishani River, the same river whose lower course flows through the Patanowä-teri region. What I did not know while this recording was taken was that there were *two* villages known as Konabuma-teri: both were Shamatari groups, closely related to each other. Both informants were aware of the distinction, but neither felt it was important enough to mention. Finally, the second Konabuma had been occupied earlier by a distinct Yąnomamö group, who also used that designation for themselves, giving a total of three places called Konabuma and three Konabuma-teries. I present a free translation with comments on the tone of voice used by myself (NC), Kąobawä (K) and the old woman, Yanayanarima (Y). I have also added coments on the accuracy of some of the statements they made in 1965, based on information I subsequently gathered over the next six years. In 1965, of course, I assumed that the information was true—until I could prove otherwise. It is not essential to be able to recall the names that occur in this transcription. Note the constant reference to wars and fights, and the often vague answers to specific questions. Observe how Kąobawä helps keep the old woman on the right track. The session had been in progress for some hours at this point:

NC: Why did you abandon Konabuma-teri?

Y: Because the Aramamisi-teri shot at us all the time. They raided us and chased us away.

NC: Did you separate there into several groups?
Y: Yes, we split into many groups. They chased us with sharpened staves.
NC: Where did the Aramamisi-teri live at that time?
Y: Over there. [A very characteristic informant response that assumes that you know where "over there" is]
NC: On the Shukumöna River?
Y: [Saracastically] "Yes! Nowhere else but there!
NC: In the headwaters?
Y: Right in the very headwaters of the Shukumöna River, that's where the Aramamisi-teri lived. [A false answer]
NC: Did the Karawatari [a distinct Yąnomamö group] live downstream from them?
Y: Yes, they were on a branch further downstream.
NC: Were there other Yąnomamö in the Shukumöna River area then?
Y: There were no others.
NC: Just two groups? The Karawatari and the Aramamisi-teri? No others?
Y: Yes. The Karawatari then ran to the other side and Ohiriwä and Ebenewä also ran away over there, as did Baushiwä. That's all. [These two men represent a *third* group, known as the Kohoroshitari, although it is not obvious from her answer.]
NC: To the Shukumöna River?
Y: Not there—to another, different, big river across the Shukumöna.
NC: What big river?
K: [Interrupting] A large branch of the upper Shukumöna River.
NC: Did the Aramisi-teri raid often?
Y: They raided constantly and drove us out!
NC: At Konabuma garden?"
Y: Yes.
NC: When you left Konabuma, did you split up? Did the "real" Konabuma-teri go to one place and your group to some other place? [I am obviously confused because she is discussing one of the other Konabuma-teris.]
Y: [Impatiently] We *all* ran away together!
NC: Where to?
Y: [Mind wandering, not paying attention] When we lived at Boraböwei garden they chased us out.
K: [Interrupting, seeing that she did not answer the question] He said: Where did you live next after leaving Konabuma?
Y: [Still not paying attention] We went to Konabuma.
K: [Repeats my question to her once more] Where did you go next after leaving Konabuma?
Y: Here—they went to Amarokomaböwei River next.
NC: Did the Konabuma-teri also go there?
Y: They didn't come along. [Probably referring to a different Konabuma-teri]
NC: Where did they go—or didn't they go anywhere?
K: [Interrupts] They didn't go with them.
NC: Where is the Amarokomaböwei River? A branch of the Mavaca?
K, Y: Yes, a branch of the Mavaca over in that direction [pointing]. [A false answer]
NC: Did you make a new garden there?
Y: Yes. They still live over at Manöni garden. [A false answer]
NC: What was the name of the village then?
K: [After a pause, repeats my question] What name did the group assume when they lived there?
Y: Waraoba-teri. They are still called that. [She probably means Mövaraoba-teri.]

NC: Were the Reyabobowei-teri among them then?

Y, K: Yes—they all lived together, including the Mǫmariböwei-teri.

NC: Who else lived there?

K, Y: Reyaboböwei-teri, Mǫmariböwei-teri, and Sibarariwä-urihi-teri [another name for Mishimishimaböwei-teri or Möwaraoba-teri] . . . they all lived together there. Nobody else.

NC: What place did they go to after they abandoned Möwaraoba-teri?

K: No! They are *still* there today!

Y: They never left that place.

NC: Where were you living when the Reyaboböwei-teri split away from others?

Y: Back at Boraböwei, when we all fought with arrows, they left. The Aramamisi-teri shot us with arrows and attacked us with sharpened staves.

K: Sibarariwä's older brother—when Reyaboböwei-teri still lived among them —fought with him and they left.

NC: At Boraböwei River?

K: Yes.

NC: Are the Reyaboböwei-teri related to the Karawatari?

K, Y: No! They lived together long before that. The Reyaboböwei-teri are truly a part of the original Aramamisi-teri group! [Implying that the Karawatari are not]

NC: Are the Reyaboböwei-teri *mashi* [in this context, "very close agnatic kinsmen"] to the Aramamisi-teri?

K, Y: [Excited, satisfied that I am getting the point] Yes!

NC: Are they closely related to Sibarariwä's group?

K, Y: No! [An obviously false answer for reasons I do not yet understand]

NC: Does Sibarariwä live at Amarokomaböwei River today?

K: Yes! [False]

NC: There are other groups, though, such as the Möwaraoba-teri . . .

K: [Interrupting] Yes! That is another name for Sibarariwä's village!

NC: [Misunderstanding his comment] There are two groups there?

K: No! Two names for one group . . . Sibarariwä-urihi-teri *is* Möwaraoba-teri! [Mishimishimaböwei-teri] There is another group, further away, called Börösöwä-urihi-teri. They are not a part of the other group.

NC: Are they closely related to Sibarariwä?

K: No! [A false answer. He contradicts this shortly.]

NC: To the Aramamisi-teri?

K: Yes! Yes! They are closely related [*mashi*] to the Aramamisi-teri!

NC: What is Sibarariwä's village called today, Möwaraoba-teri?

K, Y: Yes! That is the right name!

NC: Have I ever seen the Amarokomaböwei River?

K: No. You have never seen it.

NC: But I have gone very far up the Mavaca, and I saw the trails that people made along the river up there.

K: No! You actually saw the trails of Börösöwä's village, not Sibarariwä's. They *all* live up there. They split into several groups, each going to a different place. Some were chased out in wars and went to Paruritawä garden. [This answer conflicts with his statement above, where he denied a close relationship between these two groups.]

NC: Are the Reyaboböwei-teri and Armamisi-teri all Shamatari?

Y, K: Yes!

NC: Where did the Aramamisi-teri live at first, on the Shukumöna River?

Y: They lived on the Shukumöna River.

K: [Interrupts, corrects her] He means long *ago*.

Y: At Aramamisi. [*sic*]

NC: Where is that?

Y: Where I said it was.

K: [Realizing that her answers are not very helpful] Where the Hasuböwä-teri live today, way up the Orinoco River. It is on the same side of the Orinoco, near its headwaters.

NC: Was there a river called Aramamisi?

K: There was a large mountain there called Aramamisi.

Y: [Comes alive again, adds sarcastically] Not a river, you idiot, a *mountain*! They lived away from the rivers.

NC: Did the Reyaboböwei-teri live with them then?

Y: Yes! They were the same people! Reyaboböwei-teri *is* Aramamisi-teri! [There are some half-dozen villages to this day that are known as "the Aramamisi-teri."]

NC: Yeisi-teri also?

K: Yes! The Yeisi-teri and Aramamisi-teri all lived together then!

Y: [Repeats her answer casually] Reyaboböwei-teri is related to Aramamisi-teri.

NC: [Attempting to get her to confirm K's answer] The Yeisi-teri are also related to Aramamisi-teri?

Y: Yes.

NC: [Deliberately asking about something I know to be false to see if she is paying attention] Ashidowä-teri also?

K: [Interrupts] No! They are related to the Hasuböwä-teri!

NC: [Questioning] When the group lived at Aramamisi mountain, the following groups were there: Reyaboböwei-teri, Mǫmariböwei-teri, Yeisi-teri . . . and others?

K: No others. [A false answer]

NC: When they left Aramamisi, where did they go?

K: [Repeats my question to Y]

Y: They went to Shirakoböwei mountain when they got chased away.

NC: Is there also a garden by that name?

K: No. That is the name of an area.

NC: What large river is it near?

K: None—it is in the middle of jungle.

NC: Is it anywhere near the Shukumöna River?

Y, K: No!

NC: The Orinoco?

K: Yes, closer to there.

NC: Why did they leave Aramamisi?

Y: Because they fought with clubs and were furious.

K: And because others were at war with them.

NC: What others?

K: I don't know their names.

Y: [Interrupts excitedly] I know them! They were called Shi̥howä-teri. Also, when they lived at that place, the Kabroba-teri were always sending *Oka* magic, and they fled in fear of that as well and went next to Shirakoböwei.

NC: They all went to Shirakoböwei from Aramamisi mountain. Did many people live at Shirakoböwei?

Y: [Exaggerating the quantity with intonation] *Many*. They all got chased there by the Aramamisi-teri [*sic*], who were themselves very numerous. [She is saying that the "Aramamisi-teri" chased the "Aramamisi-teri."]

K: Also, there were the Konabuma-teri who lived with them at Shirakoböwei.

NC: [Thoroughly confused because there are several "Aramamisi-teris" and unaware that there are three Konabuma-teris] Who are the Konabuma-teri related to? The Aramamisi-teri?

Y, K: Yes! They are *all* related to each other!

NC: Are the Konabuma-teri related to the Reyaboböwei-teri?

K: Yes. They are truly the same people! Their respective big men are also related to each other as brothers.
NC: Did the Konabuma-teri also go to Shirakoböwei?
Y: Yes! They also lived there with the rest, having fled there in fear.
NC: [Thoroughly mixed up by now, but realizing that my two informants are growing weary of my monotonous questions, I decided to give them reason to believe that I am beginning to understand so that they will take heart and continue the session, so I state something neutral and true.] This is certainly a large group of closely-related people! Konabuma-teri, Aramamisi-teri, Reyaboböwei-teri, Yeisi-teri, Mǫmariböwei-teri . . . are there even more?
K: [Pleased that I am apparently catching on] Yes! Börösöwä's group—and his father's group, and all the big wheels in those groups—they *all* lived there and are as one!
NC: Where did the Konabuma-teri separate from the others? At Shirakoböwei?
K: [Looks at Y and repeats my question]
Y: Downstream from there—that's where the Konabuma-teri separated.
NC: Where?
K: [Seeing that she is not going to give an intelligent answer] Back at the place where they all lived together as Aramamisi-teri—that is where they fissioned, at the time when they lived together in a single group.
NC: Did they separate from the rest by themselves? Was Börösöwä's group among them?
K: No. Although they all, including the Aramamisi-teri, became separate groups and proliferated from a common origin, the Aramamisi-teri fought with sharpened clubs against the others [Börösöwä's group] and they split away from them.
Y: They chased them away and ran some of them through with sharpened staves.
NC: Could you explain that to me again?
K: Back at Aramamisi mountain, when all of the *big* wheels lived together, the following—Aramamisi-teri and Waumanawä's group—all lived together there and then separated into different groups. This happened when some young men were fooling around with sharpened staves and throwing them at each other. The Aramamisi-teri killed a young man [accidentally] from Börösöwä's group [Waumanawä's group] and this caused the fight that led to the split, and why Waumanawä's people fled.
NC: Who fled?
Y, K: Börösöwä's group! [Meaning Waumanawä's group]
NC: Where did they flee to?
Y, K: To the Mavaca River region.

This informant session went on for several more hours that day and resumed the next day. We had been working for about an hour on the second day. I was thoroughly confused, since it was making very little sense to me; the Konabuma-teri seemed to be everywhere, as did the Aramamisi-teri, but I had not yet discovered the simple source of the confusion. The following brief transcription reflects the frustration and anger that was beginning to characterize this session, anger on the part of all of us. It also provides the simple answer to the confusion.

NC: Why did the Reyaboböwei-teri separate from the others?
K: [Impatiently, sharply] Because they were fighting so damned much!
NC: Because the Aramamisi-teri were shooting at them in their raids?

K: Yes.
NC: What was the fight about?
K: [Growing very impatient and angry] *Kuwi*! [How in the hell should I know? would be, with the intonation he gave it, an appropriate translation. It means, literally, I do not know.]
Y: [Also getting edgy] Don't just say *kuwi*! It was because of this kind of stuff! [Pointing to a bowl of peach-palm fruit in my hut]
K: [Excitedly remembers] Somebody cut down and ruined the peach-palm trees that belonged to someone else!
Y: Yes! Because of peach-palm trees, that's why they began shooting at each other. They also [deliberately] ruined all the sprouts of newly-planted trees for spite!
NC: Then the Reyaboböwei-teri *also* lived at Boraböwei?
K: [Very weary and annoyed that I have not yet gotten this straight] The *whole bunch* lived there. [Neither informant bothers to identify who is included in "the whole bunch" and both are annoyed when I ask about specific groups, the entire point of the informant session.]
Y: [Sarcastically] It should go without saying that they *all* lived there, *including* the Reyaboböwei-teri!
NC: Where is this river called Koyeta, somewhere near Konabuma?
K: It is on the other side of that region.
NC: Did the Konabuma-teri also live at Koyeta?
K: [Impatiently] No!
Y: Sibarariwä also lived at the Koyeta River, out of fear [of the Aramamisi-teri].
NC: Was it there that the Reyaboböwei-teri split away? Or was it at Konabuma?
K: [Growing more annoyed] Yes, at Konabuma! By the time that Sibarariwä and his father went to Koyeta to live, the Reyaboböwei-teri had already split away from them!
NC: Did the Konabuma-teri live in the Shukumöna River area at this time?
K: No.
NC: Where, then, did they live?
K: [Angry] They lived at their *own* place: Konabuma!
NC: Including the Reyaboböwei-teri?
K: No! Over in the other direction, at the *other* place called Konabuma . . ."
NC: [Interrupts, suspiciously] Do you mean that there was *another* place called Konabuma?
K: [Surprised at this question] Yes.
Y: Yes, there were two places called Konabuma.
NC: [Wearily, disgusted, gives English summary: The major problem is that there was more than one place called Konabuma.]
NC: [Deep sigh because I have to start all over again to distinguish the two Konabumas in the previous several days' of informant work] Where was the other Konabuma? Was it an area? A mountain? A garden? A river?
K: Yes.
NC: [Temper welling up] Yes What?
K: [Also growing angry] Konabuma *garden*!
NC: Where was this other garden called Konabuma?
K: It was up the Mavaca River.
NC: On what river?
Y: [Sarcastically, as if I should have known from the beginning that there were two Konabuma gardens] Don't ask "what river," you fool!

So I began again from the beginning: the two places called Konabuma were so thoroughly confused in my notes at this point that it was easier to start over than to try to unscramble the confusion. Clearly I had to develop a more effective means of identifying places and gardens; I had to have more specific references.

I can fairly say that Kąobawä and Yanayanarima should have recognized the source of the confusion earlier. Some informants are much better than others at recognizing—or even anticipating—potential problems such as this, and go out of their way to draw attention to the pitfall at the very outset. For example, several years after the above tape recording was made, after I had forgotten about this particular issue, I was working on the same settlement pattern data with Dedeheiwä, brother of the old woman above. When he came to the Konabuma-teri, he began by saying something like: "There were *two* places called Konabuma; I am talking about the one that was on the Shanishani River."

I used many different informants while collecting the information on Shamatari settlement pattern, employing the techniques, types of questions, and format exemplified in the preceding transcript. In some cases I questioned the same informant several times, particularly if his or her story did not appear to be

Figure 2.4—Dedeheiwä sitting on a log as we work in his garden.

consistent. The net result was a series of only partially relatable and partially consistent, independent accounts of the various fissions and migrations of the numerous villages located south of the Orinoco River. Some informants emphasized specific gardens or events for idiosyncratic reasons, while other emphasized others. Still, there were many points in common among all the accounts, such as the size of the original Aramamisi-teri group and the fact that almost all the villages to the south of the Orinoco derived from that group. Some individuals—such as the now dead headman Matakuwä whose name means "Shin bone"—also stood out as being exceptionally prominent men in the early history of the Shamatari (see Chagnon, 1966, for a discussion of Matakuwä), which suggested to me a new means for collecting settlement pattern history that was more specific, and a means that would help me keep identically-named gardens separate from each other. Therefore, I began collecting the names of all the prominent men who were associated with each garden and simultaneously pursued the subsequent moves made by particular men as they abandoned each garden in turn.

This approach worked much better because it enabled me to keep identically-named gardens separated in my notes, but it also contained a source of confusion that sometimes muddled the picture: whenever prominent men in particular villages split away from each other to found new groups, it was not a simple matter to detect this. To do so would have involved asking the informant, for example, "Where did Maamawä, Orakawä, Makurutawä, Aṇyobowä, Amokuwä, Horoshowä, and Yamoiwä go when they abandoned the garden called Bohoroabihiwei?" Worse yet, it would have involved asking about each man specifically, "Where did Maamawä go when he abandoned the garden called Bohoroabihiwei?" and so on, a time-consuming task when there are *several hundred gardens* involved and as many as six or eight prominent men associated with each one. Moreover, my informants would only reluctantly give me the names of these men in the first place, and would soon become irate and upset if I constantly mentioned their names in every question. In view of this, I compromised and inquired about just one or two men in each place, the ones who seemed to be the most prominent—either because of their renown or their prominence in terms of number of children, or both—and whose names occurred frequently in the course of other interviews. This carried the risk of not discovering the precise garden at which one of the prominent men separated from the others, but subsequent interviews usually filled these gaps. Once I had converted most of my genealogical and settlement pattern data to IBM cards and could return each year with computer printouts of long lists of names, gardens, and relationships, I could work for days with any particular informant—there was no end to the detailed questions I could ask. I was often oblivious to the discomforts of my various companions and would urge them to remain long after they had grown weary of endless questions, particularly when I had asked the same questions on previous occasions as I checked and cross-checked conflicts. After a while our efficiency would fall off and, after several hours of work with one informant, just about any question would be met with an affirmative answer. Thus I had to spend additional time checking the cross-checking until I arrived at a suitable length of time for the interview sessions. To a man who preferred to be out hunting or working in his garden—or just relaxing in his hammock—four or five hours of intensive questioning was not a happy way to spend the morning. Looking back at the countless days that my informants spent with me, I must admire them for their patience for what was not always a pleasurable enterprise for them. On more recent field trips I attempted to arrange interviews so that no single informant spent more than three or so hours at one sitting, and the quality of the data was generally higher as a result.

This problem was particularly noticeable if the long lists reflected in any way a "natural" sequence to the informant, that is, if the lists were gardens that were arranged more or less into the appropriate occupation sequence. To alleviate this, I arranged the gardens alphabetically, and it was very obvious to the informant that I was not merely repeating a list he had given me earlier and that his task was merely to confirm it by answering affirmatively to each question. Instead, he had to concentrate at each question and make a decision *each* time.[2]

A few examples from tape transcriptions will show how I employed these minor refinements—using the names of prominent men at particular gardens, alphabetizing the gardens, and pursuing the history of particular men—to improve my data on settlement pattern. My informant in this case is Dedeheiwä, who was always anxious to demonstrate his knowledge. His status in the village (Mishimishimaböwei-teri) depended, in part, on his reputation for "possessing the truth," as he so often put it when he periodically reminded me of his skills. This recording was taken in June 1970.

Abibunawei Garden

NC: Did the Mǫmariböwei-teri make Abibunawei garden?
D: Yes, Shiitawä cleared it.
NC: Why did he abandon it?
D: Because my village shot them up there.
NC: When he abandoned it, where did he and his group go?
D: They cleared Mǫmariböwei garden next. [Their present site]
NC: Why were you at war with them?
D: [Repeats question aloud to himself] Because of a woman . . . Yoaiyobemi. We fought about her after we took her by force from them. Then we started shooting at each other.

Amarokoböwei Garden

NC: Amarokoböwei garden: did the Karawatari people make it first?
D: Yes.
NC: At the river called Widobihiwei? a branch of the river called Karaweshi?
D: [Excitedly] Yes! Yes! Yes!
NC: Why did they abandon Amarokoböwei?
D: Because the Doshamosha-teri shot them up. They shot them up with arrows. They almost wiped them out completely.
NC: Where did they flee when they abandoned this place?
D: When the Karawatari abandoned Amarokoböwei garden they fled way far away [He points to the south.] and ultimately joined the foreigners over there, on the upper Karaweshi River [in Brazil]. They joined the foreigners

[2] Alphabetizing the names of people and then collecting their parents' names is an analogous technique I used in improving the accuracy of my genealogies.

actually on the Kumishiwä River. A few of them also joined the Kabroba-teri . . . just the "leftovers." The man called Yonowä joined the Kabroba-teri.

Amiana Garden

NC: Amiana garden—who cleared this place? Did the man called Ishawawä first clear Amiana?
D: Yes.
NC: When he abandoned it, did your group move into the area and clear new gardens there?
D: Yes . . . when he abandoned Amiana we made Konabuma garden . . .
NC: Are you related [through males] to Ishawawä?
D: Yes! That is the pure truth!
NC: Then the Karawatari people never made Amiana garden first?
D: No, the Karawatari never made Amiana first.
NC: Are the following men the ones who are [agnatically] related to you, and the ones who made the garden: Ishawawä, Iroroba-teri and Mahewä?
D: Yes, that's right!
NC: Are you yourself related to these men through males?
D: Yes! Yes! I already told you that. Those men are the first ones who cleared Amiana garden.
NC: Where does Mahewä live today?
D: Way over there, at the place called Shekerei—that's where he died.
NC: Was he the one who first made Amiana garden?
D: No! He first made Shihenaishiba garden! He never lived at Amiana. He lived at Shihenaishiba garden! [Here he contradicts his answer above.]
NC: Did the man named Iroroba-teri make Amiana garden?
D: Yes! Yes! Yes!
NC: Where does he live today?
D: At Konabuma. Konabuma. Konabuma. He made that place. He died—shot full of arrows by the others—the Doshamosha-teri shot him, at the Shukumöna River. He was out in the woods when they shot him, but he lived at Konabuma at the time of his death. That was on Örata River, not the Konabuma on the Shanishani River that you know about already. Iroroba-teri once lived at Amiana garden also, and was one of the men who first cleared it—Ishawawä also.
NC: What was Iroroba-teri's father called?
D: [Whispers] Wadubashiwä! Makoma was his mother.
NC: When they abandoned Amiana garden, where then did the group go next?
D: When they abandoned Amiana they next cleared Konabuma garden. They were living at Boraböwei when they cleared Amiana. They abandoned Amiana because of raiders.
NC: Because of the raiders from Bisaasi-teri?
D: No! No! No! Because of the Aramamisi-teri raiders. They lived at Shamashiitaoba garden then. They kept raiding at Amiana, so the people there went to Konabuma and made new gardens.
NC: Did you yourself also live at Amiana?
D: Yes! Yes! Yes!
NC: Did Sibarariwä live at Amiana then?
D: No! No! No! He was not yet born at that time.
NC: Is Amiana garden the place where you held the treacherous feast for the Bisaasi-teri?
D: [Pauses and thinks] "Uhhh . . . Bosihorihoritawä is the place where they tricked them. That is a different garden. It lies in the middle course of the Washäwä River near Amiana garden—on the other side of the same hill from it.

NC: Who made Bosihorihoritawä garden?

D: [Hisses a cautious whisper] Riokowä made it! Wauwamawä also! Dokonawä also! Robaiwä also!

NC: When they abandoned Bosihorihoritawä garden, where did they flee?

D: They went to Bo̜remaböwei from there.

NC: Why did they leave Bosihorihoritawä garden?

D: Because they held the treacherous feast for the Bisaasi-teri there and expected them to retaliate. They were afraid that if they stayed there, the [Bisaasi-teri] raiders would come and shoot them.

This particular informant, Dedeheiwä, persistently uses a grammatical feature of the language that sometimes confuses and thwarts my attempts at getting to the truth: he says "No" when he means an emphatic "Yes," and unless I am paying very careful attention to his intonation pattern, I sometimes miss the meaning. The following brief example illustrates this linguistic booby-trap. It also provides some background information to the variables I had to weigh when I considered making first contact with the village of Iwahikoroba-teri, for the sorcery accusations discussed below were directed against me. I will describe this in more detail later.

Bookona Garden

NC: Who made the garden called Bookona?

D: [Whispers softly] Narimanawä made Bookona garden!

NC: Did Börösöwä help him?

D: [Whispers emphatically, making his intonation difficult to identify] No! When Bookona was first cleared, Oramamowä also cleared it. [The "No" here means "emphatic yes," as the continuation of the work shows.]

NC: Did Aramawä help clear it?

D: Yes!

NC: Who else helped clear it?

D: [Emphatically, impatiently] Börösöwä helped also! Boraböwä, Dokonawä . . . [Note that the man called Börösöwä *did* clear the garden.]

NC: When it was first cleared, these men did the clearing?

D: Yes—when it was cleared for the very first time.

NC: Where did they go when they abandoned Bookona garden?

D: They went to Habromaböwei when they abandoned Bookona. They went back there and cleared more gardens at Habromaböwei. They still live there today.[3]

NC: Why did they abandon Bookona garden?

D: Because someone was practicing harmful magic against them by blowing *oka* charms through tubes at them. The foreigners who live here [at the mouth of the Mavaca River] are the ones who bewitched them and caused deaths.

NC: Do you mean *foreigners*, the ones who live right here?

D: Yes. These are the ones I mean.

NC: Which ones, specifically?

D: Just the "foreigners" here. [Deliberately evasive—the "foreigners" were *me*.]

NC: Not the Ya̜nomamö who live here?

D: Yes, they probably are involved too.

[3] In 1971 I succeeded in making first contact with this group near this garden. See Chapter IV and Chagnon, 1971.

Thus, as I used these various direct techniques and numerous informants of all ages and from different villages, a consistent picture of the Shamatari settlement pattern began to emerge. I kept updating my map as new gardens came to light. Figure 2.2 shows how the names of the headmen were associated with the garden names in my notes.

INDIRECT APPROACHES TO SETTLEMENT PATTERN

After I had collected demographic data, genealogies, census, age, birthplace, and so on on the several Shamatari villages of interest to me in my study, I then began using a more indirect approach to confirm the patterns that were discernible from the direct methods of interview, and choose which of several versions fitted all the facts the best. The demographic data were relatable to the political histories because I would obtain the following kinds of information about the people in the genealogies: (1) place of birth, (2) place of puberty ceremony for all females, (3) present village of residence, (4) place of death if dead. The answers to these questions also produced the names of additional gardens that my informants failed to mention earlier, usually gardens that were occupied only briefly. I would obtain the names of the important men at these new gardens and add a card to my files with the garden in its proper alphabetical position.

As my work progressed, and after I had estimated the ages of all the living residents of the several villages I visited in the Shamatari area, I could then generate a probable garden sequence by arranging my census data age-estimates against the stated place of birth of each individual. The sequence of garden occupation determined by this technique was totally independent from the sequence given to me by informants who recounted the history of the Shamatari, but it confirmed the latter sequence (see Figure 2.8). There were, to be sure, a few discrepancies in the two sequences. One source of error had to do with the fact that my age-estimates were merely the crudest of approximations: I had to make these estimates since the Yạnomamö do not count with precision past two. The demographic data also provided a means to check on the implied length of occupation of specific gardens, since I also collected data from women about the gardens where they had their *yọbömou* (first menses) confinement. Thus, if my demographic data implied that a garden had been occupied fifteen years—a time interval based on the distribution of my estimated ages of all people born there—I could check to see if any females born there also had their puberty ceremony there. If any of them did, there was ample reason to believe that the garden was occupied not less than twelve years.

Another source of error or discrepancy in the sequence of garden occupation as determined by demographic data was the occasional inclusion of individuals who were born at ancient garden sites while their parents were visiting that garden long after it had been abandoned. I attempted to overcome this by getting the name of the garden where they actually had their village, irrespective of the garden they were visiting when their children were born.

Finally, there is always some error involved because the informant does not know the answer but provides one anyway. It is not possible to check and cross-check every bit of information, however desirable that may be. My first attempt at using the demographic techniques to verify the settlement pattern of the Mishimishimaböwei-teri resulted in failure. My informant for birthplaces was Dedeheiwä, who "guessed" a good deal about some of the birthplaces. When I compared the ages of all people born at specific gardens, there was an unacceptable degree of error. I therefore collected the birthplaces again from other informants, working in public on the second occasion—taking advantage of everybody's information. This is one instance where the reliability of the data appears to have improved by working in public.

OTHER CONSIDERATIONS

The Mavaca River basin has been occupied by at least three distinct groups of Ya̧nomamö: the Karawatari, the Kohoroshitari, and the Shamatari. Villages of all three groups were at war with each other for long periods of time, and it is important to know where the various villages and populations were located with respect to each other at specific points in time.[4] To obtain this data, I used the Shamatari population as the point of reference and determined the approximate location of the other two groups by asking questions like: "Where were the Kohoroshitari when your group lived at Boraböwei?" By selecting a series of gardens that covered a substantial period of time, continuous relative locations of villages of the several major populations could be approximated. (Figure 2.7 summarizes these data.)

I have been using an inexpensive, hand-held compass to fix the approximate locations of the numerous gardens in the Shamatari region. By taking bearings to all gardens from several different locations, a set of lines can be drawn using a protractor; their intersections give the approximate location of the garden. For example, the garden called Miomaböwei is W 170° N of "A" (Bisaasi-teri), W 290° N of "B" (Mishimishimaböwei-teri) and W 225° N of "C" (the confluence of the Washäwä River with the Mavaca River). Using points A, B, and C and the origins, the three bearings intersect at the approximate location of the garden Miomaböwei.

There is considerable error in this crude technique: some informants are off as much as 10 to 15 degrees when their information is compared on two different occasions. Also, the exact locations of points "B" and "C" are contributory factors to the error: neither is known with any accuracy![5] Still, a rough location of the gardens can be determined using these techniques. For the moment I have to rely on the less accurate magnetic bearings and distances measured in "sleeps" to locate most of the gardens, since I do not intend to visit each and every place to obtain

[4] The groups are *presently* multivillage populations. Never did any multivillage groups fight *as groups* against other, similarly ordered clusters. It is clear in informant statements that terms like "Karawatari" mean *particular* villages of the Karawatari cluster.

[5] I fixed the position of these points in 1972 by using a theodolite and star shots. The complicated calculations have not yet been made and will be published elsewhere.

precise coordinates. Considering most of the kinds of questions I wish to answer, the rough locations are accurate enough.

Figure 2.5, taken from one of my recent field books, shows how I kept some of my notes on the various gardens and what kinds of data—genealogical, biographical, geographical, and historical—I tried to include in each reference. Points A, B, and C in the figure refer to the three places mentioned above where I took the magnetic bearings. This is only a portion of the information I have on each garden. I used this information as a reference in the field for quickly identifying gardens mentioned by informants in various contexts, particularly for identifying gardens that I did not know by heart.

The reader should now be in a position to appreciate the kinds of data I collected to approximate the settlement pattern of the Shamatari population and the various techniques I used to obtain the data. The following maps summarize only major historical–geographical factors in the reconstructed settlement pattern of the Mishimishimaböwei-teri. I caution the reader once again that the maps are only approximations to the actual locations that were significant in the history of the Shamatari.

RECONSTRUCTING THE EARLY HISTORY: FACTUAL, METHODOLOGICAL, AND THEORETICAL CONSIDERATIONS

The mechanical procedures for collecting genealogical and demographic facts should now be clear insofar as my own field methods are concerned. Let us now take a broader look at the methodological and theoretical issues to which these facts apply.

Mishimishimaböwei-teri is just one of some dozen or so villages whose inhabitants are known, collectively, as "the Shamatari" to their immediate neighbors. The term "Shamatari" is somewhat vague and applied inconsistently by Yanomamö to a number of distinct groups, whether or not they are related historically to the Mishimishimaböwei-teri. For example, Kaobawä's group—the Bisaasi-teri—is considered to be "Shamatari" by the Yanomamö to the north of him, but he denies the identity and claims that the "true" Shamatari live further to the south.

As I use the term here, it embraces all those villages that originated by fissioning from the ancestral village known as Aramamisi-teri, a large settlement that was located somewhere between the headwaters of the Rahuawä River and the Shukumöna River (see Figure 2.7, below) approximately 75 to 100 years ago. To this day, several existing villages are called "Aramamisi-teri" because of their historical and genealogical identification to the earlier group. The identity "Shamatari" could also be defined in terms of *lineal descent* from a handful of prominent men who were associated with the early Aramamisi-teri settlement (see Chagnon, 1966). This raises a number of theoretical and methodological issues concerning the nature of lineality in a political context, native taxonomies of nonlocal groups and, by extension, the relationship of population factors to group definition, group

Page 6

GARDEN VILLAGE OR RIVER	LOCATION	FOUNDER	A	B	C
Bunimaböwei-täka	2 hrs w of Mǫm. on br. of Haoyaoba	Shiitawä, Nabörawä, Wabusiwä; came here from Breiiriböwei	140		80
Dąfamoböwei-täka DAADAAMÖ BÖWEI-TAKA (CORRECT SPELLING)	Near headwaters of Mavaca, near Ironasididioba-täka	[Ishawawä], [Matakuwä], [Kaharariwä], [Warasiwä], Dedeheiwä and Sibarariwä. Fought here with clubs and Dedeheiwä went to Mishimishi. while others to Ironasididioba, nearby. See yellowdog originals for names	150	90	
Daraima-täka	N. of Orinoco	[Watemosiköwä], Shamashiadima and adult sons.	250		
Darakawä-täka	Darakawä-u, br. of Shanäshani near Patanowä-täka	[Orakowä], [Wishawä], [Shamawä]	200	290	
Dokoriböwei-t	n. br. Washäwä; its head is near head of Darakawä of Shanishani-u	Two sets of bearins from Mavaca on two occasions: (A) Head Lower (B) Head Lower	 170 145 210 180	 290	
Doshamosha-teri Also called Aramamisi- or Yeisi-teri.	s. of Shukumöna-u on Karaweshi-u	Bosibrei (Kreiibuma); Itoböwä, Sheroroiwä, Kǫwäawä, Yawarahiwä. Came here from Bohoroaböwei. Once were called Yeisi-teri.	178	270	220
Doshamosha-teri Also called Nakiaiyoawä-teri by Patanowä-teri	180 due south of Patanowä-teri.	The Patanowä-teri claim that there are many shabonos in the region where the Doshamosha-teri live.			
Dudurumaböwei-täka	Waröta-u, w. side near headwaters	Dedeheiwä, Möawä, who split from Sibarariwä in clubfight precipitated when Möawä took his yuhabö as wife (incestuously)	160	160	

Figure 2.5—Facsimile of field ledger showing my notes on garden, village, or river; location; founder and bearings.

dispersion, and intervillage warfare. I will only introduce the issues here and show how the facts, methods, and theory interrelate.

One of the major methodological issues has to do with categorization of supralocal cultural entities—clusters of villages with a common origin if you will—and how these entities are, in native "emic" views, often determined by political context that conflicts with the general notion of lineal descent held by the same natives. For example, Kạobawä has always insisted that the residents of Mishimishimaböwei-teri are "true" Shamatari because most of the prominent men there are lineal descendants of the man known as Matakuwä, one of the most significant headmen in the history of the Shamatari. This claim is amply demonstrated in the next two chapters. However, when I brought Kạobawä and some of his brothers to Mishimishimaböwei-teri in 1970 (see Chagnon, 1973 [film] *Magical Death*, and Chagnon, 1973, for a partial account of this important meeting), he and one of their headmen—Möawä—had a long, nervous discussion of the alleged Shamatari identity of Möawä's village. Möawä himself is a patrilineal (son's son) grandson of Matakuwä. I was astonished during this discussion to hear Möawä deny the identity Shamatari, and even more astonished to hear Kạobawä agree with him. They were manipulating and denying lineal descent principles that both knew to be valid, and principles that both subscribed to under "normal" conditions. The reason that they were doing so could be understood only if you knew their past political dealings, the most significant event being summarized

Figure 2.6—Kạobawä (standing) and his brother (squatting) diplomatically agreeing with the Mishimishimaböwei-teri that the "Shamatari" indeed live somewhere else. This was their first peaceful contact in over twenty years.

as follows: In 1950 the Bisaasi-teri were invited to a feast by the Mishimishimaböwei-teri, who, with their close kinsmen, the Iwahikoroba-teri, treacherously set upon them with their staves and other weapons and killed a large number of men and wounded many more, including Kạobawä's father (who later died of the wounds). Kạobawä and the other Bisaasi-teri held the "Shamatari" responsible for this deed. Their meeting in 1970 was the first peaceful contact in twenty-odd years, and it was a very nervous meeting indeed (Chagnon, 1973). Möawä, by publicly "denying" his Shamatari descent, made it possible for the meeting to take place, thereby giving Kạobawä and the other Bisassi-teri a convenient escape: they could continue to denounce the Shamatari publicly while at the same time be overtly friendly to Möawä. He was exonerated from complicity in the deed only if his lineal identity could be manipulated in such a fashion.[6] Should the two groups become intimate friends and allies,[7] the vigor with which both groups deny the Shamatari descent of Möawä will increase, for it permits them to overlook a powerful reason for continuing their hostilities. Thus, the immediate political expediency has temporarily led to a widespread denial of what all concerned privately hold to be true. Kạobawä, back in his own village, still calls Möawä a "Shamatari" and, indeed, chuckled for some time when I played for him the recording of his conversation with Möawä—the one in which he denied Möawä's Shamatari identity. "He is, of course, a true Shamatari," laughed Kạobawä, ". . . I was just saying that in his presence for the hell of it!"[8] But, by then, Kạobawä knew how much time I had spent collecting "Shamatari" genealogies and knew I was party to an inside joke. It caused me to wonder about some other occasions that I played different tapes and heard him laugh, and was not party to the joke.

Möawä's identity, considered "emically" (Harris, 1968), is, in this very particular context and only in public at specific times, that of "Non-Shamatari." The context is clear and the political reasons make the fiction perfectly understandable. We all do it ourselves in our own culture, and from time to time we all deny in public what we privately hold to be true. The social situations in which we operate demand it.

Other situations are not as clear-cut as this, and therefore the methodological issues are more difficult to resolve by recourse to supplementary ethnographic data. One particular issue in my own fieldwork and analysis has to do with the definition of groups in both a temporal and a spatial context, and how native "emic" views are involved. It is an ethnographic fact that the Yạnomamö manipulate and "fudge" identities when it comes to classifications of a political–lineal order. This is clearly related to political context, and the principles seem to be that attributed identity varies as advantage in political dealings can be taken: if it

[6] Möawä had not personally killed anyone in this incident, although members of his group in fact had.

[7] In 1972 their mutual relationships, after three years of sporadic visiting, were cooling off, in part a consequence of the treatment that Rerebawä and I received from Möawä in 1972. This is discussed in the last chapter.

[8] Imagine the consequences of a novice fieldworker attempting to establish, in public interviews, the Shamatari identity of various individuals during this period of time. See below for a more elaborate example of the same kind of field problem.

is to one's advantage to agree that Möawä is *not* a Shamatari, then he is obviously not a Shamatari—at least in one's public statements. But what about the claim that the next village over is "not Shamatari" when in fact all the genealogical evidence clearly shows that it is? Even here, supplementary data—genealogies in this case—can guide the ethnographer's decisions. But what about more distant villages, where the population has not yet been related, genealogically, to the ones under consideration, and may not ever be? When the ethnographer's concern is to document settlement pattern, population growth and dispersal, and the nature of village fissioning, it is important to identify all subunits of the population, and where he must rely on native "emic" categories where genealogical information runs out, boundaries around the population of reference might be drawn in the wrong place. The definition of groups eventually becomes critical to a number of theoretical considerations, in particular, possible ways to analyze and interpret the warfare patterns.

Let us look at the problem of defining population blocs from the historical, developmental dimension—from the perspective of how Yạnomamö populations grow, fission, and disperse. The first portion of this chapter described how genealogical and historical data were employed to establish the pattern of settlement movement, with the emphasis on the methods used to collect native historical accounts and use them in conjunction with demographic information such as birthplaces and places of death. These methods have enabled me to trace a large number of presently distinct villages back to a handful of "mother villages"—ancient groups that ultimately gave rise to the present populations living in widely-scattered villages. Figure 2.7 shows the approximate distribution of these "mother-villages" or "population hearths" approximately 75 to 100 years ago. The next two chapters will give more details of the growth pattern, but a few general comments are in order here. First, the members of particular villages in each "bloc" hold specific attitudes about their similarities and differences: Kạobawä lives in Bisaasi-teri village of the bloc labeled "Namowei-teri" on Figure 2.7, and overtly acknowledges that he and his group are related historically and genealogically to a number of other villages. I have documented the accuracy of this claim both genealogically (see Chapter 3) and with the techniques described in this chapter. Further, he asserts that his group—the Namowei-teri—are distinct from the Shamatari: they are *shomi*—"others," "unrelated peoples," "different." This also can be documented by the ethnographer: there are nuances of pronunciation, usage, subtle myth variations, minor differences in style of headmanship, and so on that distinguish Namowei-teri groups from Shamatari groups.

Second, there are striking differences between the Namowei-teri as a population and the Shamatari as a population in the reproductive characteristics and rate of population growth and expansion (to be discussed in detail in Chapter 4). The Shamatari are growing and expanding at a greater rate than the Namowei-teri.

Third, despite the observable differences in rate of growth and dispersal, the pattern is essentially the same in both the Namowei-teri and Shamatari populations: villages grow to a certain size and fission into two or more smaller villages, each locating itself in a new region at some considerable distance from the others. At this point I must let firsthand knowledge guide my speculations about the

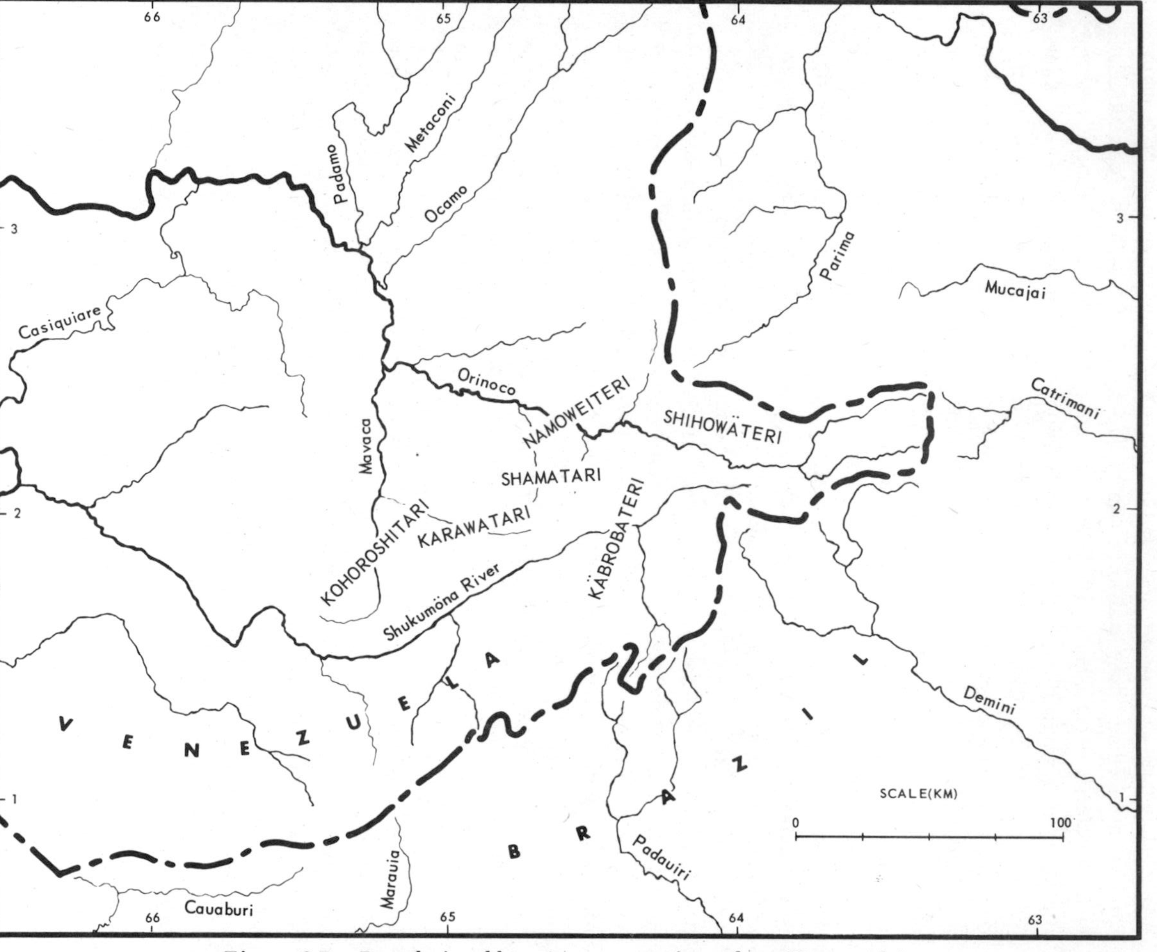

Figure 2.7—Population blocs (on a map of southern Venezuela).

other population blocs, for I do not have enough substantial genealogical and/or native historical data on them to describe their pattern of growth and dispersal. Thus, the early history of the Shamatari and the Namowei-teri, as given by numerous informants from both populations, asserts that both ancestral groups had wars with people known as "Shịhowä-teri" and "Käbroba-teri."[9] I can only assume that these ancient groups have themselves undergone a population growth and dispersal similar to that characterizing the Shamatari and Namowei-teri, and that today they are represented by several distinct villages each. Similarly, the "Kohoroshitari" and "Karawatari" are probably represented today by several villages, although I have not collected the kind of data required to document it.[10]

Fourth, there has been a gradual movement of the "population blocs" in a southwesterly direction, away from the Orinoco River toward the Brazilian border.

We are now in a position to examine some of the theoretical and methodological issues raised by these data. Let us pretend to be archaeologists 500 years hence, and that the several "population blocs" had at least one identifiable culture trait, pottery for example, that varied slightly from group to group. The pattern represented would be quite similar to patterns of settlement found by contemporary archeologists who excavate in the Tropical Forest region of South America (see Lathrap, 1970). What would emerge is a pattern of "population" movement, and it would not be unreasonable to speculate that population pressure built up, taxed the carrying capacity of the ecological niche, led to warfare and the expansion of territory-seeking have-nots, who moved by force into the territories of their neighbors and forced them, in turn, to move further. We will return to this briefly.

When the pattern of population growth and the process of village fissioning are examined in more careful detail—in a temporal/developmental perspective, the notion and definition of "population blocs" emerges in a somewhat different light. The several populations given in Figure 2.7 do not appear, on closer scrutiny, to be that distinct from each other if the Yạnomamö "emic" views are examined in the context of how minor differences are exaggerated by them on the one hand, and how villages come into existence on the other. That is to say, if we let the ethnographic facts recognizable today be our guide for interpreting the past events of this area, it seems very likely that the "population blocs" of the last century were themselves just discrete components that could all be traced back to a common "mother" village. They all have a common geographical point of origin (see Chagnon, 1966; 1968c) and, considering their dialect similarities, very likely a common historical origin in the recent past. It is not unlikely that as recently as 200 years ago the several population blocks represented only discrete villages that fissioned from a common source.

I have described, briefly, how the several population "blocs" were established

[9] See Chagnon, 1966, for additional discussion of some of the conflicts that the ancestral Namowei-teri had with the "Shihowä-teri" and "Käbroba-teri," two of the population blocs shown in Figure 2.6. The Shamatari also had contests with these same peoples.

[10] Some informants say "Kohoroshi-*teri*," not "Kohoroshi*tari*," suggesting that it was a single village, not a large, multivillage bloc.

by using native accounts of their and their ancestors' history. That is, I have accepted their view and emic categories in constructing Figure 2.7, which itself is a set of population definitions that the informants "inherited" from their parents and grandparents. It is not possible to rigorously verify or dispute these categories using field techniques. It is possible, however, to view them critically against conntemporary "emic" practices as relates to categorizing other groups. I have given one example of the Yąnomamö denying in public what they privately hold to be true. Let me now turn to an example of the Yąnomamö denying both publicly and privately what I, the ethnographer, can demonstrate to be true. The example relates directly to the problem of defining the components of a population "bloc."

Nearly all of my Shamatari informants vigorously denied that the people of Yeisikorowä-teri were in any sense related to them as a group, although a few individuals from time to time made unsolicited comments about their "brother" or "grandfather" in Yeisikorowä-teri, etc. My informed Bisaasi-teri sources—men like Kąobawä—argued that the Shamatari were deceiving me, and that the Yeisikorowä-teri were in fact a splinter village from an earlier group—a village known as Konabuma-teri. By using interview techniques such as those exemplified earlier in this chapter, I could not get my Shamatari informants to acknowledge that the Yeisikorowä-teri were their close relatives or that they had a common origin. It is important to know that my Shamatari informants were from villages that were currently at war with the Yeisikorowä-teri, and had been for many years. Furthermore, I would not have the opportunity to verify their accounts, since Yeisikorowä-teri was a very remote, uncontacted village and I did not plan to go there. Thus, to place them definitely within or outside of the Shamatari "bloc" I had to rely on Shamatari informants.

The only way I was able to resolve this conflict was to reconstruct the composition of the ancient village of Konabuma-teri and obtain the names of all the residents of that defunct group. I elected to obtain the information from several old women who had been abducted by the Bisaasi-teri from that population many years ago, suspecting that their perspectives, unlike those of the contemporary men who lived in Shamatari villages, would not be hardened and crystallized by events that happened subsequent to their abduction from the earlier population.

After I had as complete a "census" as I could get, I then asked the old women to recount the names of the children of the prominent people who constituted the "census" and, following that, the names of their childrens' children, until I had exhausted their information on the population that lived at Konabuma-teri.

Next, I asked them and informants from Shamatari villages to give me the current village of residence of the (presumably) living people whose names were provided by the old women. About half of the old Konabuma-teri population was said to be living in the present village of Yeisikorowä-teri and the other half in the village of Iwahikoroba-teri, which confirmed Kąobawä's account. It was clear from the genealogical relationships that the Yeisikorowä-teri were as closely related to my original, reluctant Shamatari informants as they were to the people of Iwahikoroba-teri, from whence my original Shamatari informants fissioned to form their own villages, and to whose residents they openly acknowledged common ancestry and common history. Thus, while they openly acknowledged close agnatic relationships to the Iwahikoroba-teri, they denied the same agnatic relationships to the Yeisikorowä-teri. Only when I confronted my original informants with detailed genealogical information that demonstrated the relationships—relationships they had earlier insisted did not exist—did they reluctantly concede that, yes, those rotten bastards in Yeisikorowä-teri, were, like the Iwahikoroba-teri, their true "*mashi*." Until I investigated the matter in this fashion, my own mental diagram of the distribution of "population blocs" contained the Yeisikorowä-teri as a tentative separate bloc by itself, sticking out like a sore thumb, with no history, and no demonstrable relationship to other villages.

I have enough genealogical and native historical data to be able to demonstrate that the other "blocs" are not as intimately related in recent times as the Yeisikorowä-teri are to the Shamatari. Still, there has been some intermittent exchange of people—women given in marriage or small factions leaving one group to join the other—which implies that the separate populations have had a small but constant influence on each other's recent past. Significantly large lineages in some Shamatari villages are in fact the consequence of this kind of exchange with, for example, the Karawatari population. Other kinds of data suggest that the Karawatari, the Kohoroshitari, and the Shamatari may have once been a single population. My oldest informants, when pressed to consider this possibility, tend to agree that this is very likely, but do not assert it with any confidence because it harks back to a time ". . . when Moon's blood spilled on earth and created men . . . ," a time that no informant is willing to speculate about in any detail. Corroborating my suspicion that the Karawatari have common ancestors with the Shamatari is the fact that a number of acknowledged Shamatari villages have, according to my informants, recently "joined" the Karawatari in villages to the south (probably in Brazil) and have become one, a highly unlikely event if the Karawatari are in fact completely unrelated to them.

Looking at the pattern of distribution of population blocs from the point of view of particular villages and how they grow, fission, and relocate themselves, other theoretical and methodological issues develop: are clusters of closely related villages "expanding against" other clusters, or is that just a superficial artifact of something more complex? The overall pattern is for villages to grow to a size too large to be effectively held together with the indigenous political mechanisms and then to fission, usually into two groups. One of the groups usually remains in the same spot and the other moves off some considerable distance, several days' walk away if the fission took place in a violent clubfight that led to deaths, or perhaps within a day's walk if the circumstances leading to the fission were not so violent. The tendency is for the newly-arisen groups to keep a healthy distance between themselves, and between themselves and other, more remotely related villages. Thus, there is a conspicuous aversion to move around or "behind" villages on their periphery. One does not find, for example, a Namowei-teri village surrounded by Shamatari villages. Two recently separated villages may enter into war with each other and avoid each other by locating themselves as far from each other as possible, but neither will "leap-frog" around villages whose members are either very remotely related or totally unrelated. Thus, the prior existence of villages at one's periphery constitutes a very real boundary, and all Yąnomamö groups, except those at the very periphery, are socially "circumscribed" in the sense that neighboring villages constitute a barrier as effective as a chain of mountains or a desert (Chagnon, 1968c; Carneiro, 1961; 1970). One consequence of this pattern is that any given area will contain villages that have a common origin. The villages may all be exceedingly hostile to each other, but they constitute a "bloc" in the sense I am using the term here. Another consequence is that if any population growth and village fissioning takes place within the area, only two alternatives are possible: either the newly arisen groups must relocate themselves closer to each other than they would like, or they must move closer to unrelated groups. The general tendency in the Namowei-teri area and the Shamatari area is to follow the latter course, and this usually leads to conflicts with the unrelated neighbors. I have explored some of the theoretical consequences of this pattern in other publications (Chagnon, 1968b; 1968c; 1972). Here, I want to draw attention to the *pattern* of expansion that results and how it relates to assumptions about primitive warfare and population density, both ethnographically and archeologically.

The morphology or structure of the population movements is that "groups" or "blocs" expand and "push" other groups away. In areas elsewhere in the ethnographic world, a strong case can be made that expansion is related to population density, and that population density, in turn, is related to ecological carrying capacity or resource shortages. A good example might be the Nuer expansion against the Dinka (Evans-Pritchard, 1940; Sahlins, 1961). The point I wish to make with these data and the ecological adaptation of the Yąnomamö is that while the pattern of expansion is the same as that documented in areas where resource shortages can be shown to exist, the genesis of the pattern is not relatable to population density or resource shortages in such a simple way. Indeed, resources cannot be shown to have anything to do with the pattern of Yąnomamö expansion described here, especially as regards the genesis of warfare and its role in determining the pattern. Yąnomamö warfare does indeed figure intimately in the development of the pattern, as warfare elsewhere, where shortages of resources are well documented in similar expansion patterns, but the practice, intensity, and "causes" of warfare in the Yąnomamö case cannot be convincingly shown to be related to resource shortages. An attempt to do so would amount to special pleading to preserve a model that does not account for the facts. My own bias was to do essentially that, but to defend the model I would have to accept the preposterous notion that a population density of the magnitude of some 0.01 people per square mile caused a "stress" on the carrying capacity. Walking several days between hostile villages over terrain that abounded in game and cultivable land leads one to take a more commonsense view of the issues and take note of the tarnish on the otherwise shiny models that apply well elsewhere, but only with gross distortion of facts here. The current population density in the region under discussion is extremely low today, and a generation ago it could only have been much lower, and before that, when most of the "expansion" took form and "population blocs" began to differentiate, it could only have been ridiculously low insofar as its relevance to the causes of intergroup warfare and expansion are concerned.

In brief, this data raises some fundamental issues regarding the relationship between primitive warfare, population density, territorial expansion, and ecological carrying capacity. While it is clear that the warfare pattern can account for the distribution of villages in space and how they relocate over time, it is also clear that Yąnomamö warfare does not arise "automatically" because of excessive population density in areas with limited territorial or other resources, unless one is prepared to accept some bizarre claims that swidden cultivators tax their resources at ridiculously low population densities.

What is at issue, in a nutshell, is the nature of primitive warfare and how or why it comes into being. The argument I would make from this data and other, related data is that tribal warfare is not a tropismatic response to resource shortages and population density. A general anthropological tendency is to assume that the "steady state" or "normal" condition among tribesmen is one of peace, as, for example, the model of expansion and warfare given by Lathrap (*ibid*): tribesmen become warlike when there is no farmland or when game animals are scarce. This is, essentially, an "ecocentric" or "biocentric" assumption about the nature of tribesmen and tribal culture.

There is another way to view tribal warfare, one that squares more convincingly with the ethnographic facts. Warfare is everywhere a means to political ends, but is not everywhere reducible to direct competition for scarce resources. That is to say, it everywhere has sociopolitical attributes, and something quite fundamental about the nature of warfare might be wrought from looking more carefully at the phenomena in a "sociocentric" way. (See Service, 1962, for a discussion of "sociocentric.")

In all tribal groups (see Sahlins, 1968, for a definition of tribal culture), local communities are "sovereign" in that the political behavior of their members is not dictated from above by supralocal institutions. The preservation of this political sovereignty seems to be the universal unstated goal of all tribesmen, the *sine qua non* of tribal culture. The most important single means to achieve this, borrowing a phrase from Hobbes via Sahlins (*ibid*), is usually a *political stance* called "Warre"—the chronic disposition to do battle, to oppose and dispose of one's sovereign neighbors. In tribal cultures the world over, there is a general attitude held by local group members that their neighbors, being remote spatially and genealogically, are therefore less moral or less human than themselves. One suspects his neighbors of sorcery, witchcraft and chicane, and treats them accordingly. The range of reaction to neighboring groups is wide, but whatever its precise form it is usually characterized by chronic suspicion and fear. Briefly stated, the range is from trade to raid, but even in the former, trade is hedged in and dominated by ritual and ceremonial, a reflection perhaps of the awesome danger accompanying association with potential enemies. That the relationship between sovereign political groups should also take the form of raid—warfare—is not surprising. In some cases the warfare can be related to competition for scarce resources, in other cases it cannot, but in *all* cases the contests have political dimensions and attributes. Warfare is, indeed, the extension of tribal politics in the absence of other means. These other means are supralocal institutions that bind groups peacefully to each other, and tribal culture by definition lacks them. Thus, hostility towards one's neighbors is of the essence of tribal culture.

Among the Yąnomamö, we are dealing with a situation where "Warre" has, for reasons other than the distribution or availability of resources, taken on the quality of actual warfare. We are dealing with something characteristically tribal —pursuit of political goals by means of violence, a deliberate attempt to keep as much space as possible between one's group and that of suspicious neighbors. With distance there is security and sovereignty. If the soundness of theory is measured by the ability of that theory to predict, then a knowledge of population density would not be a very robust basis for prediction in this case. Ironically, knowing who stole whose wife or killed whom on a raid would be a much more powerful basis of predicting the Yąnomamö response to the event.

Let us return to the observable characteristics of the population blocs. Just as the village of Mishimishimaböwei-teri shows some striking differences when compared with other Shamatari villages, so also do the Shamatari as a cluster of interrelated villages display some striking demographic differences when compared to other, similarly defined population blocs, such as the Namowei-teri villages. In particular, the Shamatari are growing at a faster rate and have expanded over a much larger area than have the Namowei-teri in the same period of time. This, also, raises some interesting theoretical issues. It is beginning to look as if there is a population, supravillage quality or set of characteristics that is "inherited" by each village by virtue of the fact that it is Shamatari in origin rather than Namowei-teri. In other words, there appears to be something characteristic of Shamatari demography that has important implications for Shamatari village organization. The differences are slight, but detectable. They may be due to chance and the normal variation that one can expect in populations of this order of magnitude. Whatever their provenience—stochastic or deterministic—they have the potential of conferring on whole populations a sociocultural advantage in realm of intergroup competition, and by extension, group selection or survivability.[11] For the moment there is no "group competition" as such, for the dozen or so Shamatari villages each act independently and jealously pursue their own political goals. Still, their higher birth rate (to be discussed in Chapter 4) and subsequent dispersal of newly generated villages implies that they would have a tremendous advantage should, for example, territoriality become an important factor in this area. Given that Yąnomamö land is finite, and given the passage of a sufficient amount of time, one would expect that the Shamatari would eventually impart their cultural and biological attributes to the Yąnomamö tribe as a whole, provided that their greater survivability were translated into a greater dominance over their neighbors. I have documented the nature of Yąnomamö expansion outward from the "center" of the tribe (Chagnon, 1968b; 1968c; 1972). Should this pattern continue, then the tribal "center" would eventually become more and more "Shamatari"-like and whatever biological or cultural peculiarities they possessed initially would eventually become tribal characteristics. When the impact of the Shamatari on the composition of some Namowei-teri villages is

[11] See Lewontin (1965) for a discussion of group selection for biological populations. I am indebted to William G. Irons for drawing my attention to Lewontin's article and specific points I raise that relate to group selection.

examined (see Chapter 4), it becomes clear that this process is already under way. Thus, all cultural (and biological) characteristics would be preserved and diffused, irrespective of their contribution to or inhibition of group survivability, provided that one or a few were clearly conferring on the population a marked advantage. For example, no one would argue that the waxing and waning of pottery styles in archaeological horizons were in themselves the "cause" of population growth and expansion merely because they were associated with the human groups that proliferated. A question then arises: how do we identify the underlying causes of population growth and village fissioning and the expansion of some groups at a rate higher than that observable among its neighbors? What demographic or cultural traits are conferring the advantage? As we shall see in Chapter 4, this question can be cast in purely demographic terms and partially answered from that perspective. Ethnologically, there appears to be more to it than can be satisfactorily resolved with just demographic data and refined descriptions of the data in terms of survivorship, birthrates, and deathrates. And that, incidentally, is what my fieldwork and theoretical interest in the Yąnomamö are all about. That is why I spent months and years collecting genealogies, demographic data, and native accounts of settlement history.

Three aspects of the demography and culture stand out as crucial variables when the characteristics of population blocs are examined from a causal perspective.

The first has to do with reproductive performance: how many children are sired by men and born to women. This establishes whether or not the population is growing (considering, of course, survivorship), and leads to investigations along other lines. To wit, and second, the lineal composition of villages, which appears to have a considerable amount of interdependence with reproductive performance. On the one hand, the high variability in male reproductive performance enables particularly fecund men to leave many (lineal and cognatic) descendants. Considering some of these descendants from a sociological perspective (the lineals), whole areas—such as the Shamatari area—are characterized by greater or lesser lineality, which has a profound impact on political behavior. On the other hand, the lineal composition of groups has a feedback effect on reproductive performance. Given the marriage rules and nature of reciprocity between lineages (*The Fierce People*, Chapter 2), larger lineages seem to have an advantage in acquiring larger numbers of women as wives for their male members. Therefore, the males of these lineages will have larger numbers of children and continue to perpetuate the lineal bias that was "inherited" by their generation.

Third, the marriage rules themselves enhance or detract from the rate at which lineages grow and proliferate. Particular kinds of prescriptive marriages bind dominant lineages together and contribute to their potential for further growth. The number of cognatic descendants a particular man in the ascending generations left comes into play here, as these determine the potential and actual number of cross-cousin marriages that take place in any village.

Thus, the population characteristics, ethnologically speaking, are not easily reducible to single "causes" such as growth rate. The cultural matrix within which reproduction takes place is constantly affecting the purely biological dimensions of the process, and interacting with them. Lineal descent, marriage rules and practices, and fertility are all interrelated and constitute a system that has many dimensions and ramifications. As we shall see below, only a portion of them can be identified and quantified. It should be noted that warfare is largely a separate, but relatable, factor in the demographic basis for group composition and solidarity.

To exemplify both the Yąnomamö attitudes toward their neighbors and the techniques I used to establish the relative geographical and genealogical relationships between villages of the several "blocs" given in Figure 2.7, I give a transcript of one interview I had with Dedeheiwä. He traces lineal descent back to "Karawatari" ancestors. His father and father's brothers married into the "Shamatari" population in the previous generation, that is, they "fissioned" from the Karawatari for reasons I was unable to establish, and "fused" with the ancestors of the Mishimishimaböwei-teri. At the present time a large fraction of the residents of Mishimishimaböwei-teri and Ironasi-teri are descendants of these inmarried Karawatari. (This is shown in the schematic diagram, Figure 2.9, below.)

NC: Where did you live when you were very young?
D: Shortly after birth, when I was very young, I lived at Boraböwei.
NC: Where did the Karawatari live at that time?
D: They lived at Shekerei.
NC: [Not believing him] No! . . ."
D: Don't tell me "no!" When *they* lived at Shekerei, *we* lived at Boraböwei!
NC: Are *you* related [through males] to the Karawatari?
D: [Excitedly] Yes! Yes! Yes! Yes!
NC: Are you a Karawatari?
D: Yes! I am truly a Karawatari. I am one of the few true descendants of the Karawatari around.
NC: Are you *truly* one of the Karawatari [lineal] descendants?
D: Yes! Yes! Yes! Yes! It is the truth!
NC: Did your ancestors split away from the Karawatari?
D: They split away, split away, split away. My own ancestors split away in the past and left the Karawatari.
NC: Where—what garden—did this occur?
D: Over in that area [pointing], at Shihenaishiba garden.
NC: Did your ancestors and the Karawatari ancestors live together at Shihenaishiba garden?
D: Yes! Yes! Yes! Yes! Yes! My true ancestors were attacked mercilessly at Kayurewä garden by the Aramamisi-teri. Then my ancestors, the ones attacked, fled in fear away from that place and moved [to the south] right past the very spot where this garden [Mishimishimaböwei] now lies.
NC: Right here? At Mishimishimaböwei?
D: Yes! Yes!
NC: Did they live here, right at *this* place?
D: Yes. They lived right *here*!
NC: What other gardens did they make in this area?
D: Over there [pointing].
NC: Did they live in the headwaters of the Rahuawä River?
D: Yes! Yes! Yes! In the *very* beginning they lived in the upper Rahuawä River—before I was even born.
NC: Before you were born did your actual ancestors live there with them?
D: [Begins to whine and whisper, for he is discussing his *own* dead ancestors] Yes! My true *shoabe* [greatgrandfather?] . . .

NC: [Suspecting who he means, whispers a name to verify] "Shamawä?"

D: [Whines, painful expression] Yes! Yes! Yes! That is the *shoabe* that lived at Yoroawätari, at Sherekasiba, at the edge of the slope at Yoroawä garden, at the river called Yurita, at the base of the mountain called Shadimoba. Wakusiwätari also live there. Then my *shoabe*, Shamawä, [sic] took over that place [from Wakusiwätari]. Then another of my *shoabes*, who is really from the ancient past—Maruwediwä—went to a garden called Sherekasiba, at Buuta River, at the falls called Käräbä, and lived there. Then they were subsequently chased away from that place by the Aramamisi-teri, who then lived up the Rahuawä River. At the mountain called Hukowä—where the Aramamisi-teri lived—they gave chase and drove my ancestors out. My ancestors went next to a place called Irota, a place called Ąbia, where the present Hasuböwa-teri came to live in recent times; my *shoabe*, Shamawä, did this. The Hasuböwä-teri later came and made new gardens in that same area. Then my ancestors moved next to the Shanishani River, my *shoabe*. They made the next garden at Darakawä River. Later, at Ihiramawä garden, they shot and killed my *shoabe* . . . the Aramamisi-teri shot him. A man called Maamawä did it; Maamawä shot and killed him. Deiyowä, another man, was also killed at that time. This was before I was born. They killed him before I was even born. They shot and killed him at Shihenaishiba, at Kayurewä garden—at Shamata garden. [These gardens are all very close together.]

NC: Did the Karawatari ancestors also live there, at the place you are talking about?

D: Yes, they lived there at one time.

NC: Did those Karawatari ancestors of yours split away *there* and join the ancestors of this [Mishimishimaböwei-teri] village?

D: Yes.

NC: At what garden did they join this group?

D: At the garden called Bohoroabihiwei [or Bohoroaböwei].

NC: You don't say!

D: Yes—at Bohoroabihiwei garden. It was there that they joined my *shoabe* [Matakuwä; he tapped his shin; the name Matakuwä means shin.] and lived with them. Then there was a big clubfight with the Aramamisi-teri over some peach-palm trees. This fight took place at Bohoroabihiwei, when they all lived there. Maamawä also lived there. A man called Amoköniniwä—also called Amoköwä—lived with them but he went away to the Boraböwei area. It was at that place that I was born.

NC: Where did the Karawatari live at that time?

D: Over there [to the south] at Shekerei . . . they had already left the area and had gone to Shekerei.

NC: Then when your group lived at Boraböwei, the Karawatari had *already* established their garden at Shekerei?

D: Yes! Yes! Yes! Yes!

NC: Did they ever live in the Moshada River area?

D: [Pauses] No . . . the Kohoroshitari lived over there.

NC: Is that true?

D: Yes!

NC: Wait! What garden did the Karawatari abandon when they made Shekerei?

D: They lived at Shihenaishiba before they made Shekerei.

NC: Do you mean that they fled *all the way* from Shihenaishiba to Shekerei?

D: They ran away from Shihenaishiba and . . .

NC: Did they make other gardens next?

D: Yes . . . Bahaböwei garden on the upper Shukumöna River.

NC: Where did they go from there?

D: They went to Shekerei after abandoning Bahaböwei.

NC: Are the Aramamisi-teri and Kohoroshitari closely related to each other?
D: Yes! Yes! Yes! Yes! They [Aramamisi-teri] chased them away from there [pointing to Shanishani River area].
NC: Where did their war first begin?
D: Way, way up there, in the very headwaters of the Shukumöna River . . . past the spot where the headwaters of the Rahuawä River come close to the branches of the Shukumöna.
NC: Did they all once live together way up in that region?
D: Yes . . . then they fought with each other with arrows and had a war, and then the Kohoroshitari fled.
NC: Why did they fight?
D: Don't ask a silly question like that! Women! Women! Women! Women! They screwed all the time and made a noise like: wha! wha! wha! wha! when they screwed. Women!
NC: After the split, where did the Kohoroshitari make their next garden and village?
D: They lived next at Moramana garden.
NC: When they abandoned that garden, where did they go?
D: They went next to Konabuma and cleared gardens there.
NC: Is that true? Do you mean that they were the very *first* people to clear gardens at Konabuma?
D: Yes! The Kohoroshitari were the first to clear gardens in that area.
NC: Where did your group live when the Kohoroshitari cleared Konabuma?
D: Boraböwei! Boraböwei! When we lived at Boraböwei, they lived at Konabuma!
NC: Did your group fight and make war with the Kohoroshitari?
D: Yes! Yes! Yes! Yes!
NC: Where did you first start shooting each other?
D: There, at Konabuma.
NC: What was the cause of the fighting?
D: "Cause," my foot! We fought for revenge!
NC: Revenge?
D: Yes! Yes! Yes! One of the Kohoroshitari we got there was called Kakawawä!
NC: Why did you kill him?
D: Don't ask such silly questions! We fought with them over women!
NC: Did you chase them away during this war? Were you born yet?
D: I wasn't born yet. Our group chased them to the Moshada River, to Mahareaböwei garden, and killed this many of them [holding up several fingers] in that area, the Moshada River area. It is over there [pointing].
NC: Did they live there when you lived at Boraböwei?
D: Yes! They were there when we were at Boraböwei. Their headman was Ohiriwä. Yarakawä was another big wheel in their village. They then fled to Mamoheböwei, right at the spot where we are today. They once gardened here.

The remainder of the transcript describes the locations of the various gardens where the Kohoroshitari and Karawatari groups lived while the Mishimishima-böwei-teri ancestors migrated into the region abandoned by these groups. It also describes a bitter war between the Karawatari and Kohoroshitari, naming some half-dozen specific individuals from each group who were killed by raiders from the other. The overall picture that emerges is that the Shamatari villages moved into areas vacated by the Karawatari and Kohoroshitari as they moved south and where they continued to fight among themselves. Gradually they ceased to have any continuing contact with the Shamatari. Thus, by approximately

1940, Shamatari history is dominated by political situations that arise between villages *within* the Shamatari population itself, punctuated occasionally by serious conflicts involving specific Shamatari villages with specific villages from adjacent Yąnamamö populations.

SHAMATARI SETTLEMENT PATTERN

Now that we have defined the relationship of the Shamatari population to other, similar Yąnomamö populations, we are in a position to take a more detailed look at the settlement pattern of the Shamatari proper.

Figure 2.8 shows the geographical locations of the several major regions that were or are occupied by the Shamatari. Those regions presently occupied are shown with a star next to them. The early history of the Shamatari group begins at the area called Aramamisi. My firsthand field experience has been confined to the six villages in the westernmost portion of the map, villages that are presently located in the areas designated as Reyaboböwei, Mishimishimaböwei and Habromaböwei.

These fourteen areas are *general regions* that were occupied by various Shamatari groups as they fissioned and spread from Aramamisi to the south and west. Each area contains many different gardens, some of which are given in Appendix D. I have employed either the names of old garden sites, rivers, or presently-existing villages to designate the regions. Thus, Toobatotoi, Ąbruwä, Doshamosha, Mishimishimaböwei, Habromaböwei, and Reyaboböwei are taken from names of presently existing Yąnomamö villages found in those regions today. Aramamisi is taken from the name of a prominent mountain in that area. Horoina, Yoboböwei, Boraböwei, Konabuma, Amiana, and Roena are taken from names of specific gardens in those areas, and Moshada is taken from the name of the river along which most of the gardens in that area were located.

The arrows shown on Figure 2.8 linking each region to the others give the sequence and direction of population movements among the Shamatari. For example, the village of Mishimishimaböwei-teri is located in the area designated as *Mishimishimaböwei.* Within this area they separated in very recent times from the village of Ironasi-teri, also located within the Mishimishimaböwei area. Before these two groups lived in this area, they lived at gardens in the Moshada area. While living in the Moshada region they themselves separated from their close relatives, who moved to the Roena area and then to the Reyaboböwei area, where they, in turn, separated to give rise to the villages Reyaboböwei-teri and Mǫmariböwei-teri.

Before the Moshada region was occupied, the collective group—Ironasi-teri, Mishimishimaböwei-teri, Reyaboböwei-teri, and Mǫmariböwei-teri—lived as a single village in the Konabuma region. They began separating into two distinct groups while they were in the Konabuma region, but the actual, final separation took place later, in the Moshada area.

Before they lived at Konabuma, the group occupied the Boraböwei and Yoboböwei regions. Most of the oldest members of all four villages were born in these

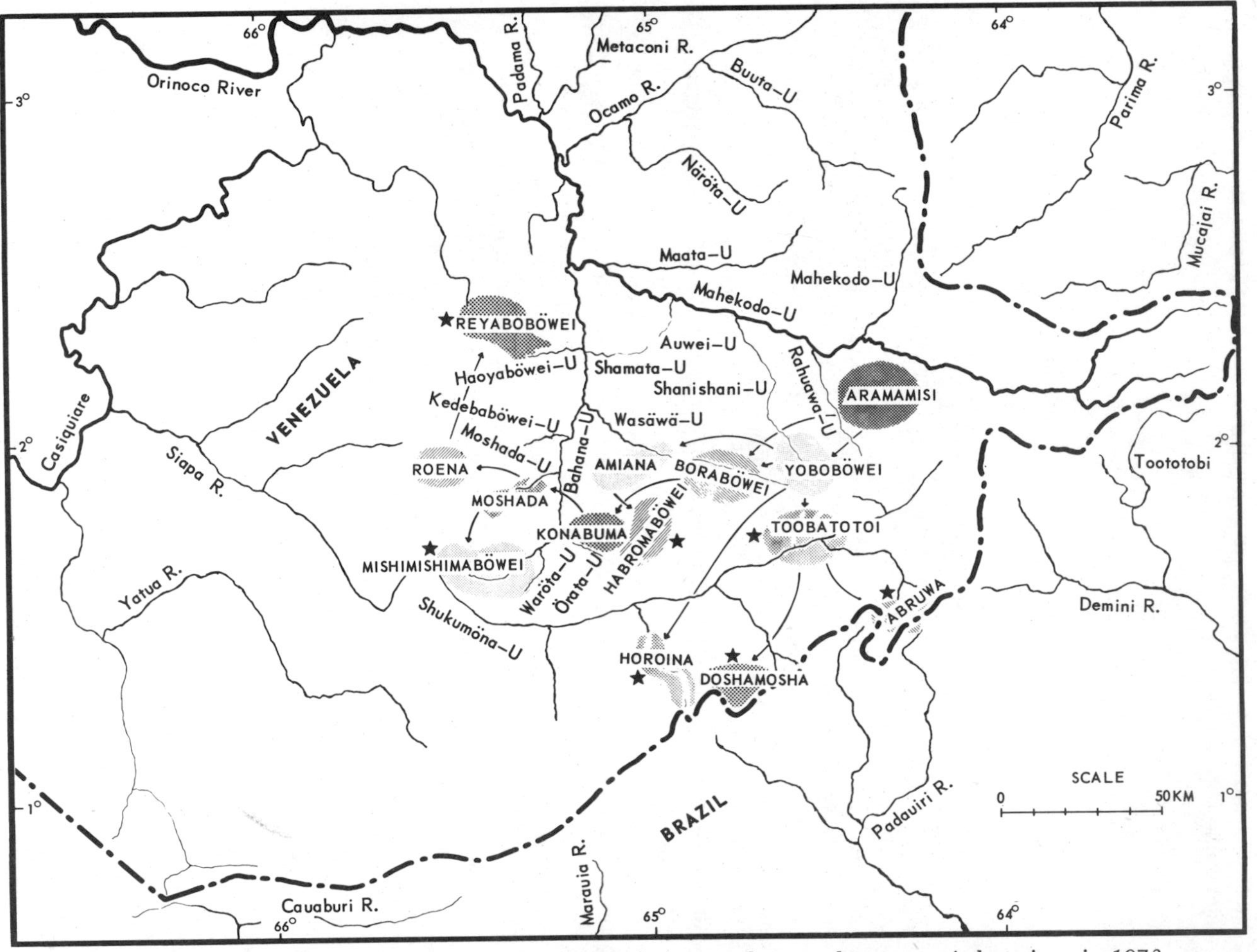

Figure 2.8—Shamatari settlement pattern. Stippled areas and stars show occupied regions in 1973.

general areas. All history prior to the Yoboböwei occupation is secondhand information. My informants know by hearsay from their long-deceased elders only the most general facts about the events, places, and people that refer to the portion of their history that took place in the Aramamisi region.

The gardens in the Yoboböwei and Boraböwei areas are rather continuously distributed, so there would be considerable justification for combining these two areas. However, after a portion of the group—the ancestral Mishimishimaböwei-teri—left the Yoboböwei region, other groups continued to make gardens in this region and left it only much later. Again, the precise movements, fissions, fusions, and recombinations that took place here are far from clear. It appears that some groups separated from a larger village only to recombine later with it, or with a group that had split off from it.

This process is still going on today in all of the regions, and provides a clue to the complexity of early Shamatari settlement pattern. In 1969, for example, a large fraction of the village of Ironasi-teri (Mishimishimaböwei-teri region) separated from the main group and left, in anger, to join their close relatives, the Reyaboböwei-teri, from whom they had separated more than 25 years earlier. They lived with the Reyaboböwei-teri for about a year, until they had a serious fight over women, and returned to their original group in the Mishimishimaböwei area, where they patched up their grievances. Several women from the group had babies while living in Reyaboböwei-teri. An anthropologist who would later attempt to reconstruct the settlement pattern would be confused by the inclusion of a number of young Ironasi-teri who were born in Reyaboböwei-teri, particularly when all other data show that the two groups had been separated for 25 to 30 years when these few individuals were born. Some of the "fogginess" in the settlement pattern as I have given it in this chapter is due to events such as this.

Figure 2.9 shows schematically the fissioning of the Aramamisi-teri population into its presently occupied villages.[12] These are listed along the bottom of the diagram. I know with considerable detail and accuracy only that portion that deals with the first six: Mishimishimaböwei-teri, Ironasi-teri, Mọmariböwei-teri, Reyaboböwei-teri, Miomaböwei-teri and Habromaböwei-teri. My data on the remaining villages, including geographical locations, are not complete. Filling in these gaps will be the objective of later fieldtrips. Finally, there may be additional villages not given in Figure 2.9. It is not clear to me that some groups—"Mokarita-teri," "Hịomisi-teri," "Nakiaiyoawä-teri," and "Narimoböwei-teri"—are to be given separate village designations or whether they are included in the villages as I have listed them in Figure 2.9. At the present they exist in my notes as merely names of Shamatari villages. They may be independent villages, or they may be alternative names for villages I have already listed.

Figure 2.9 also includes the two populations that I have been calling "Karawatari" and "Kohoroshitari," indicating that they might possibly have a

[12] This diagram was drawn before I went into the field in 1972. I collected additional data then that modifies this scheme slightly, particularly that portion of the diagram that describes the fissioning of Yeisikorowä-teri.

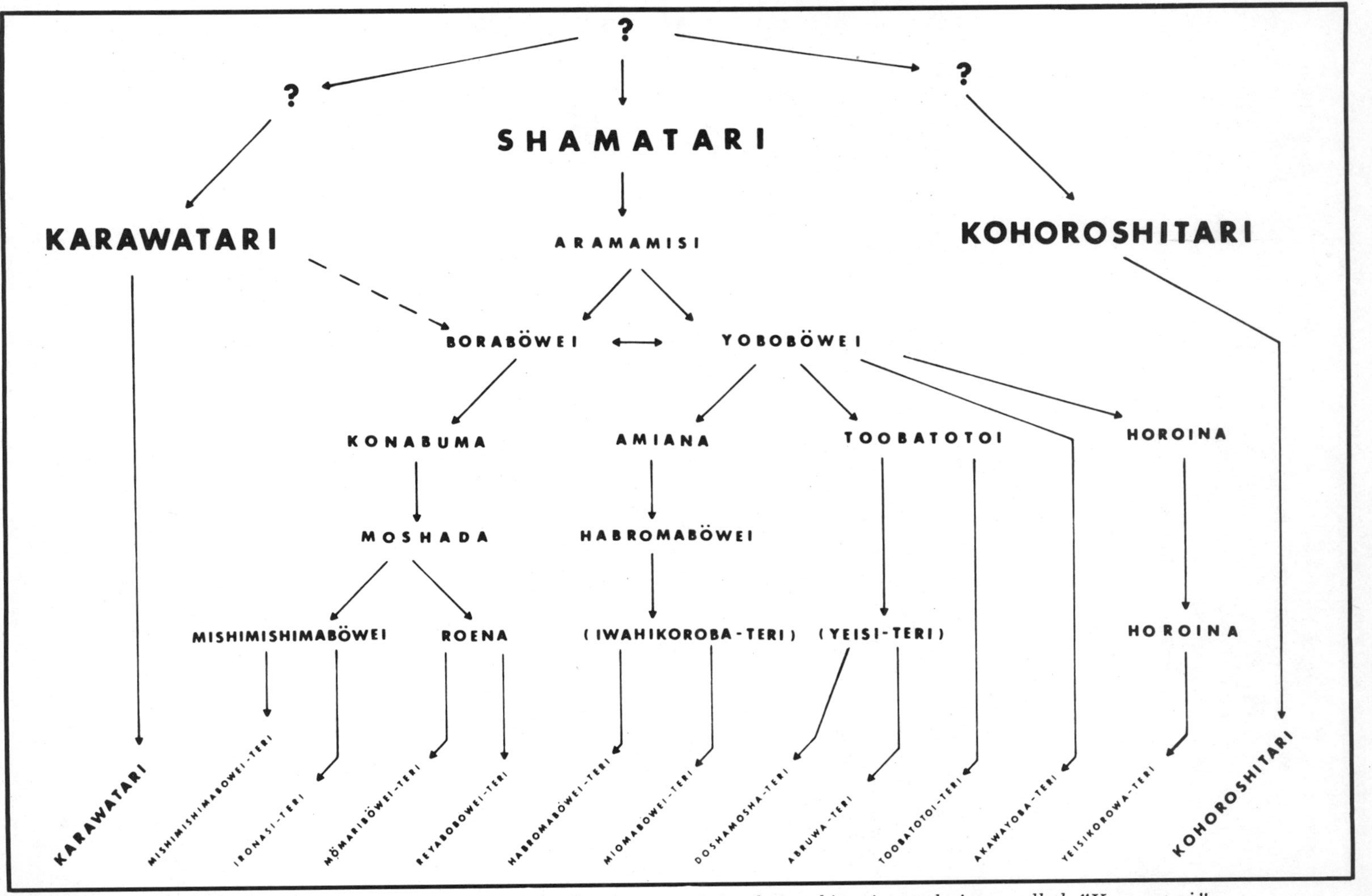

Figure 2.9—Schema of Shamatari fissions showing putative relationship of populations called "Karawatari," "Shamatari," and "Kohoroshitari."

common origin with the Shamatari. It is clear from genealogical evidence that the Karawatari group contributed in more than just a minor way to the present populations of some of the Shamatari groups. It is likely that similar evidence will subsequently show the same thing for the Kohoroshitari. Although I have indicated that the Karawatari and Kohoroshitari have not fissioned in Figure 2.9, it would be safe to assume that each of these groups has a political history at least as complicated as that shown for the Shamatari, and their populations are, today, subdivided into numerous independent villages.

3 / Genealogies, notes, and data organization

It is clear from the reconstruction of past political accounts given by older informants that no Yąnomamö village exists in isolation, free of the historical matrix that determines the attitudes held by its residents about its neighbors. Each village is biologically and historically related to its neighbors. Past events, especially wars and killings, account in large measure for the nature of the attitudes held by the members of any Yąnomamö village toward the members of neighboring villages. It is possible to demonstrate that *historically*, villages A, B, C, and D have a common origin and the ancestors of all contemporaneous groups once lived as members of the same village at some distant point in time. Similarly, another cluster of villages may have an historical relationship of the same kind. But because of the nature of the immediate political needs and the intensity of feelings that members of each group have for the members of other groups, I often encountered perplexing discrepancies in individual accounts of their own political identity and the identity of other villages.

For example, after spending nearly two years studying in detail the history and composition of the Bisaasi-teri, I was startled one day when a young man of some twenty-five years angrily denied being a "Bisaasi-teri" or a "Namowei-teri." He had just been in a clubfight with members of his village, and was attempting to distinguish himself from everybody else in the village by denying any political affinity to them. His young peers, who took his side in the clubfight, also vehemently supported his contention. He argued that he was from a different group, although I knew from older, more reliable informants that he had been born among the Patanowä-teri (actually, at Shįhota) and had never spent any time outside of that group. The reason he argued thus was that his father's father's father had originally come to the Namowei-teri population to seek a wife, and remained there for the duration of his life. All of his descendants also lived among the Namowei-teri and everyone considered them to be indisputably Namowei-teri. Yet this young man insisted, because of his father's father's father's origin, that *he* was not. I checked this information out with Kąobawä, who acknowledged that the young man's greatgrandfather did indeed come from a non–Namowei-teri population, but Kąobawä insisted that his descendants, by living so long with the Namowei-teri, had "become Namowei-teri." The young man, explained Kąobawä, was angry with everyone because of the clubfight and was not telling the "truth." He insisted that he was a Namowei-teri, and that was that, and that his two ascending agnatic kinsmen were as well.

Apart from raising some interesting and important questions about the relationship between "place of residence" and the nature of "lineal descent," this example and other, similar ones startled me, for it indisputably showed how conditional the beliefs relating to descent and filiation were to *immediate* events. I had long been aware of the shifting, ambiguous relationship between residence and descent, and had come to the conclusion that while place of residence was occasionally important in conferring political identity, descent through the male line was consistently more important in deciding political and domestic behavior. Now I had a good case that showed how important specific transient events were in causing the individuals in question to manipulate agnation and place of residence to their immediate advantage for some particular reason. There was another pattern that complicated this picture even more. That had to do with the relationship between (1) length of residence, (2) size of group, and (3) place of residence in the context of political identity by descent. The agnatic group from which this young man came was quite large and represented a significant fraction of several Namowei-teri villages. The "founder" of the lineage may have come from a different group, but because he left a number of descendants in the Namowei-teri population who, in turn, left additional descendants over several generations, the group had "become" a Namowei-teri group. The important factors were that (a) they were numerous, (b) they had lived in the Namowei-teri population for several generations, and (c) the males of the group were important politically because they represented a large group.

This incident, and several like it, led me to realize how important it was to systematically collect data on reproductive performance and on birthplace for living and dead. Reproductive performance would yield the size or relative importance of a kinship group in village histories, while place of birth, once the gardens had been identified as to population, would supplement my knowledge of the political affiliation of individuals insofar as geographic provenience was concerned.

The previous chapter described how I manipulated the geographical data, once it was collected, to arrive at a notion of the settlement pattern. Here I describe how the same kind of data is related to questions of kinship, descent, and political identity and how I collected and organized the data as I investigated genealogies.

Accurate genealogies are fundamental to an understanding of Yąnomamö social organization, intervillage political relationships, and past history. Collecting this information may have been the most boring, tedious, and time-consuming task of my fieldwork, but the resulting data have constituted the most important single source of information on many different aspects of the culture. More is embedded in Yąnomamö genealogical data than merely biological relationships.

I described in Chapter 1 of *The Fierce People* some of the problems I initially had in Bisaasi-teri collecting genealogies, and how some of my more resourceful and mischieveous informants collaborated with each other to the extent of inventing and consistently using false names and other information regarding the kinship nexus of that group. I do not wish to repeat here the description I gave in *The*

Fierce People, nor do I want to reflect the tedium and frustrations of genealogy collecting by reciting *all* of the problems and *all* of the techniques I used.

Still, if my experience is to provide a lesson for others who work under similar circumstances, I must cover some of the issues. To do so with a minimum amount of inconvenience to the reader, I will summarize the experience in terms of "lessons" I learned.

Because of the large number of questions I get from graduate students and field workers regarding my note-taking system, I will give a brief description of the system I used, one that took many months to work out after trying numerous other alternatives. I do not suggest that it is the best one; it is merely one that I found useful in my own situation.

I will also comment on the use to which I put IBM cards and computer technology as an adjunct to organizing my data and how computer techniques have been helpful to me in *collecting data* during return field trips.

Finally, I will show how genealogical data can be used to confirm settlement pattern information, as given in the previous chapter, and how it can describe the extent to which two or more groups can be said to be related politically, historically, and biologically.

Genealogies

By way of justifying an incomplete documentation of the problems raised in the field regarding the collecting of genealogical data and otherwise programmatic statements of my opinions on the subject, I think it is appropriate at this juncture to comment on my experience, and, therefore, my qualifications to discuss the subject in this shorthand way.

I have spent nearly three years living in Yąnomamö villages since 1964. I have visited some forty or fifty different Yąnomamö villages. I cannot be more specific than this on the number of villages, since the entire notion of village would have to be discussed at some length. For example, some of the villages I have visited no longer exist as separate entities, having been reabsorbed by the groups from which they originated. Others have since subdivided and are now two or even three distinct villages; do I count these two or three times? Forty or fifty villages, however, comes close to defining the range of experience I am discussing; it is not "a few" or "several."

During these visits I met approximately 3,000 Yąnomamö individuals, all of whom I have in my genealogies. A rough estimate of the total number of individuals in my genealogies would be of the order of 10,000, which includes living and dead persons. To be sure, not all of the genealogies are equally good; the reasons for this will become clear below. At this juncture I wish to say that on the basis of this experience, I have run into many problems and challenges, and if I appear to be giving them insufficient documentation, it is only because space forbids and, besides, they are quite boring. I will summarize only the more recurrent and serious ones.

By the time I began to make an intensive effort at collecting the genealogies of the Shamatari groups, I had learned some important lessons in Bisassi-teri and other villages. Knowing from the outset what the problems were helped me immensely, so the field research went more efficiently as I applied techniques I developed in my early work. I knew that my informants would lie under some circumstances and be truthful under others. I knew it would be difficult to work around the name taboo, and I knew that important gains would be made only after I identified the good informants. As happened in Bisaasi-teri, the early good breaks came from informants who might be considered "aberrant" or "abnormal," outcasts in their own society, individuals like the twelve-year-old Karina, who guided me to Mishimishimaböwei-teri the first time.

In initiating my intensive work on the Shamatari I had one very important advantage that I did not have in my earlier work on the Bisaasi-teri. The Shamatari were a different people from the Bisaasi-teri, and well known to them. Under these circumstances, I could obtain the *real* names of the Shamatari by using reliable Bisaasi-teri informants with whom I had already established rapport. With accurate names, I was independent of any informant who gave them to me, and I could go to other villages where the names would be recognizeable. I learned from this the most efficient procedure to follow: to obtain the genealogy on a particular group by collecting it, wherever possible, from people who did not belong to that group or, alternatively, were not living with that group. In my Shamatari work, therefore, I had genealogies of every village before I actually lived in or visited the village.

Once in the village, Mishimishimaböwei-teri for example, I could not expect to easily get the true names of the residents from the residents themselves. Still, I had to identify and "genealogize" the individuals who were living in the villages but who did not occur on the genealogy. I had to resort to earlier tactics, such as "bribing" children when their elders were not around, or capitalizing on animosities between individuals, or photographing the people and taking the photos to other villages for identification.

One other factor also worked to my advantage among the Shamatari. My base of operations was in Bisaasi-teri, where I had a mud-walled, grass-roofed hut. There were a number of Shamatari in Bisaasi-teri, young people who had recently married into the village, or old women who were captured from the Shamatari long ago. Once they were aware of the fact that I knew the true names of people in their villages it was possible to use them as informants to check the accuracy of what my Bisaasi-teri informants told me. As a technique, this can be likened to removing the informant from his village and working with him elsewhere, except that the informants were already elsewhere to begin with. Logically, I expanded this and would bring informants from their own village to work with me in my mud hut. Once out of their village and aware that I already knew the names of everyone in their village, most of these informants would cooperate with me. After several such experiences I knew who the best ones were, and used them more than the others. They always knew beforehand what kind of "*Ribromou*" (working with paper)[1] we would be doing, so it was *not* a matter of tricking them into coming a long distance and using them as "captive" informants. Most of the informants were very cooperative outside of their village.

[1] From the Spanish *libro*—(book).

Ten thousand circles and triangles later, here is what I think is important to know about collecting Yąnomamö genealogies.

1. *Never assume that a new informant will tell the truth.*

This dictum applies to information about members of his own group as well as that about members of other groups. With specific reference to the informant's group, the dictum could be rewritten to say: Always assume that he *is* lying.

Whenever it is possible, I check the consistency and accuracy of a new informant before I invest too much of my time with him. I normally have him give me the genealogical relationships of a group of people that I know to have certain names and to be related in certain ways. If his version is the same as the version I obtained from reliable informants, I proceed further with the new informant.

In some circumstances it is not possible to follow this dictum. For example, my collaborative work with medical–genetics colleagues[2] obliges me to take them to distant villages that I may have never visited before, or may have visited only once or twice; in some cases I never have an opportunity to return to these villages because of other commitments. One of my tasks is to provide my colleagues with minimal genealogies for use in family studies of inherited genes. Since the genealogies are necessary, I am often in the position of having to select my informants from among total strangers and accept what they say. I rarely have an opportunity to return and check their accuracy.

In 1970, while waiting at a mission airstrip for my medical colleagues to arrive from Caracas, I used two young men from a distant village as informants for the genealogy of their group. They were visiting the mission and wanted to ride back to their village in my canoe when I took the medical group there to collect blood samples. I had met both young men before. Since I had to wait at the mission several days, I took the opportunity to get a head start on the genealogy of their village.

I spent ten hours a day for two days working with these new informants. They, of course, collaborated with each other and told me a consistent story. This meant that they were either telling me the truth, or were lying consistently. I suspected the latter, but had no way to check on them: I did not have an accurate genealogy of that village to test them with. I devised a new strategy. I managed to get one of them alone for awhile to create a situation in which one did not know what the other told me. Then I worked alone with the other for awhile. When I resumed work with both present, neither was certain what the other had privately told me. I slipped into the long list of names and relationships they had given to me the names and relationships of people from a different village, scattering this new, extraneous information among the facts they had given me.

As I checked the information with them, they confirmed the false information as readily and convincingly as they did the information they had given to me,

[2] See bibliography for references to publications that resulted from this collaboration. A good summary can be found in Neel, 1970, and Neel, Arends, Brewer, Chagnon *et al*, 1971.

insisting in every case that the person in question lived in their village and had the parents that I recited. Both informants assumed that the other had given me the new information in private, and each tried to cover up for the other. I then told them what I had done, after I was convinced that they were lying. They both groaned and left without demanding the pay I had promised. They did not ride with me back to their village. This incident was after 30 months of experience with the same thing; some anthropologists never learn.

2. *On once-only visits to a new village do not try to collect genealogies by using names.*

The probability that the Yąnomamö will lie to foreigners about their real names is so high that it is foolish to attempt to work with names they give you during a brief visit. Much of my collaborative work with medical–genetics colleagues takes place in circumstances such as this. In these cases I write identification numbers on everybody and use kinship terms to discover the *probable* biological relationships among those who are alive.

While this procedure reduces the temptation to lie, it does not remove it entirely. There is so much reluctance even to acknowledge the fact that a particular person's father or mother is dead that informants will often attribute a child to a resident living sibling of the deceased real parent, or a cousin, or an uncle. You simply do not know.

Working with kinship terms and identification numbers has another built-in disadvantage; it is not possible to get more than one generation of genealogical depth.

The accuracy of such "one-day stand" genealogies probably varies from very poor to very good. There is simply no way to tell in the field if the informant is lying, except in the obvious cases where a forty-year-old man swears that another man, age thirty-five, is his "true" son, or worse yet, his father. The Yąnomamö, incidentally, appreciate the distinction between biological and sociological paternity or maternity and are very much aware of the fact that I am after the former when I collect genealogies. The kinship system gives social statuses, but there is a good deal of correspondence in biological and social definitions (Chagnon and Levin, ms.). The fact that they are not *completely* isomorphic is the reason why I have very little confidence in genealogies that are collected this way.

For the past two years I have been using a Polaroid camera to take identification photographs of all (living) individuals who appear in my genealogies. This has greatly facilitated genealogical work and has the potential of allowing for "immediate" checks on accuracy: the photographs can be brought to other nearby villages and the people identified by different informants.

3. *It takes many months of intensive work to collect an accurate genealogy.*

I have no confidence in genealogies that are collected (among the Yąnomamö) in less than six months of intensive work *under the right circumstances.* One of the circumstances is that the person collecting the genealogy speaks the Yąnomamö language tolerably well when he begins the genealogy. Otherwise, it takes longer than six months.[3]

It is possible to collect a good genealogy in less than six months, but not from a group that is entirely unknown to the fieldworker at the outset, when he has to rely on new informants. It takes months to establish rapport with individuals in a new group and to discover who the good informants are.

I am now working with a population that includes a large number of villages (see Chapter 1), many of which are still uncontacted by outsiders. But because they have ancestors in common with people I already know and have genealogies of, and because the living people in these uncontacted villages are known to my informants in other villages, I can, at this point, collect an accurate genealogy on these new groups in just a few weeks. I already have the genealogies of their ancestors, so the problem comes down to accurately identifying the living members of the village and relating them to the already existing genealogy collected elsewhere. The months required to establish rapport with informants and find out who the good informants are have already been invested.

To give a concrete example, in 1971 I made first contact with a large Shamatari group that is related to the Mishimishimaböwei-teri. They had never seen foreigners, but they know who I am and what I am like. I also know who they are, and when I arrived at their village I had with me accurate names and genealogical relationships of at least 80 percent of the group. The problem was to associate the names in my field book with the faces in the village. I did this by taking pictures of the faces and carrying the pictures back to Mishimishimaböwei-teri for accurate identification. While in their village I estimated ages, noted all new children and found out who their parents were, and obtained birthplaces of everyone. None of this required the use of names. Thus, in a two-day visit to their village I obtained 99 percent of the information I needed to give a very accurate genealogy of the group. The other 1 percent may take an additional few weeks.

4. *It takes at least three reliable, knowledgeable informants to give a meaningful genealogy; at least one must be older than fifty and at least one must be from a different group.*

These conditions are the only ones that permit me to obtain accurate cross-checks on genealogical data, and the only way I can be certain that the names are accurate. These are just *minimum* requirements. None of my "best" genealogies, such as those I have on the Namowei-teri and the Shamatari populations, were reached with less than dozens of informants in each case.

I have had the occasion to inspect genealogies that were collected by missionaries. Most missionaries use just one informant, usually a fairly young informant, and often take his word as final. However, where I have genealogies on the same group, I note that the missionary versions are usually quite deficient. I mention this because it is possible to be convinced, unless the genealogy is cross-checked sys-

[3] My French colleague, Jacques Lizot (1970; 1971a; 1971b), who is working among the villages to the north of the Namowei-teri and Shamatari, concurs in this. We *both* discarded as useless most of the genealogical data we collected during the first six to nine months of our respective work (personal communication).

tematically by informants from other groups, that the missionary version is accurate. In most cases the missionary is convinced that because he collected his version in his village, where he has spent more time than a "casual" visitor, his version must therefore be correct or more accurate. For the purposes to which missionaries put their genealogies—keeping track of individuals by family groupings—their versions are usually adequate. For social and biological analyses, they are often not.

5. *Men are better informants for genealogical relationships than women.* While this might not be a popular position to take at the present stage of social evolution in our own culture, it happens to be true of my Yąnomamö field experience. I suspect that the reason has to do with the fact that genealogical information is the repository of a great deal of political history, and politics is the domain of Yąnomamö men. Women tend to remember accurately the genealogical relationships of both males and females equally well, but for a few generations. Men are able to give genealogical relationships back further in time, but the further back they go the fewer female links they can give. This might be due to the patrilineal bias in the culture, but it is more often due to the frequency of abducted females with unknown genealogies who occur in the ancestral generations. Women are better for certain kinds of demographic work, such as infanticide, total number of births, the sex of infants who died shortly after birth, and so on. Men often forget about children who died before adolescence.

6. *Do not accept an informant's statements about his own close kinsmen, and do not solicit them.*

I make every effort to avoid embarrassing my informants or hurting their feelings by asking them about their close kinsmen. However, accidents occasionally happen, especially when I am working with long lists of names, and I may inadvertently ask an informant about someone on the list who is very closely related to him. I can usually tell from his reaction that I have erred, but once in a while I cannot. The answers, even from my best informants, are usually not accurate. When I start from scratch on a genealogy of a group with an informant of that group, a situation I normally try to avoid, I usually ask him to give me the genealogy of people who are not of his father's agnatic group. I try to get the genealogy of my first informant from someone else, and avoid asking him about people who are closely related to him.

The fact that the Yąnomamö are willing to give genealogically relevant information about others led me to exploit this by attempting to collect such information from people who were known enemies of the subject village. There is, in fact, no better way to get an accurate, reliable start on a genealogy than to collect it from the enemies. In exploiting this technique, I normally obtain the *accurate* names of both the living and the dead on the first attempt. Later, when I am working in the village or with an informant from that village, I check the accuracy of the first account, since while the first informant may have been willing to use the correct names, he might not have known all of the genealogical relationships as well as people who were actually from the group. For this work I usually try to find an informant who has married into the village, one who is familiar with all of the people and their true genealogical relationships. Ideally, the second informant is also related to the people, but only distantly; then he is usually willing to mention the names of the dead once he knows that I already know them. Most of these types of informants are people who have married into the village from different, but related, villages and are, in some respects, outsiders. This helps to explain, incidentally, why some of my best informants are something of outcasts; often they are not from the population with which I am dealing and are, for that reason, somewhat mistreated and willing to be frank about the names and relationships of their covillagers.

For Mishimishimaböwei-teri, which is genealogically quite homogeneous, I had very unusual luck. My best informant, Dedeheiwä, shares very few ancestors with most of the people in that village; he is descended from a small group of Karawatari (see Figure 2.8, Chapter 2) who married into the Shamatari population several generations ago. After I gained his confidence, it was very easy to get excellent, accurate information on the ancestral Shamatari or check the accuracy of the information I had obtained from others. The people in question in the genealogies were well known to him, but were not his agnatic kinsmen. For example, the 280-odd residents of Mishimishimaböwei-teri (1971 census) were largely descendants of the father of the man called Matakuwä. 83, or 36 percent, were lineal descendants (through males) and—184, or 80 percent, were cognatic descendants. Yet Dedeheiwä was neither an agnate nor a cognate. Consequently, I was able systematically and quite easily to verify and improve the genealogical information with him. By extension, he was a good informant for most of the other Shamatari groups whose composition heavily reflects the fecundity of Matakuwä's father.

7. *Every genealogy must be checked thoroughly by informants from different villages.*

This is very tedious, time-consuming work, and implies a system of note-keeping in the field that permits of thorough checks in an efficient manner. There is very little to say about the techniques involved in checking genealogy save that they are identical to or extensions of techniques used in collecting the genealogy. Nothing, however, is more satisfying than to work for months with reliable informants from two different villages until I have the genealogy of some third group nearly worked out to my satisfaction and *then* collect identical information from a totally different informant from a fourth village. My techniques are now such that I rarely find my reliable informants contradicting each other, although I still find occasional conflicts that cannot be resolved by working with a given pair or set of informants. At that point I find a different informant. Many of these conflicts are resolved when I discover that all informants were telling the truth, but each informant used different names for the people in question.

Alternate names are a serious problem when it comes to checking the accuracy of genealogies. Many Yąnomamö have two or more names, and in some cases the alternate names are not known to people in distant villages. I have even run into situations where not only does a particular individual have several names, but both of his parents likewise have multiple names. In working with numerous informants, the permutations and combinations are numerous when each uses a different set of names. The net result may be as confusing as assigning three distinct children to a given set of parents when in fact there were merely three names for a single person. Again, the parent combinations imply multiple marriages for several distinct individuals, when in fact there is only one marriage of two people, each with several names. Back in the United States I convert every name to a discrete 5-digit ID number, but in the field I must work with Yąnomamö names. Tracking down the alternate names becomes a very serious, time-consuming problem when the total population of names (in the Namowei-teri and Shamatari populations) approaches 4,000. In some cases, the alternate names for individual "X" may be identical to names use for individuals "Y" and "Z," so it is not possible to merely discard them as they are found, for this raises the possibility of discarding a real individual with a different set of parents. The apparent conflicts in the data also increase when X's alternate names are identical to the true names for Y and Z, who have different parents entirely. The problem then expands to determining if the three sets of parents (of X, Y, and Z) are different people. The parents of X, Y, and Z may themselves have alternate names, and these must be sorted out before the identities of X, Y, and Z are clearly established. While in the field I retain alternate-name identities and have memorized many of the more important ones. Still, it is a serious problem and unless the informants know the alternate-name identities, they may insist that other informants have lied to me. This raises the delicate matter of confronting my informants with data that others have given and implying that someone is lying. This can insult an informant who has gone out of his way to be conscientious and honest, and therefore I always attempt to resolve the conflicts by soliciting independent opinions from other informants.

One additional way of checking the *biological* accuracy of a genealogy, at least among living individuals, is to consider the blood group genes and attempt to see if the child can possibly be the offspring of the stated parents. To do this requires blood samples of both parents and the child, and most anthropologists do not normally have this kind of information at their disposal. In my Yąnomamö work I have collaborated with geneticists and have such information available. Several years ago we did check the genealogies of some fifty children in one village using these techniques. The results were very good; five children of the fifty *might* have been the offspring of different parents. In two of the cases, the Yąnomamö themselves had previously told me that they were not sure which of two putative fathers was in fact the genitor, since both cohabited with the mother at the time of conception; the test was made only for one of the two possible fathers. In two other cases, the child could not be excluded on the more reliable blood group genetic systems but was excluded by genetic systems that were known to involve larger than acceptable laboratory typing errors; it was not certain whether the genealogy was in error or the serum and laboratory techniques deficient. Finally, one child was definitely excluded by the reliable genetic system. On a subsequent field trip I investigated this and learned that the woman in question was having an affair with another man at the time of conception and he might possibly have been the father.

Caution and common sense are in order when using paternity–exclusion techniques to test the biological accuracy of genealogies. Few people realize the magnitude and kind of errors that inhere in blood-group determinations, and many assume that since test tubes are used, these techniques are by definition more scientific and more reliable than informant statements. It is possible for two different laboratories, for example, to disagree on blood types by as much as 10 percent for some genetic systems, even when each analyzes a fraction of the same blood sample with the same reagents. The source of error might be difference in the age of the blood sample when it was analyzed, minor difference in technique used by the respective technicians, inadvertent mixing up of the samples, or errors in transcribing information when lists are made. When different blood samples from the same individual are taken, and different reagents used for particular genetic systems, the error might even be greater than 10 percent. Finally, laboratory techniques cannot be used when one or both of the parents are dead or unavailable for blood typing, which is most often the case in genealogy work. Where the difference between sociological and biological paternity is relevant in any population, and it is among the Yąnomamö, paternity-exclusion tests are useful as checks on their biological awareness. In general, they seem to be very cognizant of biological paternity and when they are willing to report it accurately, they usually do so. In other societies the distinction might not be meaningful or relevant.

8. *Work privately while collecting genealogies.*

In Chapter 1 of *The Fierce People* I discussed some of the consequences of working publicly to collect genealogical information. As a technique, it is unwise in almost all circumstances because of the name taboo and the tendency of the Yąnomamö to conceal true names by inventing false ones. However, in a few circumstances it was possible for me to work in public, particularly to obtain accurate names of people in distant villages. One such circumstance involved the use of Polaroid photographs that I took of individuals in village "X" and later showed to the residents of village "Y." For example, in 1971 I contacted the previous uncontacted village of Iwahikoroba-teri, whose genealogies I knew even before I arrived there (Chagnon, 1971). I took identification photographs of everyone and later showed them to the residents of Mishimishimaböwei-teri. I let everyone in the village look at them in public and discuss them while I went on with other work. The men examined them all first, and when they grew weary, the women then looked at them. Later, I selected individuals—children, men, and women—to give me the names of everyone in the photographs. I noted these names on the photos and checked their accuracy with others in the village, getting identical names or alternate names. Since they knew that I already knew the true names, they were frank and straightforward. Besides, they did not particularly like the Iwahikoroba-teri, even though they were closely related to them.

Still, I had to work privately with reliable informants to get the names of their deceased ancestors or to check them; the ancestors were the same for both the Iwahikoroba-teri and the Mishimishimaböwei-teri.

9. *Start a new genealogy with the families of the headmen.*

Yąnomamö social organization is such that the headmen will normally come from the largest, most prominent kinship group. It is most efficient in starting a new genealogy to ask the informant first to give you the names of all the prominent men in the village. By getting the names of the brothers and sisters and children of these men, I usually have 80 percent of the village on the genealogy in very short order. Some villages are more variable in their lineal composition than others, depending on the amount of intervillage marriage; it takes longer to obtain a list of residents in these circumstances.

10. *Collect the genealogy by agnatic kinship grouping.*

My informants always gave me genealogical information that was organized by them into agnatic kinship groupings, whether or not I requested it in that form. That is how they themselves organize the information and how they prefer to give it. I found that it was more efficient to allow the informant to exhaust his information about kinship groups before interrupting him to track down the affinal links. Figure 3.1, a photograph of notes I took while working with Karina on the Mishimishimaböwei-teri group, is a good example of this. He began by giving me the genealogy of the several prominent men I requested him to discuss: this is shown in the upper half of the paper as two distinct agnatic groupings. Then he said he could not remember any other individual of the same "*mashi*" and told me: "*Hei ai a mashi, shomi; a da tabraba!*" ("This is going to be another, different, agnatic kinship group: write it down next!") This was an unsolicited statement, but since it indelibly expressed the way he organized the information in his own mind, I noted his statement down at the time. The genealogy, incidentally, is not especially accurate in a biological sense, but the names are accurate and the agnatic grouping real. It was the first time I had worked with this informant, who was only about twelve years old.

By following each kinship grouping out to its ultimate conclusion I occasionally get off on the wrong track. It turns out that in some cases only 5 percent or so of the people in a particular lineage are in the village whose residents I am hoping to get on genealogies. Thus 95 percent of the effort is spent on a different village. If I do not have any immediate interest in the second village, this seems like an enormous waste of time. I still continue to do it. I have long since discovered that such information is invaluable in demonstrating the genealogical links between groups and it enables me to state very precisely how villages are biologically and socially interrelated.

After exhausting my informant's knowledge of a particular village's inhabitants by pursuing the genealogical links through the male line, I track down individuals who have married into the group from the outside. Often they have few or no relatives in the village, and a "shotgun" approach is all that I can rely on: the "Who else lives there?" kind of question. It is important to note the village of origin of such individuals, since it reminds me that it might be a waste of time to try to track down their genealogies if they came originally from very distant villages that are not well known to my informants. Unless I do this a serious

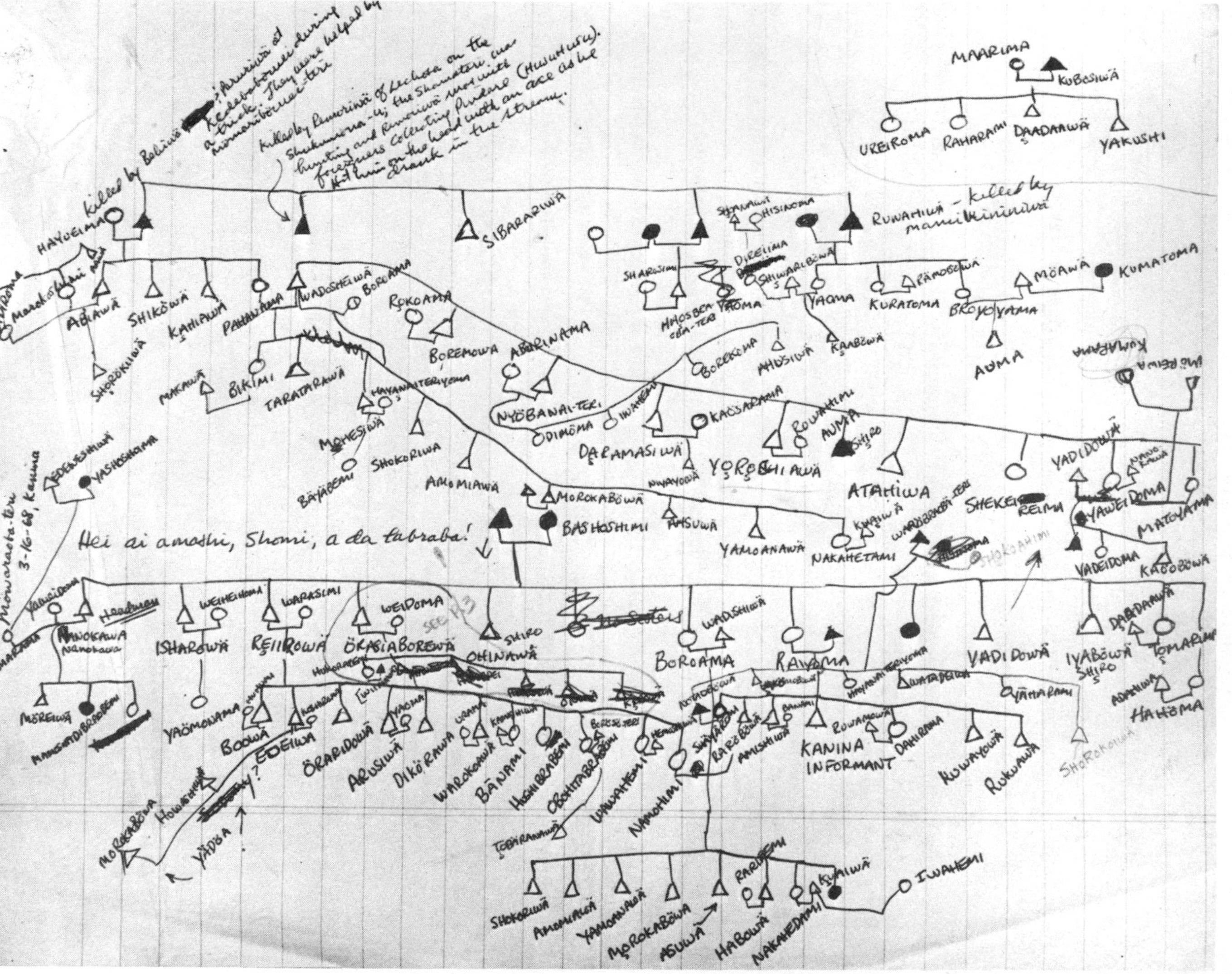

Figure 3.1—Facsimile of notes: a genealogy drawn from Karina's data

problem emerges later, when all the names are pooled together and I make lists of individuals. If their village of origin does not occur on the list, I spend many fruitless hours trying to find informants who know the genealogical links of these people.

This list of ten "lessons" should suffice to give the reader an inkling of the types of problems that I face in collecting accurate Yąnomamö genealogies, and how I attempt to work around them with specific techniques. The list is not exhaustive.

Needless to say, circumstances have developed in my fieldwork where I have not always been able to follow the dictates of my own experience, especially in those instances when I visit villages for just a brief time and do not return to verify genealogical information that I collect during the course of the visit. The net result is that I have at least three different grades of genealogical data qualitatively different bodies of information that reflect the degree to which I have adhered to the above dicta. The "poor" grade of genealogies can be used with confidence only for such simple analytical purposes as citing the number of individuals of which sex and what age who live in a particular village. They can also be used, but with less confidence, for family studies and other demographic analyses. Poor grade genealogical data result from situations where I do not know my informants, do not know the people in the village, and do not have an opportunity to cross-check the data later with other informants in other villages.

I also have another body of genealogical data that might be described as "fair." For this type of data I have usually used informants who are reliable and who, in the past, proved to be knowledgeable and accurate. The data can be easily improved and are worth making an effort to do so. In their present condition and degree of completness, they can be used for some kinds of social analyses, such as types of marriages, size of sibships, distribution of lineal relatives by village, and some kinds of demographic statements. In brief, they can, with considerable effort, be transformed into "good" genealogies; it does not require starting from scratch and does not require a long, painful search for good informants.

The "good" genealogies are those collected under the circumstances described above in the ten lessons. It is only in these that I have any confidence for most analytical purposes. Approximately one-fourth to one-third of all of my genealogical data fall into this category.

"THE" INFORMANT

Many anthropologists speak of "their informant" as if what they know about "their people" comes exclusively from one individual. This is probably rarely the case in most anthropological fieldwork, although it is probably true for certain kinds of "secret" or privileged information in every field situation. It should be apparent from the foregoing discussion of genealogy collecting that in my case I have no *single* informant whose single version I accepted as an article of faith.

In the *The Fierce People* I described two men, Rerebawä and Kąobawä, as people whose word I learned to trust on certain matters and who were very good informants. They were not, however, the only informants I used, nor were they always the best for all kinds of information. Still, they—and individuals like them among the Shamatari—continue to be reliable sources to whom I turn, people from whom I can generally get a good "first draft" of some kinds of information. In very few cases, however, do I accept the word of a single informant, even Rerebawä or Kąobawä, without attempting to check it with another person.

The few cases where checking is unnecessary involve such things as mythology, where I was more interested in what a *particular* man said about certain spirits and ancestors than I was in what my translator said was "actually true." The Yąnomamö use phrases and archaic words in myths that do not occur in normal, everyday conversation, so I must always listen to a taped myth with other informants, and have them translate the archaic or mythological sayings to colloquial Yąnomamö. In many instances the translator interrupts and claims indignantly that the original informant is not telling the myth "correctly" and insists that I listen to his version. The point of the exercise is not to look for the "true" version, since each group has it own "true" version, but to collect particular versions, whether or not the second informant subscribes to the version he is helping me understand. Since I do not want to dissuade the second informant from pointing out falsehoods, this raises problems in certain areas of my fieldwork and often strains my relationships with particular informants who resent the fact that I am bothering to record and transcribe a "false" version, and feel I am not particularly interested in their "true" version.

With respect to my fieldwork among the Shamatari, I have developed relationships with particular individuals who, like Rerebawä and Kąobawä, usually give me very reliable information on all matters, or at least do not deliberately attempt to lead me astray. It takes a very long time to establish these relationships among the Yąnomamö and I cherish them, for both personal and practical reasons. A good informant is an enormous asset and saves all manner of time and frustration. I use these informants frequently and attempt to initiate work on new topics with such people. In some instances I also accept *their* word where, as in genealogies, several informants give conflicting information. Learning, then, to trust certain informants comes from a feeling that is acquired by living in the field for a long time, a feeling that cannot be accurately described nor taught in classrooms. It is partially intuition and partially experience gained in the field, working with particular people on particular kinds of information. These relationships also depend on personality, what I am as a human being and what the informants are like: idiosyncratic factors lead me to develop warm, friendly relationships with some individuals and not with others.

All of this is to say that very little of my ethnographic data in general is the product of "the" mythical single informant, and none of my "good" genealogical data is. It should be apparent from the material presented in *The Fierce People* and in this chapter why this should be the case.

As a generalization, I would say that it is best for potential fieldworkers to start their fieldwork with the assumption that they will have to check the accuracy of their informants, rather than assuming that an informant will be honest, truthful, and candid. In some societies I am sure that fieldworkers will find that most informants can be trusted, but it *does* require checking to make this discovery. In other societies, such as the Yąnomamö, it will be necessary to proceed from the assumption that all new informants will initially deceive you and that you will have to develop procedures for checking and cross-checking them. Until reliable informants emerge, which depends on factors that are unique to each situation, it will be necessary to work on this assumption. There are probably very few societies where an anthropologist can never develop relationships with individuals that result in a mixture of friendship and fruitfulness. On the other hand, there are probably some anthropologists who could not develop such relationships in any society.

Whatever the case may be in any given field situation, it is always desirable to have several different informants and, consequently, several different perspectives on the phenomenon being investigated. The comparative method in anthropology should begin with the data—in the field.

GENEALOGICAL NOTES

The problems of collecting and checking genealogies described above are peculiar to my own field situation because of my anthropological interests and the reaction of the Yąnomamö to them. They may not be frequently encountered elsewhere. However, one set of problems that is universal among fieldworkers who collect large bodies of genealogical data is the development of an efficient note-taking and data organization system. I will describe my techniques here, hopefully providing a model that will have utility in other, very different, field situations.

Initial Genealogy

As stated above, I always attempt to collect the genealogy of some group by using informants in distant villages. The first several drafts of the genealogy I regard as the "initial" genealogy.

I usually collect initial genealogies on 8½-by-11 paper, either a sheet torn from a bound tablet, or a sheet of punched loose-leaf paper taken from a standard three-ring binder. Punched paper has proved to be the most convenient because I can store and manipulate the data more efficiently. Genealogical information taken from different informants can be kept separate, and data bearing on particular villages can be kept together. If it is necessary to travel to distant villages, the relevant data can be easily removed from the binder and carried along. If the data were all in a bound book, I would risk losing the information during the trip if, for example, the canoe tips over. The lesson in this is to develop a system that permits the transportation of selected portions of the data, leaving other information at a base camp. If the portable data is unique and valuable, it is advisable to photograph it with a fine-grained film and leave the film behind; if no mishaps take place, the film can be discarded.

Paper quality is an important consideration, as are types of writing "implements." This may seem silly, but it is embarrassing to return home with notes that are no longer legible because the paper later absorbed moisture and the ink ran. It is also frustrating to attempt to write on soggy paper with a lead pencil that tears the paper and leaves no clear image, or to reach a distant village and discover that your brand-new, 25-cent ball-point pen is dry and your paper wet.

I found that the most suitable paper is top-grade heavy bond with high rag content. Because of the very serious moisture and insect problems, I had to store my stationery reserve and my notes in cracker tins and/or plastic envelopes or bags. The tins were the most successful containers, since most of the paper-eating ants, roaches, and crickets were also plastic eaters. I kept the particularly valuable items in tins, added reheatable silica gel and occasionally sprayed a small dose of insecticide into the tin to keep the insect population down.

Soft lead pencils, either mechanical or wood, are the most foolproof writing items. They leave a dark, legible record and the writing does not run when the notes absorb moisture or fall into the river. Hard lead usually tore the humidity-softened paper. I used ball-point pens extensively and had an assortment of different colors. Color-coding enabled me to keep separate the information that several different informants gave me while checking lists of peoples' names: informant "A" was in blue ink, "B" in black, "C" in lead, and so on. In this connection, the most unsatisfactory pen was always the one with red ink. For some reason the pigment in red ink tends to run and blur, even when the paper has not been submerged in water. In the tropics, paper absorbs enough moisture to cause ink to run, even long after the notes are taken. I prefer to use the more expensive ball-point pens, such as the Parker. The refills contain much more ink, they write consistently, do not leak, and do not dry out after a few months of idleness. I normally have a quantity of cheap 25-cent ball-point pens as a reserve, but I found that they are quite unreliable: they all—irrespective of the brand—tend to leak, dry out, and last an inconsistent length of time. Fountain pens are not suitable for taking notes in the tropics.

Figure 3.2, an example of a portion of an initial genealogy on 8½-by-11 punched loose-leaf paper, shows some of the kinds of information I normally obtain. It is dated and contains the names of the three informants who provided the information. Note that I have made comments on some of the kinship relationships of people who appear in the genealogy. The comments are "negative" information in a sense; the two men "called each other brother without cause," that is, were sociologically brothers but not biologically brothers. While the informants were unable to specify the parents by name, they *did* know that the two men did not have the *same* set of parents. This tells me that when other informants claim that the two men had the same set of parents, I should suspect the information, even though the first set of informants could not provide me with the data. I do not normally collect kinship terms, which give sociological relationships, while I am collecting genealogies. I have found that informants rarely lie about kinship terminology, and therefore is is relatively easy to collect this kind of information while using a wider range of informants. Thus, I do not have to wear my best informants down by collecting information from them that could just as easily be collected from other people. In some circumstances, on the other hand, I specifically want this kind of information from my best informants for sociological reasons, but I always collect it at a different time.

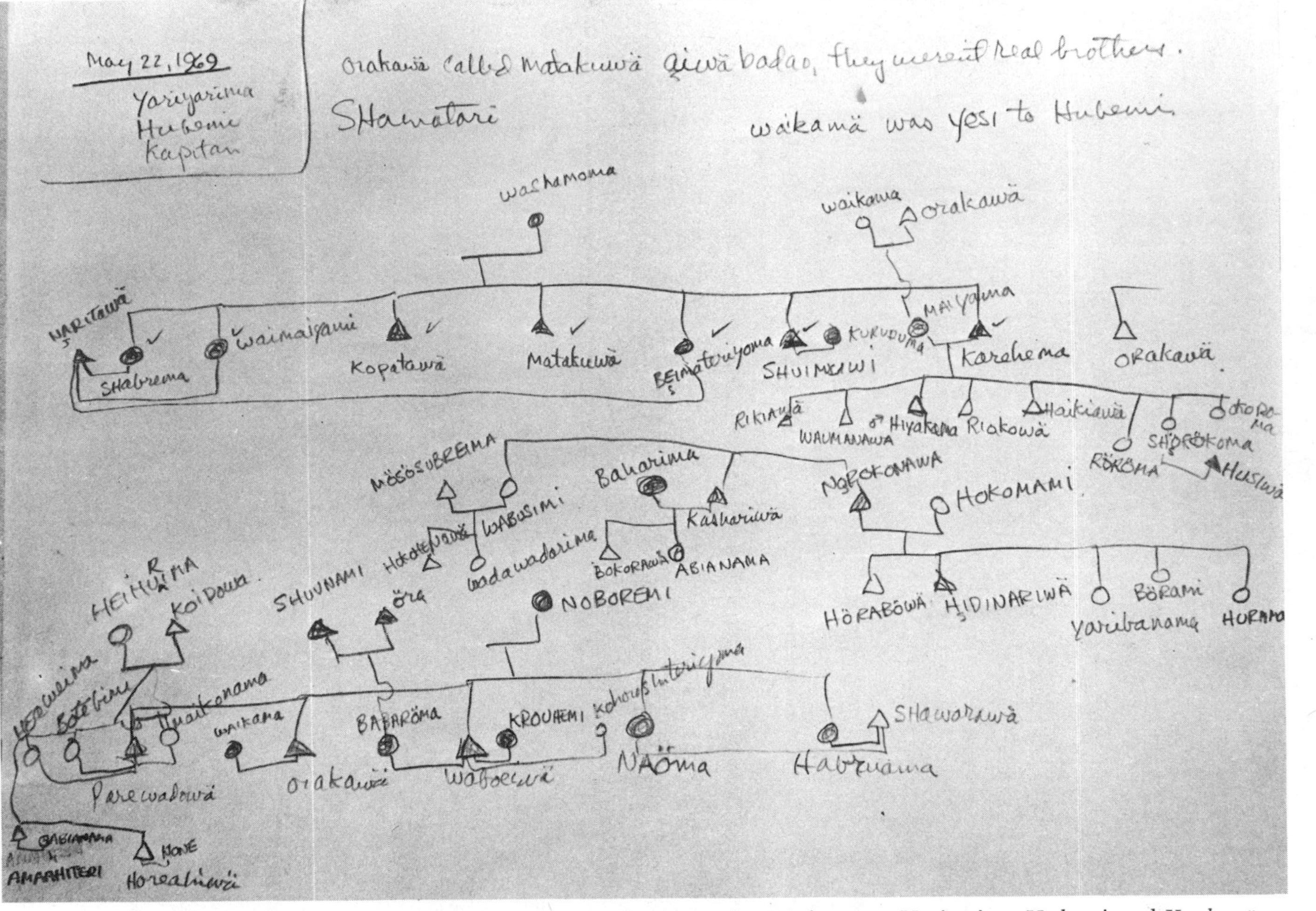

Figure 3.2—Facsimile of notes: a genealogy drawn from information from informants Yariyarima, Hubemi, and Kąobawä.

Systematizing the Data

After exhausting my informant's knowledge on an initial genealogy—which may take from one to five or more three-hour sessions, depending on the age of my informant, the extent of its knowledge, and the size of the group being investigated—I then work alone and systematize the information that occurs on the 8½-by-11 sheets. I make a 4-by-6 card of every individual whose name appears on the initial genealogy, stating his name, sex, parents, and spouses. When I have completed this, I then alphabetize all the cards and eliminate duplicate, nonconflicting information. I then check with the informant for errors, conflicts, and omissions. When the names are given to the informant in alphabetical order, he is obliged to make an independent decision on each one and state the mother, father, and spouses. I found that by doing this I always discovered a few cases where the informant initially attributed most of a man's children to one or two of his wives when in fact there were other wives not mentioned by the same informant on the initial genealogy.

Once everyone has been put on a 4-by-6 card, I then determine the village of residence, birthplace, cause of and place of death if dead, and so on. Figure 3.3 is an example of the types of information and format I kept on 4-by-6 cards. My own system is such that for demographic-genealogical data, each *portion* of the 4-by-6 card is reserved for particular kinds of information. The individual, Horeahiwä, was born at the garden called Konabuma, located on the Tohomita branch of the Shanishani River. This tells me that he was not born at the other Konabuma on the Örata River. He presently lives in the village of Yeisikorowä-teri, whose garden, Ishawari, is located on the Arimawä branch of the Mrakanahirereoba River, which flows into the Shukumöna River. I later cross-check this information in my garden files to make sure I know the locations of the gardens and rivers. Horeahiwä married Kawedema, who was his parallel cousin and therefore

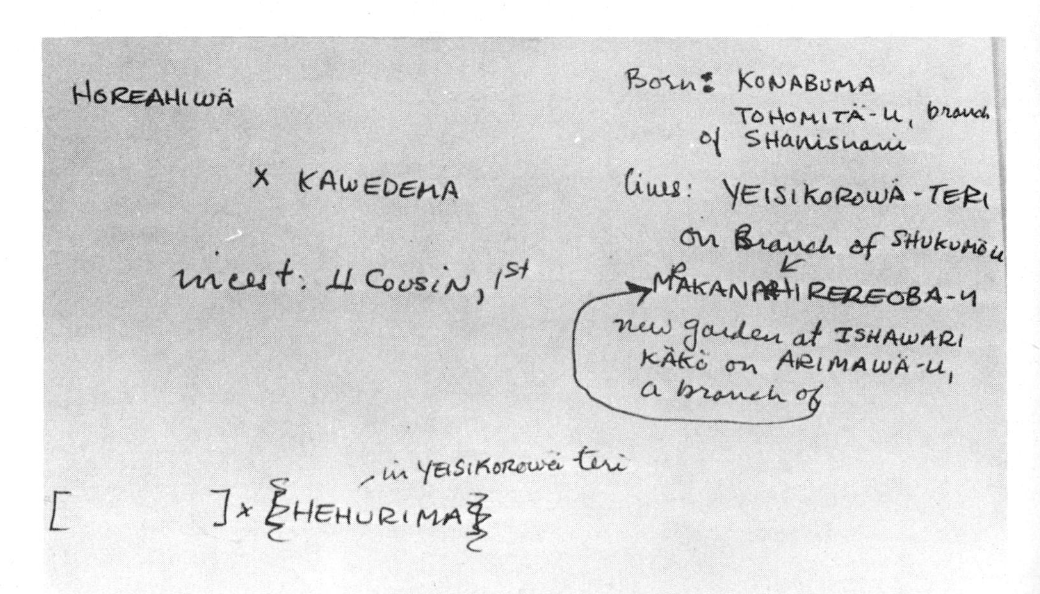

Figure 3.3—Facsimile of a 3 x 5 data card on individual named "Horeahiwä."

his classificatory sister. This was an incestuous marrige by genealogical inspection and by informant's statement. Normally it is too time-consuming and distracting to check on things like incestuous marriages while collecting the initial genealogy, but because the genealogy was given by agnatic kinship grouping, it was obvious from the initial genealogy that the marriage was incestuous.

Horeahiwä's father is dead, indicated by brackets in the lower left-hand corner of the card. My informant did not remember his name, or refused to tell me. Horeahiwä's mother is Hehurima; she also lives in Yeisikorowä-teri. My informant initially said she, too, was dead but then changed his mind. Since Yeisikorowä-teri is an uncontacted village and I have not met any of its residents, I do not know the man Horeahiwä and cannot accurately estimate his age. I normally include the sex and approximate year of birth immediately after the name, and if I have already assigned an identification number, this also follows the name. If I separate the deck into individual cards and pool it with other cards, I put the informant's name and date he gave the information somewhere on the top of the card. Otherwise, I identify the entire deck with a single card and bind it with a rubber band.

I have not gone to the expense of printing up 4-by-6 cards with the required format stated. For one thing, I rarely know how many I will need while in the field, and since I use 4-by-6 cards for other kinds of data, it is simpler to use blank cards and develop a consistent format that is memorized. For another, the format would be printed on bond paper, which is not as rugged as standard 4-by-6 cards.

I made the mistake of using several different sizes of card on different field trips. I recommend that others decide on *one* size and stick with it; 4-by-6 is very convenient, because related stationery supplies such as file boxes, indexed cards, accordion-style expanding files with alphabetical pockets, and so on, also are available.

Once the cards are filled out, all of the data transferred from the 8½-by-11 initial genealogy sheets, and the cards all alphabetized, I then make a list of all the people, leaving space between names for later additions. This requires a considerable amount of time, especially if it is all done by hand. A very useful and practical field tool is a portable typewriter, such as the compact Olympia SF DE LUXE, which I keep at my base camp. By using the typewriter, I can prepare the lists more rapidly and obtain carbon copies that can be used as the basis from which I check the first informant's statements with several other informants. I can also leave a copy of the list behind at my base camp for safe-keeping. Thus, the first list might be the information I obtained from a young informant who knew only the names accurately, but was not positive about genealogical links in the ascending generations. Figure 3.4 is an example of such a list, which shows the gaps that I later had to fill by working with other informants. I then use the list with multiple informants, as many as three or four informants on the same list or carbon copies of the list. I keep their respective additions and changes separated by using different colored ball-point pens or pencils. At this point I correct the deck of 4-by-6 cards and add new ones for those whose names did not occur in the initial genealogy. Then I separate the dead from the living and keep two lists. By this time it is necessary to go to the village and make an initial census, which uncovers new people. Then I start over with older informants

Ręirowä's group in Reyabobowei-teri: 11J0900

Census data collected in Mǫmaribowei-teri, 1969 February. This group was part of Nanokawä's at Ironasi-teri. They got angry with him and fled to Reyabobowei-teri for refuge. Lost women to protectors.

Age-Sex		Name	ID	Spouses	Father	Mother
1.	M	Aswä	11J09__		Horabowä	Habruanama
2.	M	Ąbiawä	11J09__	Didiroma	[Shihewä]	[Hayuweima]
3.	F*	Aburinama	11J09__	Roobowä		
4.	F	Amima	11J09__	Ręirowä	Wąterawä	Mabimi
5.	F	Aramatateriyoma	11J09__		Börösö-teri	Ibokoma
6.	M	Auyauwä	11J09__		Börösö-teri	Ibokoma
7.	F	Bänami (4 x 6 card)	11J09__	Katarowä	Ręirowä	Amima
8.	F	Barekimi	11J09__	Henaköshö-waniwä	[Waboiwä] demö?	[Wadubama] demö?
9.	F	Barokomi	11J09__	Ręirowä	Wąterawä	Mabimi
10.	M	Börösö-teri	11J09__	Ibokoma Obohitabrabemi	[Bisaasiwä]	[Maanama]
11.	M	Bouwä	11J09__		Ręirowä	Koneshami
12.	F	Brärämа	11J09__		Ręirowä	Barokomi
13.	M	Dąiwä	11J09__		Hemoshiwä	Wawahemi
14.	F	Didiroma	11J09__	Ąbiawä	Horabowä	Habruanama
15.	M	Dikörawä	11J09__		Ręirowä	Amima
16.	M	Ętewä	11J09__		Ręirowä	Koneshami
17.	F	Habruanama	11J09__	Horabowä	Wąterawä	Mabimi
18.	F	Haruma	11J09__	[illegible]	Horabowä	Habruanama
19.	M	Hemoshiwä	11J09__	Wawahemi	[Matakuwä]	[Taobemi]
20.	M	Henaköshöwaniwä	11J09__	Ohinarima Barekimi	[Bisaasiwä]	[Maanama]
21.	M	Horabowä	11J09__	Habruanama		
22.	M	Horedowä	11J09__	Tireiima	Ręirowä	Amima
23.	M	Iabowä	11J09__		[Shihewä]	[Hoakomi]

Figure 3.4—Facsimile of a typed list from my notes, titled "Ręirowä's group in Reyabobowei-teri: 11J0900."

and try to push the genealogical data further back. I revert to 8½-by-11 loose-leaf paper as in the case of initial genealogies, this time focusing on ancestral generations. Gradually the genealogy becomes more and more complete, and more and more complicated.

Standardized forms for the alphabetized lists of names are very convenient for additional reasons. Figure 3.5 is an example of the form I bring with me into the field. A list of 2,500 names on a form such as this is much easier to carry

Figure 3.5—Facsimile of a "before" and "after" list taken into the field for correction and updating, entitled "Shamatari that are Dead or Not in Key Villages."

SHAMATARIS THAT ARE DEAD OR NOT IN KEY VILLAGES LISTING TO CHECK CONFLICTS

DEPT ID	SERIAL	NAME	SEX	AGE	FATHER	MOTHER	SPOUSES	BIRTHPLACE	COMMENT
	4	ABIANAMA	2		1KASHARIWA	1BAHARIMA	AMAAHITERI		
	6	ABINAIEMA	2				SIBARARIWA		
	6						1RUAHIWA		
	11	1ADAHIWA	1	944	1KOHERASHIWA	1BOKEOBEMI			
	16	1AHAIMA					1KANAHITAWA		
	16	1AHAIMA					TOOMITAMA		
	22	1AHDEIWA	2		1KOHERASHIWA	1WEIONAMA	1ABURINAMA		
	22	1AHDEIWA	2		1ISAWAWA				
	22						1YOBONAMA		
	23	1AHDEWASIWA			1KOHERASHIWA	1WEIONAMA			
	24	1AHIDOMA					1RIAKOWA		
	30	1AIKAMA					1ORAWAWA		
	32	1AIYAKAREMA					1MATAKUWA		
	32						1KOPATAWA		
	35	1AIYAKORAWA	1		1MAKOWAIYOWA	1HOKABEMI	YAWADOAMA		
	40	1AIYOBOWA	1		1MAKOWAIYOWA	1HOKABEMI	1AROKONAMA		
	48	1AKAWAIYOWA	1		1MAARIMAFATHER	1MAHEKOMI	1UWAMONAMA		
	49	1AKIAMA					1ROSIWA		
	50	1AKOIWA	1		1SHIHEWA	1SHOSHOMA	1IKAIEMA		
	53	AMAAHITERI	1		1KOIDOWA	1HEIHURIMA	ABIANAMA		
	65	AMOAHIMI	2		1PAREWADOWA	1BOTEBIMI	1HIDINARIWA		
	66	1AMOKIMI					1SHIROWA		
	67	AMOMIAWA	1		WADOSHEWA	BOROWAMA	NAMOHIMI		
	68	1AMONONAMA					WIDIDIMAUWA		
	69	1AMOTAWA	1		1SHAMAWA	1MANAKASIMI			
	70	AMOTAWA	1		HAIKIAWA				
	72	1ANADOREMA	2		1KOPATAWA	1HEKURAIYOMA			
	75	1ANOTAWA	1		1SHAMAWA	1MANAKASIMI			
	80	1ARAHEWA	1		1ARAHEWAFA	1ARAHEWAMO			
	81	1ARAHEWAFA					1ARAHEWAMO		
	82	1ARAHEWAMO					1ARAHEWAFA		
	90	ARAMAWA	1		1KAREHEMA	1WAIYAMA	MAIYAHARIMA		
	94	1ARAWAIEMA	2		1KOPATAWA	1AIYAKAREMA	1TUUNAWA		
	94	1ARAWAIEMA	2		1SHAKOIWA	1MARASHAMA	1DEIDEIWA		
	94	1ARAWAIEMA	2		KASHIWA	BUHIOMI	1TUUNAWA		
	96	1ARIKEWA	1	935	1TUUNAWA	1ARAWAIEMA	HUKUMANIMA		
	96	1ARIKEWA	1	935	1DEIDEIWA				
	104	1AROKONAMA	2		ESKOIWA	HAIKIOMA	1AIYOBOWA		
	110	ARONAMA	2				1HAROAWA		
	111	AROROIMA							
	120	1ASHIDOMA	2		1IRO	1MAMASITOMA	1RIAKOWA		
	120						1RIKIAWA		
	140	1AYAKEMI			1KOPATAWA	1WAWARIMA			
	149	BABAROMA	2		NIOOKEWA	SHUHUNAMI	1WABOEIWA		
	149	BABAROMA	2		1ORA	1SHUUNAMI			
	153	1BAHANAMA	2		1SHIHEWA	MAYUEMA	1KOYEITATERI		
	153						WADOSHEWA		
	154	1BAHARIMA					1KASHARIWA		
	159	BAHORAMA	2		YAHOHOIWA	UDUANAMA			
	160	BAIKAWA	1		1NARITAWA	1SHABREIMA			

DEPT ID	SERIAL	NAME	SEX	AGE	FATHER	MOTHER	SPOUSES	BIRTHPLACE	COMMENT
Suabora	4	ABIANAMA	2		1KASHARIWA [IROKOBOTARI]	1BAHARIMA	AMAAHITERI	[illegible]	lives there ... in Mowaraoba
Yaiya	✓(6)	ABINAIEMA	2				✓SIBARARIWA		
	6						✓1RUAHIWA		
Shoriwa	11	1ADAHIWA ✓	1	944	1KOHERASHIWA	1BOKEOBEMI ?			
yaiya	16	1AHAIMA			?		1KANAHITAWA ✓	aramamisi	
	16	1AHAIMA					~~TOOMITAMA~~	Borabowei	
Shoaya	22	1AHDEIWA	2		1KOHERASHIWA ✓	1WEIONAMA ✓	1ABURINAMA ✓		
	22	1AHDEIWA	2		1ISAWAWA [illegible]				
	22						1YOBONAMA		
	23	1AHDEWASIWA			1KOHERASHIWA	1WEIONAMA ?			
	24	~~1AHIDOMA~~ False name					1RIAKOWA		
	30	1AIKAMA ?					1ORAWAWA		
	32	1AIYAKAREMA					1MATAKUWA		
	32						1KOPATAWA		
Shoriwa	35	1AIYAKORAWA	1		[MOMOWA] ~~1MAKOWAIYOWA~~	1HOKABEMI ✓ correct	YAWADOAMA ✓	Aramamisi	
Shoriama	40	1AIYOBOWA	1		~~1MAKOWAIYOWA~~ ✓	1HOKABEMI ✓	1AROKONAMA ✓	aramamisi	lives in Karawatari
Shori	48	1AKAWAIYOWA ✓	1		1MAARIMAFATHER	1MAHEKOMI	1UWAMONAMA ✓		
	49	1AKIAMA ?					1ROSIWA ?		
Nakanaya	50	1AKOIWA	1		1SHIHEWA ✓	1SHOSHOMA ✓	1IKAIEMA ✓	Borabowei	
ABAWA	53	AMAAHITERI	1		1KOIDOWA ✓	1HEIHURIMA ✓	ABIANAMA ✓ ?		lives in Horoina
YAOYA	65	AMOAHIMI	2		1PAREWADOWA ✓	1BOTEBIMI ✓ ?	1HIDINARIWA ✓	Konabuma	Horoina
Suabiye	66	1AMOKIMI					1SHIROWA ✓	[illegible]	This fellow [illegible]
Shoriwa	✓(67)	AMOMIAWA	1	940	WADOSHEWA ✓	BOROWAMA ✓ ?	NAMOHIMI ✓	Kohoroshitari	Stolen from Kohoroshitari [illegible]
abami	✓(68)	1AMONONAMA			~~[illegible]~~ ?		WIDIDIMAUWA		
	69	1AMOTAWA ?	1		1SHAMAWA	1MANAKASIMI			
Hakamaya	✓(70)	AMOTAWA ✓	1		HAIKIAWA ✓	[TOOMITAMA] ✓			in Wabonabowei
	72	1ANADOREMA ?	2		1KOPATAWA	~~1HEKURAIYOMA~~			
	75	1ANOTAWA ?	1		1SHAMAWA	1MANAKASIMI			
Haya	80	1ARAHEWA	1		1ARAHEWAFA ?	~~1ARAHEWAMO~~ ?	[MOIMOIMI]		
	81	1ARAHEWAFA					1ARAHEWAMO		
	82	1ARAHEWAMO					1ARAHEWAFA		
sabri	✓(90)	ARAMAWA	1		[BROMAWA] ~~1KAREHEMA~~	[ARAMA] ~~1WAIYAMA~~	MAIYAHARIMA ✓	aramamisi	Habonabowei
See ORAWIMA	94	~~1ARAWAIEMA~~	2		1KOPATAWA	~~1AIYAKAREMA~~	1TUUNAWA		
	94	~~1ARAWAIEMA~~ False info	2		~~1SHAKOIWA~~	1MARASHAMA	1DEIDEIWA		
	94	~~1ARAWAIEMA~~	2		KASHIWA	BUHIOMI	1TUUNAWA		
Ithiriya	✓(96)	1ARIKEWA	1	935	~~1TUUNAWA~~	~~1ARAWAIEMA~~	HUKUMANIMA ✓	MAHAMATARI	Reyaboboei
	96	1ARIKEWA	1	935	1DEIDEIWA ✓	ORAWIMA	[illegible]		in Mowaoteri
	(104)	1AROKONAMA	2		ESKOIWA	HAIKIOMA	1AIYOBOWA	Konabuma	Mowaraoba
	✓(110)	ARONAMA	2		ISHIWEIWA [DEIDEIWA]	[AREKIMI] [SHIRIBIMA]	1HAROAWA [HARIAWA] ?		
Yesiya	111	[YAROROIMA]							
Taiya	120	1ASHIDOMA ✓	2		1IRO ✓	1MAMASITOMA ✓	1RIAKOWA ✓	Aramamisi	Kr was found up [illegible]
	120						1RIKIAWA		
	140	1AYAKEMI ?			1KOPATAWA	1WAWARIMA			
	149	BABAROMA ?	2		NIOOREWA	[SHUHUNAMI]	1WABOEIWA		
	149	BABAROMA ?	2		1ORA	~~1SHUUNAMI~~		KOYEITATARI	
Yuhava	153	1BAHANAMA	2		1SHIHEWA ✓	HAYUEMA ✓	~~1KOYEITATERI~~		
	153						WADOSHEWA ✓		
	154	1BAHARIMA ?					1KASHARIWA		
owanni	✓(159)	BAHORAMA	2		YAHOHOIWA ✓	UDUANAMA ✓		[illegible]	Mowaraoba
	160	BAIKAWA	1		1NARITAWA ✓	1SHABREIMA ✓			in Karawatari

for ten hours than boxes containing 2,500 4-by-6 cards, and the lists are much more convenient to work from. Again, the Yąnomamö do not have an alphabetized cosmos, so when I check the accuracy of genealogical information from an alphabetized list, the informant must make a considered judgment at every question. I found that by working directly from initial genealogies the informants tended to give affirmative answers to almost all the questions, merely because the initial genealogies reflected native categories of kinship groupings.

In the Village

I have found from experience that it takes many times more effort to collect an accurate genealogy of a group by attempting to do it while living in the village of that group. The problems are very much more serious, lying about names and relationships is more frequent, and personal discomfort more intense. There are always a few pushy individuals who constantly demand axes, machetes, and cooking pots while I am attempting to work in the village, and when I refuse them these items, they often set about to sabotage or otherwise prevent me from working efficiently. Probably 90 percent of the residents of the village do not object to my *trying* to get this kind of information, provided that I do not flagrantly use their names aloud. But there are always a few, usually a handful of young men between eighteen and twenty-five years old, who are chagrined because I did not give them enormous quantities of trade goods on request, and who vindictively attempt to thwart my genealogy collecting attempts. It is for these reasons, among others, that I attempt to have as much of the initial work done as is possible before I visit the village.

One of my first tasks while visiting the village is to estimate the ages of everyone whose name occurs in my list. To properly identify the individuals, I whisper the name into my informant-guide's ear, who translates it to a teknonymous usage, such as "father of so-and-so," again whispering to someone else. Presently the individual is pointed out, and I note his or her age, write an identification number on the arm or chest with a felt-tipped marker, and go to the next name.

I always whisper the name to my informant; I have too often come upon names of people who were killed or died recently to be enthusiastic about using the names myself. The mere mention of such a person is enough to put the entire village in a very ugly mood. Occasionally I have no choice, and I have to read the names from the list. These situations often result when my informant, after reaching the village, refuses to help me identify the individuals as he agreed to do before we left on the trip.

In 1971 I contacted the Iwahikoroba-teri, a particularly notorious group that had repeatedly sent messages out to surrounding villages that they intended to kill me if I should ever visit them [described in Chagnon, 1971, and in Chapter 4]. None of the informants who provided me with the genealogical information was with me when I reached the village, and I had to whisper the names into the ear of one of the individuals from that group. As luck would have it, the second person I called for was the young widow of a man who had been killed by raiders just a few weeks before my visit, and when I asked, aloud, for her husband, the situation became very tense. Thus, although I had a very accurate genealogy that took me years to put together, I could not use it because of the potential hazards to my health!

The problems are dependent on the amount of contact the group has had with outsiders. In the above case, this was the first contact, and the overall situation was quite strained. In other, similar, situations, where at least some of the village residents have seen or visited foreigners, the problem is less serious. They are more likely to excuse an occasional slip-up and tolerate the mentioning of a recently deceased person.

After I have estimated the ages of everyone on the list, I photograph every individual with both a Polaroid and a standard 35mm camera. If I do not know the people well, I write identification numbers on both their arms and on the photograph. I use the 35mm camera because Polaroid photos are often very blurry in poor light conditions, sometimes to the extent of being almost useless. I made the mistake of purchasing the most inexpensive Polaroid with a fixed lens: I urge others who use the Polaroid to get a more expensive model—one with an "indoor" and "outdoor" setting on the lens. The 35mm shots, when developed and enlarged, are very easy to match up with the Polaroid pictures and these prints, usually much clearer than the Polaroid prints, can be taken to other villages on later field trips and used for identification purposes. Figure 3.6, which shows both the Polaroid and the standard 35mm photograph, shows why it is necessary under poor light conditions to take both types of pictures. The light was so poor when I took the Polaroid photograph that it was almost impossible to identify the individuals in the picture. The 35mm print, taken within seconds of the Polaroid photo, is much clearer and can be used on later field trips for identification purposes. Incidentally, I took the Polaroid print to Mishimishimaböwei-teri to see if the residents of that village could identify individuals on the Polaroid pictures. They consistently gave me specific names for the individuals, even though the print was almost obscure. On a later trip, after I had the 35mm photos developed and enlarged, I brought the clearer print to the village and obtained confirmation of the original identifications! Once the Yạnomamö learn to read photographs, they are very skillful at correctly identifying the individuals shown in them.

I did not begin using the Polaroid camera until 1969, knowing that the Yạnomamö are not fond of being photographed. I have been chased around the village on a number of occasions by irate people wielding clubs and firebrands, people who were very upset because I was attempting to photograph specific events—particularly cremations. However, their reaction to the Polaroid camera and prints was very different because the procedure was not mysterious and they could immediately see the results. They actually enjoyed seeing themselves and others in the prints. I inaugurated the technique in Mishimishimaböwei-teri, starting out very gingerly because I was not certain what the reaction might be. Rerebawä was with me at the time, and I let him take a few pictures of me for the amusement of the others. Then I took a few pictures of him for everybody to look at, deliberately including a few people in the background, arguing afterwards that they "accidentally" got themselves into the picture. When I discovered that the reaction was enthusiastic, I let one of the headmen take a few

01 SEBREDOWÃ M 50
02 " Son M 12
03 " " M 5
04 " " M 7 = OWABÖWÄ

pictures of me and of the others in his village. They enjoyed these photographs immensely, and in no time they were dragging various people out of their hammocks to have me take their photographs. At this point I enlisted several enthusiastic children to make the rounds of the village with me and point out everyone who had not had their photos taken. These children, like most Yąnomamö, had excellent memories, and my youthful assistants quickly pointed out all those who were not included in my collection of Polaroid photos, and they did so much more quickly than I could have by checking my list. They assumed the obligation of assuring that nobody escaped, which resulted in a 100 percent photographic sample of the village in a matter of hours.

I taped the ID photographs to 8½-by-11 sheets of punched loose-leaf paper, two photographs to each sheet (see Figure 3.7). I filed the sheets in a nylon post binder, numbering each photograph sequentially. After my youthful assistants assured me that I had taken everyone's photo, I systematically went through the photos with the children and had them identify the people by name, writing the name under the photograph and checking the name off my alphabetized list. I also indicated on the list the number of the photograph, which enabled me to quickly locate the person's photo. (See Appendix A; the photograph numbers are given in column 7.)

An unexpected bonus was that the Polaroid photographs provided an extremely efficient means of rapidly discovering the names of people who no longer lived in the village, and the alternative names of those who appeared in the photos. Whenever I ran into a name in my list that had no corresponding photograph number, I would simply ask the children to find the photograph for me. I would then add the new name to the identification. Figure 3.7, reproduced from my 1969 Polaroid files, shows two men. The man in photograph 44 has four names, but I knew him in my genealogies by just one or two names. In other cases, I was able to resolve once and for all cases where I was not sure if two names meant two people, or that one person had two names.

Another unexpected bonus of using the Polaroid the first time in Mishimishimaböwei-teri was the discovery of a few people who did not exist at all in my genealogies, people who had no living relatives in the village, or people who were so colorless that all of my informants had simply forgotten to mention them. In Mishimishimaböwei-teri, a group that I knew quite well before I took their photographs, it was not necessary to write down the identification numbers on the arms of the people, since I knew most of the 280-odd individuals quite well by the time I took their photographs. In other villages, where I did not know the individuals by both face and by name, I wrote the ID numbers on their arms or chests as well as on the photographs.

Among the Yąnomamö, it is desirable to take each person's photograph as a separate picture. This is not always possible, especially in the case of women and infants, who tend to be more reluctant than men to be photographed. The danger in having many people in the same photograph is that if one of the individuals

Figure 3.6—Photographs for identification: comparing polaroid to 35mm photos of an Iwahikorobateri man called Sebredowä and his sons.

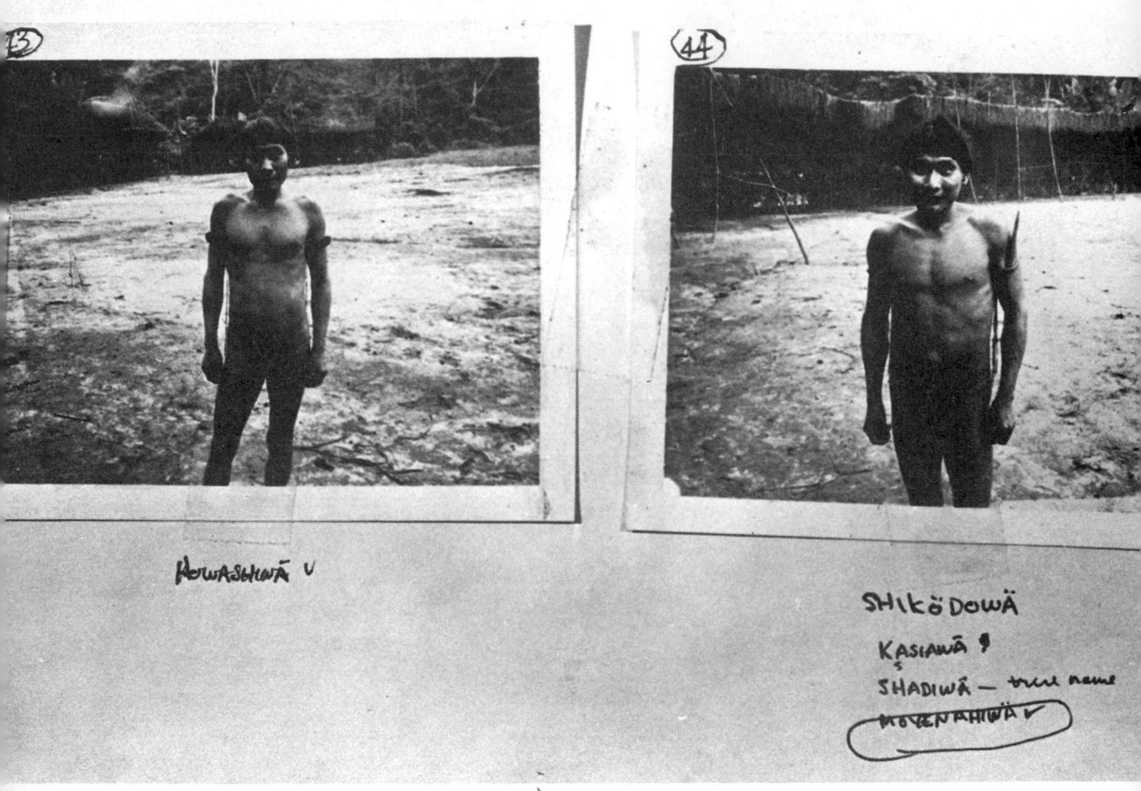

Figure 3.7—Polaroid photographs of two men, one man having four alternate names.

dies, the entire photograph is useless for identification purposes in that village; showing it to others would be worse than saying the person's name. In 1971 I photographed one of the headmen of Ironasi-teri, a splinter group of the Mishimishimaböwei-teri. He was with two of his adult sons. A few weeks later he died of a respiratory infection, and everyone in Mishimishimaböwei-teri insisted that I destroy the photograph. I anticipated their reaction beforehand and had ripped that particular photograph from my files, leaving a conspicuous gap for everyone to see. I actually hid the photograph elsewhere. Since I also took a 35mm at the same time, I can now enlarge just the faces of the two sons and make separate prints of them. I know the individuals fairly well, but will not see them for a few years. When I visit their village again, I may have forgotten their names, but I will know just where to look should it become important to document who does what in the village while I am living there, and document it without causing them embarrassment by asking for names.

Demographic Data Complementing Genealogies

With the lists checked for alternative names and the identification photographs taken, I normally complete some of the demographic and geographical inquiries next. This included collecting information on place of birth, actual number of present spouses and reasons for discarding other spouses, whether marriages were incestuous, new births, the location (garden) of puberty places for all females, and where in the village each individual lives. For the deceased, I work privately with selected informants, usually in a remote corner of the garden, and determine the place and cause of death. For this work I rely on people who have demonstrated their reliability in the past, older people who have been my informants for some considerable time. Ideally, these people come from a group in question, but not always. I occasionally have to work elsewhere with an informant from an adjacent group, one who is related to the people in question, but not too closely related.

The tape recorder is a useful tool for some of this type of informant work, especially the cassette type of recorder. If time is an important consideration, it is more efficient to tape the information than to write it down by hand. If a cassette tape is used, the information can be located very quickly and later transcribed to written form. Also, similar kinds of information—birthplaces, for example—can be kept on the same cassette. The tape cassette reserved for birthplaces can be identified as such, and removed or inserted into the recorder when needed, without rewinding the tape. For example, it is possible to tape record birthplaces of the residents of Mishimishimaböwei-teri for 20 minutes and remove the cassette, replacing it with another that deals with the location of gardens. A few days later I might be working with the birthplaces of the Ironasi-teri, and I simply put the first cassette back into the recorder and begin taping that information. With 5-inch reels of ¼-inch tape, this is not possible without creating insurmountable storage problems, and wasting enormous amounts of time (and quantities of heavy batteries) rewinding the tapes to their appropriate positions.

The type of information I often record on tape is data that I collect about each individual, usually when I have long, prepared lists (computer printouts) of individuals. By working with lists and with cassette tapes, it is possible to quickly collect enormous amounts of information on things like birthplaces, place of puberty, place and cause of death, and so forth. Some of this work can be done in public, as when I use numbered identification photographs; I merely record the photograph number and the place of birth of the individual shown in the photograph, and do not have to say the names of people aloud. Other kinds of information require that I use real names, and I must work privately. I always carry an inexpensive earphone attachment with me so that I can transcribe portions of this information while I am in the village; the insertion of the earphone plug automatically turns off the speaker of the recorder, and I can transcribe very juicy and very secret information while sitting in the middle of a crowd of people—provided that the earphone jack does not accidentally come out! It is embarrassing to have the recorder suddenly blare out the name of some deceased ancestor of half of the village, and I look like a fool striking my defenseless tape recorder, enjoining it to be more polite and considerate of people's feelings.

Some tape recorders do not begin recording until the tape has begun to advance, which takes a few miliseconds after the "on" switch is activated. In working from prepared lists, I did a great deal of stop–go recording, and until I learned to pause a moment before speaking, I inadvertently lopped off parts of names or numbers, creating additional, but minor, identification problems.

Another category of information that I collect very rapidly and efficiently by using the tape recorder in conjunction with Polaroid photographs is kinship terminology. I decide beforehand, from genealogical inspection, which individuals I want to use as "ego" in the paradigms. I select informants of both sexes and from the major kinship groups represented in the village, and obtain from them the specific kinship term they use for every other individual in the group. (The kinship usage of six individuals in Mishimishimaböwei-teri is given in the last six columns of Appendix A.) The selected informant looks at the photograph and "tells the microphone" what kinship term he uses. This data is useful, among other things, for detecting incestuous marriages.[4] I also attempt to get individuals from a wide range of ages for this type of work; I use very young informants for getting the maximum information about kinship terminology for ascending generations, and very old informants for maximum information about junior generations. In some instances I have even used toddlers as "informants" by asking one of their parents what he or she would call such a person. Finally, and in private, I collect kin terms used for long-since-dead ancestors.

I have given the "ideal" sequence I usually try to follow when I collect genealogical information. Frequently the field situation is such that I actually finish some portions of the "ideal" sequence before I even begin earlier portions. Again, recent changes in my field techniques have caused me to alter some of the stages in collecting genealogical information. The Polaroid camera, for example, has been something of a revolution in my field techniques, and I am still exploring the potentials of this tool. With the Polaroid, it is possible for me to visit a group that I know only poorly, take their photographs and then go to a distant village where I can obtain reliable identifications of the people in the photographs. On the basis of one visit to the group I could, with the right informants from neighboring groups, make a very thorough and accurate census and genealogical study of that group in a very short time. It is unlikely, however, that I will use this technique to any great extent in my projected work, since I plan to confine it to the Shamatari population where I already have a large amount of data that were obtained over many years by cruder, more time-consuming methods. Here, the Polaroid will be useful mainly as a means of accurately identifying individuals whose correct names and genealogies I already know.

One additional use of the identification photographs, whether Polaroid or standard 35mm prints, has to do with ethnographic film. In 1971 I invited my filming colleague, Timothy Asch, to join me with a sound man—Craig Johnson —in the field. I took them to Mishimishimaböwei-teri where we shot approximately 80,000 feet of 16mm color, synchronous sound film, focusing largely on the

[4] Note in particular in Appendix A the variations in usage for the two brothers, individuals 0178 and 2194. Theoretically they should have identical usage for all individuals in the village, but incestuous marriages have led to the observed variation. I am exploring this further elsewhere (Chagnon and Levin, ms.).

families of the two most prominent men of the village. There will be individuals in this footage whose names I will no doubt forget over the years that we plan to work on the film and edit it into teaching resources. With the identification photographs I can match faces in the film to names, and therefore to genealogical relationships, and be able to specify very accurately the kinship relationships of everyone who appears in every sequence that was shot in that village. (The identification photographs are given in Appendix E, so that this book can be used as a supplement to the films I intend to produce with Asch over the next several years. The photographs are the key for entering the genealogical lists of Appendix A.)

THE COMPUTER

I urge all budding fieldworkers to take a course in basic computer applications and collect and record their data with the intention of later punching it on IBM cards and handling it by computer means. I was well advanced in my fieldwork before I learned to appreciate the potentials of the computer, and how it could be used to aid me in the field.

I have made many return field trips to the Yąnomamö: I have returned every year since I began my work in 1964. This has allowed me to go over old data and find the conflicts and gaps. After several field trips, however, the quantity of accumulating data became so great that it was no longer possible to clean it up between field trips. In 1968 I began punching some of my data, particularly genealogical data, on IBM cards and manipulating it with the computer. Normally the computer is used *after* the data have all been collected, and its use is largely for analytical purposes. In my own situation, I was able to use the computer for cleaning up data between field trips and, therefore, as an aid to efficient collection of data. To this point, I have largely confined my use of the computer to data organization and systematization and am only now making a large investment in computer analysis. (See MacCluer, Neel, and Chagnon, 1971, and Chapter 4.) For example, the tedium of converting rough, initial genealogy notes into lists by making handwritten cards is largely a thing of the past. I know who the good informants are and do not have to constantly check them in the field. Now I punch the data directly onto the IBM cards when I return from each field trip and sort the cards by machine. It is possible to obtain printouts of this material in a very short time—minutes—and to quickly identify conflicts, gaps, and inconsistencies. The time I would have spent in the field doing this by hand can be spent collecting additional data. On the next field trip I correct errors, gaps, and conflicts with the same informants.

The printouts also reduce the risk that I will spend valuable time in the field collecting information that I have already gathered. As I collect initial genealogies I can quickly check the printouts to see if the people mentioned in the genealogy already exist in my printouts. Until I began using computer printouts, I did waste a considerable amount of time going over ground that I had already covered thoroughly. When the population of names approaches 4,000 entries, it is not an easy matter to recall whether or not you have collected specific genealogical information on particular individuals.

Once I recognized the utility of the computer and the speed and accuracy of data retrieval, I converted much of my previous genealogical data to IBM cards. The format I used for obtaining printouts for my field ledgers is as follows:

Columns 1-7	Identification number used by my medical colleagues to label their specimens and findings. I normally include this in my field ledger in the event they get word to me that they need a repeat blood specimen from individual "03A0054." For my own purpose, I use a shorter, more efficient number that does not include a letter. Four digits are sufficient to enable me to include 9,999 individuals in my data. The seven-digit number that refers, for example, to Möawä is 11H0734. The first two digits tell my colleagues that it is a Yąnomamö as opposed to a Shavante, for example, and the sample was taken in 1969. The letter tells them the village of Yąnomamö where the individual sample was taken. The last four digits refer to the individual, but only three digits are necessary: no village exceeds 999 people. However, my medical colleagues do collect biological data in other populations in which the local groups do exceed 999 people, and they must keep their files consistent.
Columns 8-12	Identification number that I assign for computer manipulation. Möawä's number is 1240.
Columns 13-27	Ego's name: Möawä. Since he is alive, his name begins in column 14. Were he dead, I would precede his name with the digit "1" to indicate that fact.
Column 28	Sex: Möawä is a male, so I punch the digit "1" in this column. Females are indicated by the digit "2."
Columns 29-31	Age: I use year of birth; Möawä was born in approximately 1936, so I punch the three digits "936" in these columns. Putting the complete year of birth uses one additional space wastefully.
Columns 32-45	Father's name: Möawä's father was Ruwahiwä, but he was killed by the Bisaasi-teri many years ago. To indicate the fact that he is dead, his name begins in column 32 with the digit "1."
Columns 46-60	Mother's name: Möawä's mother is not dead, so she occurs, beginning in column 47, "Abinaiema." For her, column 46 is blank—until she dies.
Columns 61-74	Spouse's name: Möawä has several spouses, but only one of them can occur on a card. His oldest living spouse is normally included on the original card; in this case, it would be "Daeyama." Möawä has had six different spouses, so five additional cards will follow the original entry, each with his identification number (4 digits) and the name of the spouse. This information, of

course, will be in the same columns as the original card information for the same categories.

Columns 75-77 Birthplace: Only three spaces are allotted to this parameter. I have assigned a three-digit number to all known Yạnomamö gardens, and as I discover new gardens I continue assigning three-digit numbers to them. On Möawä's card, these columns would contain the number 124, which corresponds to the garden called "Konabuma-Örata"—to distinguish it from the garden by the same name, Konabuma, located on the river Shanishani. The second garden, "Konabuma-Shanishani" is numbered 199. At the present, I have over 300 identifiable gardens that relate to the Namowei-teri and Shamatari populations.

Columns 78-79 Place of residence: For Möawä, it is Mishimishimaböwei-teri, a village to which I have assigned the number "16." Thus, these columns would contain just the two-digit identification.

Column 80 Population of origin: Möawä is a Shamatari, so I punch "1" in this column. If he were a Namowei-teri, I would punch a "2" here, as I did, for example, for Kạobawä. At the present, I am concerned mainly with the two populations "Shamatari" and "Namowei-teri" and use only two digits. The Shamatari are those people born at any garden founded by someone who is, by genealogical identification, a Shamatari, and whose parents are genealogically Shamatari as well. Thus, when Möawä visits Bisaasi-teri with his family, and his wife has a baby while on that visit, I would punch a "1" in the column for the baby's identification card and assign the number "16" as place of birth—Mishimishimaböwei-teri. On a biographical card, handwritten, I would note that the child was *actually* born while his mother was visiting Bisaasi-teri. Serious errors and misrepresentations would occur if the baby were entered in my records as having been born in Bisaasi-teri and comes from the Namowei-teri population. Thus, birthplace in my data technically means the village of residence of the parents when the child was born.

This format, I re-emphasize, is used only to obtain printouts that I take into the field: it contains names and, therefore, wastes a good deal of space as a format for analysis. For analysis, only numbers are required for ego, parents, and spouses.

One of the first steps at systematization I made was to determine if everyone in the population of names was listed as "ego" in columns 13 through 27. This told me whether I had genealogies on everyone, and quickly told me where the gaps and conflicts were. One of my colleagues, Dr. Jean MacCluer, wrote a program for me that took each card and systematically rearranged the information as follows: wherever an individual had a spouse, a new card was printed with the spouse in the ego column and the original ego in the spouse column. Wherever an individual had parents, the father was printed in the ego column and the mother in the spouse column and vice versa. Thus, three new cards were generated from a single card. The resulting printout was an exhaustive list of every person who ever occurred in any genealogy. It led to the discovery of marriages that had previously escaped my attention, usually by listing a set of parents also as spouses to each other. It also clearly showed where I had to concentrate my efforts in future field trips: many people had no parents listed.

There were a number of pitfalls and problems. IBM cards have 80 spaces, so all information must be contained in a short space. Yąnomamö names, which must be used in the field, are variable in length. It was not possible to use the card efficienctly wherever names were required. For data analysis purposes, I convert every person to a four-digit number, which allows me room to include 9,999 people in my analysis. Thus far I have kept comfortably below five digits since I am presently working with only a fraction of my total data and a fraction of the Yąnomamö population. It is possible that projected fieldwork by myself and my students will ultimately yield numbers of egos in the vicinity of 10,000, at which point I must change my identification system.

For checking the accuracy of genealogical information with Yąnomamö informants, I must continue to deal with names rather than numbers. Each year I bring updated, bound printouts to the field in large ledger books, printouts of village composition, and printouts of pooled villages. Much of the space in the columns is devoted to names—ego, father, mother, and spouses. It would be desirable to also include information such as birthplace, village of residence, and population of origin as *names* in each individual's entry, but there is not sufficient space to write these out. Thus, I must use numbers that are equivalent to specific gardens, villages, and populations. Figure 3.8 is an example of one page of this kind of printout.

There is no efficient way to alphabetize data of this kind because the card-sort machines all take a great deal of time. While the computer can do it much faster, it is very expensive and a very inefficient use of the computer that I used from 1968 to 1972. Accordingly, I alphabetized all of the cards on a card-sort machine and had the computer assign numbers in sequence to each card, giving a numerical sequence that paralled the alphabetical sequence. With this done, I could rapidly put the cards into alphabetical order by sorting them by number. This greatly facilitated the manipulation of the accumulated data, but once new data were added, the system no longer worked: new people came after the original alphabetized list, so their names and new ID numbers did not permit alphabetizing by sorting according to ID number. I will change identification numbers after I stop collecting data so that the alphabetical sequence and the numerical sequence will again be parallel.

Another initial problem had to do with the unavoidable pooling of good and bad data. It was not desirable or possible to keep the bad data from getting onto printouts and causing additional work. When I converted all of my early genealogical data to IBM cards I punched *every bit of information* I had, including the material I knew to be suspect, because I wanted to make sure I had an exhaustive list of everyone in the populations I was studying. The expected result eventually caused an additional amount of field time spent rechecking information that I had previously checked and corrected. At this point I know my informants so well that I rarely bring home and punch up genealogical data that is bad. I can usually determine in the field whether or not I am getting meaningful, accurate data, and unless it is good, I simply do not punch it up.

DEPT ID	SERIAL	NAME	SEX	AGE	FATHER	MOTHER	SPOUSES	BIRTHPLACE		COMMENT
11I0859	949	KODEAMITERI	1	947	1TUUNAWA	1TIHUAWEIMA	OWAMONAMA	124	1	
11H0776	950	KODEDEARI	1	940	ISHIWEIWA	1BARORAMA	UDUWANAMA	118		
11I0862	958	KOHARAROMA	2	949	1WAYUHEMA	1KOHAMA	BUNIMANAWA	128	1	
11H0767	836	KOHARAWA	1	919	1WABAIYOWA	1WORAEIMA	SHAROSIMI	108	1	
11H0767	959	KOHARAWA	1	919	1WABAIYOWA	1WORAEIMA	SHAROSIMI	108	1	
	959						DORORAMA			
03H0749	963	KOHERENAMA	2	954	NOSHIOMAAWA	WISHARIOMA	WAROWA	139	211	REAL NAME = KORISHIWA
		KOHERENAMA	2		NOSHIUMAAWA	WISHARIOMA			1	
11H0707	2289	KOREBOWA	1	966	YAKAHAIWA	SHEKERAMA		165	1	= BUKUMANIWA
		KORÖSÖNAWA	1	970	KODEDEARI	UDUWANAWA			1	
11H0717	1021	KOSHIROMA	2	944	1KAROWA	BARAMI	HOWSHIWA	111	1	
11H0749	1025	KOSHIWA	1	949	ISHIWEIWA	1BARORAMA	ROAHIMI	118	1	
	1026	KOYAKOBOWA	1		YAKAHAIWA	WAHAKAIMA			1	
	1936	KOYAKOBOWA	1		YAKAHAIWA	WAHAKAIMA			1	
11H0703	1028	KOYOKAROWA	1	964	YAKAHAIWA	WAHAKAIMA		128	1	
11H0703	1936	KOYOKAROWA	1	987	YAKAHAIWA	WAHAKAIMA		128	1	
		1KREIINAWA	1		BARAWAWA	MABEMI			1	
11H0754	1046	KUAIEWA	1	936	1KOKOBIRAWA	1YEIIMANAMA	NAKAHEDAMI	108	1	
11H0777	1062	KUMISHIWA	1	939	1RUWAHIWA	1HIYUMA	ROENAMA	116	1	
		KUNIAMA	2	958					1	
11I0877	1063	KURADOMA	2	950	SIBARARIWA	1WAREHIMA	RAMOBOWA	127	1	
		KURATOMADA	2	969	RÀMOBOWA	KURATOMA			1	
11H0722	1065	KURIANAMA	2	958	YOINAKUWA	SINABIMI		141	1	
11J0928	1081	MABEMI	2	910	1MATAKUWA	1MAMOKAHIAHAMI	DEDEHEIWA	108	1	= MABIMI
	1081	MABEMI	2	910	1MATAKUWA	1MAMOKAHIAHAMI	WATERAWA	108	1	= WEIONAMA

Figure 3.8—Facsimile of a computer printout from a field ledger, showing kinds of information checked on return trips.

I now have graduate assistants punch much of the data.[5] Since my handwriting is not always legible and they are unfamiliar with Yąnomamö names, new people are "created" and old ones transformed in the data punching. Since I am not intimately familiar with all Yąnomamö by name, I end up with a few individuals that are not recognized by the Yąnomamö when I mention their computer printout names. Also, the computer does not print out diacritical marks, and I cannot always tell from a printout how the word should be pronounced. On one occasion I was working with a very reliable informant using an IBM printout that listed everyone in the village by name. When I came to the individual "Häämä" I pronounced it "Haama." My informant didn't recognize it at first but when I gave the person's parents, he laughed at my pronunciation and said: "You mean Häämä!" Then he asked me who gave me that name, and I had to try to explain how the *makina* (computer) did not write "straight." Has comment on that was something to the effect that "the computer is just like Yąnomamö—it lies."

The net result of the inclusion of a misspelled name in the printouts is that the name proliferates and is included in many different printouts, ego in some, father in others, child in others, and so on. Accordingly, it must be retained for the moment as an "alternate" name for someone, even though it is known to be a typographical error.

Now that much of my genealogical and demographic data is on IBM cards, it is possible to obtain rapid, accurate summaries of large bodies of data, summaries that say a great deal about Yąnomamö social organization and settlement pattern dynamics. For example, by sorting on the column that gives place of birth, it is possible to obtain quickly a list of all individuals in Mishimishimaböwei-teri who were born at each garden. Figure 3.9 was drawn from such a list, modified by grouping the gardens into regions. Pooling all Shamatari from all villages and sorting on birthplace is also another way to check on the fissioning of villages as described by informants in interviews: individuals who live in presently distinct villages were born at the ancestral locations before fission separated them.

Dozens of applications are possible once the data are cleaned up and corrected. To mention just a few, it will be possible to make statements about cause of death by lineage identity, cause of death by geographical region, comparisons of mortality between villages or lineages among the Shamatari, comparisons of mortality between the Shamatari and the Namowei-teri, biological relationships of all people in the village to all others, comparisons of the kinship categories with biological relationships, types of marriages by both biological identification of spouses and lineage identification, geographical distance in kilometers between places of birth of all married people, distances in meters within the village of all people related in specific ways—and a host of other intriguing analyses. Chapter 4 lists additional applications in the area of data analysis, and also explores some of the above-mentioned correlations. (See also Chagnon and Levin, ms.) The use

[5] Since 1970 I have been fortunate to have the skillful and enthusiastic assistance of Michael J. Levin in this aspect of the work. Many of the printouts and data summaries in this book were prepared by Levin with the many useful computer programs he developed while he was associated with my project at the University of Michigan. He will describe his several programs elsewhere.

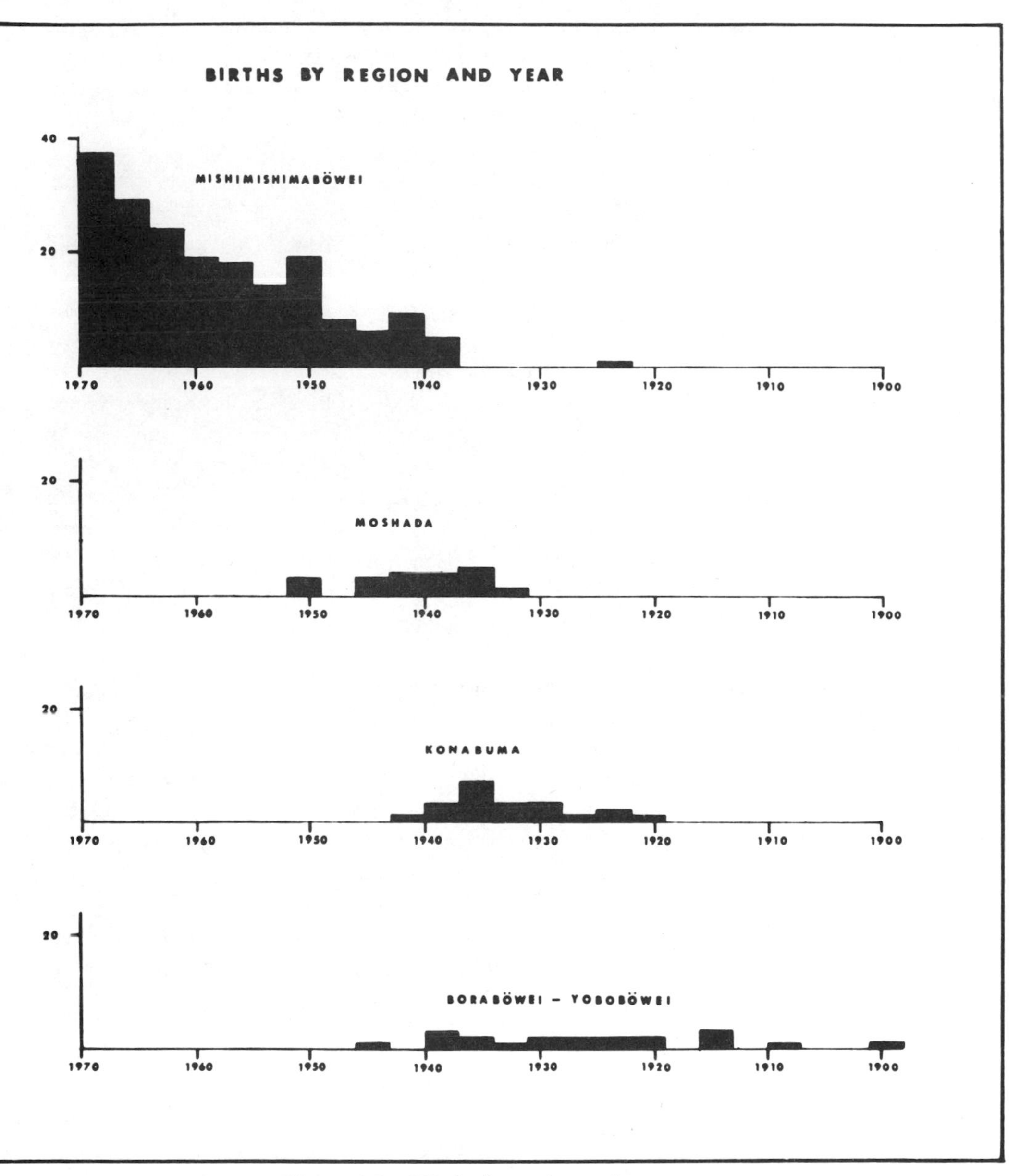

Figure 3.9—Births by region and year.

of simulation programs will also lead to new insights into the social system. For example, it is possible to define the parameters that determine marriage, using estimates based on actual Yąnomamö behavior. (See MacCluer, Neel and Chagnon 1970, for an example of this kind of computer analysis.) What impact particular parameters have on the marriage behavior can be assessed by varying the values of the parameters and altering the restrictions. It is possible, for example, to explore what would happen if male egos were allowed to mate at random with any female not in their lineages and compare the result with the actual marriage behavior found in the same population (see Chapter 4). In this way a good estimate of the demographic basis for marriage patterns can be made and an important insight into the "effect" of the jural marriage rules can be gained.

I conclude this chapter by giving examples of data that were treated with computer techniques to show some of the practical uses to which such techniques might be put in handling genealogical and demographic data.

The previous chapter discussed the history of Mishimishimaböwei-teri and documented earlier fissions and the process of population dispersal. The genealogical data discussed in this chapter can be used to verify and explore the sociobiological dimensions of this process. Figure 4.4, p. 153, illustrates how the process of fissioning has affected the distribution of particular segments of the lineage. It contains information showing exactly how the fissioning affected this particular lineage: beneath each individual is his identification number and the number of his current village of residence. All those with the number "16" live, for example, in Mishimishimaböwei-teri, and they can be found in Appendix A by means of identification numbers.[6] Thus, the genealogical data, which can be quantified (Chapter 4), confirm the historical and settlement pattern data and, by using computer techniques, they can be rapidly and efficiently converted to graphic diagrams to illustrate population processes and their genealogical consequences.

Examining the birthplaces of the Mishimishimaböwei-teri and clustering the individual gardens into regions, a similar verfication of the historical data emerges. Figure 3.9 shows the distribution of the number of individuals born in particular regions by age. As is clear, the birthplace and year-of-birth data confirm the settlement pattern discussed in the previous chapter, subject, of course, to the kind of "fog" in the system described therein. In general, the oldest people were born at the gardens occupied further back in time, and younger people were born at gardens more recently cleared and abandoned.[7] The "youthfulness" of the population is clear in Figure 3.9: most of the Mishimishimaböwei-teri were born at the most recently occupied gardens. This is explored in more detail in the next chapter.

[6] Figure 4.4 was drawn before I conducted my 1972 field research. I discovered a number of genealogical links in 1972 that will ultimately expand the lineage as drawn in Figure 4.4. See Chapter 4 for a discussion of these new data.

[7] Compare Figure 4.4 to Figure 2.8, p. 84.

4/Analytical objectives and field data

I have described in considerable detail "*how*" I collected and organized large quantities of genealogical, demographic, and settlement pattern data. I have not discussed "why" I did it. Lest it appear that anthropologists spend their time in out-of-the-way places of the world meticulously accumulating esoteric information merely for the sake of recondite debates at annual conventions, I will put forth in this chapter a number of analytical examples based on a provisional examination of some of the data discussed in the previous two chapters. This will show how apparently unrelated data fit into a broader picture and how, in particular, detailed genealogical information constitutes the fundamental basis from which a host of important theoretical issues can be discussed.

The issue that intrigued me most of all has to do with the relationships between village fissioning, social organization, and demography. The Yąnomamö represent one of the last opportunities to explore the process of tribalization and document its salient characteristics. I refer to that period in time when human populations made a transition from hunting and gathering economy to agriculture, and how the stability and productivity of the new economic order gave rise to a sharp increase in the rate of population growth and, as a consequence, expansion of groups into regions previously unexploited by agricultural techniques. This is not to say that the Yąnomamö have recently made such a transition. Rather, I draw attention to the general characteristics of Yąnomamö economy and social organization and suggest that a thorough study and analysis of population growth and village fissioning as they take place in this tribe can shed light on similar processes elsewhere in both time and space.

That the Yąnomamö represent one of our last, fleeting opportunities to carefully document the interrelationships between demography, social organization, and aboriginal population dispersal has also had an effect on my field work. I spent a great deal of time collecting the data hoping to obtain enough to address problems that lend themselves to statistical analysis. The Yąnomamö, like all tribesmen, are doomed, and soon they will be swept aside and decimated by introduced diseases as Western civilization penetrates deeper and deeper into the remaining corners of the world where it has not extended itself. This has already begun in portions of the Yąnomamö area: since 1964, when I began my fieldwork, the regions where this type of demographic research can be done have been drastically reduced. There are blocs left where this is still possible. By 1975 most of these will have disappeared. The culture will remain intact for some years to come, but fundamental changes will have taken place in demographic characteristics because of the introduction of diseases (see Neel et al., 1970), the increasing influence of missionaries and government agencies, the increased mobility brought about by introduced canoes and motors, the disappearance of alliance systems based on exchanges of native goods and women, loss of political sovereignty and a host of other factors. In brief, it is still possible to collect data that can illuminate more general problems. In a few years it will not be.

VILLAGE FISSIONING AND POPULATION GROWTH AMONG THE YẠNOMAMÖ

Given the size of the body of data I collected and the complex nature of interaction betwen the variables, it is almost impossible to explore the relationships between demographic phenomena and village fissioning unless computer methods are used. One method I intend to employ will be to arrange villages in increasing order of size and look for patterns in demographic characteristics, marriage, lineage composition, and other social features. Robert Carneiro (ms.), also keenly interested in the process of village fissioning, suggests that the frequencies of villages of various sizes imply something fundamental about the fissioning process and the growth pattern that leads to the kind of distribution observed. He is currently pursuing this along mathematical lines and is exploring the possible use of computer methods to study the problem from that perspective. My own emphasis will be on more specific organizational patterns found in one tribe. The histories of the villages and populations that I discussed in Chapter 2, coupled with the known composition and genealogical links discussed in Chapter 3, can be used to reconstruct villages before and after fissions. While ignoring births and deaths, a rough idea of prefission composition can be obtained when two recently fissioned villages are pooled together. Up to a certain point, even births and deaths can be controlled for the purpose of the analysis. In addition, I have documented cases of village fissioning as they happened during my fieldwork, and I know the composition of the village before the fission occurred. The procedure will be to first identify the demographic and social parameters that influence either the probability or outcome of fissions, estimate their values, and then turn to computer techniques to simulate the population over long periods of time, starting with known characteristics of a real Yạnomamö population and eventually letting the computer "replace" it with an artificial population. If, after several hundred simulated years and several hundred simulations the artificial population still has characteristics similar to those found in the real population, then I am on the right track. If not, back to the drawing board—or the field.

This chapter deals with my current attempt to cope with these methodological problems, drawing on the rough data at a time when I know that it will require, perhaps, a year or more to identify and rectify all of the errors and inconsistencies in the data. Therefore, the discussion will often lead to questions that are as yet unanswered or might never be answerable with this body of data. The point, however, is not to answer specific questions, but rather, to demonstrate how an anthropologist goes about the business of testing theory through the analysis of his data. This can be done very effectively by discussing work that is "in progress" rather than highly polished, finished products whose neatness and symmetry are often misleading and do not often disclose the nature of the analytical paths that were followed to reach the final conclusions. Finally, I intend this demonstration to show how closely related the fieldwork methods are to analytical procedures and the theoretical objectives.

THE EXPANSION OF THE SHAMATARI AND NAMOWEI-TERI

Geographical Considerations

Among the Yąnomamö, the process of population growth and its consequence, village fissioning, has two major and readily documented aspects. One is an increase in the number of people and villages, and the other an increase in the amount of area over which this population is distributed, given that population density remains constant. Let us consider the geographical aspects here.

One obvious difference between the Namowei-teri and the Shamatari is that the geographical area containing the Shamatari villages is much larger. Figure 4.1 shows the difference. The area is drawn around the most peripheral villages in their approximate 1972 locations, and measured by polar planimeter. The histories of past village movements (obtained from informants) goes back approximately 100 years for each population. Both populations began as single villages in the same general region, indicated by a star on Figure 4.1. Today, the Shamatari villages are found scattered over a much larger area—larger by a factor of 6. Calculating the "population density" for the two populations, there are 0.42 people per square mile in the Shamatari region and over twice as many (0.90) in the Namowei-teri region. Enormous tracts of land, most of it cultivable and abounding with game, is found between villages in both regions. Whatever else might be cited as a "cause" of warfare between the villages, *competition for resources is not a very convincing one.* The generally intensive warfare patterns found in aboriginal tropical forest cultures do not correlate well with resource shortages or competition for land or hunting areas (see also Carneiro, 1961): the Yąnomamö are *not* aberrant insofar as warfare intensity and abundance of resources are concerned.[1]

Another measure of the dispersion of Shamatari villages is the distance between them. It is probably misleading to use 1972 as a date for comparing intervillage distances, for three of the Namowei-teri villages were within sight of each other at that time. If we use 1968 as the date, the comparison would include the now defunct village of Monou-teri: its members fissioned and all rejoined the two Bisaasi-teri villages that year. Again, the members of one of the Shamatari villages

[1] See Vayda, 1961, for a criticism of various South Americanists—Murphy and Steward —who posited other "causes" for intensive warfare in this ethnographic province. While this is not the place to labor the issues, I wish to point out that Murphy and Steward are keenly aware of ecological interrelationships and were not overly impressed with ecological causes for the warfare patterns in the tropical forest cultures.

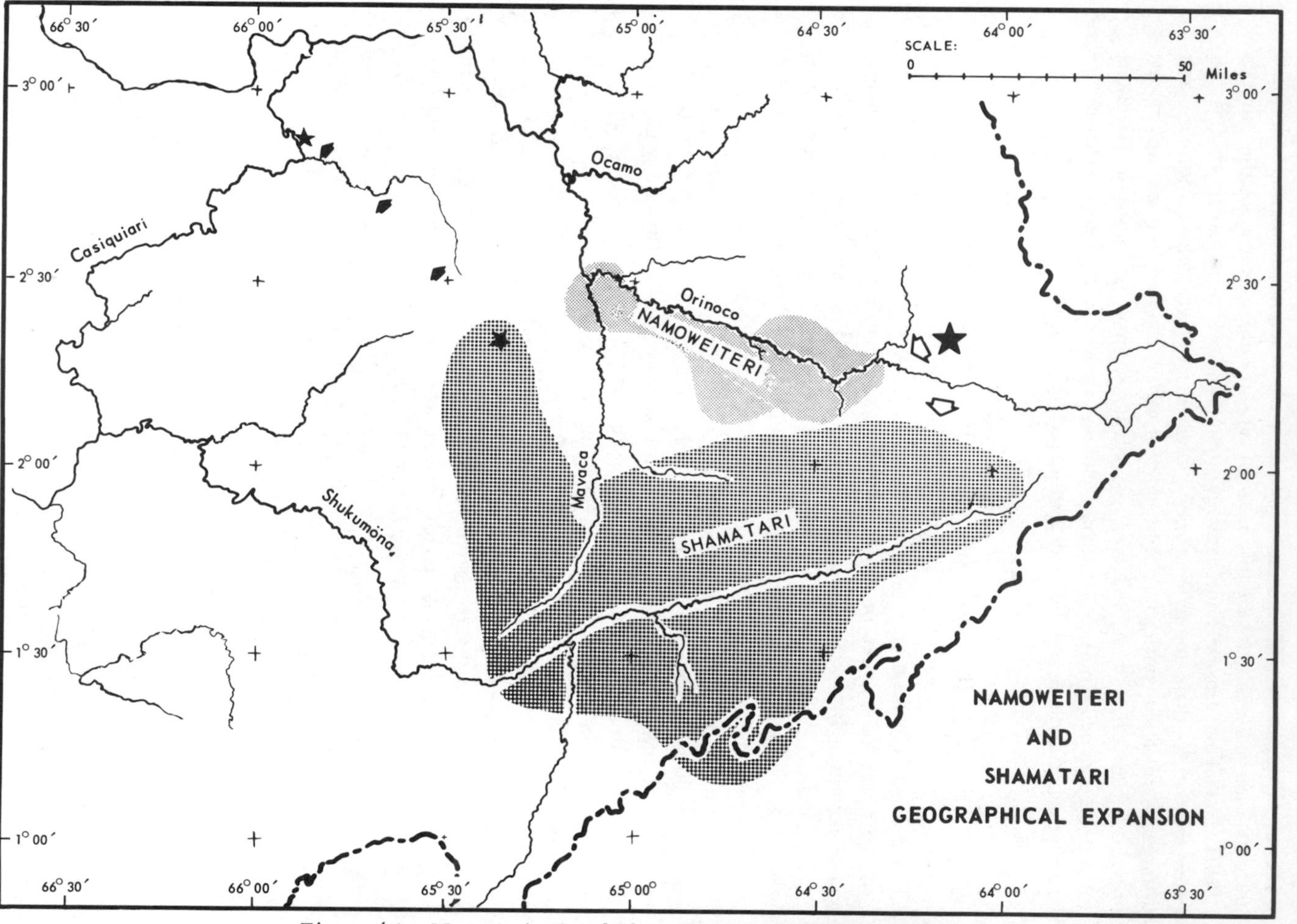

Figure 4.1—Namoweiteri and Shamatari geographical expansion.

—Mǫmariböwei-teri—migrated in 1972 an enormous distance away from their previous location to escape what they felt were mounting war threats from the Bisaasi-teri and the Reyaboböwei-teri. Using 1968 as the date for comparison, the (approximate) average distance between Namowei-teri villages was 30 miles compared to 50 miles for Shamatari villages. We are here dealing with large differences, and it is clear that Shamatari villages are much further apart than are Namowei-teri villages. A consideration of the mortality in warfare suggests that the intensity of warfare characterizing each area might be the major factor accounting for this difference. Warfare intensity, estimated from mortality figures, is higher among the Shamatari. This leads to a conclusion that will, no doubt, perplex some of my colleagues: the Shamatari have more warfare and a *lower* population density than the Namowei-teri—and their villages are more widely scattered. The relationship between warfare intensity and population density is not a simple one in these populations. In fact, without the historical accounts given to me by the informants the warfare would make very little sense at all.

Demographic Considerations

There are some important demographic differences between the Namowei-teri and the Shamatari. One question that comes immediately to mind is: if the Namowei-teri and Shamatari populations began as a single village approximately 100 years ago and one population is represented by some twelve villages containing approximately 2000 people and the other by only five villages containing approximately 700 people, what caused this difference? Two kinds of answers suggest themselves immediately, and the truth may lie somewhere in between. The first possible explanation is that the Shamatari village was vastly larger than the Namowei-teri village 100 years ago. The difference in the sizes of the present population represents a factor of nearly three, that is, there are approximately three times as many Shamatari as there are Namowei-teri. It is possible that the Shamatari village was three times as large as the Namowei-teri village 100 years ago, and that both populations grew at approximately the same rate, preserving the initial difference in size. If the Namowei-teri village contained 100 people and the Shamatari village contained 300, and both grew, for example, at a rate of 10 percent per generation, after five generations the difference in the sizes of the two groups would still be three.

One fact that consistently conflicts with this hypothesis is that my informants all assert that the original Namowei-teri village was very large: ". . . about the size of Patanowä-teri . . ."[2] None of my informants ever saw the old village, of course, and base their estimates on what their parents and grandparents told them. Since there is no reason to believe that Yąnomamö villages in the past had a different range in size from what we find today, there is little reason to believe that if the original Namowei-teri village was "about the size of Patanowä-teri," that the original Shamatari village was three times the size of Patanowä-teri. I

[2] Patanowä-teri had a population of over 200 people. It recently lost some of its members when a fight resulted in the fissioning of a small dissident group. They rejoined the Bisaasi-teri.

cannot accept the conclusion that the Shamatari village contained over 600 people, or anywhere near that number. Shamatari informants claim that the original Shamatari village was large, but their conception of large, like that of the Namowei-teri, is based on present standards of village size. No Yąnomamö village, so far as I know, has ever existed for any length of time after it reached a population of 200 to 250 people.[3] Mishimishimaböwei-teri in 1971 was very exceptional with a population of 281 people. In 1972 it had 230 people, but with visitors from Ironasi-teri, it was temporarily over 400 while a ceremony was in progress.

A second possible explanation is that both "original" villages were approximately the same size, but one of them grew at a different rate than the other (or its members survived at a different rate).

There is considerable support for this explanation. This can be seen in the reproduction statistics given in Table 4.1 which summarizes the reproductive performance of males and females in (1) the population of deceased Namowei-teri and Shamatari; (2) the population of the ten villages of Shamatari (09, 10, 14, 16, and 21) and Namowei-teri (05, 06, 07, 08, and 18) at the present time; (3) the population of Mishimishimaböwei-teri in 1972 and (4) the reproductive performance of living females in both populations who are thirty-six years old or older.

If the present numbers of Shamatari and Namowei-teri can be accounted for in terms of different growth (or survival)[4] rates, the figures should show that the Shamatari population outproduced (or outsurvived) the Namowei-teri. This is clearly the case in the reproduction figures shown in Table 4.1. Looking only at the performance of dead individuals from both populations, the Shamatari males and females consistently outproduce the Namowei-teri males and females, indicating that differential growth rates rather than initial difference in village size accounts for the present difference in size of the two populations. Equally revealing is the difference in the standard deviations of the males and females on the one hand, and the two populations on the other. The data clearly show that Shamatari as a population contains exceptionally productive individuals who contribute large numbers of offspring to the next generation, whereas the incidence of such exceptional individuals among the Namowei-teri is much lower. We will return to this below and explore some of the consequences in lineage dispersion and marriage types. One point of interest in the statistics is the higher variance among males as compared to females. This shows the consequences of the fact that some males have many wives, and produce many offspring, while some males have one or no wives, and produce few offspring. The lineal "impact" of a man

[3] I am speaking of pre-contact only. Some villages in Brazil, in permanent contact with missionaries, are said to exceed this.

[4] The data came from my genealogies. While I have made an attempt to obtain all live births for everyone, I am sure that I have not gotten all of them. This is especially true for the deceased. Thus, the genealogical data represents survival of offspring more than total number of offspring. I believe that survival rate has been approximately the same in both populations (until the recent advent of European contact in some of the Namowei-teri villages and the introduction of new diseases). Since I cannot prove this, it is necessary to qualify statements about reproduction in terms of possible survival-rate differences between the two populations.

TABLE 4.1 REPRODUCTIVE PERFORMANCE

	A				B				C	
					Villages 5, 6, 7, 8, 9, 10, 14, 16, 18, 21					
	Deceased				*Living*					
	Shamatari		*Namowei-teri*		*Shamatari*		*Namowei-teri*		*Mishimishimaböwei-teri*	
	M	*F*	*M*	*F*	*M*	*F*	*M*	*F*	*M*	*F*
No. of Parents	85	107	94	95	99	121	117	147	37	45
No. of Children	586	486	442	370	371	393	377	413	123	130
Average	6.94	4.54	4.70	3.90	3.75	3.25	3.22	2.81	3.32	2.89
Variance	53.37	10.1	11.3	6.9	10.2	5.2	6.3	2.6	12.3	4.5
Standard Deviation	7.4	3.2	3.3	2.6	3.2	2.3	2.5	1.6	3.5	2.1

	D	
	Living Women, Age 36 or Older	
	Shamatari	*Namowei-teri*
No. of Women	36	46
No. of Children	178	170
Average	4.94	3.70
Variance	5.94	2.57
Standard Deviation	2.4	1.6

on Yąnomamö social organization can be very high compared to that of women; some men have as many as twenty or thirty children, but female reproductivity is limited by the gestation and lactation periods.

An examination of the reproductive performance in present villages indicates that the trend, detectable in the deceased population, has continued into the present: the living Shamatari continue to have more children than do the Namowei-teri. Both the males and females have a higher average. Looking only at the reproductive performance of women (column D of Table 4.1) who are near or at the end of their fertile years, the same picture emerges: the Shamatari outproduce the Namowei-teri.

Finally, in Table 4.1, column C I have given the reproductive performance of individuals in the village of Mishimishimaböwei-teri, based on the village composition as of 1972.[5] This, the largest of the Shamatari villages, falls somewhat below the average for the total Shamatari population for both male and female reproduction. An hypothesis suggested by these data might be: as a village grows to be very large, its members begin to limit their reproduction by such measures as increased infanticide or increased abortion. My data on this are so inadequate as to make any arguments based on them mere speculation.

A third possible reason for the presently much larger number of Shamatari might be the absorption of other groups, particularly whole villages. I have no evidence that the Shamatari are any different in this respect than the Namowei-teri. Both groups have incorporated segments from other populations, and the numbers involved in each case are comparable.

Summarizing the demographic information with respect to the population growth, it seems clear that the Shamatari are distinct from the Namowei-teri in their reproductive achievements, and that the present difference in total population size is more likely due to differences in reproductive (or survival) rates than to initial differences in the sizes of the founding populations. These data show that both the ancestral Shamatari and the present Shamatari have reproduced, on the average, at a higher rate than have the Namowei-teri. I conclude that both groups began approximately 100 years ago as a single village and the process of population growth and village fissioning were the same for both, with the exception that because of a higher reproductive (or survival) rate, the Shamatari population grew more rapidly and fissioned more often than did the Namowei-teri. Therefore, there are now many more Shamatari people and villages distributed over a much larger area. If the difference in average number of children for females thirty-six years old or older is considered, and if this difference has been characteristic over a hundred years, then the present difference in population size could be attributed to the differential reproductive performance among women in the two populations. The Shamatari women, according to my statistics, *presently* bear 33 percent more children than the Namowei-teri women.

[5] The composition of this, like all villages, changes from year to year. Appendix A gives the residents of the village in 1971, when Timothy Asch and I shot 80,000 feet of film there. I use the 1971 population so that this publication will more effectively complement the films that will come out of this footage.

VILLAGE COMPOSITION: LINEAL CONSIDERATIONS

Village fissioning can be affected by many things. One of these is the composition of the group in terms of kinship and descent. This is an issue regarding "solidarity" and the kinds of kinsmen among whom one lives. The genealogical data, when arranged by lineal descent patterns, can be related to this problem.

The villages of both populations vary in their composition quite markedly: some are dominated by one or two lineages, both politically and statistically, while others have a much less regular composition. One of my early suspicions was that there was a fairly simple relationship between lineage composition and stability, such that larger villages showed a pattern distinct from smaller villages. For example, my experience among the Namowei-teri villages led me to suspect that larger villages tended more toward a dual composition, and that smaller villages had a more heterogeneous composition. Patanowä-teri, recall (from the discussion in *The Fierce People*), was largely comprised of two and only two lineages, whereas the Bisassi-teri villages departed significantly from a composition that reflected duality. An obvious question, therefore, was: did villages fission after reaching a certain size *if* their lineal composition was either very dual or markedly different from duality, or did fissioning lead to greater or lesser duality? An examination of the data from the Shamatari population, at least at this juncture, suggests that the relationship between village size, fissioning, and lineal composition is somewhat more complex, and that it is not possible to conclude, from the considerations of lineal composition and size alone, whether the process of village fissioning leads to an increase or a decrease in duality. I am here speaking of total composition, including infants. When lineal composition is compared for adult males, there is a correlation between village size, fissioning, and composition.

The high reproductive performance of a few males in the Shamatari population has had an important impact on its lineal characteristics. One man in particular, the fabled Matakuwä—"Shinbone"—that Kạobawä described as one of the "original" Shamatari (Chagnon, 1966), has left a very impressive mark on the population. Indeed, it is small wonder that in the minds of many Yạnomamö the "Shamatari" are nearly synonymous with Matakuwä's *mashi* (patrilineal relatives and descendants). Matakuwä sired forty-two children. Moreover, many of his brothers and sons also had many children—one of his sons had thirty-three. Their children, in turn, were also very fecund. The net result is that a very large fraction of the Shamatari population are lineal descendants of Matakuwä's father, and an even larger fraction are cognatic descendants. Table 4.2 summarizes the lineal and cognatic descendants by generation, starting with Matakuwä's father as the apex. The distribution of these descendants by village is discussed below.

The dispersion of Matakuwä's lineage in the Shamatari area can be seen most graphically in Figure 4.2, a pedigree of the *lineal* descendants of the lineage founder, individual 1222. This diagram was drawn before my 1972 fieldwork and does not contain a number of individuals that I can now relate lineally to Matakuwä. In fact, Matakuwä (individual 1221, near the top of the figure) is shown

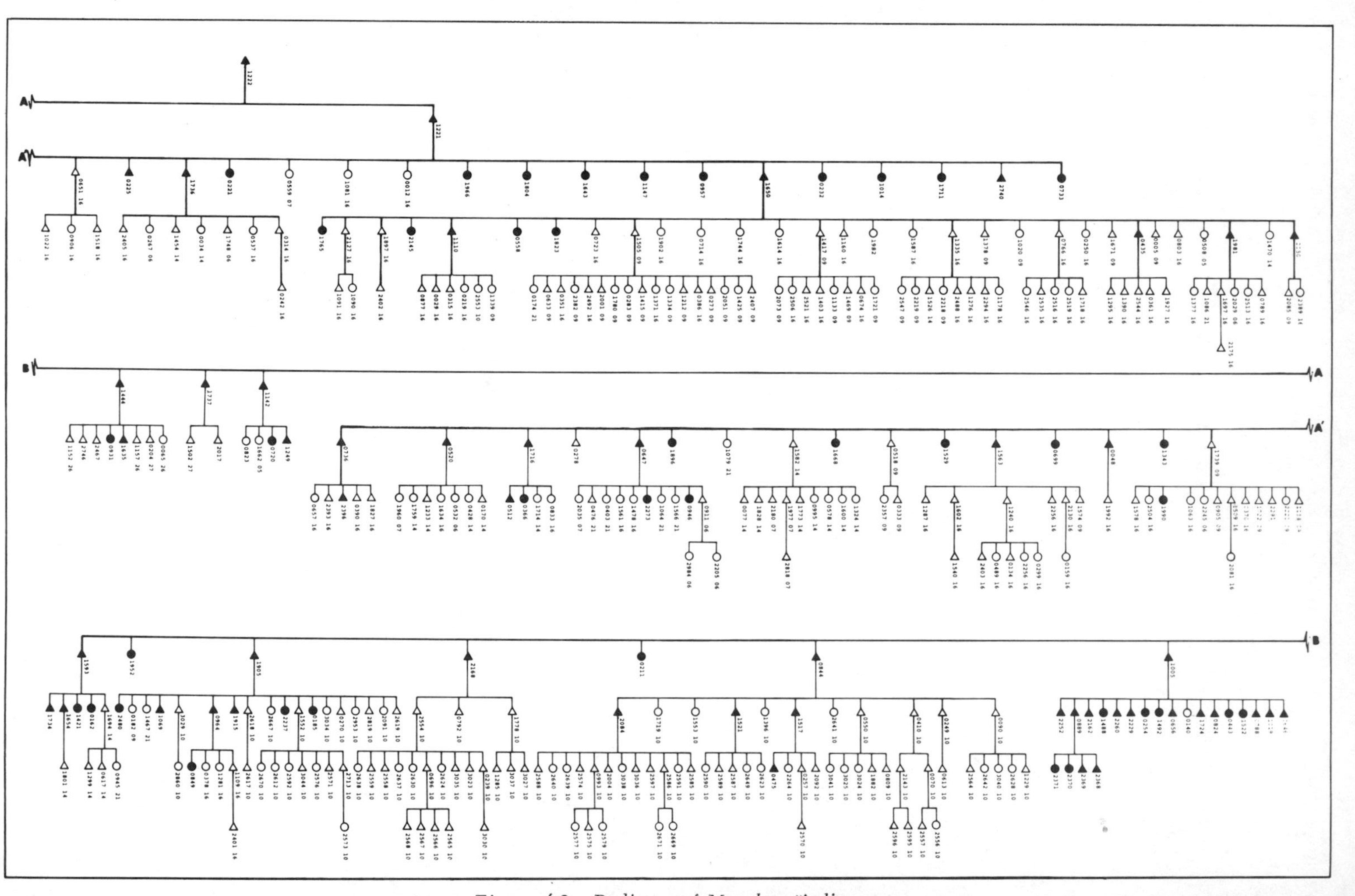

Figure 4.2—Pedigree of Matakuwä's lineage.

TABLE 4.2 DESCENDANTS OF MATAKUWÄ'S FATHER IN ALL VILLAGES (By Generation)

	Lineal	*Cognatic*
Generation I	12	12
Generation II	109	118
Generation III	161	326
Generation IV	92	176
Generation V	5	17
Generation VI	0	0

here with only thirty-four children.[6] The new individuals, added in 1972, represent an earlier fission that led to the founding of a yet uncontacted set of villages not considered here.

Two points can be made about the pedigree. First, the descendants are found in all of the Shamatari villages, but are more highly concentrated in some. Thus, the historical data (Chapter 2) on fissions are confirmed by the present distribution of people in the lineages. The same pattern holds for the other Shamatari lineages (see below for statisitcs). Second, segments of the lineage tend to stick together when the village fissions: clusters of brothers remain in the same group and separate from their parallel cousins. This pattern was discussed at length in Chapter 3 of *The Fierce People.* Below each individual in the pedigree shown in Figure 4.2 is a six-digit number. The first four digits are the identification numbers of the individual, and the next two are the village designations as given on Figure 2.5.

Table 4.3 presents the same data (including the new data) in statistical form. Thirteen lineages are shown along the top as headings for rows. The five Namowei-teri and Shamatari villages are then listed along the left margin as headings for rows. (The totals for villages are not accurate—some individuals have been left out because the data are not cleaned up yet.)

These are the largest lineages in both populations; the first seven lineages are Shamatari and the next six are Namowei-teri.[7]

The first and most obvious fact of importance is that Matakuwä's lineage is by far the largest in this selection of villages. He has additional (lineal) descendants in other villages not included here, as indicated in Table 4.4.

Second, Matakuwä's lineage, as well as several others, has a very wide distribution among the villages. There are only two villages where individual 1222 does not have lineal descendants—Hasuböwä-teri and Patanowä-teri. It is likely, as the data are gradually cleaned up, that some of his lineal descendants will be found there as well.[8] It is clear that the villages shown here contain many people

[6] The new individuals are, however, included in Table 4.2.

[7] There are some Shamatari lineages, not included, that are larger than the smaller Namowei-teri lineages shown here.

[8] The village of Hasuböwä-teri is shown as having 142 people that are not included in the thirteen lineages, but I know that most of the 142 people are Shamatari or descendants of Shamatari. My Hasuböwä-teri and other informants were not able to specify the genealogical links, and I spent far less time working on this group than on the others. I plan to return there to fill in this gap.

TABLE 4.3 DISTRIBUTION OF LINEAGES BY VILLAGE

	Lineages														
	Shamatari							*Namowei-teri*							
	1222	2968	2936	0081	1443	0200	2700	2954	2886	1598	2856	0916	1829	Other	Totals
Namowei-teri Villages															
05	2	3	2	0	1	0	0	39	21	1	5	8	1	20	103
06	7	2	5	0	0	0	0	17	35	2	5	11	0	3	87
07	6	1	5	1	0	0	0	28	9	5	0	3	18	10	86
08	0	0	1	0	1	0	0	7	6	39	2	1	0	142	199
18	0	4	0	1	1	0	0	64	81	8	29	0	0	11	199
Shamatari Villages															
09	92	24	11	1	12	1	14	2	0	0	0	0	0	18	175
10	101	1	1	30	0	1	1	0	1	0	0	0	0	59	195
14	17	16	28	0	1	34	4	0	1	0	0	0	0	10	111
16[a]	83	37	24	1	47	1	18	2	0	0	0	0	0	18	231
21	10	54	7	0	0	1	1	1	0	0	0	0	0	6	80
Totals	318	142	84	34	63	38	38	160	154	55	41	23	19	297	1466

[a] The figures for Mishimishimaböwei-teri in this distribution are for the year 1972.

who have agnates in some or most of the other villages, and, incidentally, why informants from any village know a great deal about the older people in other related villages.

Third, the Shamatari villages are, quite naturally, dominated by Shamatari lineages and the Namowei-teri villages by other lineages, reflecting the fact that both groups are the end product of a process of village fissioning that can be traced back approximately 100 years to a single village in each case. A major difference between the two populations is the degree to which the lineages dominate the population. Matakuwä's lineage accounts for 38 percent of all the population in all the Shamatari villages, but the largest single Namowei-teri lineage only accounts for 23 percent of the total number of Namowei-teri.

Table 4.4 gives the composition of villages by percentage of village belonging to the largest, two largest, three largest, and four largest lineages. Compared to the Namowei-teri villages, the Shamatari villages appear to be more dominated by a single large lineage. Looking at the distribution for the two largest lineages, the Shamatari villages also tend to be more "dual" in composition. This pattern continues; 82 percent of the members of the Shamatari villages, on the average, belong to the four largest lineages, whereas only 68 percent of the members of the Namowei-teri villages, on the average, belong to the four largest lineages of that population.[9]

Table 4.4 underscores the point raised at the beginning of this section. There appears to be no simple relationship between village size and lineal composition. One of the smallest villages (21) has the "most lineal" and "dual" composition, and one of the largest villages (08) has the least.

Mishimishimaböwei-teri (1972 census) has only moderate domination by one lineage: 35.9 percent of the group belongs to Matakuwä's lineage, including the most dominant headman—Möawä. He, however, exercized a degree of authority over the village that is not predictable by the modest fraction of the village that belonged to his lineage. I will discuss this further in Chapter 5, but at this juncture I point out that the statistics with reference to lineal composition say very little about the "strength" of leadership and authority wielded by headmen. These tend to be more a function of personal charisma. The statistics, however, do indicate whether the prominent men's lineal identities are consistent with group composition. It is theoretically possible for particularly aggressive men from smaller lineages to be the "real" headmen, but in practice this rarely happens. In general, village composition by lineage reflects politics: the most prominent men in the village invariably come from the larger lineages, usually from the largest single lineage. If there are two or three very large lineages, there will be men from them who are very significant in the domestic and political affairs of the village.

Each village, therefore, has a number of important men, but usually one of them will be more important than the others, and this man usually belongs to the largest lineage. As the lineage grows larger in the village, there will be several men—agnates (brothers or classificatory brothers)—who compete with each

[9] Calculated by averaging the averages for the five villages of each population.

TABLE 4.4 DISTRIBUTION OF POPULATION BY LINEAGE SIZES AND VILLAGES (In Percent)

	Villages									
	05	06	07	08	18	09	10	14	16	21
	Namowei-teri					*Shamatari*				
In Largest Lineage	37.9	40.2	32.5	19.6	40.1	52.5	51.8	30.1	35.9	67.5
In 2 Largest Lineages	58.2	59.8	53.5	23.1	72.9	66.3	67.2	55.9	56.3	80.0
In 3 Largest Lineages	66.0	72.4	64.0	26.1	87.4	74.3	67.7	71.2	72.3	88.8
In 4 Largest Lineages	71.0	80.4	70.9	27.1	91.5	81.1	68.2	85.6	82.7	90.0

other for leadership. Mishimishimaböwei-teri, in the recent past, has fissioned and re-fused in fights between Möawä and some of his agnates, Nanokawä, Reirowä[10] and Sibarariwä in particular. These men now live in Ironasi-teri, where Möawä's (Matakuwä's) lineage is very dominant. If the residents of Ironasi-teri (09) and Mishimishimaböwei-teri (16) were pooled together to reflect what their composition was like before they fissioned, it is clear how dominant Matakuwä's lineage would be. Forty-three percent of the village would be members of the same lineage, and the village would include over 400 people. More significant than the fraction of the village dominated by one lineage, however, would be the fact that Möawä and Nanokawä would be living in the same village, as would Sibarariwä, and they would be fighting constantly.

Table 4.5 gives the distribution of adult males by their lineal identity in the villages.

Two points can be made about this distribution. First, when the two populations are compared, the Shamatari, again, tend to be more lineal in village composition; more of the adult males in the Shamatari villages belong to the largest single lineage. Second, there appear to be more intermediate-sized lineages in the Namowei-teri group. Among the Shamatari, the composition of villages appears to be slightly different: most of the villages have one or two relatively large lineages, and most of the village males belong to them. This implies that political and domestic affairs are dominated by one or two groups of agnates, and suggests that there should be more cohesion. Another way of saying this is: given the marriage practices and nature of competition that leads to fissioning, the ideal composition—from a solidarity or group harmony consideration—would be a village with two dominant lineages. The next best would be a village with one dominant lineage plus a hodgepodge of individuals who do not fall into lineages of any size, such as the lineage structure of village 08 in Table 4.5. The worst possible combination would be a village with a group of several (more than two) lineages, none of which is clearly dominant. I suspect that the Shamatari villages have grown to larger sizes because of the kinds of lineal composition they maintain.

Finally, Table 4.3 (p. 136) includes information that enables us to examine the Shamatari villages in another way. Note that villages 14 and 21 do not have Matakuwä's lineage as the single largest lineage, but are dominated by other lineages in terms of their composition. This pattern was discussed in *The Fierce People* (see especially the discussion of Figures 3-1 and 3-4 of that publication). To be sure, Matakuwä's lineage is represented very prominently in both villages, but it is secondary in statistical and political significance to other lineages. It is this kind of situation in which ambiguous examples of descent and political identity arise. Some case materials I collected imply that the Yąnomamö view villages as lineal descent units, while other informants do not endorse such a view. If we assume, for sake of argument, that the Yąnomamö do classify villages as single lineages, then many of the ambiguous examples become much clearer. It would be possible for a Yąnomamö, depending on the circumstances, to be a member of village 14 or 21 and deny being a Shamatari *if* he equated "Shamatari" with

[10] Reirowä died in 1971. See Chapter 5.

TABLE 4.5 DISTRIBUTION OF MALES 20 YEARS OLD OR OLDER BY LINEAGES AND VILLAGES (In Percent)

	Villages									
	05	06	07	08	18	09	10	14	16	21
			Namowei-teri					*Shamatari*		
Adult Males in Largest Lineage	38.9	39.1	26.3	23.1	42.0	47.8	60.6	41.2	38.1	78.6
Adult Males in 2 Largest Lineages	77.8	56.5	52.7	28.2	74.0	65.2	84.8	52.9	59.5	85.7
Adult Males in 3 Largest Lineages	88.9	69.6	68.4	30.8	94.0	73.9	84.8	58.8	76.7	92.9
Adult Males in 4 Largest Lineages	94.4	78.3	73.7	30.8	96.0	78.3	84.8	64.7	83.8	92.9

Matakuwä's lineage. He might even argue that his entire village, which separated from Mishimishimaböwei-teri, is a different *group* entirely. He would ignore the fact that they separated from the "true" Shamatari, as well as the fact that a significant portion of his village is comprised of Matakuwä's lineal descendants. In other circumstances the same person might argue precisely the opposite.

In short, I have many examples which suggest that the Yąnomamö view other villages as essentially single lineages, but in most cases I also have supplementary data about the circumstances that show how the context has influenced the statements of the informants. It is as though some fissions have as one of their objectives the establishment of a group with a different lineal identity, but because of marriage patterns and interlineage obligations, all new groups reflect the composition of the original group to such a large degree that the new groups are hardly more than a diluted version of the original. Then, depending on the circumstances of the fission and the motives of individuals, the agnatic relationships are "manipulated" according to the political needs of the moment. Thus, Möawä can deny being a Shamatari in order to make peace with Kąobawä, or particular individuals can deny being related to or having any affinity to groups they, at the moment, are at war with.[11] Möawä might have insisted on not being a Shamatari to Kąobawä by choosing to ignore a generation of relationship. He told Kąobawä that the Shamatari were living in Ironasi-teri; he might have meant that Sibarariwä, Matakuwä's son, was living there. Möawä, being only a grandson, was "non-Shamatari" for that occasion, a convenient fiction accepted publicly by Kąobawä, again, for that occasion.

These issues are too hoary to discuss in any detail in a publication of this sort, especially when only a portion of the data is given and not all of that is in final form. Still, it is important to realize how genealogical data, when manipulated in various ways in analaysis and if collected with some purpose, relate to broader, more general theoretical issues, such as the relationship between ideology and composition on the one hand, and the contextual nature of informant statements about ideology on the other. What is at issue here is precisely the same thing pointed out by Sahlins (1963; 1965) several years ago in his review of *Social Structure in Southeast Asia*: You cannot assume that statistics about group composition will tell you directly the nature of the ideology about descent and residence rules. The growing importance of methodology in social anthropology, and the increased use of statistics, suggest that this problem—attempting to deduce qualitative generalizations from quantitative facts—will be with us for some time.[12]

VILLAGE COMPOSITION: COGNATIC CONSIDERATIONS

The magnitude of the impact of lineage 1222 on the Shamatari population is eclipsed only by the cognatic effects. Of the Shamatari included in the five villages of Table 4.6, 75.4 percent of them are descended from Matakuwä's father through

[11] Another notable example of this latter type of fiction is the political and lineal identity of the village of Yeisikorowä-teri not included in the villages shown in the tables, but shown on Figure 2.8 and discussed in Chapter 2.

[12] The relationship of group composition to group ideology in the context of Yąnomamö political affairs will be developed in another publication.

either the male or the female line—*three-quarters of all Shamatari have him as an ancestor*! Moreover, his impact on the Namowei-teri has also been great, due mainly to the inclusion in that population of many abducted Shamatari women and their descendants. There are presently eighty-four people in the several Namowei-teri villages who trace descent from individual 1222—over 12 percent.

An inspection of Table 4.6 shows that the Shamatari impact on the Namowei-teri population has been greater than the impact of the Namowei-teri on the Shamatari. Two reasons account for this. First, the Namowei-teri villages have been more successful in abducting women from the Shamatari. Second, they have also been more successful at obtaining marriageable women from the Shamatari than the latter have at getting women in return. Most of this latter effect has been due to the activities of the Bisaasi-teri and their success at getting women from villages 14 and 21 in recent times (discussed in *The Fierce People*, Chapter 3, p. 79).

The total contribution of individual 1222 to the entire population (all ten villages) is startling: 45 percent of the entire population are descended from him in some way. If multiple relationships are considered, the picture is even more startling. Of the some 1,500 living people in the ten villages, 45 percent are related to him at least by *one* link, but some people are related in several different ways. There are nearly 1,000 total relationships between the present living population and individual 1222!

Comparing villages by lineal as opposed to cognatic descendants, the Shamatari villages contain far more people related cognatically to Matakuwä's lineage than they contain lineal descendants. For example, only 12.5 percent of the members of village 21 are lineal descendants of 1222, but 95 percent of the members are cogantic descendants! This startling figure reflects the way the village fissioned, and how many of the women in village 21 were descendants of 1222. In Mishimishimaböwei-teri, there are twice as many people related to 1222 through *either* the male *or* the female line as there are people related only through the male line.

Cognatic descendants are significant in the context of marriage patterns, for the frequency of cross-cousin marriage—the prescriptive form in Yąnomamö society—is very much a function of the number of cognatic descendants left by any individual in previous generations. Indeed, the actual number of cousin marriages may have more to do with the number of grandchildren a man (or woman) left than the stringency of the marriage rules themselves: you can't marry a cross-cousin, no matter how onerous the rule, if you don't have one. Conversely, given some demographic structures, it may be difficult to avoid marrying a consanguine, and *any* preference or prescription results in frequent cross-cousin marriage.[13]

How important the reproductive behavior of individuals in the second ascending generation was to the frequency of cousin marriages became apparent when I participated in a computer simulation of the Yąnomamö population with Dr. Jean MacCluer and Dr. James V. Neel (MacCluer et al., 1971). Dr. MacCluer had developed a very sophisticated Monte Carlo program that simu-

[13] I am presenting this in a publication with Michael Levin (Chagnon and Levin, ms.).

TABLE 4.6 DISTRIBUTION OF COGNATIC DESCENDANTS BY VILLAGE

	Lineages													
			Shamatari							Namowei-teri				
	1222	2968	2936	0081	1443	0200	2700	2954	2886	1598	2856	0916	1829	*Other*[a]	*Totals*[b]
Namowei-teri Villages														
05	30	18	27	18	14	3	0	13	72	11	12	13	3	0	234
06	19	19	27	3	9	14	0	21	60	4	13	30	12	0	231
07	26	12	25	14	6	14	4	33	41	10	1	26	23	0	235
08	3	2	8	39	1	0	0	17	28	113	6	2	0	0	219
18	33	19	81	13	5	0	14	99	161	31	54	4	12	0	526
Shamatari Villages															
09	162	98	108	28	19	3	52	2	3	2	0	0	0	0	477
10	129	30	45	75	0	2	12	0	2	0	6	0	0	0	301
14	66	65	94	15	1	75	37	0	2	0	0	0	0	0	355
16	184	103	74	40	81	6	33	0	4	0	0	0	0	0	525
21	76	67	57	9	0	2	7	0	0	0	0	0	0	0	218
Totals	728	433	546	245	136	119	169	185	373	171	92	75	50	0	3311

[a] The individuals who are not demonstrably related cognatically to the founders of these lineages have not been counted.

[b] Individuals may be related cognatically to more than one of the lineage founders.

lated the Yąnomamö population in terms of reproduction and marriage. I provided estimates of the essential parameters—age at marriage, reproductive performance, marriage rules, and so on—based on my early observations and data on the Namowei-teri population. The observed frequency of cross-cousin marriage in the real population was approximately 15 percent; that is, I could show by genealogical links that 15 percent of the marriages were between cross-cousins. The early simulated runs were puzzling because the frequency of cross-cousin marriage was very low. No matter how we weighted the various parameters, we could not get the simulated marriages to yield a frequency anywhere near 15 percent. MacCluer examined the relationship between the fertility of men and that of their sons, and it became quite obvious that the high frequency of cross-cousin marriage in the real (Namowei-teri) population was due largely to the fact that two very fecund men produced a large number of offspring, and that some of their sons, in turn, also produced large numbers of offspring. Thus, the number of potential cross-cousin spouses in the third generation was very high. When this demographic fact was put into Dr. MacCluer's program, the simulated population approximated very closely to the marriage behavior observed in the real population, using the original estimates of the several demographic and social parameters. This is one clear-cut example of how the methodology—computer analysis in this case—led to an understanding of a phenomenon that might not have been recognized otherwise. Now, with hindsight, it seems obvious that the frequency of cross-cousin marriage is very closely related to the differential fecundity in ascending generations and is not a simple function of marriage prescriptions.

Villages can become biologically and socially very heterogeneous in their composition and still retain a political identity that reflects past fissions. For example, the village of Monou-teri, discussed in *The Fierce People*, contained a great many individuals who were, by cognatic descent, related to Matakuwä and other Shamatari lineage founders. Yet no Yąnomamö regarded the Monou-teri as "Shamatari," and the notion would have been absurd to them. The adult males of Monou-teri were from the dominant Namowei-teri lineages (2954 and 2886), and the village fissioned from the Bisaasi-teri. (See Figure 2-8, p. 43 of *The Fierce People*.) Using the "gene count" method (following Hiorns et al.), I can show that nearly 40 percent of the genes in Monou-teri came from the Shamatari population. Not surprisingly, when my medical colleagues collected blood samples in Monou-teri and later had the computer "assign" the village to that group of villages to which it was most closely related biologically, it assigned Monou-teri to the Shamatari population (Ward, 1970; 1972). A similar situation developed in the genetic analysis of village 05 (discussed in Chagnon, 1972; see also Neel, Arends, Brewer, Chagnon et al., 1971).

Relationships through the female line can become important when new alliances begin to develop between previously hostile villages. When Kąobawä made his first friendly contact with the Mishimishimaböwei-teri in many years (discussed in Chapter 5) one of the more important steps in the relationship developed through a cognatic tie. Dedeheiwä's sister had been abducted by the Bisaasi-teri ancestors many years earlier, and was married to Kạobawä's "father" (father's brother). Her (biological) son was therefore a (biological) nephew (sister's son) to Dedeheiwä, as well as being Kạobawä's "brother." While the early friendly gestures were developing, the man in question figured very prominently in the emerging alliance, and many of the impending relationships between both villages were phrased in terms of this cognatic relationship. After they developed, the young man in question—a political nobody—was no longer involved in the politics. But, for a brief period of time, he was the most significant tie between the groups—the Mishimishimaböwei-teri visited "Dedeheiwä's nephew" whereas the Bisaasi-teri visited "Shadadama's uncle." Recall that this tie is very important in the Yạnomamö kinship sytsem. (See the photograph in Figure 3-3, page 62, of *The Fierce People.*)

Again, when I contacted the Iwahikoroba-teri for the first time (discussed in Chapter 5) my entree was via cognatic ties: another abducted Shamatari woman, who also married one of Kạobawä's father's brothers, was the focal link. She and her son—a different brother to Kạobawä—came with me. She went to visit her brother, the headman of the village, and her son went to meet his mother's brother.

Much of the visiting between villages that are at war is possible only because of these kinds of cognatic ties. An inspection of Table 4.6 from this perspective shows how interconnected all the villages are, and why an existing kinship nexus between distant populations can be renewed and rather rapidly developed into intimate ties between large groups of people in the village involved.

The extension of both lineal and cognatic relationships across many villages also makes it possible for intermarriages between the groups to follow prescriptive patterns, often when the women involved have been abducted.

The most important point to be made out of the discussion of village composition, both from a lineal and a cognatic viewpoint, is that each village is historically, socially, and biologically a part of a much larger whole. Its composition and size are only the temporary consequence of a continuous process of population growth and fissioning, and its current political relationships cannot be clearly understood unless the greater nexus is known. While the members of each distinct village strive to preserve and emphasize their political autonomy and sovereignty, much of their behavior is understandable only when their position within the larger framework is clearly defined. An important methodological issue emerged from this. Anthropological fieldwork has traditionally emphasized the intensive study of *single* communities as the *sine qua non* of field methodology. I am convinced that had I limited my fieldwork to an intensive study of just one village, I would know and understand a great deal less about Yạnomamö warfare, social organization, marriage, and politics. Again, by having returned over and over again to visit the same groups at different points in time I have been impressed by how important the process of village growth and fissioning is in the social life of the Yạnomamö, and how misleading my results would have been if predicated on a single visit to one village. There is an important dynamism in the population that cannot be easily detected on a short visit to one village, and an enormous variability in population structure, marriage patterns, and political relationships in both time and space (Chagnon, 1972). This might not be true in other field situations, where population growth is not a characteristic affecting tribal dynamics. Among the Yąnomamö, this process is one of the more important facts of life.

THE STRUCTURE OF MARRIAGE IN YĄNOMAMÖ VILLAGES

I discussed the relationship between marriage patterns and village fissioning in *The Fierce People* from the perspective of how marriage ties between lineages keep the composition of the resulting new villages similar in kind to that of the parent village. (See Figs. 3-1, 3-4, and 3-5 of *The Fierce People*.) I showed how the strength of the reciprocal marriage obligations between lineages led to fissions along predictable lines, and how agnatic ties weakened as they grew more remote.

The arguments apply to the process of village fissioning among the Shamatari. Now, after accumulating more detailed data, I am in a position to attempt to look for other kinds of relationships between village stability, village fissioning, and marriage patterns. Even with the task enormously simplified by the use of computers, the amount of work required is still very great, and the problems numerous.

There clearly is an important relationship between village fissioning and the kinds of marriage patterns found in the village, both before and after the fission. I showed in *The Fierce People* how variable the patterns of prescriptive marriage are, especially in the amount of prescriptive marriage. But there is also a great deal of variability in the structure of prescriptive marriages themselves, and villages can be characterized by various amounts and kinds of subtypes. Only time and effort will tell how the variability in the structure of marriage patterns relates to the probability of village fissioning, and an exhaustive analysis of the problem will require computer simulations of the kind mentioned earlier.

But before any attempt at simulation can be made, it is necessary to identify the important parameters and to estimate their values. Marriage practices are just one component affecting the process of fissioning, and to give an indication of how complicated it is to "measure" them and their consequences, even with computer techniques, let us consider the structure of marriage in Mishimishimaböwei-teri.

To simplify the demonstration, let us consider marriages from the male spouse's genealogical ties to wives. Table 4.7 gives the distribution by age category for all marriages by males in Mishimishimaböwei-teri. The frequency of multiple marriages is given along the top, for example for the men between the ages of thirty-six and forty-five years, two of them have had only one wife, three have two wives, two have had three wives, and one has had six wives, etc.[14] The figures in

[14] The largest number of contemporary wives for any man, so far as I know, is five. The record number of wives for any man in these two populations is fourteen—that includes all wives, past and present.

TABLE 4.7 DISTRIBUTION OF SPOUSES FOR MALES IN MISHIMISHIMABÖWEI-TERI

Ages of Males	*Number of Spouses* 1	2	3	4	5	6
6–15	3	0	0	0	0	0
16–25	11	1	1	0	0	0
26–35	12	4	4	0	0	1
36–45	2	3	2	0	0	1
46–55	0	0	0	1	0	0
56–65	0	0	0	1	0	1
66–	0	0	0	0	0	0
No Age	2	0	0	0	0	0
Totals	30	8	7	2	0	3

the matrix of Table 4.7 represent the *total* number of marriages a man has had and do not mean that he presently has that number of spouses. Appendix B identifies contemporary spouses. The fifty men in Mishimishimaböwei-teri have been married a total of ninety-three times for an average of 1.86 marriages each. Of these ninety-three marriages, forty-nine of them have been with women who are genealogically related to their spouses. That is, 53 percent of all marriages are consanguineal.

Within the forty-nine cases of consanguineal marriages there are many ways men are related to their spouses. In most cases, many genealogical links exist between the spouses. For example, the individual Shiwaniböwä (ID 1697) is related to his spouse, Yaoma (ID 2173) in the following ways. She is his (1) FaFaFaDaDaDa, (2) FaMoFaSoSoDa, (3) FaMoMoSoSoDa, (4) MoMoFaDaDaDa, (5) MoFaFaFaSoSoSoDa, and (6) MoFaFaMoSoSoSoDa. That is, he is related to her by six different genealogical routes. One of the stumbling blocs in "measuring" or "quantifying" Yąnomamö marriage patterns emerges from a consideration of the various types represented by these six relationships. Figure 4.3 (Case 1) reduces the six types to essentially four paradigms. Considering the rules of descent, the marriage presciptions and the kinship terminology, three of the four paradigms represent appropriate, prescriptive marriage patterns. Subtypes "A" and "B" are marriages of individuals whose parents are cross-cousins; subtype "C" represents MoBrDa marriage. Only subtype "D" cannot, on the basis of inspection, be related to Yąnomamö marriage prescriptions. If anything, it would be incestuous. However, in small, highly inbred populations such as this, one can expect that relationships between spouses will be numerous and not all of them are to be reckoned with for the purposes of analyzing marriage behavior.

Attempting to relate the marriage of this pair of individuals to the arena of village stability and solidarity for the purpose of characterizing the entire village in terms of its distribution of marriage types, we immediately run into a problem of "counting" this marriage. If our hypothesis is that village stability is somehow related to the kind of marriage patterns found among its members,

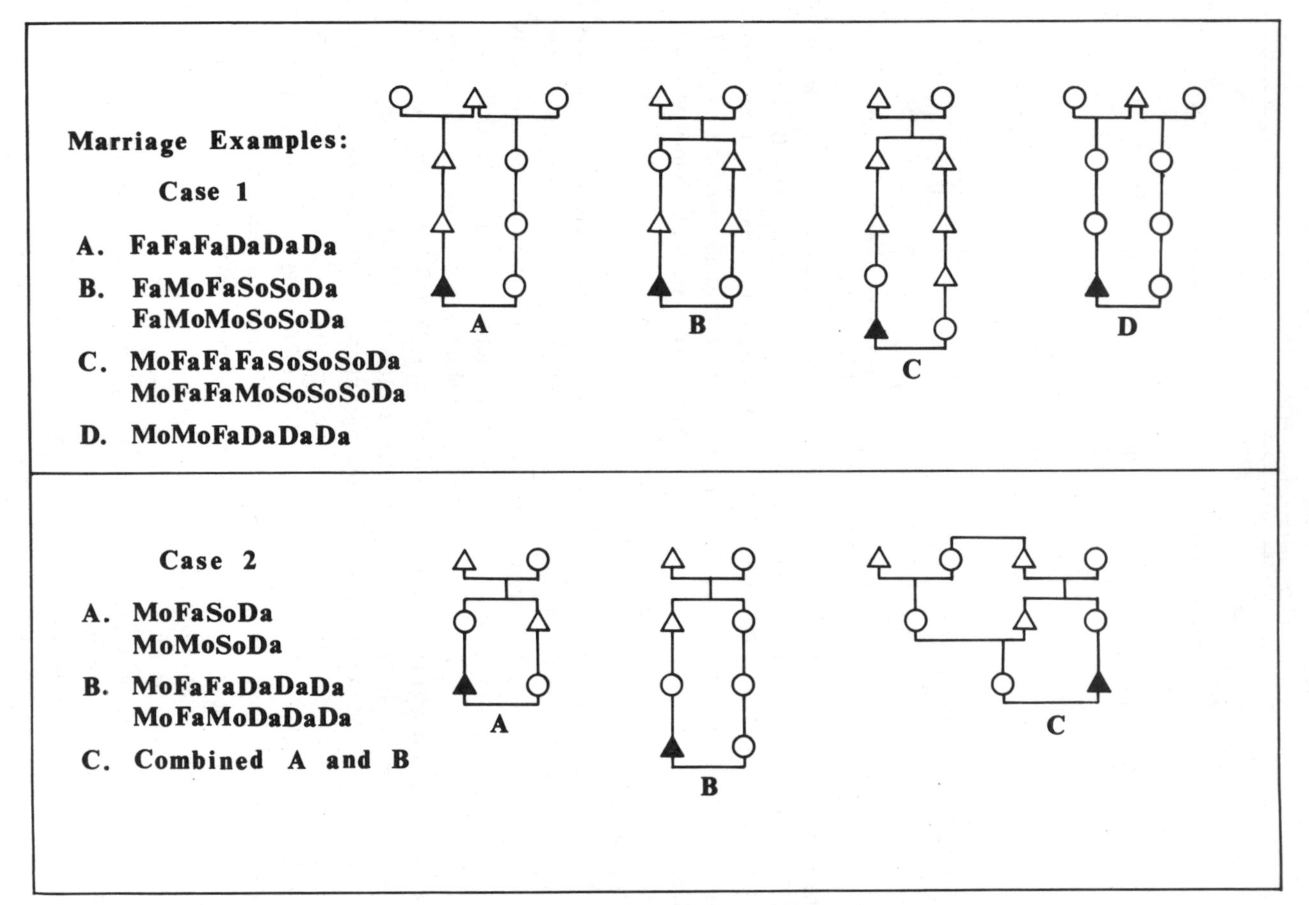

Figure 4.3—Marriage examples.

how do we consider this and many other similar marriages? What if our hypothesis is that a village with a high incidence of MoBrDa marriages is more "stable" than a village with a lower incidence? This particular marriage in fact would count as an example of MoBrDa marriage (subtype "C"), but it also represents other legitimate marriages as well.

One of the problems in analyzing marriages only from the perspective of individual pairs of individuals is that previous marriage arrangements in ascending generations are not given any weight. That is to say, the obligations between segments of lineages created by prior marriages are not evident when marriages are reduced to individual paradigms. Consider, for example, the paradigms in Figure 4.3 (Case 2). Individual 67 is related to his wife, individual 1334, as (1) MoFaSoDa, (2) MoMoSoDa, (3) MoFaFaDaDaDa, (4) MoFaMoDaDaDa, (5) FaFaFaFaSoDaSoDa and (6) FaFaFaMoSoDaSoDa. Two of the paradigms ("A" and "B") represented are given in the diagram; the third drawing ("C") shows how these two can—ought to—be put together. It shows that the father of 1334 married his FaSiDa while, in the next generation, individual 67 married his MoBrDa.[15] Whether or not it is either desirable or possible to treat each marriage paradigm as a separate "type," independent of previous marriages, is at the heart of the issue of village solidarity as "measured" by marriage types. Case 1 could be rearranged in a similar fashion to show the marriage alignments in ascending generations.

I repeat, there is the question of how many times marriages such as the ones shown in Figure 4.3 (Cases 1 and 2) should be counted. Does one count each married couple only once and equate the selected marriage's impact on solidarity with that generated by a marriage between two individuals who are related only once, as MoBrDa/FaSiSo? Surely the multiple genealogical connections between spouses in the former, more complex pattern of marriage reflect a greater degree of intergroup obligation based on several generations of exchange. Yet the opposite proposition—that a first cross-cousin marriage generates more "solidarity" than a second cross-cousin marriage—is not entirely without support.

In order to deal effectively with the "measure" or "measurability" of marriages in this and similar populations, it might be necessary to utilize a statistic that describes the amount of relationship between any two pairs of married individuals. The same statistic can be also used to express the relationship between any two pairs of individuals, however they are related. One such measure is the "coefficient of coancestry" developed by Sewall Wright (1922). It is used by geneticists to characterize inbreeding, and measures the probability that a child will receive a gamete from each parent that is identical, by descent, from an ancestor common to both parents. It is calculated by the following formula:

$$f=[(1/2)^{n_1+n_2+1}\ (1+F_A)]$$

where n_1 is the number of generation links to the common ancestor through one parent and n_2 is the number of generation links through the other parent. F_A is

[15] When the data are all cleaned up I will be in a better position to document how regularly FaSiDa and MoBrDa marriages alternate generation after generation. At the present there is a suggestion that this pattern occurs with relatively high frequency.

the inbreeding coefficient of the common ancestor. This value can be largely ignored in populations such as the Yąnomamö where the purpose is to examine only recent generations and where genealogies are not remembered beyond four generations or so.

Utilizing only the portion of the formula that counts relatedness down from a common ancestor in a marriage paradigm such as those shown in Figure 4.3, the resulting statistic, while not the same as the "inbreeding coefficient" as used by geneticists, can be very useful to cultural anthropologists who wish to characterize marriage patterns with some numerical value. The resulting number, for most anthropological purposes, is quite useless unless the genealogies are consulted. There are many ways that a particular value of f can be reached. Thus, the value of $f=0.0625$ is the numerical measure of a first cross-cousin marriage, but it is possible that the same value could be gotten when two individuals marry who are *not* first cross-cousins but who have many, more remote, ancestors in common. But when the genealogical composition of a village or cluster of villages is known, the statistics becomes very useful, when viewed against the genealogies, to express a measure of the group's "relatedness," particularly when broad characterizations are made. A village comprised of a hodgepodge of small lineages and characterized by a great deal of influx from other, unrelated groups, will have a low average value for f when all marriages within the group are considered. Conversely, a village that is dominated by a large lineage and whose ancestry includes a few very fecund men will have a much larger value of f for its marriages. Table 4.8 gives the distribution of the values of f as defined above for all actual marriages. It is clear that the Shamatari villages are characterized by marriages that are more consanguineal than are the marriages in the Namowei-teri villages —about 250 percent more. The impact of a few founders such as Matakuwä's father in the Shamatari population accounts for most of the difference represented in the statistics: the Shamatari villages contain individuals who are more closely related, so that their marriages have, on the average, a higher value of f when compared to Namowei-teri marriages.

Extending this argument to the specific problem raised at the beginning of this chapter, if the probability of a village fissioning is a function of group solidarity based on either the amount of relatedness within the village or the nature of marriages between related spouses, then the values shown in Table 4.8 are compatible with the conclusion that larger villages will be comprised of close kinsmen and characterized by more consanguineal marriages. The Shamatari villages *are* larger, which means that fissioning is inhibited by *something*, and they are more consanguineal in composition. It is not unlikely that the *something* in question is the amount of relatedness of spouses (or the structure of that relatedness).

A statistic such as the one just described only tells part of the story. If village solidarity were merely a matter of total relatedness among co-residents, then the statistic would be very useful by itself. However, it is clear that the structure of relationships within a village has an effect on solidarity. For example a man's first cross-cousins—(his *shoriwä*) are related to him as measured by the f statistic, in precisely the same way that his first parallel cousins are related to him. Both types of cousins have a value of f of 0.0625, yet his cross-cousins are,

TARLE 4.8 COEFFICIENTS OF RELATEDNESS BY VILLAGE[a]

Villages	*Average Relationship between Spouses*	*Population Average*
05	0.0135	
06	0.0085	
07	0.0130	
08	0.0097	
18	0.0127	0.015 (Namowei-teri)
09	0.0359	
10	0.0153	
14	0.0359	
16	0.0198	
21	0.0396	0.0293 (Shamatari)

[a] The coefficients of relatedness are based on the definition given in this chapter. The figures are for all marriages in each village, including those where no genealogical links are demonstrable between spouses. The figures shown here arc for male egos.

essentially, his allies while his parallel cousins are his "brothers" and, depending on the circumstances, his competitors as well. Again, there are many types of "cross-cousin marriage," particularly those involving second cross-cousins, that would be indistinguishable from each other if the value of f alone were used to describe their relationship. A second cross-cousin marriage, when compared to the genealogical paradigm of a first cross-cousin marriage, involves the interrelationships of a larger network of people; this might affect the degree to which the degree of cousin marriage adds solidarity to a village. Second cross-cousin marriage raises the possibility that there have been exchanges between lineages over two or more generations. Thus, the number of lineages within a village determines, in large part, the structure of marriage types; their political dominance with respect to each other leads to patterns of exchanges between particular lineages. The net result is that a second cross-cousin marriage between members of a strong and a weak lineage might have a different inhibiting effect on the process of village fissioning when compared to the same kind of marriage between two very large, dominant lineages or two very weak lineages.

The lineage composition of a village brings us back to the discussion of the potential "solidarity strength" of the first versus second cross-cousin marriages. If, for example, cross-cousin marriage creates stability and if all cross-cousin marriages found in a village are between members of the less significant lineages, then the frequency of cross-cousin marriage—first or second—alone is not a good measure of that village's "solidarity." Given the demographic structure of the Yąnomamö population and the differential reproduction of a few individuals such as Matakuwä, it is unlikely that recently absorbed lineages will have more complex types of consanguineal marriages than the initial lineages. What can happen, however, is that the newer lineages might have proportionately more *first* cross-cousin marriages with segments of other lineages, and this might enhance the strength of the relationships between particular segments within the village while at the same time detracting from the general solidarity. I reproduce here the "ideal" marriage pattern presented as Figure 3-1 of *The Fierce People* (Figure 4.4 here). The situation I am describing, with respect to the diagram, arises when a lineage—"W" in this case—is incorporated by a village as shown in Figure 4.4. The village, prior to this incorporation, was dominated by Lineages "X" and "Y," and the exchanges and reciprocal obligations between them in marriage held the group together. Over time, however, the closeness of consanguinity in marriage between individuals of Lineages "X" and "Y" might decline; their marriages might reflect earlier solidarity by representing many different kinds of complex consanguineal links, but it is possible that the links are not "close" in a genealogical sense. Again, as the village grows, and segments of large lineages take form and lead to competition between adult agnates, disposition of women in marriage might show a bias: ambitious groups, in an attempt to build their political following, cede women to more remote groups to bind them in marriage to their own political interests. While this might be expedient while the village retains its composition and size, the "dilution" of consanguineal ties in this fashion might later constitute a weakness in lineage solidarity when the village fissions. Thus an ambitious cluster of men from a dominant lineage, "X" for example, might give women to a newly incorpoarted lineage, say, for example, Lineage "W" of Figure 4.4. The newly incorporated members of lineage "W" might have far fewer accumulated links with Lineage "X," but the ones that exist might be closer and stronger. Thus, the solidarity between Lineage "W" and that segment of Lineage "X" into which its members married might be very high when compared to the "general solidarity" within the village or within Lineage "X." In fact, it might constitute a source of weakness in overall solidarity, since men of lineage "W" compete with men of Lineage "Y" for women of Lineage "X."[16] Once fighting erupts within a large village, it becames chronic and ultimately leads to fissioning. Thus, when the village fissions, a fraction of the "X" Lineage will move to a new location with most of the members of Lineage "W."

An examination of the lineage composition of the villages presented in Tables 4.3 and 4.4 suggests that this is precisely what happens. Take, for example, the composition of village 21. Comparing the composition in terms of sex and lineage, it is clear that the village, while containing a significant number of individuals from Matakuwä's lineage, is dominated by lineage 2968, a different lineage. Almost all the adult males in the village are from that lineage. Making this analogous to the ideal marriage pattern under discussion, lineage 2968 has done what Lineage "W" has done. When the number of actual *first* cross-cousin marriages in the two villages is compared, it turns out that there are proportionately

[16] A graphic example of the competition between three lineages will be presented in a 16mm film, *The Axe Fight*; the film depicts a fight with axes, machetes, and clubs in Mishimishimaböwei-teri. While on the surface the fight is over an incident involving the refusal to share food, the groupings of the contestants in the fight reflect their lineage identity and marriage alliances (Chagnon and Asch, n.d.).

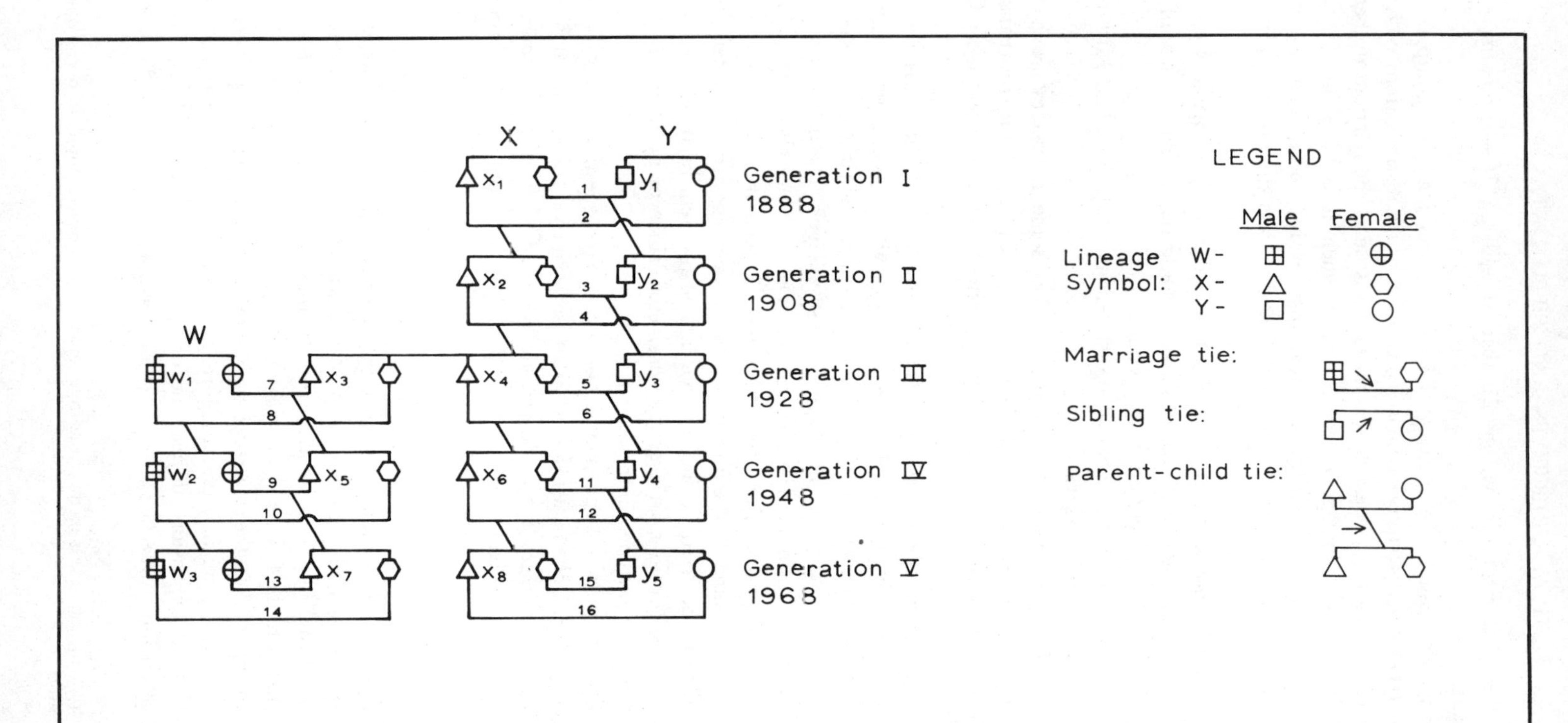

Figure 4.4—Ideal social structure.

more of these marriages in village 21 than in village 16—approximately 20 percent more.

This raises the issue of evaluating the contribution made to group cohesion by various *types* of prescriptive marriages, types that are distinct from each other in degrees of biological closeness. It also raises the issue of the relationship between kinship, biology, and marriage types at a time when it is becoming almost an article of faith in some anthropological circles that kinship and biology not only do not mean the same thing, but to suggest that one reflects the other in any meaningful way is to commit a serious offense, especially in discussions of marriage types. While I will not argue that social relationships in Yąnomamö society can be directly read from biological relationships, it would be foolish, in view of these data, to ignore the obvious connections between them.[17]

Some of the more frequent types of prescribed marriage found in Mishimishimaböwei-teri are shown in Figure 4.5.

One of the first and most obvious facts is that some marriages are included in several different types of cross-cousin marriage. In estimating the parameter "frequency of cross-cousin marriage," how does one count these marriages? Once? Four times?

A second fact that should emerge also has to do with the measure of the frequency of prescriptive marriage. If the process of village fissioning is a function of the amount or frequency of prescriptive marriages, what can we say about the frequency of prescriptive marriage in this village? There are twenty-four cases of first cross-cousin marriage of the FaSiDa and MoBrDa types: 25 percent of *all marriages* are of these two types and 49 percent of *all consanguineous marriages* are. But some of these cases are single marriages that represent several types. Are they to be counted once or twice? The problem becomes even stickier when second cross-cousin marriages are considered, since many of the first cross-cousin marriages are included in these types.

Third, there is quite a large number of types. The question is not so much a matter of "if" the Shamatari follow their prescriptive rules, but "how" they follow them. All villages may not include some of the variants shown here, especially if they are small villages, or if there has been only a brief history of reciprocal exchanges between lineages. A classification of villages by marriage types will have to consider the diagnostic types, and whether the types occur in all villages.

Fourth, it should be pointed out that the "common ancestor" in many of the marriage types shown in Figure 4.5A is Matakuwä (or his father), underscoring again the fact that the reproductive performance in ascending generations is intimately related to the frequency of cousin marriage.

Finally, to show that the marriage types are actually more complicated than they appear in the upper half of the figure, the lower half of the diagram, Figure 4.5B, provides an expansion of just one of the marriage types (type "10"). It also draws attention to the fact that the computer does not do all of the work for

[17] I am exploring the details of these interrelationships in a different publication (Chagnon and Levin, ms.).

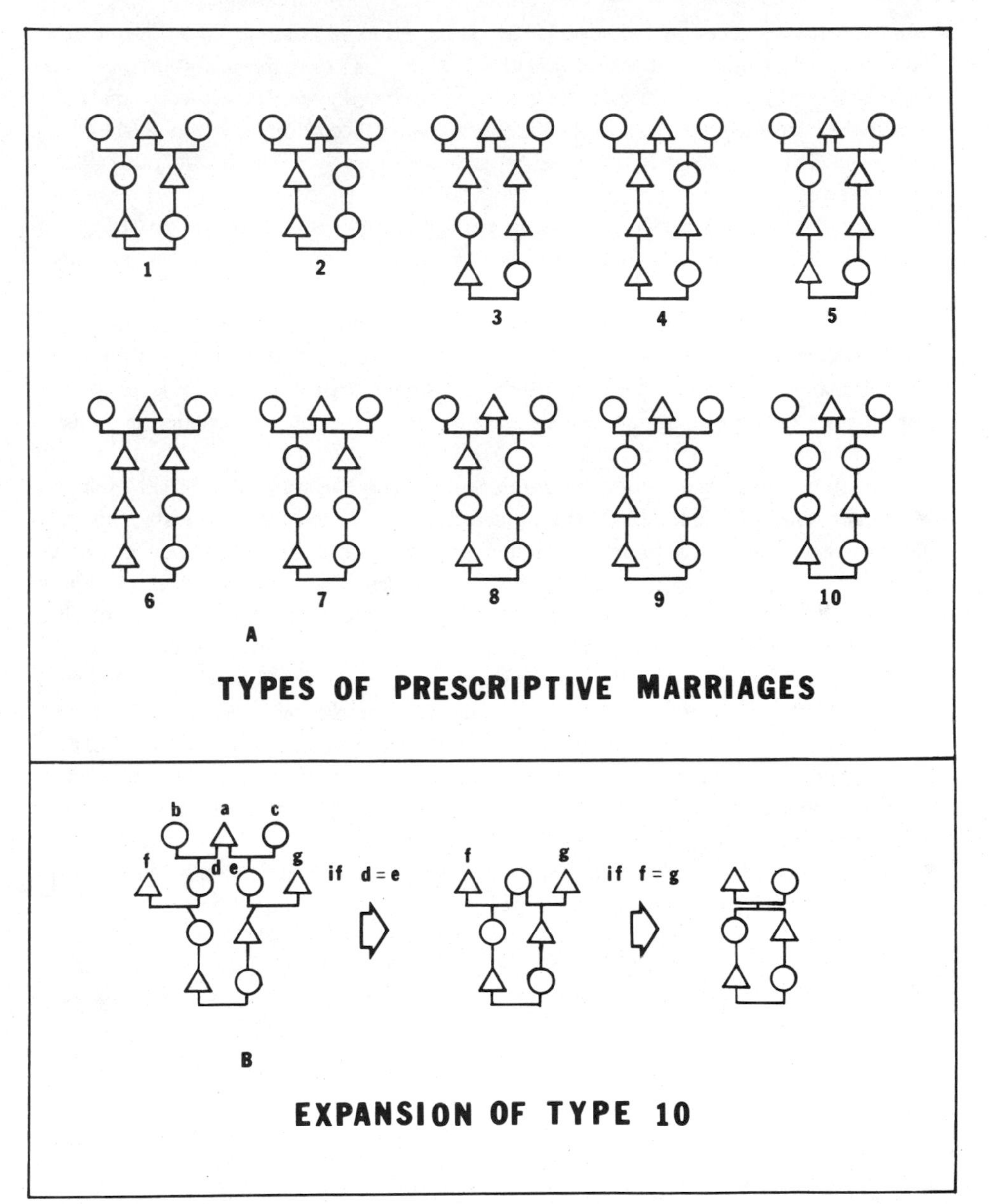

Figure 4.5—Types of prescriptive marriages.

the anthropologist. The computer lists in a matrix all examples of particular genealogical connections between spouses. In this task it is infallible and annoyingly accurate. But it does not (thus far in the development of the programs) distinguish which marriages have complicated interrelationships with other marriages. Figure 4.5A expands marriage type "10" and shows how this type, in some individual cases, reduces to other types of prescriptive marriages. Thus, the analysis is not a simple matter of examining the matrix of a computer printout that summarizes the various marriage patterns for each village. Rather, each marriage must be examined as a particular case and treated accordingly. Most of the four-generation types shown in Figure 4.5A can be similarly expanded to other forms of marriage.

These figures and data cover only a portion of all consanguineous marriages in Mishimisimaböwei-teri. I have not, for example, discussed incestuous marriages or "marriage by capture." These, too, might be related to village solidarity and the probability of fissioning. I documented one case of a fight in Mishimishimaböwei-teri that was over an incestuous marriage by Möawä, and everyone seemed to agree that this was the "real" cause of the fission that followed. The frequency of incest, therefore, might be a relevant consideration in predicting village fissioning.

Incestuous marriages might be significant in another way. Most cases of incest involve men who are *waiteri* and who can flout the rules with impunity, men such as Möawä. Two expressions I frequently heard while investigating incestuous marriages were: "He was a real *waiteri*! He married his own *yuhabö*!" or, "Only those who are *waiteri* commit incest!" On one occasion, while I was chatting with Rerebawä about something totally unrelated to marriage and incest, he commented: "When my son grows up and becomes a man he will be very fierce. He'll probably commit incest a great deal." One of the most difficult parameters to measure in the context of village solidarity is the role that the headmen play in keeping large villages together. It is clear to me that their degree of *waiteri* has very much to do with their leadership, and perhaps one measure of it is the amount of incest they commit!

As the genealogical data and marriage pattern data are gradually cleaned up, a number of important theoretical issues can be examined regarding the "structure" of marriage in populations of this kind. A recent paper by Morton et al. (1972) argued that "marriage rules" have very little effect on the amount or nature of inbreeding in tribal populations. The crux of the argument, which was very elegant in a mathematical sense, was the assumptions made about the demographic characteristics of tribal populations; the assumptions were unreasonable. Where there is a high degree of variation in male reproductivity, different kinds of conclusions must be drawn. Preliminary analyses with the data in their present state of untidiness show that marriage rules very clearly affect the structuring of inbreeding. If the residents of Mishimishimaböwei-teri are selected at random, one male and one female, and allowed to "marry" in a simulation, a procedure that can be efficiently accomplished with computer programs, some interesting results emerge. First, the amount of inbreeding does not change very much, but the structure of marriage certainly does. It has been shown that in most human populations there is, despite incest prohibitions of the same kind, approximately the same amount of cross- and parallel-cousin marriages (Hajnal, 1960). This is not the case in the Yąnomamö population: the marriage prescriptions very clearly channel the marriages into various and legitimate categories.

The Shamatari are quite distinct from the Namowei-teri when marriages are simulated without any restrictions. What emerges is that the Namowei-teri inbreeding coefficients fall markedly below the value found in actual marriages, indicating that the marriage rules have a considerable influence on the amount of "inbreeding" in some Yąnomamö villages, and the "structure" of marriages in all villages. Thus, the computer methodology, when applied to these genealogical and marriage data, will lead to some important theoretical insights into the relative contribution that "marriage rules" and demographic characteristics make to the kinship structure of populations. That marriage rules, marriage practices, and demography are intimately related was shown quite some time ago by Rose (1960) for the Groote Eylandt Aborigines of Australia. Unfortuantely, Rose did not have computer techniques at his disposal for his analyses, and his conclusions suffered from his failure to give proper weight to the categorical rather than the genealogical definition of prescribed marriage types.[18]

OTHER CONSIDERATIONS

There are a host of other factors that relate to village fissioning and stability, not all of which are easily quantified or, if quantifiable, are very difficult to document accurately.

One of these is the intensity of warfare (Chagnon, 1968a; 1968b; 1968c). There appears to be a close correlation between the intensity of warfare, the existence of large villages, and the practice of selective female infanticide. The sex ratios found in villages at the periphery of the tribe indicate that where warfare is less intense, so also is the practice of female infanticide. There, the sex ratios, when compared to villages near the center of the tribal distribution (such as all of those discussed in this monograph), indicate that there are relatively more females in the population. The Shamatari and Namowei-teri populations are more heavily involved in warfare, and the age/sex distributions reflect the stronger selection against female offspring. The data are presented in Table 4.9 and Figure 4.6, which give the population distributions in ten-year intervals and percentages. Table 4.9 gives the distribution in numerical terms; Figure 4.6 shows the same data graphically in age/sex pyramids.[19]

It is clear that there is a severe shortage of females in both populations, particularly in the younger age categories. The "bulges" in the pyramids reflect more the inadequacies of the age estimates I made than mysterious selective pressures against particular age groups. I tend to estimate young adults more often as twenty-five years or thirty years than twenty-three or twenty-eight years. I have attempted to take cognizance of kinship terminology and other factors that would enable me to rank siblings, but it has not always been possible to be

[18] I am exploring some of the relationships between demographic characteristics, observed marriage types, and simulated marriages (with a number of restrictions) in a different publication (Chagnon and Levin, ms.).

[19] See also Chagnon, 1972.

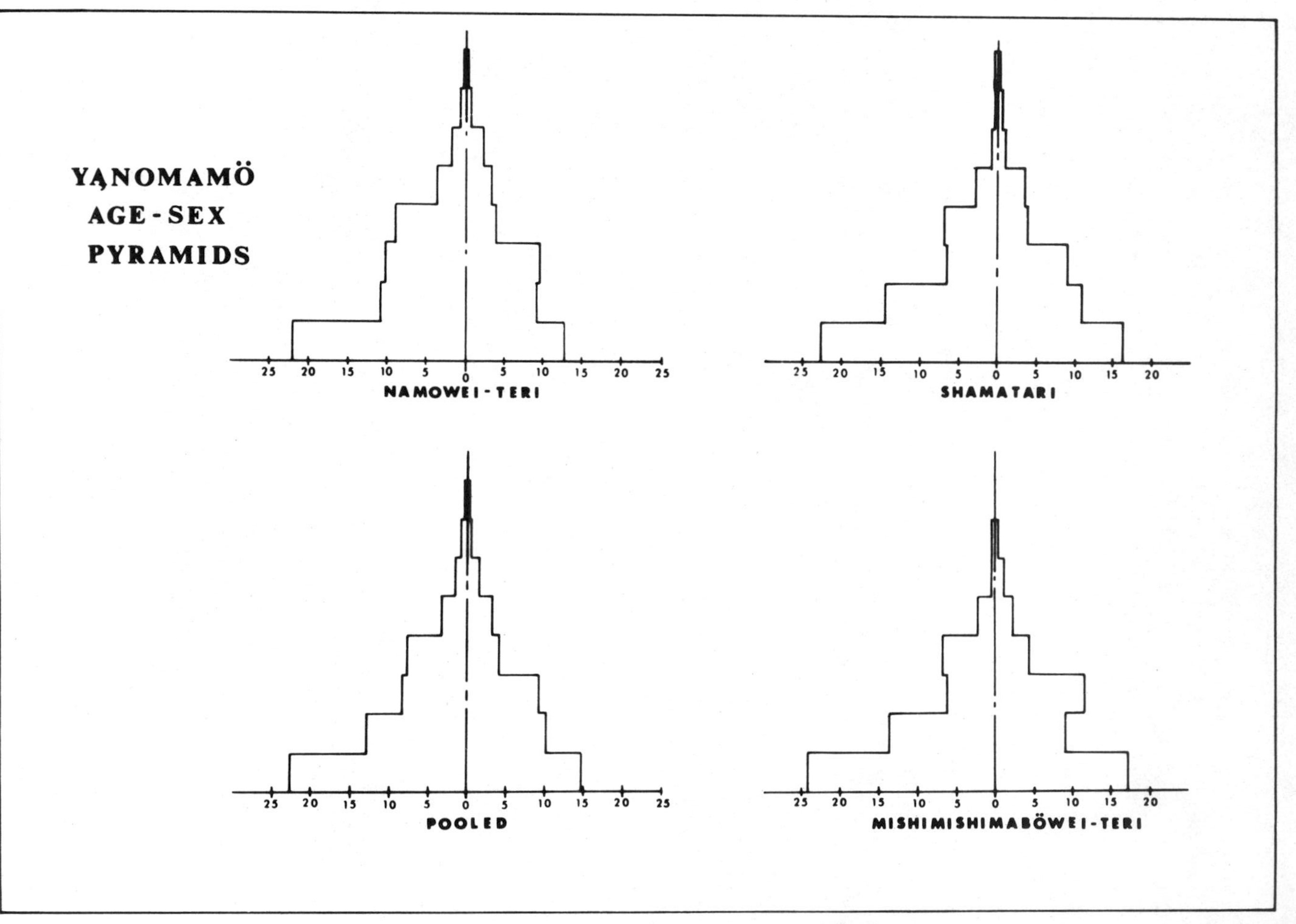

Figure 4.6—Yąnomamö age-sex pyramids.

TABLE 4.9 AGE/SEX DISTRIBUTION

Age Intervals	*Namowei-teri* M	F	*Shamatari* M	F	*Pooled* M	F	*Mishimishimaböwei-teri* M	F
0–10	22.1	12.7	22.9	16.2	22.7	14.6	24.3	17.2
11–20	10.8	9.2	14.5	10.9	12.8	10.1	13.9	9.0
21–30	10.2	9.6	6.6	9.0	8.4	9.3	6.4	11.6
31–40	9.0	3.9	6.7	3.9	7.9	4.0	6.7	4.1
41–50	3.6	3.1	2.7	3.4	3.2	3.3	2.2	2.2
51–60	1.9	2.2	0.8	0.8	1.4	1.5	0.4	1.1
61–70	0.5	0.6	0.7	0.2	0.6	0.4	0.4	0.4
71–	0.1	0.3	0.1	0.4	0.1	0.3	0.0	0.0

systematic. Still, I am confident that I can distinguish between males and females below the age of ten and those who are fifteen and older: the shortage of females in the younger age categories is not an artifact of my "guessing" ages incorrectly, or systematically missing female children in my census. It is real.

The data are consistent with the argument that intensive warfare leads to large villages and increased female infanticide. There is, of course, feedback in this interrelationship. Much of the fighting has to do with the acquisition of women, who are in short supply. Note that the sex ratios in older age categories are not nearly so biased in favor of males, reflecting the fact that warfare selects primarily against males. Thus, by the time the cohort reaches age thirty to thirty-five, there are approximately as many males as there are females.

Finally, the data show that the Yąnomamö are a "young" population. The pyramids are large at the base and rapidly become narrow, indicating fairly high loss of infants. Particular villages, because of local factors, show a great deal of variability in demographic characteristics; some of them are fairly narrow at the base and imply much less loss of infant life. Infant mortality is usually very high when the populations are obliged to move often to avoid their enemies; if the population remains sedentary for relatively long periods of time, the demographic characteristics change. In populations this small, the changes can be very abrupt in a short period of time. As a measure of the "youthfulness" of the population, less than five percent of the people are older than fifty years, whereas 60 percent of the people are twenty years old or younger.

The age/sex structure of villages can have an important relationship to village fissioning, particularly for villages in the intermediate size range. Size alone cannot be taken as an infallible predictor of the probability of fissioning unless the distribution of the ages and sexes of the group are carefully considered.

The number of adult males in the village is very important, and the variability in this is very high. (See Chagnon, 1972, for data.) A village with very few adult males but many women and children is less able to fission and yield two militarily viable groups than a similarly sized village with proportionately more adult males. Some of the villages discussed in this chapter are sufficiently large so that this is not a major consideration. A few, however, are too small to fission and produce two viable groups, and several, while large enough, have marginal numbers of adult males. The age/sex structure for these would be critical.

The intensity of warfare is difficult to measure. One of the problems is that wars wax and wane from one decade to the next, but the probability of war remains fairly high. It is as much due to the chronic *fear* of raids as to the *actual frequency* of raids that villages remain large. A longer-term measure of warfare intensity is perhaps more relevant than a count of raids per village over a short period of time. The number of individuals killed over a long period of time is one such measure. Table 4.10 gives the distribution of causes of death in the two populations. Note in particular that proportionately more Shamatari men have died violently than Namowei-teri men, and if this accurately reflects the intensity of warfare, then there is more of it in the Shamatari area.

From these statistics, it is clear that warfare has a more pronounced impact on the Shamatari population than on the Namowei-teri. Over 30 percent of the adult males die in warfare as compared to about 24 percent among the Namowei-

TABLE 4.10 CAUSES OF DEATH

	Shamatari		*Namowei-teri*	
	M	*F*	*M*	*F*
"Natural" Causes	0	0	0	2
Epidemics[a]	3	14	6	11
Dysentery	1	1	14	5
Warfare	52	5	44	9
Duels[b]	1	1	5	0
By Husband[c]	0	0	0	1
Snake Bite	1	3	4	2
In Childbirth	0	0	0	1
Respiratory Infection	1	5	3	0
Hayaheri[d]	0	1	6	1
Old Age	7	4	8	3
Sorcery[e]	27	11	15	5
Crushed by Falling Tree	1	0	1	0
By *Hekura*	6	5	13	20
Shawara	28	55	66	70
Wayuwayu[f]	1	9	0	0
Measles	0	1	0	0

[a] Many of these deaths are due to malaria; during periods when malaria was particularly virulent, any death was attributed to it.

[b] Chest-pounding, clubfights, axe-fights, and so on.

[c] Killed by husband for real or imagined wrong.

[d] This word, literally, means "pain" or "painful." Presumably the deceased suffered intensive pains in the abdominal region.

[e] These are mostly adult deaths. It is difficult to get large amounts of data on infant deaths.

[f] This is a Shamatari word meaning essentially the same thing as the Namowei-teri word "Shawara"—epidemic. I have distinguished between them to keep an account of informants' precise wording. I have also distinguished these two "causes" from "epidemics" because much of the data under the latter rubric were collected when malaria was rampant. The three categories could be pooled together for most analyses.

teri. Counting both males and females in both populations, nearly 20 percent of all deaths are attributable to warfare. By anybody's standards these are impressive facts.

The totals given in Table 4.10 differ somewhat from the figures I have published elsewhere (for example, Chagnon, 1972). This is an artifact of the present condition, of the data; Table 4.10 does not include a number of individuals whose IBM cards have blanks in the column that identifies them either as Shamatari or as Namowei-teri. When these corrections have been made, the totals will change again, but the pattern will probably remain as it is given here.

Perhaps the most difficult parameter to measure is the role of leadership in holding villages together. I am convinced that villages in this area of the tribe grow to be large because headmanship is strongly developed. There is a correlation between size of village and, for lack of a more precise term, "strength" of headmen. Strong leaders like Möawä add a great deal to the stability of the village, and manage to keep order and organization a jump ahead of the smouldering conflicts that threaten to tear larger villages apart. The leadership here, however, does not differ in kind, only in quantity. That is to say, Möawä's status has been acquired, as have the leadership positions in all Yạnomamö villages, but because he is a particularly forceful and aggressive man, he has established himself in rather dictatorial ways over his group. Möạwä is a very young man, and it has been only in the past few years that he has managed to acquire a large following. His history prior to that was one of constant fighting with several of his agnates, and fissioning away from them with just a few followers. All of this is to say that he insists on having his way in matters; while he was younger, and perhaps less competent compared to his agnates, his insistence probably led to repeated disputes and his separation from the larger group. Now, however, he is polished and has demonstrated his force, and large groups of people have reconstituted themselves in his village. He is, as the Yạnomamö refer to headmen, ". . . the one who *really* lives here." Like strong leaders in other large villages, Möawä depends a great deal on his aggressiveness to keep the village intact. He, like other strong leaders in Patanowä-teri and Hasuböwä-teri, has had to, from time to time, settle disputes by killing the individual who caused them.

These are very drastic measures, but they might represent the additional leadership element required to allow a village to grow from 150 people to 200 or more people. Quantifying this element is, perhaps, impossible, and it may be that only subjective evaluations are possible. That leaves me rather in the position of accurately measuring the first 5,200 feet of a mile with a surveyor's chain—and pacing off the last 80. But I am not even sure if the quantifiable data represent that large a fraction of the total mile. If it turns out, after I have cleaned up all the data and made the analyses suggested here, that there are too many loopholes or non-correlations to predict village fissioning in any meaningful way, I will, at least, have made a detailed *description* of that process in one population, a description that can be used in making comparisons with other populations.

5 / The difficulties of being relative when you are a relative of the one-who-lives-there

This chapter deals with some of the nonquantifiable aspects of fieldwork—the quality of the field situation, if you will. In particular, it describes some of the personal relationships that I developed with important political leaders in several Yąnomamö villages and how these personal ties affected the nature of my work and the conditions under which the data were collected. It deals largely with political leadership and leaders, some of whom were friendly and generous in their dealings with me, and others of whom were less than friendly—to the point of threatening to or actually attempting to kill me. I am hard pressed to describe the nature, quality, and dimensions of leadership in Yąnomamö society. These range from barely detectable attributes in small villages to oppressively conspicuous qualities in very large ones.

Perhaps the most revealing way is to describe some of my experiences with particular leaders among the Shamatari, which stand in contrast to the kind of relationships I described in *The Fierce People*—(my relationship with Kąobawä, for example) during my early fieldwork. Headmanship among the Shamatari differs from headmanship among the Namowei-teri, but the differences do not lend themselves to a statistical, quantitative approach. Kąobawä, like many headmen, was magnanimous, wise, and munificent. Yet there was no mistaking his force and political poise once the idiom of leadership was known. Dedeheiwä of Mishimishimaböwei-teri was of the same mold. But Möawä, Dedeheiwä's son-in-law, was more of a tyrant in his style. I had seen headmen develop and wield great authority as the warfare patterns and considerations of defense and security called these powers into being, and I had watched the same men gradually relax their autocracy, almost with a sigh of relief, as the crises waned. These tended to be older, more experienced leaders in Namowei-teri villages, men who competently rose to the occasions presented by their culture and who were no more and no less firm than the situations required. They were men who were confident of their abilities and who proudly brooked no impudent dissent from men less proved than they.

What follows is an account of how some of these people affected my work and how one in particular affected me.

At the end of a monograph written for students and potential fieldworkers, it would be desirable and pedagogically elegant to conclude by suggesting that if one follows procedures and methods similar to those discussed herein, success will be inevitable. But I end, however, with the admission that I did not completely achieve all that I had defined as my professional obligations or my personal objectives. The reasons for falling short of these self-defined goals are complex and manifold, but they are the kind of reasons that are all too often ignored by potential fieldworkers when they contemplate and design their field projects. In my case, they have to do with personal values to which I subscribe and how these were at odds with the personal values and behavior of one Yąnomamö headman; this ultimately developed into an intolerable situation for me. While my formal training and disposition were such that I could live patiently in a different society for one or two years, by the time that three years had elapsed my patience had begun to wear very thin. Toward the end I felt irresistible compulsions to lay aside my professionalism and responsibilities as a "dispassionate observer" and give free rein to my passions: in a few instances I wanted desperately to be a Yąnomamö for just ten minutes and do unto others as they were doing unto me. It was then that I realized it was time to take a break from the routine of yearly return field trips.

I have spoken to many anthropologists who have spent years with other peoples and who, at the end of their fieldwork, could no longer continue because of similar intense feelings and personal difficulties with the people among whom they had lived. It appears to be a characteristic problem among fieldworkers who spend two or more years in intimate daily contact with people whose values and attitudes differ markedly from their own, anthropologists who have learned the native language well enough to appreciate some of the subtleties that repetitiously define the attitudes and, frequently, the contempt that the native people have for them. Anthropologists rarely discuss these things in print, or in public, but they are problems that all potential fieldworkers should consider seriously. Both as representatives of their culture and as idiosyncratic examples of it, all anthropological fieldworkers have a limitation regarding how much of a particular kind of different culture they can comfortably live with before they begin having personality difficulties, both at home and in the field. The methodological point in all this is to plan your research objectives so that they can be accomplished in the length of time allotted. My own personal feelings are that two years of field research should be planned as a minimum, but that the design should include a break at the end of twelve to fifteen months.

I am speaking now of field situations where the research must be conducted in a native language that can only be learned in the field. A much shorter field project can be conducted with equally meaningful results if the work can be conducted in a language that can be learned before going into the field, or a language that is closely related to the native language of the fieldworker.

I have described and explained some of my methods, objectives, and results in this monograph. To make what I consider an important point for fieldworkers, I conclude by describing the more significant reasons and events that led me to conclude that it was time for me to temporarily stop fieldwork, even though my objectives had not all been achieved. I will return to the Yąnomamö again to check on specific loose ends and to help my students initiate fieldwork in specific areas of the tribe, but never again will I singlehandedly attempt to do so much in so many different villages for one project.

The main problem had to do with what the Yąnomamö call *madohe*—material possessions that can be given in trade. More accurately, it had to do with their constant preoccupation with acquiring *madohe* and how they viewed me in the context of being first and foremost a provider of *madohe*. Their pursuit of *madohe* was intimately bound up in a system that defined the relative status of giver and receiver of goods. In addition to having real, practical value, the trade goods often, but not invariably, reflected, when they passed from one person to another, a kind of pecking order and hierarchy. It is a subtle system, and the more I lived with it the less I liked it, for everything came to hinge on a more or less chronic giving of goods either to establish interpersonal relationships or to maintain them. Apart from the annoyance of having to interrupt my work to dig through my possessions to locate fishhooks or matches when they were requested, it became tedious to weigh the implications of giving or withholding the items at each request. Just as it was important to give under some circumstances, it was likewise important to withhold under others. It is marvellous to discover a classic economic/status system such as this—but quite another to live in it.

The relationship between giving and status is dependent on the situation and the individuals involved. Giving does not by definition improve one's status. To give a machete to a man freely without his solicitation will add to the status of the giver. The giver will, all things being equal, be cherished as a generous man. But all things are never equal, and that is the whole point of the relationship between giving and status. To give the same machete to the same man when, for example, he *demands* it "or else" creates a situation latent with status implications that go far beyond the immediate, vis-à-vis relationship with that man. It then becomes important to know when to withhold items. The system goes beyond goods. To put it into Lévi-Straussian terms, it includes goods, women, and services. Since I had no women to exchange, my involvement was restricted to goods and services.[1]

Complicating this picture were the monopolistic attitudes of the members of all the Yąnomamö villages. Each group wanted me to visit them and only them and resented the fact that I took possessions to other Yąnomamö. They made no attempt to conceal this attitude. They publicly defended and justified their desires by accusing their neighbors of chicane and thievery, in some cases while visitors from the villages so denounced were actually present. "*Bä noshi ömabou*!" they would say to me—"We want you all to ourselves!"

Finally, there was a characteristic pattern regarding the relationship between me, trade goods, and the members of any given village. At first contact with the new village I would bring a quantity of assorted trade goods for the known leaders and important men in the village. In this I followed Yąnomamö precedent. Thus I established a basis for additional friendly visits and could begin productive work

[1] The Yąnomamö knew I had a daughter, for my family spent three weeks with me in Bisaasi-teri in 1965. Many of the Bisaasi-teri men seriously proposed that I "give" my daughter to one of them.

in the village. With each subsequent visit the expectation of trade goods increased as more and more men made requests that could not be ignored.[2] The general relutance to cooperate with me unless the flow of trade goods went directly to individuals also increased.[3]

Requests for trade goods would, initially, be reasonable, somewhat hesitant, and only moderately passioned: "Shoriwä! I am poor and in need! Give me a machete so I can clear a garden!" With time, the requests increased in frequency and urgency and would be appended with hints that friendly behavior might be withheld unless the goods were given: "Shoriwä! Give me a machete and an axe! And be quick about it or I will be angry!" With some individuals the requests would evolve into demands with specific appended threats. In some cases, the threats would be relatively transparent and easy to ignore, as from a boisterous sixteen-year-old youth who is merely emulating tougher people: "Shori! Give me your knife or I'll hit you with this stick!" In other cases, they came from mature men with established reputations for doing what they threatened. These requests were not easily ignored and could not be taken lightly.

The Shamatari, among whom most of my most recent fieldwork was concentrated, were known to be notorious for the extravagance and sharpness of their demands, and not a few Yąnomamö who had occasion to trade with them complained about it. For my own part, I found this chronic pecking and demanding of *madohe* very depressing, and increasingly difficult to live with as time wore on.

In brief, my acceptance in villages hinged very largely on the quantity and kind of goods I dispensed, as did the amount of cooperation I could expect. There were always a few individuals who became good friends and informants, but it would be folly to assume that this was completely independent of the possessions they acquired by so doing. With few exceptions—Kąobawä and Rerebawä being the most notable—my "acceptance" among the Yąnomamö was a function of

[2] There is a general escalation in quantity of goods requested in all villages that I have repeatedly visited over several years. My anthropological fieldwork can be accomplished with relatively small quantities of goods. However, I was associated with a multidisciplinary study that involved the interests and research of many other people, a study that by nature required that maximum data and samples be collected from each village in the shortest amount of time possible. One of my responsibilities to my colleagues was to insure that this in fact happened. One unfortunate consequence for my continuing anthropological interest in many of the villages was that I was identified by the Yąnomamö as an inexhaustible fount of goods. Thus, to assure the complete cooperation of entire villages for some of our studies I had to give goods to men, women, and children. The positive effect was that the "team" could visit villages like Mishimishimaböwei-teri with me and in three days have all the material and data they came for. The negative effect was that all my subsequent visits to this village were disappointments to the Yąnomamö because I did not come with equivalent quantities of goods.

[3] One example of how Yąnomamö attitudes affected my personal behavior in my own culture regarding direct compensation to individuals from which I requested favors happened in Caracas and was very embarrassing for me. I was walking with my friend and colleague, Professor Jose María Cruxent. I wanted to have a photograph taken with both of us in it, and I asked a small, passing boy if he would be so kind as to push the button on my camera as he pointed it in our general direction. He was startled by the request and taken aback. Then I unwittingly blurted, in Spanish, exactly what a Yąnomamö would say to me or I to him under the same circumstances: "Te pago." A rough English translation is "I will pay you." As soon as it came out I knew it didn't sound the same in Spanish or English as it did in Yąnomamö, and Professor Cruxent delicately chided me for being "... very Yankee." The fact is that I was being very Yąnomamö.

material possessions. To be sure, my fluency in their language was amusing and interesting for them and this had some appeal and attraction, but cooperation was almost always determined by possessions. A deaf-mute who generously disposed of large quantities of desirable items would have been more appealing and attractive.

More than the depressing constancy of giving goods and withholding them as each situation developed, the threats are what ultimately wore me down. I particularly disliked threats to my life. My study of the Shamatari groups began with threats to my life and ended that way.

My increasing intolerance of these threats made me realize that I was reaching the point where my reactions would no longer be dominated by the values and precepts developed in my anthropological training, and that I might respond to them either as a Yanomamö would respond, or as I might respond in my own society under similar circumstances when threatened by a fellow citizen. I became aware of and alarmed by the very real possibility that my remaining research objectives among the Shamatari would require, say, four additional months of fieldwork but my ability to contain my growing intolerance of the threats might not last more than three.

This problem actually began emerging two field trips prior to 1972, when I began having serious difficulties with Möawä, one of the headmen of Mishimishimaböweiteri. The study of his village was central to the final objectives I had elected to pursue, and it became increasingly apparent that success would depend very heavily on how I got along with him. Möawä was the silent, intense young man whose entry into the village on the occasion of my first visit brought a hushed and uneasy suspense over the village equal only to that Sibarariwä caused by his arrival an hour or so later (see Chapter 1).

Möawä, more than any other Yanomamö I have known, was the archetypical expression of his culture's values and political ideals. He was fierce, a man of great personal courage and renown, strong, an excellent marksman, and forceful to the point of awesomeness. He took what he wanted when he wanted it, and scorned those who would pretend to impose their will on him. People feared him because he was capable of great violence and expressed it unhesitatingly. But people also looked up to him, if they were not his competitors, and did what he demanded of them. He was a man of his word, and when he spoke or commanded, people listened and obeyed. When he threatened, everyone knew he meant what he said. Because of his forceful bearing and abilities, he was able to attract a large following and hold it together. His enemies despised him, but they feared him as well. Life for the obedient in his village was secure and relatively happy, but for the competitor or politically ambitious, it was dangerous and strained. Competitors did not last long as coresidents, for Möawä's overbearing manner led to disputes and fights, and his competitors—mostly agnates—sooner or later packed up and left. At least three of his agantes—Sibarariwä, Nanokawä, and Reirowä—were very much like him, but not nearly so able or successful. There was a long history of their joining and leaving Möawä's village in recent years, a process of fusion and fission that hinged on how well they got along with Möawä.

My relationships to the village at large were largely predicated on my specific relationships to Möawä and his father-in-law, Dedeheiwä. Möawä called me "older brother" (*abawä*) and Dedeheiwä called me "brother-in-law (*shoriwä*), and in uncanny fashion, my realtionships to these men as implied in our mutual kinship usage was very characteristic. My relationships with Möawä were fairly cold and strained, but with Dedeheiwä, friendly, relaxed and easy-going.

Creating a situation unlike any other in my field experience, Möawä was a man that I almost never used as an informant but a man whom I could not, even with deliberate attempts, avoid. He watched me constantly and demanded that I sleep in his house, right next to his hammock. It was clear from the outset that he would permit no other way, and to force the issue would have precipitated a premature crisis. Indeed, toward the end, virtually every conversation or social situation was of the nature of a crisis.

Möawä was used to having his own way. After the first two visits to his village, each suggestion or request he made was a demand and had no alternative.[4] The longer I studied his group, the more blatant and excessive were the requests and demands he placed on me. My relationship to him, in response, was one of attempted avoidance and very calculated compromises that were geared to satisfy the substance of his request, but to indicate in a delicate way that there was a point beyond which I could not or would not go, at least on that occasion. Möawä was no different than other Yąnomamö insofar as his requests and demands went. What *was* different was that I felt that the probability of his doing something violent if disappointed was very much higher because of his reputation and ability. An invisible constant friction developed between us, a kind of war of nerves that had only one logical conclusion. It was a personal, undeclared contest that I knew from the outset I would ultimately lose. All I wanted was to buy time in order to satisfy my curiosity about his village and collect the data I felt were required to adequately describe the political history, genealogical ties, and demography of this and adjacent groups. To buy that time I gave in, inch by inch, to his icy and forceful requests. Each year I could feel myself losing ground and heading for a confrontation with him that I wished to avoid; in 1972 I knew, the first day I arrived, that it would be my last visit to his village for a long time—perhaps forever. Let me recount, briefly, how this situation developed and cite some examples.

From 1968 to 1970 I was able to conduct my study in Mishimishimaböwei-teri with a tolerable degree of success and a tolerable but gradually accelerating feeling

[4] Like all headmen, Möawä carefully weighed his requests and rarely made one that did not turn out the way he wanted it to. I was at first startled and then very intrigued by this consistent pattern among headmen, since it took consummate skill and ability to size up each situation, day after day, and consistently appear to have ones' orders followed and requests satisfied. Kąobawä was very accomplished at this and, in his dealings with me was very gracious and polite. Should there be any doubt in his mind that I might deny a request, it was never made in such a way that he asked for something and I refused. He would indicate, for example, that one of his friends from a distant village arrived to visit and needed a machete, but he had none to give the man. Then he would pause, look at me and say something like: "Dearest nephew, do you not have one lying around that you are not using?" It worked every time. Möawä, on the other hand, would exercise a different style, one that was harsher. He would say: "Older brother! Give that man your machete! Do not be stingy with your possessions!"

of strain with Möawä. During this time I worked extensively with Dedeheiwä, with whom I was from the start on excellent terms. In 1970, the third time I lived in Mishimishimaböwei-teri, Möawä's patience began to grow thin and he came to the point sooner than he had on previous trips: "Distribute all of your goods and leave—but come back soon with more!" I was welcome in the village only so long as I had desirable items to give, or rather, to give to Möawä. This I understood and had long since learned to live with. The delicate task was to dribble the goods out in sufficient quantities so that he was temporarily satisfied, and then give everything away to the others when it looked as though impatience would dissolve into anger. I tried to pace myself and nurse the situation along until it was time for me to leave the village, so that my distribution of goods came at a time when I had no more work projected and, therefore, required no further cooperation. The distribution of goods would always anger people who did not receive something they wanted, and it was useless to try to work any longer in the village.

Möawä was constantly manipulating the status-establishing mechanisms, turning every conversation or personal interaction into a kind of Little-League contest to see if he could browbeat me into a new promise or to show me and the village where we both stood. One annoying habit he fell into was to wait until a lesser individual made some request that I refused, and then immediately make the same demand. He seemed to seek out these opportunities, no matter how small and insignificant they were. It began with my water supply. People would sit around my hut watching me work, and periodically see what my reaction would be to a request for water. Nobody was thirsty, everybody had water, and the stream was just a few yards away. It was a pretext to test the status of individuals. I usually refused to give drinks, not because water was scarce and valuable, but because I knew that after the water came the food, then the machetes, then the hammock, then the clothing off my back, and so on. Möawä had the frustrating habit of waiting for me to refuse a drink to someone, then coming over to me and asking not only for a drink, but for my cup from which to drink. Now, it seems irrational, *even to me*, but tiny events like these took on enormous proportions in the field, and after three years grew almost intolerable because they were chronic.

My first and sudden awareness of how unpleasant Möawä was, how selfish and self-centered, came in 1970 on the first day of my visit during that field season. I always brought with me tubes of antibiotic eye ointment when I visited remote villages, and made a point to check each child's eyes, treating those whose eyes were infected. When I left the village, I gave the surplus antibiotic to selected adults around the village for future use. Eye infections are very common among babies and cause great discomfort for months. Adults occasionally get the same infection, and the eye ointment was a welcome relief because it invariably cured the infections within a day or so.

On the occasion of this visit, Möawä had infected eyes and asked me to "cure" him. I did, and immediately the others began scurrying home to fetch their children. I began putting ointment into the children's eyes, whereupon Möawä gave a cursory, authoritative order and everybody scattered: "Get the hell out

Figure 5.1—Möawä didn't care if all the children went blind: the tetracycline eye-ointment would all belong to him, as would the soda-crackers I gave the children.

of here! That medicine is mine!" He demanded *all* of the ointment I had. At first, I thought he was joking, and I told him I was going to cure all the children first and then give the adults the surplus tubes so they could cure the children after I was gone. He was unflinching: he said he didn't care about the others or if they went blind, and he forbade me to give the medicine to anybody but him. He wanted it *all* for himself. I gave him several tubes, but I saved a few tubes for my final day in the village when I gave them to more responsible men for their families.

My reaction to Möawä's stinginess and cruel lack of concern for others in the village was *not just my appraisal* of the situation. The Yąnomamö themselves felt the same way. Like parents everywhere, they are saddened when their children are sick and anguished when there is no cure for the illness. They knew that the tubes of tetracycline ointment would cure their children, and were bitter when Möawä demanded it all for himself. "Let them all go blind!" he bellowed, "This medicine is for me." The others in the village had no choice because he was the headman, and if they defied him and demanded the medicine, it could have led to confrontations. I therefore took the initiative to save them the trouble. This raises the issue of whether or not the fieldworker should do what he thinks is "right" under the circumstances and defy the "native system" by curing the sickness and making sure that everyone is cured. Or, not meddle in the "native system" and let one particularly selfish tyrant take all of the medicine while the others suffer for months. In this case, 99 percent of the population was delighted with my decision and benefited from it. I did not "destroy" or "undermine" the local authority, for it was not predicated on grounds so shifty that a few tubes of tetracycline would topple it.[5]

On another occasion I visited his village to find that everyone was out of tobacco and in great need; their crop had been eaten by insects and burned by a long spell of hot weather. I made a special trip down river to get them tobacco: it took a one-day walk out to my canoe, two days by canoe downstream, one day to trade for tobacco in villages there, two more days to ascend the Mavaca, and one more day to walk back into the village with the tobacco. When I began distributing the tobacco to the residents of the village, Möawä angrily put a stop to the distribution and demanded that I give *all* of it to him. I knew by this time that he would not share it, no matter how desperate the others might be for tobacco. I managed to give substantial bundles to a number of the more prominent men in the village, men who *would* distribute it further among their relations. I had reserved the largest portion of all for Möawä, but he was unflinching in his demand. So I gave all of the remainder to him, but he was nevertheless insulted that I had not given him the entire supply. For the next several days numerous individuals approached me to beg for tobacco that I might have hidden in my pack somewhere, but I had no more. Most of these people were very close relatives of Möawä, and I referred them to him for tobacco. They invariably scoffed and whispered that he was stingy, and would not think of sharing his tobacco with them; there was no need to bother to ask, because he would only get angry.

On another occasion I had three triangular files with me. I intended to give one each to Möawä and Dedeheiwä and to keep the third one to loan to anybody who wanted to sharpen his machete. As soon as Möawä learned of the three files, he immediately demanded them. Seeing that it would lead to a disagreement, I immediately gave one of them to old Dedeheiwä, to whom I had promised it, and one to Möawä, explaining to him and the others that the reamining one was mine, but I would loan it to anybody who wanted to use it, and on leaving, would give it away. He immediately "borrowed" it to sharpen his machete, and then announced with no small amount of authority in his voice: "This file, also,

[5] There are, no doubt, some anthropologists who would argue that what I did was, from purist grounds, morally reprehensible. I have heard such arguments made in other contexts. I am always impressed with the fact that the purists who point their moral fingers at others did their fieldwork in a library or in a place where all the conveniences of modern technology and medicine were readily available to themselves and the people among whom they lived. I do not consider it morally reprehensible to cure sickness, even at the expense of reducing my rapport with a village headman.

Figure 5.2—The happy children who collected around my section of the shabano were a welcomed contrast to the grim world of adults.

belongs to me!" I never saw it again, nor did anybody except Möawä have access to it. Similar incidents developed around hallucinogenic seeds (*hịsiomö*) whenever I brought them to the village to distribute among the prominent shamans. Möawä always demanded all of them, and I was obliged to give portions away clandestinely to others before he discovered that I had them, knowing that he would claim them all and refuse to share them fairly, if at all.

When I lived in Möawä's village I had a horde of cheerful, happy, and eager children in my house most of the day. They were a welcomed contrast to the often strained life in the adult world. They became very fond of my soda crackers or other tidbits. I would have them wash my dishes in the stream and "pay" them with crackers. They enjoyed this and took turns. No matter who actually washed the dishes or carried the water, they all shared in the crackers and we were all quite pleased with the arrangement. After several days of this on one of my trips, Möawä rose suddenly from his hammock and angrily chased all of the kids away with angry threats, pelting them with hard fruit seeds. He then turned to me and hissed: "If you have any crackers to give away, give them to me. The crackers shall be mine from now on, and don't you ever give any crackers to the brats." Möawä, too, had grown fond of crackers and my other food, and I always gave him a share of every meal I prepared. He demanded more.

Things came to a head in 1972, but to understand the intensity of my reaction to Möawä on that field trip it is necessary to understand, first, the nature of my contacts with the Iwahikoroba-teri, a village some two and a half days by trail to the northeast of Möawä's village.

FIRST CONTACT WITH IWAHIKOROBA-TERI

I contacted Möawä's village in 1968; my plan was to then contact the Iwahikoroba-teri, whom I knew from genealogical composition and political history to be closely related to Möawä's group. The Iwahikoroba-teri were very much despised by the Bisassi-teri, Ka̧obawä's people, for their treachery in 1950, when they killed many of the visiting Bisaasi-teri during a feast. Members of Möawä's village participated in that treachery, but the Bisaasi-teri were able to ignore these men as individuals when they developed friendly ties with Möawä's group again in 1970 (see film *Magical Death*). The Iwahikoroba-teri had heard about me through the Patanowä-teri and through Möawä's group, and word reached me that they were very angry because I had not visited them yet and had "denied" them trade goods that I so freely gave to other Ya̧nomamö. I had planned to contact them in 1969, but it did not work out. By 1970 there were ugly rumors that the Iwahikoroba-teri were so angry with me for not visiting them that they were going to kill me should I dare to come. On hearing these rumors in 1970, I decided to postpone making contact with them that year and sent a message to them that I was angry at their threats and would only come to their village if they agreed to treat me fairly and receive me in friendship. The Mishimishimaböwei-teri, although "allies" of the Iwahikoroba-teri, spoke very harshly about them—their agnates—and assured me that the threats to my safety were real. They told me that the Iwahikoroba-teri had also accused me of practicing harmful magic against them, and would kill me on sight for the deaths I had allegedly caused in their village with my *oka* magic.[6]

I spoke privately to Dedeheiwä about these accusations. While acknowledging that they were true, the astute old man also told me that the Iwahikoroba-teri headman, Börösöwä, would probably allow me to visit if I went there with him. Others in the village wanted to kill me, but Börösöwä was stronger than they. He agreed to discuss my visit with Börösöwä, so I delayed my scheduled attempt to contact the Iwahikoroba-teri in 1970 at Dedeheiwä's urging. I asked the Mishimishimaböwei-teri, publicly, to reassure the Iwahikoroba-teri that I did not practice magic against them or any other Ya̧nomamö, and that I wanted to visit them the following year but would not do so until their attitudes modified.

That year a number of Bisaasi-teri visited Möawä's village. They were camped, along with people from Möawä's group, somewhere between Iwahikoroba-teri and

[6] "*Oka*" is magic blown through tubes from a distance. I have never met a Ya̧nomamö who could demonstrate how it is done, but all are convinced that their enemies do it. See 16mm films, *The Ya̧nomamö Myth of Naro (Opossum) As Told by Ka̧obawä* and The *Ya̧nomamö Myth of Naro (Opossum) As Told by Dedeheiwä* (Chagnon and Asch, n.d.); the origin of "*oka*" magic is dealt with in the beginning of this myth.

Mishimishimaböwei-teri. A party of Iwahikoroba-teri hunters accidentally stumbled into their camp: thus, mortal enemies met eye to eye for the first time in many years. The Bisaasi-teri men were guests of the Mishimishimaböwei-teri, so the Iwahikoroba-teri were obliged to either ignore them or befriend them. They chose the latter course and set about exchanging whatever items they had with them at the time—bows, arrows, decorations, and so on. Koaseedema, one of the Bisaasi-teri men involved in the exchanges, gave the hunters his dog. He was invited to visit their village in the future to collect payment for the dog.

In 1971 I was told of this meeting, and decided to try to make contact with the Iwahikoroba-teri. Hubemi, an old woman in Bisaasi-teri who had been abducted from the Iwahikoroba-teri ancestors many years earlier, begged me to take her along when I went to make first contact with them. She wanted to see her brother, a man she had not seen in some forty years. Her son, one of Kạobawä's younger brothers, and another man volunteered to come along with Hubemi and me. Thus, I had three companions.

The man who had ceded his dog to the Iwahikoroba-teri the previous year had described in detail, once he got home, the precise location of the village, and my guides were confident that we could find it. The Bisaasi-teri had raided the Iwahikoroba-teri in that very area many years earlier, and remembered the streams and hills by name.

We left for the village, going by boat for one day and then walking inland in an easterly direction. There were no trails and after two days of wandering through dense thickets and swamps, we turned back: Hubemi and her son had gotten diarrhea and were not able to go on. In addition, my medical colleagues from the University of Michigan and from I.V.I.C. were scheduled to arrive soon, and at the rate I was going, there would not have been time to reach the Iwahikoroba-teri and get back to meet my colleagues at the savanna, where their plane would land. Knowing that bug-infested savanna and those colleagues, I knew that they would not be happy if they had to wait there for me several days while I wandered through the jungle looking for an uncontacted village.

For the next several weeks I participated in the annual medical studies with my colleagues in the Ocamo River basin. Then most of them left by light plane to visit a group of Yạnomamö in the savannas of the Parima "mountains," and I took one of them to Mishimishimaböwei-teri to collect samples from about sixty individuals who were not living there in 1969, when I brought the same colleagues to Möawä's village to collect blood samples. The Shamatari population was of considerable interest to them because of the amount of time I had spent studying it and the large quantities of demographic, genealogical, and political history data I had on the various villages. Ryk Ward, the geneticist who was to come with me was young, robust, and competent in jungle living, and wanted very much to come with me to Iwahikoroba-teri, which, with luck, would result in additional blood samples for a study that he was doing on migration matrices and gene frequencies. I had hoped to contact the Iwahikoroba-teri alone, accomplish my anthropological objectives, and then determine if it was feasible to bring my medical colleagues into the village to collect samples. My failure to make the contact when the old woman and I tried a few weeks earlier put me in the undesirable position of first contacting them accompanied by a medical colleague and drawing blood samples on the occasion of the first contact. I did not exactly relish the prospects of arriving at a village of particularly notorious Yąnomamö who were threatening to kill me because I allegedly practiced harmful magic against them, and immediately setting to work sticking needles into their arms. The Iwahikoroba-teri were, of course, aware that I often took other foreigners to visit Yąnomamö villages, foreigners who both cured illnesses and took blood samples. Still, I was very uneasy because of the threats to my life and their advertised conviction that I was practicing magic against them.

I agreed to bring my colleague into Iwahikoroba-teri, but insisted that I would play it by ear regarding the blood samples. There were two possible ways of making the contact. One was to go first to Möawä's village and try to persuade men of his group to take us into Iwahikoroba-teri via a known and frequently-used trail, and return the same way, stopping on the way back to collect the sixty samples in Möawä's village. The other was to take guides from Bisaasi-teri and attempt to contact Iwahikoroba-teri by following the same general route I had taken a few weeks earlier, when the old woman was along. After thinking it over, I elected to follow the latter alternative, suspecting that the Mishimishimaböwei-teri would attempt to prevent my going to the distant village to bring trade goods to the Iwahikoroba-teri that they themselves might otherwise have.

I knew that several Bisaasi-teri would go along with me, and I was delighted when Koaseedema, the man who had given the dog, agreed to come. Back in 1968, not a single soul from Bisaasi-teri would even consider coming to Möawä's village with me. Thus, in February 1971, I set off for Iwahikoroba-teri with my geneticist colleague and four Bisaasi-teri guides, including Rerebawä. As before, we wandered through thickets and swamps for two days. Finally, and with some excitement, Koaseedema announced that he knew where we were: we found an abandoned hut, which he claimed was approximately halfway between Iwahikoroba-teri and Mishimishimaböwei-teri. We found a trail that was used regularly, and then we knew that we were on the right track.

On the third day's march I began reacting violently to an insect bite, or a toxic plant, or wild food that I had eaten. Large red welts appeared all over my body, I grew weak, nauseated, and developed diarrhea. That night when we camped, my thirst became unquenchable, the itching and welts almost unbearable, and I grew so weak that I could not stagger out of my hammock the few feet to the stream to get water. From time to time I had difficulty breathing, and was growing very alarmed about my condition. I knew how important these particular blood samples were to my colleague, so I agreed to continue on toward the village rather than turn back, as I should have. At dawn I was too weak to get out of my hammock and I dozed in a fitful sleep, awakening every half hour or so when the itching and welts, which appeared in cycles, rhythmically reached their peak of intensity.

About 9:00 A.M. I was awakened by a noise in the jungle not far from our hut. It was a group of Iwahikoroba-teri hunters after wild turkeys. My guides began whispering excitedly, undecided as to whether we should signal to them. I finally gave a weak shout, and several hunters came over to our temporary hut. They stood there silently, after having been informed by the shouts of my guides that "we were *all* a bunch of foreigners, all very friendly!" They recognized Koaseedema and asked him if I were Shaki, to which he grunted affirmatively. They stared at me. I was not a very impressive sight, covered with large red welts, and too weak to get out of my hammock. I told them I was sick and that the guides were tired. I asked them to go to the village and get help to carry the packs. They turned silently and disappeared into the jungle. I then fell into an uneasy sleep, interrupted from time to time by periods of itching that were so intense that I had to bite my tongue to keep from screaming.

After what seemed an eternity, I heard shouts and we were shortly surrounded by about twenty-five young men, all with large wads of tobacco protruding from their lower lips, all nervously clutching their bows and upright arrows. It was about noon. They stared at me for some time, until I finally asked them to take up the packs and start for the village.

I learned from them that they were not living in their village, but in a temporary camp about three hours' walk from where we made our present camp. Their camp was close enough to their village so that they could easily return to fetch plantains, and abundant supplies of them were hanging in the hut rafters.

We reached their camp shortly before dusk. The walk was slow and painful, and I had to rest many times. Once I actually fell asleep for a few minutes.

We approached the periphery of the clearing at about 4:00 P.M. The carriers and guides stepped aside after signaling our approach and motioned for Ryk and me to go in first. It was one of the most unusual entries I have ever made. The villagers were afraid and not certain what to do, so at first they did not shout and growl the customary greetings, but stood nervously at a distance, silently clutching their bows and arrows, staring at us. Finally, a few of the oldest men, remembering the customary protocol, approached me cautiously and began growling and shouting their greetings, nervously intimidating me with their bows and arrows. I had enough presence of mind to switch on my small tape recorder, and on seeing this, Ryk took a few hasty photos. They eyed us suspiciously and continued to greet us. Dokonawä, one of the older men in the group, approached me carefully and began to speak softly to me, in whispers, his bow and arrows at rest. He welcomed me. I remember being surprised that they knew which of the two of us was Shaki. I asked him where I was to set up my hammock, for I was anxious to lie down, irrespective of the breach of visitor etiquette this might represent. They seemed to be collectively relieved when I spoke, and in the distance, I saw several young men clack their arrows sharply against the roof of a small hut in which a surprisingly young but obviously authoritative man lay motionless, watching me. He had the poise and demeanor of a headman and strong leader. It was Börösöwä, the man Dedehiwä had said would tolerate my visit.

I walked over and sat in the hammock next to his. The others with me followed, and as there was no room, squatted on their haunches. I asked Börösöwä if we could have a hut that would be large enough to hold us all, and he pointed to the one a few yards away. This hut also proved to be too small, and in a now comic breach of etiquette, I got up once more and asked Börösöwä if he would have a larger hut made for us, next to his. When I addressed him, I called him

Figure 5.3—Börösöwä—Iwahikoroba-teri headman. He guaranteed my safe passage against the wishes of Borahiwä and his brothers.

"*shoriwa,*" to which he responded indignantly: "You are to call me 'younger brother,' and I will address you as 'elder brother'!" The indignation was artificial. He had obviously learned what my relationship was to Möawä, and since Möawä was his "brother," I therefore had to be a brother as well. I assumed this usage, choosing the endearing term "*ǫwas*" to indicate affection. At this, a chorus of tongue-clicks responded with their approval. He then commanded a number of young men to build me a hut. They scurried out, carrying with them an extremely dull and badly worn machete of a type that I had seen only in Brazil: their steel tools came from Brazilian villages via a long trading network.

The young men soon reappeared and began chopping on the poles they had collected. I was dozing in my hammock, half delirious with rash and hives, and I heard one of my guides chuckle to himself about how clumsy they were with the one dull machete they were all using. When they finished the frame, we put up the nylon tarp we brought with us, and retired. My guides had built a roaring fire in the hut, and I recall how hot it was as I fell asleep, too weak to move my hammock or ask them to move the fire. Before falling asleep, I told some of the Iwahikoroba-teri that I would "*nohimou*" (make friends) with everyone in the morning.

The next morning my condition had not changed appreciably and I only vaguely remember the events: 15 minutes of work, rest 15 minutes; more work, more rest. I tried to use the genealogies I had spent years collecting, but as luck would have it, the husband of the second person on the list had been killed by Bisassi-teri raiders only a few weeks before my visit, and the Iwahikoroba-teri were very angry that I knew their names.

They were willing to allow Ryk to take blood samples. My task was to identify the individuals and relate them to the genealogies I had collected from numerous informants in several other villages. The most certain way to accomplish that was to use their true names, having the individual come as he was called, along with his family. But because I had unfortunately hit upon the name of a recently deceased man, their strong reaction precluded further attempts along this line. The only alternative was to ink numbers on their arms or chests with an indelible felt pen, photograph them with a Polaroid and a 35mm camera, and mark the identification number on the blood sample test tube. By showing the photographs to informants in Mishimishimaböwei-teri I could later relate the temporary identifications I painted on their chests and arms to the identifications in my computer printout.

It was a nightmare, and I can only vaguely recall what happened. My vision, because of the fever, was almost as blurry as the Polaroid photographs. I recall staggering from my hammock, attempting to look well to them, but having to stagger back. I knew they detected my sickness and could see how weak I was. The medicine I took for the rash seemed to affect my sense of time and perception and everything was fuzzy and blurry, almost unreal in the dull light and shadowless camp. Everything seemed to move slowly and grow vague unless I stared hard at it. The sounds also lacked form or sharpness and droned on and on. I was desperate to make my writing legible; my hands trembled as I wrote the black numbers on perspiring skin, and they seemed unstable when I pressed the shutter of my camera, and my arms felt like lead when I pointed them over to Ryk. I collapsed into my hammock to rest before attempting to number more of them, and gradually began to care less and less of what I knew they must be thinking: someone had blown charms on me and therefore I was as vulnerable as they. I desperately wanted to appear strong and healthy, but it was no use. I had even lost the will to try, and I shuddered to think about how far away my canoe was and worried whether I could make it back there. Then I would try extra hard and manage to get up to my feet and number another family. Thankfully, I could do that faster than Ryk could take blood samples. And, thankfully, the work came to an end: I had run out of people to number. Ryk ran out of test tubes on the 130th person, but I had numbered over 150 bodies and had probably missed another twenty more.

My companions from Bisaasi-teri told me that the sickness I had was caused by *Hekura*—they had sprinkled red coals on my skin and the welts and hives were really burns. I fell asleep pondering that theory, which had a certain logical appeal.

My itching and nausea seemed to have subsided during my early fitful sleep, and I woke up periodically when the welts appeared and disappeared in monotonous cycles, feeling a little better each time. I shone my flash around the village every time I awakened, to make sure that the whole thing was not just a dream and that I was still in a real world. The piercing beam of light would fall on sleeping people, who would look ghastly white against the blue smoke that filtered through all of the huts, irregularly scattered over a half acre of lumpy terrain. Some would awaken suddenly when the light hit their faces, and they would wince at its intensity, of a starkness and brightness they had never seen before. I shone it around to see if my companions were still where I had last seen them, and then shone it all around the village quickly, communicating that I was *moyawe*—alert. I had known my guides to do this, and understood why they did. I learned about a year later that my flashlight saved our lives.

Dedeheiwä related the following account to Rerebawä the next year, and he, in turn, told me. I recall this conversation vividly, and probably always will for the rest of my life. It was like a premature look at eternity. "*Aba*!" He always began a serious conversation by the endearing term for older brother. "Listen carefuly. The one with the white beard in Mishimishimaböwei-teri visited here while you were gone and told me this, and urged me to pass it on to you." He was talking in low whispers now, as he did when it was very serious, as if to make me listen harder. It was his equivalent to alphabetizing information and making the recipient think about each word. "He told me to tell you that you should not try to return to Iwahikoroba-teri again as you planned. Boraböwä and his two brothers will try to kill you again! Also, Tananowä has vowed to kill you if you should set foot in his village!"

I was listening intently now, and I asked him to repeat Dedeheiwä's conversation word for word; it still came out the same way. "What do you mean 'try to kill you again'?" This puzzled and alarmed me. He brought his face closer to mine and continued, taking the tobacco out of his mouth so I would hear more clearly. "While we were there last year, when the bird *Hekura* sprinkled hot coals on your skin and you had those welts all over your body, Boraböwä almost killed you." I felt myself grow weak all over, and began trembling a little. "What did he do?" I asked quietly, somewhat annoyed with myself that I had failed to detect the danger when it had been most critical, having to admit that my sense of awareness was not as keen as I had tried to convince myself it was. He continued, whispering softly, but deliberately searching my eyes to make sure he saw my awareness. "The second night we were there and after everyone was sleeping, Boraböwä and two of his brothers crept up close to your hammock.

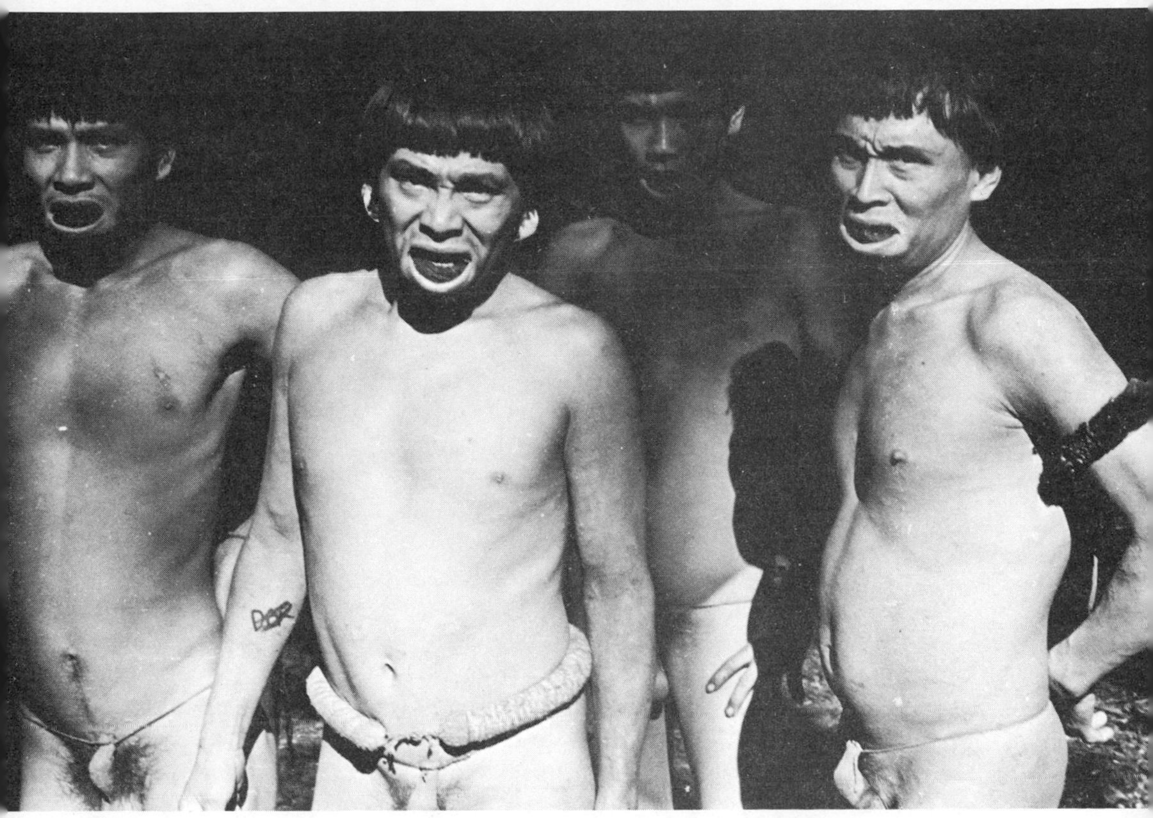

Figure 5.4—They were approaching my hammock, armed with axes, intending to crush my skull. When they saw my flashlight, they knew I was awake and they turned back. When Rerebawä told me what Boraböwä (second from left) and his brothers (on either side) had attempted, it was like a grim, sobering look into eternity.

They thought you were sleeping, but suddenly you sat up and shined your *linterna* around the village, and they knew you were *moyawe*, that you were not sleeping. They knew you kept your shotgun close to your hammock, and they became frightened, so they turned back. All of them had axes, and they were going to crush your skull while you slept!" His final comment fell like an axe-blow itself, and I was so weakened from the information that I had to sit down. I thought about anthropology and professionalism, about obligation to science. But most I thought about my wife, my son and my daughter, and what all this meant to them. My *buhii* had become not only cold, but my true me, my *bei kä möamo*, the the very center of me, was shaken badly. This is the part where all Yąnomamö fear to be shot, for the wounds are always mortal.

When we walked out of Iwahikoroba-teri, I recall that Börösöwä and his brother, Konasiwä, insisted on escorting me back to the boat. They were the two who apparently guaranteed my safe conduct.

My allergic reaction seemed to have ebbed almost as mysteriously as it had come upon me, and I felt no extraordinary fatigue or itchiness most of that day. "Where is this '*kanowä*' you ascended the river in?" asked Börösöwä, who had never seen a canoe before. "At the mouth of Jaguar River." I replied. Konasiwä knew a shortcut and discussed it with Börösöwä. "Bei! Let's go—it is getting late! The sun is almost up!" I nodded and walked out of the village, not looking back. We reached the canoe at dusk, traversing in one day what it had taken three days on the way in, three days of apparently serious wanderings away from the shortest route. But now we had fresh guides who knew the area, and we trotted most of the way, resting only infrequently.

I gave Börösöwä and his companions some twenty-five machetes to distribute in the village, earmarking one of them for Tananowä, the leader of a splinter group that I hoped to contact the following season.

We would have to travel all night in the canoe to make it to the airstrip downstream in time to get the blood samples on the plane. It was a dismal night; it began raining about 10:00 P.M. and we paddled for hours, trying to catch fitful naps in the incessant downpour. By 4:00 A.M. we were too exhausted to try to keep the canoe in the middle of the river, so we pulled it up on a sandbar and slept on the wet sand, in a cold drizzle, until it began to grow light again. The welts had all but disappeared by then. My last attack came as I fell asleep in the wet sand, and the swelling and hives were confined to my lips, where the abrasive action of the sand rubbed on them as I tried to wiggle into a more comfortable position in the cold drizzle. I left before dawn for the airstrip, reaching it some six hours later, only to learn that the airplane had been rescheduled for the following day, and that the forced march and canoe trip—nearly thirty hours long—was unnecessary. Unaware of the week's events, my medical colleagues were both surprised and disappointed to see me at the airstrip a week sooner than they anticipated, and in possession of only *half* of the blood samples I was expected to deliver. The undelivered half of the Shamatari blood samples had to wait for the following year, and again, very nearly cost me my life. Symptoms of danger appeared as soon as my recent fieldwork began, in February 1972.

I had advised my medical colleagues that to complete *my* study, I had to have four months of additional research among the Shamatari unencumbered by rigorous airplane schedules and the urgency to get perishable blood samples to point X at time Y. They would not join me in the field in 1972, but I agreed to bring the remaining Shamatari blood samples out.

MY LAST ASCENT OF THE MAVACA?

When I returned to the field in 1972, I was greeted by my friends at Bisaasi-teri who were not disappointed to know that the medical people were not coming, and that I would, accordingly spend much more of my time with them. They knew I would be taking a few trips to the Shamatari area, and they had learned to accept this as part of my irrational behavior. They had heard from Dedeheiwä of Mishimishimaböwei-teri that if I should try to return to Börösöwä's village or to make contact with Tananowä's splinter group I would surely be killed. Indeed, Tananowä, a man I had never seen, was so determined to kill me that during the context of a raid he organized earlier in the year, a raid that included my old friends, the Patanowä-teri (see 16mm film *The Feast*), he made a number of effigies of the individuals he most wanted to kill. One of them was of me. What annoyed me more than anything else was the fact that my friends the Patanowä-teri assisted in the ceremonial shooting of my effigy. It was small consolation when Rerebawä privately assured me that they did it only to please their allies, and "probably" did not really want to kill me. Irrationally, it seemed more acceptable to me to be shot by the Iwahikoroba-teri, a notorious Shamatari group whom I had never seen, than by the Patanowä-teri, whom I thought to be my friends.

I therefore decided that I was not going to attempt to contact Tananowä's village and was not going to visit Börösöwä's group again. At this point I had not yet heard about the nearly successful attempt on my life in Börösöwä's village the year before, and based my decision exclusively on the quality and content of the new rumors. How you separate rumors into categories is an art, not a science, a feeling that you learn by the seat of your pants, and one that you cannot teach to someone else.

This was to have been the year that I brought all of my census material up to date on the several Shamatari villages. The new, vigorous rumors immediately removed two of the six villages from the study. Two other Shamatari villages that I intended to visit, the Mọmariböwei-teri and Reyaboböwei-teri, I then learned, had entered into hostilities with each other and with some of their neighbors two months before I arrived, and each group had abandoned its village and had migrated far away. The Mọmariböwei-teri fled far to the west, to the banks of the Casiquiare Canal, where they hoped they could establish their first direct contacts with the foreign missionaries, and remove themselves from the wars and harassments they lived with to that point. The other village, Reyaboböwei-teri, was said to have migrated far to the south; to reach the area they were thought to be living in would have required walking for at least a week in one direction, and even then it was not certain they were living in that area. These events removed a third—and perhaps a fourth—village from my list of six that I was determined to visit on this field trip.

Early in my 1972 trip I visited the Mọmariböwei-teri on the banks of the Casiquiare Canal, but only a fraction of them were there, living in temporary smoky huts, in one of the worst mosquito-infested swamps I have ever visited. They told me about the contact they had just established with the missionaries, and how they were going to become "Christians," give up tobacco, drugs, and multiple spouses. They had just collectively been advised that all of this was "sin," they explained, and they wanted nothing more to do with "sin." They were going to stay there in that swamp and be fed and clothed by the people from God's village until their gardens began producing; they were going to learn to sing and be happy.

They looked helpless and pathetic, emaciated from their long migration through the mountains and then the swamps, dwarfed in the tattered clothing that the missionaries gave them, swatting incessantly at the mosquitoes with which they had chosen to live, free from sin. They were only a mere shadow of the people

Figure 5.5—Shiitawä, headman of Mǫmariböwei-teri before learning of sin. He had one of the most magnificent shabonos I have seen, and now he lives in a mosquito-infested swamp.

who greeted me boisterously in their magnificent, airy, and mosquito-free *shabono* deep in the jungle a few years earlier, a soverign people, strong and confident. I went through the necessary motions of counting them again and asking Shiitawä, their aging leader and old friend, a list of previously drafted questions that he, because of his genealogical ties, age, wisdom, and experience was in a position to answer. I left, feeling very discouraged at what I had seen and what I knew was happening to them, and what soon, would happen to Möawä and his people.

That left just two villages of the six I wanted to visit. One of these was Möawä's village, the one for which my data on census and composition were the most recent and most complete. The other was Sibarariwä's village, which lay only a few hours walk beyond Möawä's, and although I had never visited it, I knew almost everyone there. I had very detailed information on the composition of his village. But I had to go there to map it and collect additional information on kinship usage.

To get to Sibarariwä's village I had to pass through Möawä's. My plan was to collect the blood samples in the farthest group, after mapping their village and completing the rest of my scheduled work there, and take the samples downstream to the airstrip for shipment out to Caracas in a light plane I had hired and scheduled for a specific date. Then I would return to Möawä's village and spend a few weeks or so there, filling in details and missing information in already prepared printouts developed out of the previous year's work. I was short of trade items because I could not get everything into the light plane that originally flew me into the area; I left machetes and other items behind to make room in the plane for a dear friend of mine, Padre Luiz Cocco, a Salesian missionary, and two Yąnomamö boys he had taken out to Caracas for medical attention. My machetes would be brought in on the plane that came to pick up the blood samples, and I intended to bring some of these to Möawä's village on my return trip. Thus, when I set out for Sibarariwä's village to collect the blood samples, I had just barely enough trade goods to gain the cooperation of the members of that group.

Rerebawä came with me, as he often did, when I visited the Mishimishimaböwei-teri. He, too, was fond of Dedeheiwä—"white beard" he called him—and enjoyed participating in and watching the skillful, dramatic performances that took place daily in his village. Rerebawä told me, the year before, that he wanted to learn to be *Hekura* from Dedeheiwä, and that the old man had promised to teach him: "White beard knows the *Hekura* and the truth about them. *Wadubariwä* actually lives in his chest. He promised to give me some of his *Hekura* when I come to his village again."

After two days of canoe travel, we reached the point on the Mavaca where we had to begin walking inland to the village. We coincidentally bumped into a number of Mishimishimaböwei-teri who were returning from Iwahikoroba-teri, where they had just traded and participated in a feast. The feast also included a large group of visitors from Yeisikorowä-teri, the remote and yet-uncontatced Shamatari village that lay several days to the south of Mishimishimaböwei-teri—the people to whom the Mishimishimaböwei-teri had denied their agnatic kinship ties. I had missed meeting them but to have met them meant going to Iwahikoroba-teri.

I asked the passing men to inform Möawä and Dedeheiwä of my plans, and that I intended to "live" with them after I collected the blood samples from Sibarariwä and his group. They agreed to carry this information home and said they would send young men to carry our equipment, for there was more than Rerebawä and I could handle by ourselves.

The Mishimishimaböwei-teri were always happy to see me each year, and when I arrived, many of them came down to the river to greet me, a five-hour walk in sloppy weather, a three-hour trot in good weather. At dusk some of the young men began coming out to the river to spend the night with me and Rerebawä. They were usually so excited when word reached them of my arrival that they ran from the village to my customary riverside camp with no food and no hammocks, carrying only their bows and arrows, knowing I would share my food with them. They often reached the river after dark, and would have to spend a half hour or so scurrying around in the dark jungle to find suitable trees whose bark they would bite off with their teeth and rapidly fashion into temporary hammocks of eight or ten straps, and sleep two at a time in them.

Figure 5.6—Mǫmariböwei-teri: Shiitawä's magnificent shabono.

Figure 5.7—Now Shiitawä's people live in a mosquito-infested swamp—free from sin.

At dawn a larger party of men and boys arrived, many of them from Sibarariwä's group. I had arrived at a time when Sibarariwä's entire village was visiting Möawä's for a mortuary ceremony: they were going to consume the remains of Ręirowä, an important man of Sibarariwä's group who died "of magic" almost one year to the day earlier, when I was living in Mishimishimaböwei-teri.[7]

We unpacked the supplies and left for the village, making good time. Möawä greeted me and had the carriers put all of my possessions in his house. I explained my schedule and my plan to collect blood samples from the various members of Sibarariwä's village who had not been sampled before, and told him that I would

[7] Asch and I filmed the arrival of the man who announced to the Mishimishimaböwei-teri the death of Ręirowä in 1971. In 1972 I filmed the ceremony during which his cremated ashes were consumed. We are currently editing this footage into a film.

be coming back to his village with many possessions for him and his group after I took the blood samples out.

He appeared to understand and approve of what I was telling him, but his attention was fixed on the cluster of fifteen machetes that were lying on the ground near my pack. He wanted to know what else I brought for him this year, whether I had any tobacco (their crop had failed again) or any *hịsiomö* drugs. The machetes, I repeated, were for Sibarariwä and the others, for blood samples, but I would give one to him if he couldn't wait for my second trip; no, I had no tobacco with me, but I would surely bring large quantities back with me when I returned now that I knew they were poor and without any, and I would try to get *hịsiomö* for them as well.

While I helping a few young men construct a temporary palm-wood shelf for my packs and supplies, Möawä decided that he wanted to examine the machetes, so he cut the binding that held the three packages together, and laid all fifteen of them out on the ground before his hammock, examining each one carefully and admiringly. I told him again that they were for the other group, but that I would soon be back with many more machetes, just like the ones he was looking at, after I took the blood samples downstream. The plane would bring me many machetes. There was a crowd of men around his hammock, all of them men from his group and none of them from Sibarariwä's. His face turned solemn at the third repetition of my intended disposition of the machetes he was examining; he looked at me coldly and then, bluntly, informed me that the machetes were to be distributed to the men *he* designated, and *none*—repeat, *none* —were to be given to people in Sibarariwä's group. They were thieves and liars, he said, and they were not to have any of these machetes. These machetes were for *him* and the men in *his* village.

I knew that matters were, after these several years, finally coming to a head. He went on. I was to give *all* of my trade goods away immediately, and not to attempt to defer my distribution until I planned to leave, as was my practice in the past. Moreover, none of the *madohe* were to be given to members of the visiting group, but to be given to people that *he* named. Again, I was not to squander any of my delicacies on the children; if I had food to give away, he would see that it was eaten. He had also heard that in villages to the south, where the Yạnomamö had foreigners living among them, the foreigners gave shotguns away to the Yạnomamö in large numbers. He informed me that he had decided he wanted my shotgun.

As he made demand after pointed demand, I knew that this was going to be a delicate situation. I knew that I would not get any blood samples unless I was prepared to give trade goods in return, and I knew that as soon as I began paying for the blood samples according to *my* plan, there was going to be a serious confrontation.

That night Dedeheiwä again told Rerebawä of the attempt on my life in Iwahikoroba-teri the previous year, and Rerebawä whispered the story to me from a distance, over the jabbering in the village. I heard that the Iwahikoroba-teri—Borahiwä and his brothers—had tried to kill me. It was annoying to be reminded of the threats on my life and how serious they had become.

Figure 5.8—Before I had my hammock strung, Möawä had taken all my machetes and promised them to his particular henchmen. I knew this might be the final incident.

I fell asleep worrying only about how I would be able to get the blood samples and remain on good terms with Möawä. My murder as attempted by Boraböwä and his brothers the previous year had apparently impressed Möawä, and he had decided to drop any remaining veil of diplomacy and patience. Not only was I to distribute my possessions immediately, but I was to get my worthless self back downstream to fetch tobacco and more trade goods for him. The very nerve of me to come to his village without mountains of machetes and no tobacco, and think of giving the few machetes away to members of a *different* group!

I visited with old friends the next day, took ID photos of Sibarariwä's group and worked in the garden with Dedeheiwä, having him resolve questions that had arisen as a consequence of conflicting information obtained from several other informants on my last trip. He also identified the Polaroid photographs of those members of Sibarariwä's group that I did not know well, and filled in gaps and omissions in page after page of genealogies that I had converted to computer printout.

That night I worked late taking star shots to locate the village with astronomical data, after working for several hours with a compass and several informants who pointed out the directions to scores of abandoned garden sites. I had collected this information before, but to acquire some feeling for the consistency of informants from one year to the next and to compare the differences in informants' notions of cultural geography, I collected various sets of the same data. I avoided Möawä all that day, and went to bed long after he retired. Just to let me know he was around and aware, he shouted out at me occasionally to go to bed so he could get some sleep. I ignored him. He had developed the habit on the occasion of my last two visits of ordering me to sleep when he was weary of observing me, just one more way of letting me know he was the lord of the village. Objecting to the disturbance I made was a fairly thin pretext, since the village often would be rocking with arguments, chatter, and chanting to the point of being a roar. But that was "native" noise and didn't bother him. The thin, silent beam of my flashlight on my notebook did.

Early the next morning Dedeheiwä told me that they were going to drink the remains of "someone" and I should get ready to film it if I planned to do that. I asked him if he thought it would be advisable, and he assured me that it would —he would even stay at my side to make sure nobody became unduly abusive. *HE*, in brief, *suggested* that I film it. Under the circumstances, I would otherwise have stayed at a comfortable distance, knowing how touchy Möawä was and how volatile the entire village was with all of Sibarariwä's group camped there. I asked Dedeheiwä in a whisper if the deceased were *Ręirowä*, a guess on my part, but a logical guess in view of the kinship ties among the assembled multitudes: it had to be someone important. Dedeheiwä winced, acknowledged that this was indeed the truth, and urged me to not utter his name to anyone else in the village. Just before the ceremony began Dedeheiwä came over to tell me to prepare my photographic equipment. He was concerned about the way Möawä was treating me, and asked me privately to overlook it. He urged me to take the blood samples in the afternoon, after the ceremony was over, because people would be dispersing and would not be going directly home. This was a full week earlier than I had planned to take the samples, and there was no way, from this remote village, to change the airplane schedule I had earlier worked out. I asked Dedeheiwä if he would come with me down to Mavaca and work with me, away from the village, to complete a large number of loose ends that my premature departure would create. He agreed to come.

I filmed the mortuary ceremony, Dedeheiwä remaining at my side for most of it. A number of young men, emulating Möawä, made pointed threats while I filmed, but Dedeheiwä scolded them and told me to ignore them. Finally, when it was over, he took me back to my section of the village.

I told them that I would begin to collect the blood samples late in the afternoon

Figure 5.9—Barahiwä, stirring Ręirowä's remains into a half-gourd of plantain soup.

and continue the work on into the following afternoon. There were, luckily, a number of individuals in the village to whom Möawä ordered me to give machetes, men whose blood samples I intended to collect for a special serum study we were doing on paternity exclusions. I told these men that I wanted samples from them, their wives and their children, and would give them machetes, as my "younger brother had asked me to do."

While I prepared the equipment for sampling, all the men of the village were busy taking hallucinogenic drugs and violently striking down *Hekura* from enemy villages. Everyone seemed to be in a very ugly, unpredictable mood; there were over 400 people living in the village at that time, the largest group of co-residents I had ever seen. It was one of the most volatile situations I have ever been in. To make matters more tense, a terrible fight broke out between Dedeheiwä's wife and several of the visiting women. Hadakoama screamed at the Ironasi-teri women across the village, "You ugly bitches! Always demanding more than your share

Figure 5.10—Sibarariwä, Nanokawä, and other lineage members approach to consume their agnate's remains.

of the meat! You come here and eat us out of house and home, staying longer than you should, and shit on the people who feed you by demanding more than what they themselves eat! We work while you lie around flirting with our men. Your foreheads are filthy! You are all *Shami*!" They replied in kind, the vituperous insults growing hotter and hotter until some of the women began picking up pieces of firewood and threatened to attack their adversaries. Dedeheiwä, reeling from the effects of the *ebene*, staggered all the way across the village clearing and shouted at his wife: "Shut up! Stop insulting them! I'll have to beat you if you keep that kind of talk up!" He had to make several trips to convince her that he meant what he said.

He was well advised to stop the argument, for it was rapidly approaching the point where the women would start hitting each other with pieces of firewood—and then the fight would have extended to the men. In congregations of Yąnomamö this large, such a fight would have been disastrous, since there were many smouldering grievances. The fight among the women had to do with the distribution of the meat at the mortuary ceremony. The women from the visiting group felt that they had been slighted and had gotten less than the women from the local group—which was probably the case. There was a message in this manner of meat distribution, and it said that the visitors were no longer welcome and should return to their own village and eat their own food.

In the midst of this unhappy assembly I pondered what to do about the blood samples. It seemed unlikely that I could persuade Sibarariwä and his group to remain at Möawä's for another week, as my schedule would have liked it. I could leave Möawä's village to go to Sibarariwä's except that his group planned to split into several groups and go in different directions.

My decision was made for me when Möawä and a few of the lesser leaders told me that they had invited the Iwahikoroba-teri to come for a feast. They told me that the Iwahikoroba-teri would surely have to pass by the spot at the river where I had beached my canoe and would know that I was visiting Möawä's village. Möawä repeated to me how angry the Iwahikoroba-teri were at me, and how some of them might lie in ambush when I left and shoot me as I descended the Mavaca. A year or two earlier, a group of Yąnomamö ambushed a canoe on the Orinoco and sent a volley of arrows into it, but because the Orinoco is wide and the canoe was some distance from the bank, nobody in the canoe—neither the Yąnomamö or the Europeans—was hit. The Mavaca at this distance from the mouth was a very tiny stream, and was less than a canoe's length wide for a whole day's travel. It would have been difficult to miss at that range. They could see this information annoyed and disturbed me. If I stayed for another week I would surely see the Iwahikoroba-teri visitors and they would see me. At first, when such a possibility semed to exist, Möawä and Dedeheiwä assured me that they would make sure that the Iwahikoroba-teri would not harm me, unless they wanted a fight with Mishimishimaböwei-teri. Then when it seemed to be information that might lead to a quicker distribution of the trade goods, Möawä began hinting around that while I might be safe within the village, there would be nothing he could do to prevent the Iwahikoroba-teri from ambushing me between the village and the canoe, at the canoe, or downstream from it. In short, he was suggesting that I would be largely on my own if I stayed very long in the village.

As these hints became more pointed, I decided to collect the samples immediately and get out of there as soon as possible. I announced that I would take blood samples that afternoon and evening, and finish the work the following morning. As soon as I moved my sampling equipment over to an unoccupied section of the village, I was surrounded by about 200 pushy, impatient, angry, shouting people, each determined to get a particular item of which I had very few to distribute. They jabbed and poked me constantly for several hours, demanding payment immediately, while I methodically continued to draw the blood samples. I could not move an inch in any direction, they were crowded in so close; if I hunched over to take a close look at a vein in someone's arm, the space I evacuated was immedaitely filled wtih an equal volume of sweaty, smelly Yąnomamö body. Everyone was farting, as is the characteristic reaction to the food at feasts and mortuary ceremonies; and they were farting at very close range, 200 or so strong. There was no other range. Uncomfortable as my situation was, I recall breaking up with uncontrollable laughter at one point when I complained about the foul odor they were eliminating in such cramped quarters. One of them remarked cynically: "Farting? Who's farting? Why, we Yąnomamö do not even have ass-holes in this village, so how could we fart?"

Möawä came over when I began the sampling and repeated his instructions firmly: the machetes were to go to the men he specified, and to nobody else. He watched as I took the first few samples, so I deliberately chose men that he specified, but men whose samples I intended to collect anyway for the special paternity exclusion study. He seemed to be convinced that I was following his instructions, so he left. He came back from time to time to check on me. When I ran out of the men he had specified, I then had to choose very carefully. From my knowledge of past fights and disputes in the group when Sibarariwä and his section lived in the same village with Möawä, I knew who the men were that had stood up to Möawä and defied him. I began calling them, in turn, knowing that Möawä would be less able to prevent me from giving my machetes to these men without a fight, and knowing that these men would apply pressure on the rest of their village to cooperate with me when the machetes ran out. Instead of

Figure 5.11—Nanokawä, Möawä's classificatory brother, was himself a man of renown and had fought a good deal with Möawä. I gave him a machete, knowing that Möawä could not object too vigorously.

taking their families in turn, as I had done before, when I sampled men whom Möawä had specified, I quickly sampled the important men and paid them with machetes very quickly. I was down to one machete when Möawä learned what I had done.

He trotted over in a rage and stared in disbelief at the single machete. He glared at me with naked hatred in his eyes, and I glared back at him in the same fashion. He was clutching an axe in his hands and was shaking with anger. We stared at each other for some moments before he hissed: "You aren't following my orders, you son-of-a-bitch! And don't you ever look at me that way again!" He then raised his axe to strike and I saw how white his lips and knuckles were. Möawä hissed again: "Either you give that machete to that man over there, or I'll bury this axe in your head!"

By then it was too late, I had disposed of the machetes in such a way that I was able to get the rest of Sibarariwä's group to cooperate. Needless to say, I gave the single machete to a man he specified, but not before taking his blood sample and that of his family, whether or not I needed those samples.

I worked late into the night and went to bed long after Möawä was sleeping. I remember feeling very confident that he wouldn't try anything that night, since he was out of tobacco and he knew that I was coming back with a large quantity of it for him. After all, had I not invited Dedeheiwä to come along with me, and would I not have to bring the old man back up to the village?

The next morning I resumed the blood sampling, but there were only odds and ends of trade goods left, so the crowd was much thinner. They were impatient to have me finish so that I could get out of the village, get back downstream and collect the tobacco and more machetes for them, and get back up to distribute these items. Möawä's boldness had set a precedent, and even the youths of lowest status insulted and threatened me.

They repeatedly told me to hurry or else the Iwahikoroba-teri would surely catch me between the village and my canoe. It was noon and raining before I stopped drawing blood samples. Möawä was so desperate for tobacco that he demanded my pipe tobacco to chew. I refused, but told him I would give a canful to him at the river. He refused to walk out to collect it, but sent a youth along with me to bring it back for him.

We walked out to the canoe in a dreary rain, not quite a downpour but more than a mere drizzle. Everything was soaked by the time we made it to the canoe, four hours later.

I loaded everything and asked Dedeheiwä to get in. Another man had also asked to come along, but at the last minute, realizing how tense the situation was becoming, he decided not to come with me. What if I told the Bisaasi-teri about how they treated me? They might do the same to him. Just as I was about to push out into the current, the youth stepped forward and asked for the can of tobacco. I told him that I would not give it. If Möawä wanted it that badly, he should have come to the river to get it himself. I knew that this would anger Möawä, and I did it for that very reason. I knew already that I could not bear to spend another day in that village, and had no intention of coming back so long as Möawä lived there.

I worked downstream with the old man for longer than I told Möawä I intended to. I figured that if anybody were going to lie in wait along the riverbank to take potshots at me, he would have to wait for some time. There was no sense following a schedule that they knew. I waited downstream for about a week, working there with Dedeheiwä on things that I had intended to do in the village. By then, Rerebawä had told all the Bisaasi-teri how Möawä treated us and how he threatened to kill me with an axe. They were angry and kept telling me "I told you so!" kinds of things. Dedeheiwä, seeing that the Bisaasi-teri were growing openly angry at his fellow villagers, wanted to go home. Although no harm would have come to him, he felt uncomfortable because of the ill will that his son-in-law had created.

I dreaded the trip back upstream, and worried about it constantly. At night I would dream about raiders behind every tree, of ambuscades at every bend in the river above the confluence of the Washäwä-u, where the Iwahikoroba-teri area lay. I would have to pass through their area for at least six hours of river travel with the fastest boat I could locate, and the river would be very narrow. The Iwahikoroba-teri undoubtedly knew by now that I would be bringing Dedeheiwä back upstream soon.

For the long, trying trip back upstream I decided to leave my dugout and mount my 18 h.p. motor on my small rowboat. The dugout was too heavy and too slow for this trip. I had left supplies of gasoline hidden along the riverbank, the only way that such a small boat could make such a long trip. It could not carry enough fuel to make it up and back.

I asked Rerebawä to come along. He had grown to hate Möawä overnight, recalling the treachery of 25 years earlier when Mö̧awä's village had tricked the Bisaasi-teri and had killed, among others, the brother of his wife's father. Now he remembered these things well and decided, after all, that the Shamatari were a bunch of unmitigated bastards, treacherous to the core. He had been very disturbed by Möawä's threat to my life, and did not care if he ever saw him again. He told me that when Möawä raised his axe as if to strike me, he had taken up my shotgun and was prepared to shoot him if he tried to hit me with the axe. I know that Rerebawä would have done exactly that. I also realized that I would have defended him in the same way.

And with this, I realized that it was time for me to quit, for the causes that would provoke that kind of reaction in a Yąnomamö, and in me at this point, were not worth fighting or dying for. An argument over a banana in the right situation could lead to that kind of confrontation. The banana would be largely irrelevant, but the situation, as I had grown to understand after three years, would not be. The Yąnomamö do fight about "things" like bananas—or women—or possessions as such. I could easily fight with Möawä "over a banana," and one of us might get gravely injured, or killed. But the banana would have been only a very insignificant aspect of the fight. The real reasons for the fight would be very different and would have to do with the status system. It would be something of a gross misrepresentation to say that the cause of fight X was "bananas": the cause was political. Bananas were simply the catalyst that touched off a confrontation that had other, different, and much more complex roots. Recent trends in ethnological theory are tending more and more to crystallize around the notion that warfare among swidden cultivators must always be explainable in terms of population density, scarcity of strategic resources such as territory or "proteins," or a combination of both. The Yąnomamö are an important society, for their warfare cannot be explained in this way. South America as a culture province had its share of militant tribesmen, but in few cases in the Tropical Forest was intertribal or intervillage hostility and fighting clearly reducible to competition over scarce resources or population pressure (Carneiro, 1970). Elsewhere in the ethnographic world a better case can be made for the intimate relationship between fighting, population density, and scarcity of resources, but Highland New Guinea models do not necessarily fit in the South American lowlands. Like the American military involvement in Southeast Asia, some tribal warfare is best interpreted from its political attributes. I know of no serious anthropologist who would argue that the American military activities in Southeast Asia were a direct response to territorial shortages or protein deficiences in the United States, but there will be some anthropologists who will feel cheated if another colleague claims that Yąnomamö warfare is not related to these ecological parameters. Some of us would deny that primitive warfare can operate on the same political principles that characterize modern warfare. I find the parallels between the behavior of modern nation states and the military behavior of sovereign tribal villages very intriguing: they are common responses to common military or other kinds of threats. *Warre* did not disappear with the emergence of the nation state. Rather, it expanded in scope and continued to characterize the relationships between sovereign political bodies right to the present day. It is still with us, and causes statesmen to ponder the essence of security, and to conclude, from time to time, that the best defense is a good offense—as tribal headmen are wont to do.

Rerebawä, Dedeheiwä, and I set off for the landing on the high Mavaca where I would let Dedeheiwä off. I did not tell him, but I knew I would not be seeing him for a very long time. I did not want to return to his village, ever: not because of him or because of the way 95 percent of his group treated me, but because of Möawä and the 5 percent of the village I could no longer live with.

It was a long trip. The river had dropped markedly, and that high up in its course, it was choked with logs and deadfalls. After chopping our way through many of them we finally came to one that could not be passed without several hours of chopping. It was only a few minutes by boat below our destination, so I put Dedeheiwä ashore at this point and gave him the tobacco I had obtained. None of it was for Möawä, nor were any of the other going-away presents I handed over.

It was difficult for me to remain silent and watch the old man disappear into the jungle. I could not tell him that I would never return to his village so long as his son-in-law lived there.

Only after I returned to Mavaca did I let my feelings be "officially" known. I told the Bisaasi-teri that I planned never to return to Möawä's village. Nor would I go to visit the Iwahikoroba-teri. I was tired of having people threaten to kill me. I was alarmed at how close some of them had come. I told them that I would do "the same" to Möawä as he did to me, should he ever venture to come to Mavaca to visit. By the time this information got to him it undoubtedly had acquired embellishments and exaggerations that characterize the growth of Yąnomamö and all other rumors. I hope this was the case, and that Möawä will think twice about coming two weeks by trail to visit the villages at the mouth of the Mavaca River.

No matter how short I fell of my research objectives, I decided that I had done enough purely demographic fieldwork for the time being. I had, after all, spent three years living in Yąnomamö villages, had collected the data systematically, and had returned every year for eight years to check and double-check on the accumulated results. They amount to a great deal of information and are more than enough to do an acceptable analytical job. It is to that task that I now turn, after eight years, and try to put it all together into the patterns and configurations that I know or suspect are there.

I do not expect to return to Mishimishimaböwei-teri for a long time, if at all, but I do plan to continue certain aspects of my fieldwork among the Yąnomamö in other villages. The greatest privilege I have had in my life was to have met people like Kąobawä, Rerebawä, and Dedeheiwä and to learn from them something about the quality of their way of life, at a time when that way of life was whole, and when their villages were sovereign. Their culture will not endure for long; and its disappearance will impoverish all of us. For me, these men are more than identification numbers listed in the appendices of recondite journals. To the extent that my craft is scientific, it is necessary and desirable to quantify people, things, and culture. To the extent that people such as Dedeheiwä, Kąobawä, and Rerebawä are the subject of investigation, I, as the observer and reporter, feel an obligation to bring out their quality and the quality of their lives, to document in whatever way is appropriate and meaningful what it is like to live that style of life.

Quantity and quality are not incompatible approaches in ethnography. I am less concerned about the formalism of explanation—the models that social scientists make—than I am about the irreducible goal of explanation: to generate greater understanding of the external world. Where it is necessary to depart from the form to achieve the goal, it is desirable to do so. I have collected my share of facts and have followed the appropriate models. The job does not end there: headmanship in tribal society requires some pacing off as well as measurement.

Perhaps Möawä is an exceptional headman by Yąnomamö standards, and the strength of his character is an aberrancy. Whatever has called his qualities into being—idiosyncratic factors or micropolitical evolution among the Shamatari, a demand on leadership created by the largeness of villages—it is there, and it became something that I had to cope with during my fieldwork. Möawä was the one who really lived there, and should anyone invite himself to take up residence in that village, those were the conditions. I learned to sympathize with and understand why men like Sibarariwä, Nanokawä, and Reirowä chose to live apart from him, and had that choice been compatible with my anthropological goals, I, too, would have made it.

Scientific curiosity brought me to his village and professional obligation kept me there in circumstances I did not particularly enjoy. Individual personality characteristics led me to react emotionally to Möawä and grow to dislike him, perhaps out of envy for his remarkable competence, but more out of my own pride. As a human being with my own values and character I do not enjoy being pushed around and bullied, either psychologically or physically. Being a professional anthropologist does not oblige me to like it, or impose on me the solemn proscription to remain silent about my feelings. I would not tolerate that kind of treatment in my own culture, but I did in Möawä's. I always feared that the time would come when I would lay aside my own cloak of relativism and respond to this man as I would to someone in New York or Chicago, or as another Yąnomamö might respond in Mishimishimaböwei-teri. Those who contemplate fieldwork should consider themselves from this perspective; one cannot dismiss it lightly.

Many readers will be tempted to reduce my conflict with Möawä to a simple explanation that it represents only an ethnographer, in possession of valuable goods, giving them away in such a fashion that it was perceived by the headman as a threat to his authority and an undermining of it. This might be "structurally" defensible, but it would ignore what I feel to be, as an interested principal in the situation and as a trained observer looking back at it, equally relevant and very important facts. One such body of facts has to do with my observations on other headmen and my personal relationships with them. It was not like this. Another set of facts is that Möawä and I, as people reduced to the nature of our respective personality characteristics, simply did not mix well together. I think we both found that to be a constant source of friction.

I learned his language and the idiom of his culture's political strategies, and chaffed at the bit, knowing that I, because of my professional obligations and formally acquired relativism, had no choice on his ground but to move and bend with the blows. Perhaps it is a tribute to him that I should have become so personally touched by his quality, and so emotionally involved in my response to it. I can not help feeling that a measure of my response was due to an intensely private question: had I been born in his culture, could I have been his equal? My feelings about him are such that I would be delighted to have him come into my culture and deal with me on my terms. He would probably do very well.

I do not think that it is absurd for ethnographers to become so involved in what they do that questions of this order come to mind. Perhaps that is why some people become anthropologists: they are not sure where they fit in their own culture, and it is appealing to speculate about the goodness of fit in another time and another place. To become involved, as the saying goes, in something challenging or in an assumed simpler kind of culture where laws are said to work and cause men to behave rationally. Personally, I was quite happy to return to my own culture, and I think I understand it better. It has a kind of irrationality that my anthropological experience has taught me to live with.

APPENDIX A

Mishimishimaböwei-teri census data

Appendix A has two major uses. First, it provides to both students and colleagues a substantial body of new raw data that lends itself to quantification. The enthusiastic reception of my first book, *The Fierce People*, has created a situation where more detailed data on the Yąnomamö is now pedagogically necessary. Since the definitive work I plan to write is still several years away, I hope that this book will be an adequate intermediate step that temporarily supplements the materials I presented in *The Fierce People* and several journal articles. Dozens of anthropologically significant hypotheses can be formulated and tested from the data presented in this and in the other appendices. A wealth of supplementary biomedical data, especially genetic information, is available for Mishimishimaböwei-teri and many other Yąnomamö villages. My medical colleagues, Drs. James V. Neel and Miguel Layrisse,* are the authorities on this aspect of the multidisciplinary study we have been conducting for the past eight years.

Appendix A is essentially a census of Mishimishimaböwei-teri for the year 1971, supplemented with genealogical, geographic, demographic, and anthropological information. (A few residents are not included because of technical problems stemming from computerization procedures.) The parameters listed in the columns have been systematically checked and are not likely to change as I continue the enormous task of data cleanup. Nevertheless, I consider this a *provisional* summary, however close to the final product it may be.

Note that genealogical data for only *one* ascending generation is given for each individual listed in Column 1 as "Ego." If Ego's parents are alive and living in Mishimishimaböwei-teri, they will, of course, appear in Column 1 as residents. Depending on the age of the Ego, three, four, or five ascending generations of ancestors exist in my data. I am presently analyzing these data in the context of the wider population network in which they have their greatest anthropological/demographic significance. Several projected publications will present the results of these analyses.

Second, the data in this and the other appendices provide a detailed frame of reference for the numerous ethnographic films I will be producing with my colleague, Timothy Asch. Appendix G lists and briefly describes some of these films. One of the films (*Doing Anthropological Fieldwork in Mishimishimaböwei-teri*) complements this book in an intimate methodological way, for it describes how I conducted some of the work described here. Asch and I shot nearly 80,000 feet of film in Mishimishimaböwei-teri according to a very detailed plan that we had worked out beforehand. I knew what was generally significant in the culture,

* Dr. James V. Neel, Department of Human Genetics, University of Michigan Medical School, Ann Arbor, Mich. 48104; Dr. Miguel Layrisse, Dpto. de Fisiopatología, I.V.I.C., Apartado 1827, Caracas, Venezuela.

and what was particularly significant in this village. Thus, the 80,000 feet of film was, by filming standards, very judiciously expended and we planned from the outset to document many of the events and social interactions that will appear in the films listed in Appendix G. This is a novel step in ethnography and ethnographic filming, an experiment in filming, teaching, and research that has already yielded bountiful returns to professionally concerned teachers and students. Our first film, *The Feast*, served as our model. It, too, was the result of careful planning before we entered the field in 1968, the year it was shot. The success of *The Feast*, like the success of John Marshall's *The Hunters*, stems from the fact that it illustrates the general by focusing on the particular. Our filming in 1971 in Mishimishimaböwei-teri followed a similar pattern in that we focused on the families of two prominent men in the village, Möawä and Dedeheiwä, and showed how these individuals and their families behave in a wide range of social circumstances. The written materials will reveal the position of these people in a larger context, and we can indulge in this methodological luxury only because of the other, more traditional data that accompany the films.

DESCRIPTION OF THE DATA

The appendix contains 18 columns of information. Each column has a descriptive heading. The content and abbreviations or codes used are as follows:

Column 1: ID (Identification number). The individuals are listed in sequence by number rather than alphabetically, although there is some correspondence between identification number and alphabetization. The numbers in this column are the four-digit identification numbers described in Chapter 3 (as are the numbers in Columns 9 and 10).

Column 2: NAME.* Each resident of Mishimishimaböwei-teri is listed by his true or most commonly used name. In a few cases the names are shortened because only fifteen spaces were assigned to this parameter in my original format. Each individual occurs only once, despite the number of alternate names he has. A few children did not have names yet, so I named them after one of their parents (usually the mother, as in individual 2541, "Sharama So" [Sharama's son]).

Column 3: SEX. Males are indicated by the numeral "1" and females by "2."

Column 4: AGE. The age is given in estimated year of birth. To convert to actual (estimated) age in years, subtract from 1971. Note that the first numeral of the year of birth has been dropped, so that an entry "953" should be read "1953."

Column 5: BP (Birthplace). The numbers in this column refer to villages or garden sites, either ancient abandoned gardens or contemporary gardens. The approximate location of these gardens is given in Appendix D. In some cases the exact location of the villages or gardens is not known.

Column 6: MENS (Place of first menses for post-pubescent females). The information here is the same kind as that given in Column 5, that is, the numbers refer to garden sites or villages.

Column 7: PHOTO (Identification photograph number). Each person, with a few exceptions, occurs in the identification photographs given in Appendix E. A few individuals occur in several photographs. The numbers in this column

* The diacritical marks on the names are missing.

refer to the photograph number. See Appendix E for supplementary information.

Column 8: RES (Place of residence within the village). The numbers and letters in this column refer to the place within the village where each individual sleeps. Appendix F gives a scale diagram of the village with each frontpost of the house numbered. I divided the village into six sections, labeled A through F. Each section has a number of frontposts, each of which is numbered. The terminal letters in the codes given in Column 8 refer to what "position" within the house the individual sleeps. Where there are two hammocks, one hanging over the other, the suffix "D" refers to "down" (the lower hammock) and "U" refers to "up," the higher hammock. The suffix "S" refers to *shikö hamö*, ("at the back of the house"). Thus, where Individual 180 lives is coded as "F10S"; this means she lives in Section F of the village, at the tenth post and sleeps at the back of the house. Some children, not yet weaned, sleep in their mothers' hammocks.

Column 9: FATHER. The numbers given here refer to the four-digit identification numbers. For those individuals listed in Column 2 whose parents are still living and reside in Mishimishimaböwei-teri, the numbers given in this column can be used to locate the parents in the list (Column 1).

Column 10: MOTHER. See description of Column 9 entries.

Column 11: STAT (Marital status). The entry "S" means that the individual is single and never has had a spouse. The entry "M" means that they were once married, and therefore their marriage and reproductive information are given in Appendix B.

Column 12: LIN (Patri-Lineage). The numbers in this column identify the individuals by lineages (as used throughout Chapters 3 and 4). The oldest or genealogically most remote ancestor is used as the lineage "founder"; the numbers correspond to the identifications of these men. A few people whose ancestors come from remote villages have a "0" as their lineage. This information is useful when marriages are examined and the lineages of the spouses examined in terms of reciprocal exchanges.

Columns 13 through 18: KIN TERMS. I chose six informants in Mishimishimaböwei-teri and had them give me the kinship terms they used for every resident of the village. The informants were:

Column 13:	2194	Yọroshianawä (Male, 28 yrs old)	Lineage 2968
Column 14:	0178	Barahiwä (Male, 37 yrs old)	Lineage 2968
Column 15:	0059	Amanama (Female, 42 yrs old)	Lineage 2968
Column 16:	1478	Ramöma (Female, 30 yrs old)	Lineage 1222
Column 17:	0340	Dedeheiwä (Male, 60 yrs old)	Lineage 1443
Column 18:	1240	Möawä (Male, 35 yrs old)	Lineage 1222

They were selected for their lineage affiliation, sex, and prominence in village activities. The two women are sisters or classificatory sisters to the male informants so that the differences between Female Ego and Male Ego usage can be compared. Two of the men were brothers, a choice I made so that variation in their usage can be compared. Ideally, they should use identical terms for everyone else in the village (except for their own siblings; one informant was considerably younger than his brother, and this will account for some differences in usage). Finally, Möawä and Dedeheiwä were used as informants because they are two of the most prominent men in the village. Appendix C gives a more complete description of the kinship terminology and provides the terminological equivalents for the code given in Columns 13 through 18.

ID	NAME	SEX	AGE	BP	MENS	PHOTO	RES	FATHER	MOTHER	STAT	LIN	-------- KIN TERMS --------					
3	AAWA	1	953	113	0	141	F10D	621	400	S	2936	7	7	10	25	7	10
12	HADAKOAMA	2	933	116	0	87	F42D	1221	1159	M	1222	15	15	15	29	33	29
29	AHSOKAWA	1	958	132	0	10	C 6	1110	876	S	1222	7	7	10	7	7	10
41	AKABOREBIMI	2	926	28	141	116	A 7S	1380	1381	M	1380	15	15	15	29	33	29
59	AMANAMA	2	929	108	108	131	F 8	962	2803	M	2968	28	6	3	34	26	33
67	AMOMIAWA	1	955	113	0	53	E 4	1929	259	M	2968	10	10	7	10	8	7
134	AUMA	1	963	166	0	20	F40	1240	2678	S	1222	7	7	21	7	7	21
159	BAHORAMA	2	966	126	0	93	B 4	2130	1861	S	1222	26	32	32	32	32	32
168	BAKOANAWA	1	966	126	0	31	F 6	179	1541	S	2968	10	10	7	10	7	7
178	BARAHIWA	1	934	124	0	31	D 5	962	2803	M	2968	35	3	6	5	10	8
180	BARAMI	2	929	108	116	133	F10S	962	2803	M	2968	28	28	16	34	26	33
202	BASOKAMA	2	958	111	126	122	C 9S	1046	957	M	2936	28	36	32	6	26	36
212	BESHIEMI	2	939	124	113	38	F32	1461	1711	M	2700	28	28	35	34	26	33
218	BIKIMI	2	956	118	126	128	D 9	1929	153	M	2968	26	26	32	26	32	32
219	BIREIMA	2	956	113	0	82	C 6S	1110	876	M	1222	32	32	26	32	32	26
227	BOAOWA	1	936	145	0	36	A18	777	182	M	1443	23	19	25	27	10	8
234	BOKORAMO	1	957	113	0	8	C11S	1736	2265	S	1222	8	8	27	1	7	6
242	BORAWA	1	964	128	0	95	C11	314	958	S	1222	7	7	7	10	7	10
247	BOREKOMA	2	946	108	111	103	F14	22	8	M	2968	26	26	32	34	33	32
248	NONOKAMA	2	968	128	0	103	F14	517	247	S	2936	32	32	32	32	26	33
256	BOROSOTERI	1	929	124	0	30	C 9	222	1078	M	1443	4	4	25	19	16	19
259	BOROAMA	2	934	173	173	129	D 8D	1650	197	M	1222	36	36	34	20	32	6
282	BRAOBEMI	2	964	132	0	110	F24	2248	1614	M	2700	26	26	32	26	33	32
298	BROROYAMA	2	952	113	0	112	F40S	22	2237	M	2968	26	26	32	34	33	9
299	BIRIHOMA	2	967	128	0	112	F40S	1240	298	S	1222	32	32	32	32	32	26
312	BUKUMANIWA	1	967	126	0	144	A13S	2134	1631	S	0	7	7	10	7	7	10
314	BURIMANAWA	1	955	118	0	37	C10	1736	2265	M	1222	8	8	5	1	7	16
315	BURIWABOWA	1	962	132	0	1	F 8	1110	876	S	1222	7	7	18	7	7	10
326	DADORAWA	1	953	109	0	102	F11D	618	457	M	2968	10	10	7	1	7	7

ID	NAME	SEX	AGE	BP	MENS	PHOTO	RES	FATHER	MOTHER	STAT	LIN	KIN TERMS					
330	DAERAMA	2	948	118	132	131	C 6S	826	2801	M	2954	26	26	32	32	32	32
331	ARIMI	2	966	113	0	150	C 7D	1568	330	S	1222	32	32	32	32	32	36
332	DAEYAMA	2	944	111	128	55	F40D	340	232	M	1443	28	28	16	34	26	33
336	DARAMASIWA	1	930	108	0	63	F 4	962	2803	M	2968	35	35	1	5	10	8
337	DAPARAIWA	1	957	166	0	59	B 2B	777	185	S	1443	16	16	6	27	10	8
340	DEDEHEIWA	1	911	108	0	86	F43	222	1078	M	1443	4	4	4	19	3	19
355	DIMOMA	2	945	113	141	123	C 8	245	8	M	2968	26	26	32	34	33	32
359	DIRIMAWA	1	952	118	0	49	F34	340	3085	M	1443	16	16	1	5	10	8
361	DODOHIWA	1	961	166	0	18	F26U	435	1904	S	1222	7	7	10	7	8	10
368	DOROROAMA	2	941	164	126	117	A 8	777	185	M	1443	28	28	6	34	26	33
370	DOSORAWA	1	949	118	0	25	A 3	1739	2813	M	1222	8	8	27	1	7	16
375	DUREMA	1	951	113	0	151	C12S	2064	957	S	2936	16	8	7	1	10	8
378	EDEWESHIMA	2	953	113	119	92	A18S	964	1689	M	1222	36	32	26	32	33	26
390	HAAMA	1	957	128	0	9	F27	736	1274	S	1222	8	8	5	1	7	16
425	HAMAMOBOWA	1	968	126	0	11	A17U	2825	1124	S	2825	7	7	10	7	7	10
438	HARUBOWA	1	963	132	0	2	F10	863	180	S	2936	7	7	10	7	8	10
445	SHASHANAMA	2	966	126	0	87	F43D	340	12	S	1443	28	6	6	34	26	33
447	HASHASHIMI	2	962	132	0	115	B 6	2134	1631	M	0	32	32	26	32	32	26
449	HASHIOBEMI	2	958	113	0	52	A13D	2134	1935	M	0	32	32	26	32	32	26
473	HAYUEMA	2	916	101	101	104	F15	2430	2832	M	2430	29	29	34	15	33	15
489	HEHADOMA	2	967	126	0	145	A12	1240	1227	S	1222	32	32	26	32	32	17
517	MOSHABUMA	1	945	109	0	56	F14	863	180	M	2936	7	7	10	25	8	10
522	KOKONATEBOWA	1	923	124	0	114	A 4	222	1078	M	1443	4	4	25	19	16	19
537	HESIRAMI	2	949	113	126	95	D 5	1736	2265	M	1222	36	24	34	20	32	6
582	HISINOMA.	2	926	124	113	138	B 6	2838	2106	M	1222	36	36	34	20	30	6
610	HOMABEMI	2	965	132	0	87	F42U	340	12	S	1443	28	28	6	34	26	33
638	HORODOMI	2	941	164	0	105	F16S	1356	2673	M	81	32	32	26	34	32	26
651	HOWASHIWA	1	939	124	0	43	B 5	1221	1159	M	1222	19	19	25	4	8	4
657	HUWADAROREMI	2	964	126	0	65	F19	736	1274	M	1222	36	36	34	6	32	6

ID	NAME	SEX	AGE	BP	MENS	PHOTO	RES	FATHER	MOTHER	STAT	LIN	-------- KIN TERMS --------					
666	HUBRAABOWA	1	953	168	0	109	F22	2248	1744	M	2700	10	10	7	10	8	7
674	HUHEAWA	1	959	182	0	6	F21	793	687	S	794	7	7	10	7	7	10
687	HUKORABEMI	2	936	124	118	68	F20	1461	1711	M	2700	28	28	6	34	26	36
706	HURUMOWA	1	936	108	0	89	A 2	1856	1804	M	2968	35	35	1	5	10	8
708	HURURUAWA	1	954	169	0	41	A10	340	3085	S	1443	16	16	1	27	10	8
714	HUSIHEAMI	2	950	132	126	54	D 8S	1650	2828	M	1222	36	36	34	6	28	6
723	IYABOWA	1	944	126	0	21	D 9U	1650	586	M	1222	8	8	27	1	7	16
733	IBOKOMA	2	925	124	169	27	C 8	1221	1779	M	1222	15	15	32	29	36	32
760	IRORIAMA	2	968	119	0	60	A 4S	522	1377	S	1443	6	32	32	32	26	33
766	ISHAROWA	1	934	124	0	111	F32	1650	197	M	1222	8	8	27	1	7	1
777	ISHIWEIWA	1	901	172	0	83	A 7	222	1078	M	1443	4	4	4	19	35	19
783	IWAHEMI	2	946	123	165	103	E 4	22	8	M	2968	26	26	32	34	33	32
784	MONOWA	1	969	128	0	103	E 4	1046	783	S	2936	7	7	32	7	10	7
789	KAABOWA	1	952	113	0	29	F29	1981	1904	M	1222	7	7	10	25	8	10
803	KAHIAWA	1	959	113	0	10	F10U	1650	473	S	1222	8	8	27	1	7	6
816	KAMISHISHIWA	1	954	118	0	16	A	222	1470	M	1443	10	10	25	22	16	19
817	KANAHEROWA	1	963	132	0	7	E 5	2064	957	S	2936	16	8	7	1	10	8
833	KAOSARAMA	2	943	109	109	98	F 3	1716	2097	M	1222	36	36	34	20	32	6
834	BRAKIWA	1	968	126	0	19	F 3	336	833	S	2968	10	10	7	10	7	7
906	KEAMA	2	957	132	126	79	F34S	651	2440	M	1222	36	6	32	6	32	6
910	KEBOWA	1	931	124	0	26	F19	1461	1711	M	2700	35	35	1	5	10	8
949	KODEAHITERI	1	943	109	0	94	C 4	1856	1804	M	2968	35	35	1	5	10	8
950	KODEDEARI	1	949	118	0	50	B 4	777	185	M	1443	16	16	7	5	10	8
951	HOROINATERI	1	963	126	0	70	B 4U	950	1861	S	1443	10	10	7	10	7	10
958	KOHARAROMA	2	941	113	126	95	C10S	2064	957	M	2936	28	6	32	20	26	36
959	KOHARAWA	1	934	124	0	35	A 8U	2838	2106	M	1222	8	8	5	1	25	35
1014	KOROPINAMA	2	916	173	173	100	F	1221	864	M	1222	15	15	15	29	33	29
1020	KOSHIKIMI	2	958	132	0	76	A	1110	2209	M	1222	32	32	26	32	32	26
1021	KOSHIROMA	2	951	126	126	146	B 5	863	180	M	2936	32	32	26	15	33	26

ID	NAME	SEX	AGE	BP	MENS	PHOTO	RES	FATHER	MOTHER	STAT	LIN	-------- KIN TERMS --------					
1022	MAMOKOBREI	1	969	126	0	146	B 5	651	1021	S	1222	8	8	7	13	7	7
1025	KOSHIWA	1	953	116	0	41	F16	777	185	M	1443	16	16	1	5	10	8
1028	KOYOKABOWA	1	965	132	0	52	A13U	2134	1935	S	0	7	7	21	7	7	10
1046	KUWAIWA	1	938	124	0	126	E 2	976	2224	M	2936	7	7	10	4	8	19
1059	KUMARAMA	2	956	133	126	96	D 6S	379	366	M	2968	26	26	32	26	32	33
1062	KUMISHIWA	1	936	124	0	39	F30	1563	558	M	1222	8	8	27	1	7	16
1063	KURADOMA	2	941	113	126	81	F35	1739	2012	M	1222	36	36	34	20	32	6
1065	KURIANAMA	2	956	141	126	110	F17	2248	1744	M	2700	26	26	32	26	33	32
1089	MADOYAMA	2	938	116	0	80	F 2S	962	232	M	2968	28	28	16	34	26	33
1090	MADOYAMA DA	2	970	119	0	80	F 2S	2127	1089	S	1222	32	32	26	32	32	26
1091	KAOOBOWA	1	962	132	0	62	F 4S	1110	1089	S	1222	7	7	18	7	7	10
1099	MAIHABOWA	1	957	111	0	17	B 2D	959	1619	S	1222	7	7	10	25	7	10
1109	MAIYABARIWA	1	941	109	0	20	F23	964	1689	M	1222	7	25	21	25	8	10
1124	MAKARIOMA	2	943	186	132	92	A17D	777	185	M	1443	6	28	16	34	26	36
1125	REMOSHIMA	2	969	167	0	92	A17D	1509	1124	M	1222	32	32	26	32	32	26
1126	MAKAWA	1	931	124	0	99	F 7	976	2224	M	2936	25	25	10	4	8	19
1178	MAMOSHADIB	2	955	132	0	75	F11	1335	2217	M	1222	32	32	26	32	32	26
1206	MAROKOSHIMI	2	946	113	0	121	D 3D	621	400	M	2936	32	32	26	32	32	26
1240	MOAWA	1	936	124	0	113	F40	1563	6	M	1222	8	8	5	1	25	3
1246	MOHESIWA	1	938	124	0	42	D	1929	259	M	2968	19	10	7	10	8	7
1274	MORAMANAMA	2	921	108	124	64	F31	976	2224	M	2936	29	29	29	15	33	15
1276	MOREWA	1	965	132	0	14	D 6	1335	2217	S	1222	7	7	18	7	7	10
1278	MOPOKABOWA	1	956	132	0	48	C 5	1929	259	S	2968	10	10	7	10	7	7
1281	MOSHADAMA	2	936	109	113	92	A17D	964	1689	M	1222	31	29	26	32	33	26
1287	MOSHIWARIWA	1	944	118	0	66	F26	1563	1274	M	1222	8	8	5	1	7	6
1297	SHADIWA	1	943	122	0	44	F41	340	3085	M	1443	16	16	1	5	10	8
1312	NAKAHEDAMI	2	944	128	113	129	I 2	1922	259	M	2968	26	26	32	15	33	32
1335	NANOKAWA	1	936	116	0	85	D 6	1650	197	M	1222	8	8	5	1	25	35
1339 .	NAOOMA	2	948	113	119	96	D 7	1110	2209	M	1222	32	32	26	32	32	26

1346	NATOAWA	1	951	169	0	142	A16	522	182	S	1443	16	16	7	27	10	8
1347	NIYAIOBOWA	1	963	126	0	24	F 4	336	833	S	2968	10	10	7	10	7	7
1370	OBOHEAMI	2	951	113	141	147	F11S	863	180	M	2936	32	32	26	15	33	26
1371	OBOHITABRAO	2	951	116	132	28	C 8S	1505	996	M	1222	32	32	26	29	36	29
1377	OHINARIMA	2	943	167	118	60	A 4S	1981	2193	M	1222	32	32	26	32	33	29
1390	OKIMOBOWA	1	967	197	0	11	A 3U	435	2490	S	1222	7	7	10	7	7	10
1403	ONIWA	1	961	132	0	13	F21	793	687	S	794	7	7	18	7	7	10
1435	UWAMONAMA	2	943	118	0	124	C 4	1650	2224	M	1222	36	36	34	15	33	6
1456	RAAIYOWA	1	961	141	0	0	F23U	2248	1744	S	2700	10	10	7	10	8	7
1459	RAHAKAMA	2	949	111	128	60	A 2	522	182	M	1443	6	6	16	34	26	33
1473	RAKOIWA	1	968	118	0	35	A 9	959	1619	S	1222	7	7	0	7	7	10
1475	RAMOBOWA	1	944	118	0	33	F35	340	3085	M	1443	16	16	1	5	10	8
1478	RAMOMA	2	941	109	126	71	F41	647	1655	M	1222	36	36	34	11	32	6
1496	RASHAWAMA	2	954	169	126	110	F28	2248	1744	M	2700	26	26	32	26	33	32
1509	REIYAWA	1	944	118	0	106	A15	1739	2813	M	1222	8	8	5	1	7	6
1511	REMORIWA	1	966	132	0	12	D 3S	3088	2265	S	2936	8	8	27	6	7	8
1518	RIBOWA	1	953	111	0	132	C12	651	2265	S	1222	8	8	5	1	7	6
1539	ROENAMA	2	938	134	134	39	F31D	2103	558	M	200	26	26	32	34	28	33
1540	SHIKIWA	1	965	118	0	39	F31U	1062	1539	S	1222	7	7	10	7	7	10
1541	ROKOAMA	2	946	113	141	73	D 4	1736	2190	M	1222	36	36	34	20	32	6
1542	HEHURIOMA	2	962	132	0	79	F 6S	179	3084	S	2968	26	20	32	26	32	32
1543	YAREHEIWA	1	968	165	0	31	D 4	179	1541	S	2968	10	10	7	10	7	7
1561	POWAHEMI	2	941	109	134	71	F 7	647	1655	M	1222	36	36	26	26	32	6
1568	RUAMOWA	1	939	124	0	125	C 7U	3018	876	M	1222	7	7	21	25	8	10
1578	SIMODOWA	1	949	116	0	156	A	1563	1412	M	1222	8	8	5	1	7	16
1614	SHARAMA	2	936	116	0	154	F24	1650	558	M	1222	0	0	0	0	0	0
1619	SHAROSIMI	2	946	169	293	153	A 8N	777	182	M	1443	6	28	6	34	26	33
1624	SHAWARAKURI	1	959	132	0	22		256	733	S	1443	16	16	7	27	10	8
1628	SHAYAREMI	2	960	132	0	79	F 7S	222	1470	M	1443	26	26	32	26	28	32

ID	NAME	SEX	AGE	BP	MENS	PHOTO	RES	FATHER	MOTHER	STAT	LIN	-------- KIN	TERMS --------				
1631	SHEKEREIMA	2	941	118	132	115	A14	962	2803	M	2968	28	28	16	34	26	33
1634	SHIRIMOIMA	2	946	134	0	108	F18	520	1769	M	1222	36	36	34	6	32	6
1644	SHIBIRIMI	2	955	133	0	88	B 7S	1051	582	M	2700	33	26	32	26	33	32
1675	SHIMONEIWA	1	958	113	0	4	A14	340	3085	S	1443	16	16	1	5	10	8
1688	SHIRIRIWA	1	958	166	0	6	A15	777	185	S	1443	16	16	6	27	10	8
1697	SHIWARIBOWA	1	941	169	0	58	C 5	1981	2193	M	1222	7	7	10	25	8	10
1706	SHOENAWA	1	943	124	0	120	B 7	1461	699	M	2700	16	35	6	5	10	8
1718	SHOROKOIWA	1	959	166	0	13	F27S	1504	607	S	2936	7	7	18	7	7	10
1726	SHOSHOMA	2	901	12	12	130	D 4S	2793	2676	M	2968	29	29	29	15	29	15
1744	SINABIMI	2	937	116	276	67	F23	1650	2932	M	1222	36	36	34	20	32	6
1745	BOMABOWA	1	969	126	0	67	F23	2248	1744	S	2700	10	10	7	10	8	7
1776	TAIYOBEMI	2	966	141	0	35	A 8S	959	1619	S	1222	32	32	26	32	32	26
1795	TESHINAKUWA	1	936	145	0	51	A18	777	182	M	1443	16	19	1	27	10	8
1827	TOMOMAMOWA	1	949	118	0	32	F29	736	1274	S	1222	8	8	27	1	7	16
1834	TORAAWA	1	936	124	0	58	D 3U	222	1078	M	1443	4	10	25	19	16	19
1837	DOURAWA	1	954	113	0	45	C 6	1929	259	M	2968	10	10	7	10	8	7
1861	UDUWANAMA	2	946	26	175	119	B 4S	3086	1876	M	3086	36	36	32	34	32	32
1867	UGUSHITATERI	1	961	141	0	18	A 8D	959	1619	S	1222	7	7	10	7	7	10
1877	UMOYOWA	1	966	126	0	31	D 5S	179	1541	S	2968	10	10	7	10	7	7
1883	UREIROMA	2	967	126	0	27	C 8	256	733	M	1443	28	28	32	34	26	28
1897	UWA	1	943	116	0	40	F16	1650	2932	M	1222	8	8	5	1	7	16
1904	WABOAMA	2	946	10	126	152	F26D	777	185	M	1443	26	26	6	34	26	36
1927	WADORINAWA	1	967	128	0	155	F26	435	1904	S	1222	0	0	0	0	0	0
1929	WADOSHEWA	1	925	108	0	54	D 8	962	2803	M	2968	35	35	1	5	10	8
1935	WAKAKAIWA	2	941	118	166	52	A12	340	12	M	1443	28	28	6	34	26	33
1938	WAHARU	1	954	134	0	84	F 9	618	2273	M	2968	10	10	7	10	7	7
1979	WAKASHINAMI	2	963	0	0	134	F24S	1461	1228	S	2700	28	28	6	34	26	36
1992	WANISHEWA	1	959	132	0	46	C12S	48	1902	S	1222	8	8	5	1	10	6
[illegible]	[illegible]	[illegible]	[illegible]	[illegible]	[illegible]	[illegible]	[illegible]	[illegible]	[illegible]	[illegible]	[illegible]	8	10	10	[illegible]	8	10

ID	NAME	SEX	AGE	BP	MENS	PHOTO	RES	FATHER	MOTHER	STAT	LIN	-------- KIN	TERMS --------				
2127	YADIDOWA	2	944	116	0	62	F 2	1650	586	M	1222	8	8	27	1	7	6
2130	YAHOHOIWA	1	944	118	0	69	B 5	1563	2106	M	1222	8	8	5	1	25	6
2134	YAKAHAIWA	1	938	124	0	52	A13	2876	2086	M	0	8	8	5	1	25	35
2140	YAKARIMA	2	962	132	0	139	F14S	517	247	S	2936	32	32	32	32	26	36
2160	YAMOANAWA	1	962	126	0	17	D 8U	1929	259	S	2968	10	10	7	10	7	7
2173	YAOMA	2	953	113	0	140	C 5S	22	2433	M	2968	26	26	32	26	33	32
2175	DODOWA	1	968	128	0	140	C 5S	1697	2173	S	1222	7	7	7	7	10	7
2181	YARABOWA	1	963	126	0	23	E 3	1046	1312	S	2936	7	7	7	1	8	8
2190	YARINAMA	2	921	108	108	78	D 4	1736	1078	M	1222	29	29	29	15	28	15
2194	YOROSHIANAWA	1	943	116	0	56	F 6	962	2803	M	2968	11	16	1	27	10	8
2207	YASHUBRABOWA	1	965	126	0	36	A16	1795	1281	S	1443	7	8	7	10	7	7
2209	YAUKUIMA	2	931	124	113	97	D 7	1461	1711	M	2700	28	28	35	34	26	33
2215	YAWAROMA	2	965	132	0	149	F15	1929	259	S	2968	26	26	32	26	32	32
2217	YAWEIDOMA	2	944	116	132	74	D 6	962	232	M	2968	6	28	16	34	26	33
2218	OKO	2	965	119	0	74	D 5	1335	2217	S	1222	32	32	26	32	32	26
2234	YOAIYOBOWA	1	956	113	0	9	F42	340	12	M	1443	16	16	6	27	10	8
2248	YOINAKUWA	1	923	108	0	109	F22	1461	1711	M	2700	35	35	6	5	19	8
2256	YOKOREWA	1	946	118	0	118	A10	1563	2106	S	1222	8	8	5	1	25	16
2265	YOYOSIMI	2	941	124	118	72	D 2	222	1078	M	1443	29	29	29	15	28	29
2290	RABEKOWA	1	969	128	0	26	F18	910	1634	S	2700	10	10	7	10	7	7
2294	RIYIWA	1	965	141	0	14	D 7S	1110	2209	S	1222	7	7	18	7	7	10
2380	MAROKO	1	969	126	0	132	C 6S	1568	330	S	1222	7	7	7	7	8	8
2381	ADIADI	1	966	0	0	79	D 4S	826	2801	S	2954	10	10	7	7	7	7
2384	BABEAMA	2	969	128	0	77	E 2	1046	1312	S	2936	32	32	32	12	32	33
2399	BOROIMA	2	951	113	141	79	F 9	50	738	M	1222	32	32	26	32	32	26
2391	NONIAWA	1	970	126	0	117	A 8	959	368	S	1222	7	7	10	7	7	10
2392	EMAMI	2	969	0	0	147	F11	326	1370	S	2968	6	0	32	12	26	32
2393	HARIKANA	1	959	113	0	3	F30	736	1274	S	1222	8	8	5	1	7	6
2394	HENAKIMI	2	966	141	0	148	F11D	863	180	S	2936	32	32	26	26	33	26

ID	NAME	SEX	AGE	BP	MENS	PHOTO	RES	FATHER	MOTHER	STAT	LIN	-------- KIN TERMS --------					
2395	HENIBOWA	1	958	168	0	57	B 7S	2479	2478	S	2700	10	10	10	10	7	7
2398	KOROSONAWA	1	970	126	0	119	B 4S	950	1861	S	1443	0	10	7	7	7	7
2400	MATIO	1	969	128	0	87	F42	340	12	S	1443	16	16	6	5	10	8
2401	ARROZO	1	970	128	0	29	F28	1109	1496	S	1222	7	7	7	7	10	23
2403	SHIKOWA	1	965	132	0	91	A 7	1240	1124	S	1222	7	7	10	7	7	10
2405	USHUBIRIWA	1	962	132	0	2	D 3S	1736	2265	S	1222	8	8	5	1	7	8
2408	YAMOBEMI	2	955	111	126	115	A11	1706	582	S	2700	32	26	32	26	32	32
2488	AKAMIAWA	1	965	113	0	97	D 6	1335	1188	S	1222	7	7	10	7	7	10
2489	ARAMATATERIY	2	960	128	0	127	D 9D	1568	2999	M	1222	32	32	26	6	26	33
2490	ARONAMA	2	941	187	113	60	A 3S	777	182	M	1443	6	32	6	34	26	33
2491	ARONAMA SO	1	970	132	0	60	A 3S	706	2490	S	2968	7	7	26	7	7	0
2492	ARUSIWA	1	953	118	0	57	B 8	1505	63	S	1222	7	7	10	25	7	10
2493	AUYAWA	1	952	113	0	96	C10	256	733	S	1443	16	16	7	5	10	8
2494	BARIKIMI	2	916	145	0	61	A 4D	1905	1930	M	1222	15	15	34	29	33	29
2495	BOREKOSHIWA	1	966	141	0	5		1504	607	S	2936	7	7	18	7	7	10
2496	BOROIMA SO	1	970	126	0	73	F 9	1938	2389	S	2968	7	7	7	10	7	7
2497	DADAKEMI	2	960	132	0	87	F43U	340	12	S	1443	28	6	6	34	26	36
2498	DIAMA	2	969	126	0	115	A14	2134	1631	S	0	32	32	26	32	32	26
2499	DIDIRIMA	2	969	126	0	116	A 7S	777	41	M	1443	28	0	28	34	26	36
2500	DIKORAWA	1	951	113	0	90	A11	1505	63	S	1222	7	7	10	25	7	10
2501	DORAIMA	2	966	119	0	136	A17U	227	1281	S	1443	32	36	32	32	26	32
2502	HAAMONAMA	2	969	119	0	92	A17U	227	1281	S	1443	36	36	32	32	26	32
2503	HADOMA	2	967	165	0	71	F41	1297	1478	S	1443	26	26	32	20	32	32
2504	HAOMA	2	961	0	0	78		1739	586	M	1222	36	36	34	6	32	0
2505	HEREREWA	1	956	133	0	15	F11	618	457	M	2968	10	10	7	1	7	7
2506	HOKEIMA	2	963	119	0	68	F20	1417	687	S	1222	32	32	26	32	0	26
2507	HOOTERI	1	961	128	0	69		769	1990	S	2968	10	10	18	7	7	7
2508	HOSEI JOSE	1	969	126	0	123	C 8	1568	355	S	1222	7	7	7	7	10	8
2509	HOYATATERIYOMA	2	965	166	0	60	A 4	2482	2510	S	1443	32	26	26	32	32	32

ID	NAME	SEX	AGE	BP	MENS	PHOTO	RES	FATHER	MOTHER	STAT	LIN	-------- KIN	TERMS --------				
2511	HUKOBREI	1	951	113	0	107	F17	793	687	M	794	7	7	10	25	7	10
2512	HUKORABEMI DA	2	959	119	0	68	F20	1417	687	S	1222	32	32	26	32	32	26
2513	HUUHUUMI	2	954	182	141	61	D	1981	2490	M	1222	32	32	26	32	32	26
2514	HUUHUUMI SO	2	971	141	0	61	D	1246	2513	S	2968	36	32	7	7	8	7
2515	IBOKOMADA	2	970	119	0	27	C 8	256	733	S	1443	28	6	32	34	26	27
2516	KAUMA	2	964	141	0	34	F32	766	212	S	1222	32	32	21	32	7	26
2517	KIYAKO	1	963	132	0	57	F 2	2479	2478	S	2700	10	10	7	10	7	7
2518	KOBEWA	1	969	119	0	121	D 3D	1834	1206	S	1443	16	7	7	7	7	7
2519	KODEKONAMA	2	961	132	0	34	F32	2729	212	M	818	32	32	21	32	32	26
2521	KRAOWA	1	962	111	0	58	F20	1417	687	S	1222	7	7	10	7	7	10
2522	KUWAIYOWA	1	960	132	0	23	B 2U	824	2801	S	1222	10	10	7	10	7	7
2523	MAHOHOMA	2	970	128	0	54	D 8S	1929	714	S	2968	26	26	32	26	32	32
2524	MAMOKAKUWA	1	965	141	0	5		1504	607	S	2936	7	7	18	7	7	10
2525	MAMOSHADI SO	1	970	119	0	75	F11	2505	1178	S	2505	7	7	7	7	8	7
2526	MANOKOMA	2	970	128	0	55	F40D	1240	332	S	1222	32	32	26	32	32	26
2527	MOIYAWA	1	965	141	0	66	F26	435	1904	S	1222	7	7	10	7	7	10
2528	MOMIRAWAMA	2	966	128	0	67	F23D	2248	1744	S	2700	26	26	32	26	36	32
2529	NABAYAHIBEMI	2	969	128	0	33	F35	1475	1063	S	1443	26	26	32	26	32	32
2530	OBOHITABRA SO	1	970	119	0	28	C 8S	256	1371	S	1443	6	16	7	27	10	8
2531	OHINARIMA SO	1	970	126	0	60	A 4S	522	1377	S	1443	6	7	7	7	10	8
2533	OKOMOBOWA	1	953	113	0	101	F	1504	607	S	2936	7	7	10	25	8	10
2534	ONOMA	2	968	128	0	35	A 8	959	1619	S	1222	32	32	26	32	32	26
2535	ORA	1	966	141	0	34	F32	766	212	S	1222	7	7	21	7	7	10
2536	OSHEMOBOWA	1	968	119	0	30	C 9	256	1371	S	1443	16	6	0	5	10	8
2537	IRIBROMA	2	970	119	0	60	A 2	706	1459	S	2968	32	32	32	32	32	26
2538	RARIOWA	1	970	128	0	52	A12	2134	1935	S	0	7	7	21	7	7	10
2539	RISA	2	969	119	0	71	F 7	2194	1561	S	2968	26	26	17	20	32	32
2541	SHARAMA SO	1	971	128	0	154	F24	2248	1614	S	2700	0	0	0	0	0	0
2542	SHIRIMOIMA SO	1	970	126	0	108	F18	910	1687	S	2700	10	10	7	10	8	7

ID	NAME	SEX	AGE	BP	MENS	PHOTO	RES	FATHER	MOTHER	STAT	LIN	--------	--------	KIN TERMS			--------
2543	TOBARANAWA	1	964	126	0	24	C 9	256	1371	S	1443	16	16	7	27	10	8
2544	WABOAMA SO	1	970	126	0	152	F26	1287	1904	S	1222	0	7	10	7	7	10
2545	YAHAIMA	2	970	126	0	98	F 3	1504	833	S	2936	26	26	32	26	32	32
2546	YAMOHAMA	2	969	119	0	34	F32	766	212	S	1222	32	32	26	32	32	26
2547	YAWEIDOMA DA	2	970	119	0	74	D 6	1335	2217	S	1222	32	32	17	32	32	26
2548	YOYOSIMI SO	1	970	126	0	72	D 2	2052	2265	S	2936	8	8	27	13	7	8
3000	BUUTA	1	968	119	0	60	A 3D	706	2490	S	2968	7	7	7	7	7	10

APPENDIX B

Marriage and reproduction statistics

Column 11 of Appendix A specifies whether or not the "Ego" in any particular row is married or ever has been married. If the individuals listed in Appendix A are not now or never were married, the 11th column will indicate these facts by the symbol "S"—single. If the individuals were married at least once in their lifetime, the symbol "M"—married—will occur in Column 11.

This appendix gives a summary of marriage and reproductive performance of all those individuals in Village 16, Mishimishimaböwei-teri, who have an "M" entered in Column 11. The first person listed, Hadakoama, appears in this appendix as Ego number 0012. She was (and presently is) married to individual 0340, Dedeheiwä. She had eight children by him as shown in Column 3 below. Finally, the current status of that marriage is indicated in the fourth column. In Hadakoama's case, the digit "1" appears in the fourth column, which means that the marriage is still current. The entries in Column 4 of the present appendix are as follows:

1. Current spouse; marriage still recognized.
2. Spouse is deceased.
3. This wife is shared with another man.
4. Marriage terminated; spouse was "thrown away."

This appendix is incomplete and may show minor discrepancies with information given in the chapters. This unfortunate flaw is the result of the continuous process of updating and correcting the data: some of the text material was summarized from the computerized material during different times of the correcting process. Were I to wait until all the corrections were made, this material would remain inaccessible for several more years. Inasmuch as this book aims chieflly at methodological points, I feel that a premature disclosure is warranted. A large number of articles for professional journals are in progress, and they will contain the refinements of data accuracy that are missing here.

A number of additional clarifications are required. A number of individuals will be found in the "Ego" column here, but their "current" wives will not be found in the list. This is because some families were in the process of moving out of or into Mishimishimaböwei-teri and were undecided in 1971. Some of them still had their families in Ironasi-teri, the splinter village that fissioned away from Mishimishimaböwei-teri several times in the past. This underscores the point that recently fissioned villages undergo a process of separation that may take months or years to complete, especially if the fission did not take place during a fight in which someone was killed, as was the case here. During this time there will be individuals and families migrating back and forth trying to decide where to settle. This is often a complicated and structurally fascinating situation. One example worth noting in this connection is the case of Nanokawä, individual number 1335. He is Möawä's parallel cousin—a competing agnate. Still, he has many intimate and compelling kin ties with Wadoshewä (1929) and Daramasiwä (0336), his two most powerful brothers-in-law. Wadoshewä and Daramasiwä wanted him to rejoin the village so desperately in 1971 that they cleared and planted a complete garden for Nanokawä and his large family and invited him "home." He was living in Mishimishimaböwei-teri during most of the year, but some of his wives and children remained in Ironasi-teri. His presence in the village contributed to the strain that existed in the village, a strain that expressed itself in both hostile acts and ceremonial distributions calculated to strengthen particular kinship and marriage ties. Some of these political strains are the matrix against which a number of the films, particularly *The Axe Fight* and *Reahumou* are to be interpreted.

Another point of clarification is that the number of children listed for each marriage represents all children—living, dead, and those who live in other villages. Again, the statistics are not complete enough for some demographic applications, such as an accurate estimate of "completed fertility." Abortions and infanticide on the one hand, and infant mortality on the other, are not sufficiently well documented to warrant these kinds of estimates or characterizations. A more realistic precis of the data would be that the numbers of children given for each marriage represents those that lived long enough to have acquired a name.

Finally, the present appendix does not identify the individuals who have been abducted from other villages. This is an important phenomenon and will be treated in a separate publication.

Ego	Spouse	No. of Children	Marriage Status
0012	0340	8	1
0041	0777	1	1
0059	1110	1	2
0059	1335	0	4
0059	1504	0	2
0067	1334	0	4
0178	0537	1	1
0178	1541	3	1
0178	3084	1	4
0180	0863	6	2
0202	0314	0	1
0202	1897	0	1
0212	0766	5	1
0212	2729	1	2
0218	1126	0	1
0219	1837	0	1
0227	0378	0	1
0227	1281	4	3
0247	0517	3	1
0256	0733	4	1
0256	1081	0	4

Ego	Spouse	No. of Children	Marriage Status
0256	1371	4	1
0259	1929	7	1
0282	0789	0	1
0298	1240	1	1
0314	0202	0	3
0314	0958	1	4
0326	1370	1	1
0330	1568	2	1
0332	1240	1	1
0336	0833	3	1
0340	0012	8	1
0340	0232	1	2
0340	1081	1	4
0340	2893	0	4
0340	3085	6	2
0355	1568	2	1
0359	0906	0	1
0368	0959	1	1
0370	1459	0	4
0378	0227	0	1
0447	0651	0	1

Ego	Spouse	No. of Children	Marriage Status
0449	0666	0	1
0473	1650	5	2
0517	0247	3	1
0522	0182	2	4
0522	1377	2	1
0537	0178	1	1
0582	1051	2	2
0582	1706	1	1
0638	1897	1	1
0651	0447	0	1
0651	0758	0	2
0651	1021	1	1
0651	2190	1	4
0651	2265	1	4
0651	2440	1	2
0657	0910	0	1
0666	0449	0	1
0687	0793	3	2
0687	1417	4	1
0706	1459	1	3
0706	1935	0	4
0706	2490	1	1
0714	1929	1	1
0723	2489	0	4
0733	0256	4	1
0766	0212	5	1
0766	0607	1	2
0777	0041	1	1
0777	0182	5	4
0777	0185	7	2
0783	1046	1	1
0789	0282	0	1
0816	0174	0	4
0816	1020	0	4
0833	0336	3	1
0833	1504	1	2
0833	1750	1	4
0906	0359	0	1
0910	0657]	0	1
0910	1634	2	1

Ego	Spouse	No. of Children	Marriage Status
0949	0008	1	2
0949	1435	0	1
0949	1125	0	1
0950	1861	3	3
0958	0314	1	4
0958	2134	0	1
0959	0368	1	1
0959	1619	5	1
1014	1835	0	4
1014	2011	5	1
1014	3014	0	4
1020	0816	0	4
1021	0651	1	1
1025	1561	0	4
1046	0783	1	1
1046	0957	1	2
1046	1312	3	1
1059	1335	0	1
1062	1539	1	1
1063	1475	1	1

Ego	Spouse	No. of Children	Marriage Status
1065	2234	0	4
1065	2511	0	1
1089	1110	1	2
1089	2127	2	1
1109	1496	1	1
1124	1240	1	4
1124	1509	1	1
1124	2825	1	4
1125	0949	0	1
1126	0218	0	1
1126	1628	0	1
1178	2505	1	1
1206	1834	1	1
1240	0298	1	1
1240	0332	1	1
1240	0738	0	4
1240	1124	1	4
1240	1227	1	2
1240	2678	1	2
1246	0414	4	1

Ego	Spouse	No. of Children	Marriage Status
1246	2513	1	1
1274	0736	5	2
1274	1563	1	2
1281	0227	4	1
1281	1795	2	1
1287	1904	1	1
1297	1478	2	1
1312	1046	3	1
1335	0059	0	4
1335	0876	0	1
1335	1059	0	1
1335	1188	1	1
1335	1339	0	1
1335	2115	1	4
1335	2209	2	1
1335	2217	5	1
1339	1335	0	1
1370	0326	1	1
1371	0256	4	1
1377	0522	2	1
1435	0949	0	1

Ego	Spouse	No. of Children	Marriage Status
1459	0370	0	4
1459	0706	1	1
1475	1063	1	1
1478	1297	2	1
1496	1109	1	1
1509	1124	1	1
1539	0384	0	4
1539	0500	1	2
1539	1062	1	1
1539	2037	0	4
1541	0178	3	1
1541	0252	0	4
1561	0734	1	4
1561	1025	0	4
1561	1641	0	2
1561	2194	1	1
1568	0330	2	1
1568	0355	2	1
1578	1807	1	1
1614	2248	3	1
1619	0959	5	1

Ego	Spouse	No. of Children	Marriage Status
1628	1126	0	1
1631	2134	3	1
1634	0910	2	1
1644	1975	0	4
1644	2069	0	2
1697	2173	1	1
1706	0582	1	1
1726	1650	7	2
1744	2248	6	1
1759	1281	2	3
1795	2519	0	1
1834	1206	1	1
1837	0219	0	1
1861	0950	3	1
1861	2130	1	1
1897	0202	0	3
1897	0638	1	1
1904	0435	4	2
1904	1287	1	1
1904	1981	2	2

Ego	Spouse	No. of Children	Marriage Status
1929	0153	1	2
1929	0259	7	1
1929	0714	1	1
1935	0706	0	4
1935	2134	4	1
1938	2389	1	1
2052	2173	0	1
2052	2265	1	1
2127	1089	2	1
2127	3434	0	2
2130	1861	1	3
2130	2678	0	2
2134	0958	0	1
2134	1631	3	1
2134	1935	4	1
2173	1258	0	4
2173	1697	1	1
2173	2052	0	1
2190	0651	0	4
2190	1736	1	2

Ego	Spouse	No. of Children	Marriage Status
2190	1905	0	2
2194	1561	1	1
2209	1110	1	2
2209	1335	2	1
2217	1335	5	1
2234	1065	0	4
2248	1614	3	1
2248	1744	6	1
2265	0651	1	4
2265	1736	4	2
2265	2052	1	1
2265	2064	2	2
2265	3088	1	2
2389	1938	1	1
2489	0723	0	4
2490	0435	1	2
2490	0706	1	1
2490	1981	1	2
2494	2911	0	2

Ego	Spouse	No. of Children	Marriage Status
2494	0522	2	4
2494	0777	5	4
2505	1178	1	1
2511	1065	0	1
2513	1246	1	1
2519	1795	0	1

APPENDIX C

Kinship terminology

Yąnomamö kinship terminology conforms to the Iroquois variety of the bifurcate merging type; parallel cousins are classified with siblings and distinguished from both sets of cross-cousins, who are, in turn, lumped into a single category (discriminated only on the basis of sex).

The numbers given in Appendix A in Columns 13 through 18 correspond to the terms given below. See Appendix A for the relationships between the informants used for the kinship terms.

Before discussing the terms, let me first describe how they were collected. The Yąnomamö employ a wide variety of kinship words to refer to or address their kinsmen. Not all of these words properly constitute a system of terminology in the traditional anthropological sense: some are terms that emphasize affect or endearment and are used to exaggerate closeness of relationship to kinsmen who would, in a descriptive, formal sense, be called by a different kinship word. To provide students and colleagues alike with the complete range of verbal kinship responses, I provided, in Appendix A, the informant's actual response to the question: "What do you call this person?" At the time I asked the question, the informant was shown a photograph of the kinsman in question and told (whispered) his or her name. I tape-recorded the responses in all cases. They are listed below, corresponding to the numbers given in Appendix A.

I conducted this work in public, with a large number of onlookers listening and watching—and making certain that the informant did not, in their estimation, make a "mistake." The Yąnomamö do not attempt to deceive me on matters of kinship usage, but some informants make occasional mistakes because their minds wander or because I mispronounced a name; working in public eliminates this kind of error.

In some cases the person in question is too young to be addressed by a kinship term, or the informant has not begun to refer to the child in conversations. A common reaction was: "That baby is a newborn! I don't call him anything!" I would rephrase my question in such a way as to get the informant's (projected) usage, such as: "What will you call her when she becomes *moko*?" In some villages I even "used" very tiny infants as informants by asking the parent questions like: "What will your baby call so-and-so when he gets older?" I also used selected informants to give me their usage for people who died long ago; these two techniques enabled me to get usages extended back in time as far as possible, and projected usages as well.

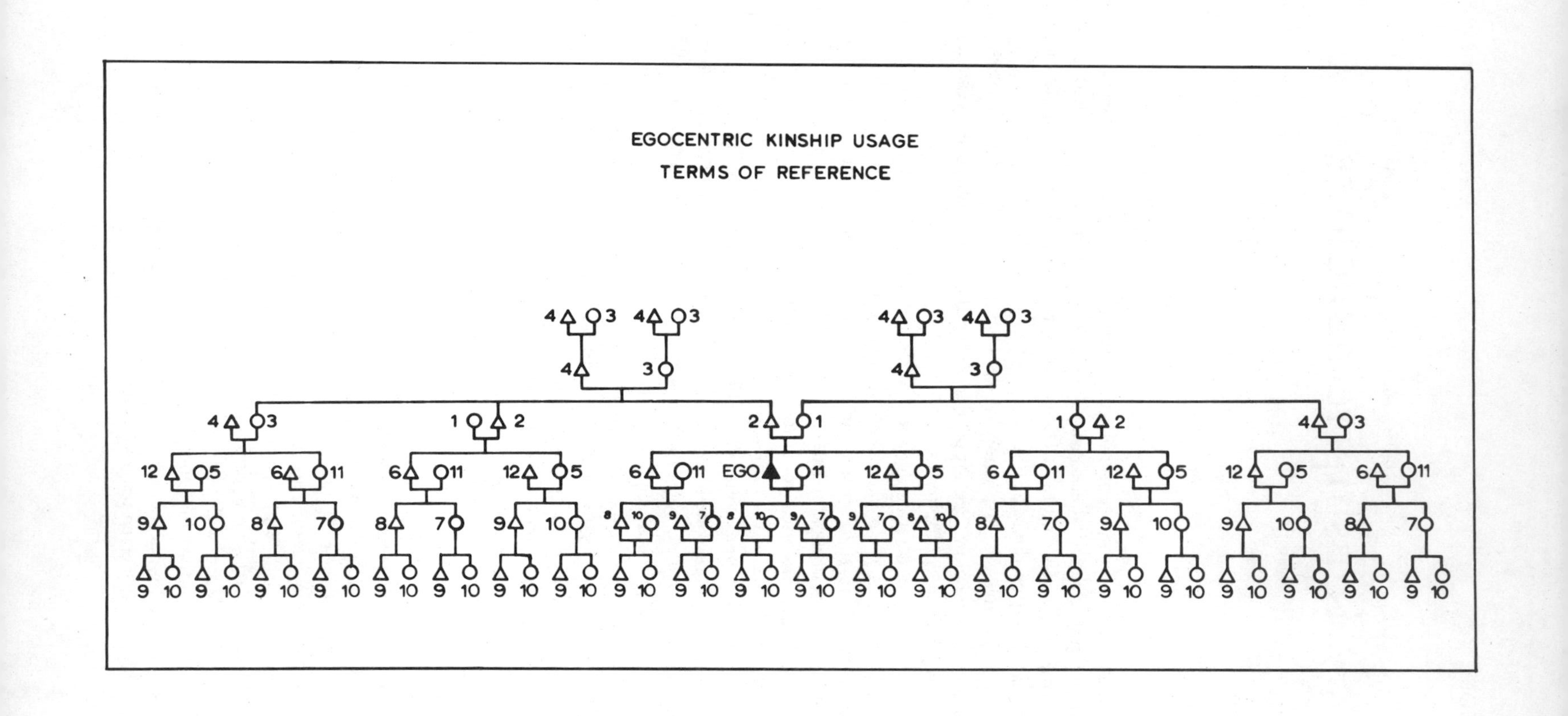
EGOCENTRIC KINSHIP USAGE
TERMS OF REFERENCE
EGO

One fact that should emerge from the set of kinship words, when viewed against the genealogical data given in Appendix A, is that there is a good deal of inconsistency in actual usage when the model of "ideal" usage (see the paradigm, page 220) is examined. These inconsistencies can usually be traced to some incestuous marriage, which necessitates a manipulation of kinship usage for some people, but there is also an enormous variation in the extent to which the manipulations are reverberated through the nexus of kinship relationships. One man may change his usage, but his brothers may not.

There is also a large amount of variation in the use of particular terms from one region to another, even where both terms are used in similar ways in two regions; the terms may even be identical in pronunciation, but have various shades of meaning in two adjacent regions. The Bisaasi-teri, for example, use the kinship term *yaöyä* to mean "my sibling of the opposite sex" (both male and female speakers). Among the Shamatari to the south, the term tends to be used exclusively by males to refer to sisters. This distinction between the Bisaasi-teri and the Shamatari is maintained, even in the face of considerable migration between the two populations. Again, among the Bisaasi-teri, male speakers distinguish between older and younger sister quite sharply, but among the Shamatari the same distinction is vague or rare in daily usage. However, both males and females in the Shamatari dialect use terms to distinguish same-sex siblings into older and younger, as do the Bisaasi-teri, and both have an unequivocal term used by both male and female speakers to designate an older brother. In brief, the criterion of relative age of siblings appears to be more vague among the Shamatari.

The range of application of particular terms that occur in different dialect areas can be very large and have important structural implications. The term *hayä* in most Yąnomamö dialects is restricted to Ego's father (or his father's brothers, mother's husbands, father's parallel cousins, and the like) but in the extreme northeastern end of the tribe, the Sanöma area, this term is also extended to father's father and other men of the second ascending generation. There seems, in addition, to be a cline in this tendency to merge lineal kinsmen of the first and second ascending generation, one that is strongest in the Sanöma area in the northeast, and gradually diminishing in a southwestward direction until, among the Shamatari, it ceases to exist. There the term *shoayä* is unequivocally applied to father's father, his siblings, and parallel cousins, and the like. In the region intermediate between these two extremes there appears to be some inconsistency, and informants will occasionally argue that the term *shoayä* should not apply to father's father, "because a man could not marry a daughter of that *shoayä*." (See Lizot, 1971b, for a discussion of this problem in the area where he conducted his research.) Among the Shamatari the term *shoayä* is used consistently for FaFa, MoFa, and all of their lineal ascendants as well. A few informants, however, insist that the father of a *shoayä* could be called *shoriwä*, and that the terms *shoayä* and *shoriwä* alternate by generation in ascending generations.

Paralleling this cline is an associated tendency in the intermediate region to ignore generation distinctions in vocative forms of kinship terms. I have heard the Yąnomamö north of the Orinoco use sibling terms in direct address to parents or siblings of parents, and Lizot reports that this is very common further to the north. This usage occurs rarely in Bisaasi-teri, where a sizeable fraction of the population has come from villages immediately to the north, but it is extremely rare among the Shamatari further to the south.

In the list of numbers, kinship words, and rough English equivalents that follow, I have made no attempt to give every possible genealogically specifiable English equivalent. The large amount of genealogical data in Appendix A, as well as the egocentric kinship paradigm that follows the list, can be used by those who wish to make such exhaustive lists.

Appendix A Term Number	*Yąnomamö Word*	*Rough English Translation or Equivalent*
1	Abawä	Older brother (male or female speaking).
2	Aịwä	Older brother (male or female speaking).
3	["Ego"]	"Me" (see Term 11, below).
4	Hayä	My father (male or female speaking).
5	Hẹaroyä	My husband (female speaking).
6	Hebarayä	My sibling (male or female speaking).
7	Hekamayä	My nephew, grandson, daughter's husband (male or female speaking).
8	Heriyä	My brother-in-law, male cross-cousin (male speaking).
9	Iba	"Mine" (implying "my true offspring"). This is not a kinship term as such, but is frequently used by both males and females to designate their true children, or to emphasize closeness to a child of a sibling (of the same sex).
10	Ihiruyä	My son (male or female speaking).
11	Kamiya	"Me"
12	Mokami	My younger female relative (male or female speaking). Emphasizes affect and endearment.
13	Mokawä	My younger male relative (male or female speaking). Emphasizes affect and endearment.
14	[No term—a punching error]	
15	Nayä	My mother (male or female speaking).
16	Osheyä	My younger sibling of the same sex (male or female speaking).
17	Owasimi	My younger female relative (male or female speaking). Emphasizes affect and endearment.
18	Owasiwä	My younger male relative (male or female speaking). Emphasizes affect and endearment.
19	Shoaiyä	My mother's brother, grandfather (either side); my father's sister's husband (male or female speaking); my wife's father (male speaking); my husband's father (female speaking).
20	Shedämi	My female relative (male or female speaking). Emphasizes affect and endearment.
21	Shedäwä	My male relative (male or female speaking). Emphasizes affect and endearment.
22	Shomi	"Different," that it, when used in a kinship context in the broadest sense, it usually means 'someone from a different, remote group' or 'someone

Appendix A Term Number	*Yąnomamö Word*	*Rough English Translation or Equivalent*
		to whom I cannot demonstrate a relationship.' It is not a kinship word as such.
23	Shoriwä	[Synonymous with Term 8; the Shamatari use the term *Heriyä* almost to the virtual exclusion of the term *Shoriwä* in daily kinship reference and address, but use the latter term regularly in formal chanting.]
24	Sioböyä	Female cross-cousin; wife (male speaking).
25	Siohayä	Son-in-law; sister's son; daughter's husband (male speaking); son-in-law; brother's son; daughter's husband (female speaking).
26	Tääyä	My daughter
27	Wąhamayä	My male cross-cousin; my husband (female speaking).
28	Yaöyä	My sister (male speaking); my sibling of the opposite sex (male or female speaking; a rare usage among the Shamatari).
29	Yayä	My grandmother (either side), my father's sister, my mother's brother's wife (male or female speaking); my wife's mother (male speaking); my husband's mother (female speaking).
30	Yeisiböyä	[Synonym for Term 29 in Shamatari dialect]
31	Yesiwä	[Synonym for Term 29 in Shamatari dialect]
32	Yuhayä	My granddaughter, my son's wife (male or female speaking); my sister's daughter (male speaking); my brother's daughter (female speaking).
33	Suaböyä	[Synonym for Term 24 in Shamatari dialect]
34	Nadohiyä	My female cross-cousin, my sister-in-law, my brother's wife (female speaking).
35	Badayä	My older sibling of the same sex (male or female speaking).
36	Hesioböyä	[Synonym for Term 24 in Shamatari dialect]

In addition to these equations, there are two usages that can not be gotten from either the above list or from the paradigm that follows. These are:

1. Wife's mother's mother = wife.
2. The children of your older sibling of the same sex must be called *older* siblings by your children, irrespective of the ages of both sets of siblings. Thus, my thirty-year-old son (male ego) would call the ten-year-old son of my (Ego's) older brother by an older sibling term, even though my son is obviously "older" in an absolute sense.

It should also be emphasized that there are no kinship terms that are exclusively affinal: all terms applied to relatives by marriage are used to designate consanguines as well. Rodney Needham (1962), an English anthropologist, has argued for the structural significance of this feature in distinguishing prescriptive marriage systems from those that are described as preferential.

With respect to sibling terms in the paradigm that follows, I have adopted a simple convention in order to make the Egocentric kinship usage consistent with

Shamatari practice. It can be argued (see Lizot, 1971b) that the inconsistency in sibling terms stems from the option to emphasize relative age for one set of usages or to emphasize sex distinctions in another, complementary set of usages, that is, that there are two sets of kinship terms for siblings. The convention I will follow in the (male) Egocentric paradigm below is this:

Yaöyä = My sister
Abawä = My brother

Whatever sibling terms are adopted for the purpose of drawing an Egocentric kinship paradigm, the system will be consistent with the Iroquois equations: sibling terms will be extended to parallel cousins.

One remaining feature of Yąnomamö kinship deserves mention. The kinship system implies, when represented in an Egocentric paradigm, that sibling terms are used by parallel cousins for each other indefinitely through all descending generations. But because of the patrilineal descent pattern, this is actually true only for the descendants of brothers through males. That is, male grandsons, descended through males, of a pair of brothers will consistently call each other by sibling terms ". . . because we are *mashi*," that is, because they are members of the same patrilineal descent group. Theoretically, female granddaughters, descended through females, of a pair of sisters should also use sibling terms for each other, but whether or not they do depends on the marriage ties of their mothers and grandmothers, that it, their usage is determined by patrilineal descent considerations. The four diagrams that follow show the problem graphically. Ego 1 will call his parallel cousin by a sibling term. Ego 2 *might* call her parallel cousin by a sibling term, but the usage cannot be predicted from the diagram because the marriage relationships are not given. Diagram 3 shows how this is

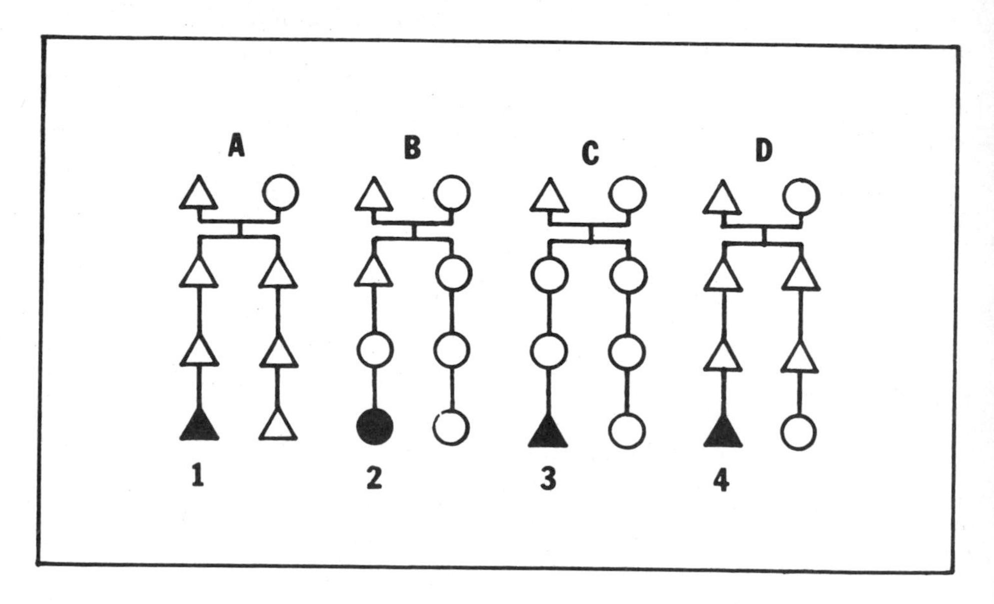

related to marriage possibilities: Ego 3 might conceivably marry his parallel cousin because of the patrilineal ties that have taken place (not shown) in ascending generations, ties that take precedence over the theoretically implied usage based on descent through the female line. An example of this was given in Chapter 4 (see Figure 4.3, case D). Finally, to underscore the significance of patrilineal descent, Ego 4 would *not* marry his parallel cousin because the relationship between them is unequivocally a sibling relationship.

The numbers on the paradigm will correspond to the following kinship terms, and are sufficient to describe the kinship system (except as noted above).

1. Nayä
2. Hayä
3. Yayä
4. Shoayä
5. Yaöyä
6. Abawä
7. Tääyä
8. Ihiruyä
9. Hekamayä
10. Yuhayä
11. Suaböyä
12. Heriyä (Shoriwä)

These are all terms of reference; the terms used in direct address are variants of these (see Lizot, 1971b).

APPENDIX D

Garden locations

The following coordinates refer to the approximate locations of the gardens (abandoned and contemporary) or villages given by numerical code in Columns 5 and 6 of Appendix A. These locations were estimated by means of the techniques described in Chapter 2: bearings were measured by magnetic compass and distances were measured in "sleeps" or by the intersection of bearings from several widely dispersed points. The fact that the coordinates appear to be within 05′ of accuracy should not be taken to be a measure of the estimate's precision. The fact is that I have not visited many of the places listed below, and even if I had, it would still have been difficult to locate the gardens on a map: there are no accurate published maps of this region. By plotting the coordinates on Figure 4.1, an approximate distribution of the gardens with respect to each other can be obtained.

Garden Number	*Garden Name*	*Approximate Coordinates*	*Comments*
010	Iwahikoroba-teri	1°40′N x 65°00′W	Recent area of occupation
012	Karawatari	1°00′N x 66°30′W	General area of occupation
026	Yeisikorowä-teri	1°35′N x 64°55′W	Recent area of occupation
028	Kohoroshitari	1°00′N x 66°00′W	General area of occupation
101	Amarokoböwei-täka	1°00′N x 66°30′W	A Karawatari garden
108	Boraböwei-täka	1°55′N x 64°50′W	
109	Botoabö-täka	1°40′N x 65°15′W	Many sites in this area
111	Bukimawä-täka	1°30′N x 65°30′W	Shukumöna River drainage
113	Dạadaamöböwei	1°30′N x 65°25′W	Many sites in this area
116	Hạtakoamöböwei	1°40′N x 65°15′W	Many sites in this area
118	Horedoböwei	1°35′N x 65°20′W	Several sites in this area
119	Ironasi	1°30′N x 65°25′W	Might be confused with an identically-named garden at 1°40′N x 65°15′W
122	Kayurewä	2°00′N x 64°50′W	Very old area of occupation
124	Konabuma	1°40′N x 65°10′W	
126	Mamoheböwei	1°35′N x 65°20′W	Many gardens in this area
128	Mishimishimaböwei	1°35′N x 65°20′W	Presently occupied
132	Nimobötotoi	1°35′N x 65°20′W	
133	Paruritawä	1°45′N x 65°25′W	
134	Roena	1°50′N x 65°25′W	
141	Ugushita	1°30′N x 65°30′W	Shukumöna River drainage

Garden Number	*Garden Name*	*Approximate Coordinates*	*Comments*
145	Yoboböwei	1°55′N x 64°40′W	Very old area of occupation
164	Habromaböwei	1°40′N x 65°00′W	Presently occupied by a fraction of Iwahikoroba-teri
165	Direi	1°35′N x 65°20′W	
166	Yọbönai	1°25′N x 65°25′W	Shukumöna River drainage
167	Hịmotabö	1°35′N x 65°20′W	
168	Dodorihesbraoba	1°35′N x 65°20′W	
169	Bọshoroböwei	1°40′N x 65°20′W	
172	Ishiwei	2°00′N x 64°45′W	Very old area of occupation
173	Shihenaishibä	2°00′N x 64°45′W	Very old area of occupation
175	Horoina	1°35′N x 64°55′W	Near Shukumöna River
182	Araböhenawei	1°25′N x 65°25′W	Shukumöna River drainage
186	Bọremaböwei	1°45′N x 65°05′W	
187	Mahanishidoböwei	1°50′N x 64°40′W	
197	Ironasi	1°30′N x 65°25′W	Presently occupied

APPENDIX E

Identification photographs

The 1971 residents of Mishimishimaböwei-teri are shown in the identification photographs that follow. Ideally, I would like to have each person on a separate photograph, but the village women are quite reluctant to be photographed alone and usually demand that their co-wives or sisters (and their older children) be included with them. In addition, the women attempt to hide the faces of their younger children or try to hide their children from me. I could only achieve a near 100 percent photographic sample of the village by compromising with the women and photographing most of them in groups, and by "hiring" young children to accompany me around the village to make sure that particular women have not concealed their babies from me. Still, a few people managed to elude me by sneaking out the back of their huts whenever they saw me approach with my camera. Some of them made a prolonged joke of it and fled more to frustrate me than out of a sense of fear.

I use these and similar photographs on return visits to villages, mostly to update my census data. This spares me—and the villagers—the embarrassment of using their names out loud. However, during the course of a year a few people die, and should they be one of several people in the same photograph, then that photograph must be removed from my notebook, and, indeed, all of the photographs must be used with great caution. One of my first tasks on returning to a village like Mishimishimaböwei-teri is to work alone with a trusted informant such as Dedeheiwä and determine whether or not there have been any deaths in the village since my last visit, and I systematically make notes in my census books and on identification photographs accordingly. However, I first determine whether or not any close relatives of Dedeheiwä have died, and remove these photographs and names before working with him.

A few of the residents of Mishimishimaböwei-teri—particularly the younger children—appear in more than one photograph. Appendix A gives, in Column 7, only one of the photographic references. The four-digit identification numbers used throughout the text and listed in Column 1 of Appendix A are given, in this appendix, beneath the individual's photograph. Where there are several people in a photograph, each person is numbered on the photograph itself with a single-digit number, and his or her corresponding four-digit identification number is given below the photograph. The number that appears in the upper left-hand corner of the photograph is designated, in Column 7 of Appendix A, as the "ID Photograph" number.

I envisioned the major use of this appendix as a supplement to the series of ethnographic films that will eventually be distributed (see Appendix G for a list of the films), films that document a large number of social and cultural aspects of this village. If used to their fullest extent, the ethnographic films and the photographs in this appendix will constitute a unique resource for students, teachers, and researchers who wish to verify, challenge, or modify the conclusions that I (and Timothy Asch) reach in both the distributed films and the published study guides that will accompany them, or to develop their own hypotheses about the behavior of the individuals shown in the films. Hopefully it will be possible, using these photographs, to identify individuals in the films who might not otherwise be identified in the study guides, or to cross-check the identifications given. Finally, we intend to deposit a complete, unedited print of all of our footage in a national film archive when such an archive is funded. This book and the appendices in it will serve as a guide to researchers in the future who utilize the film resource.

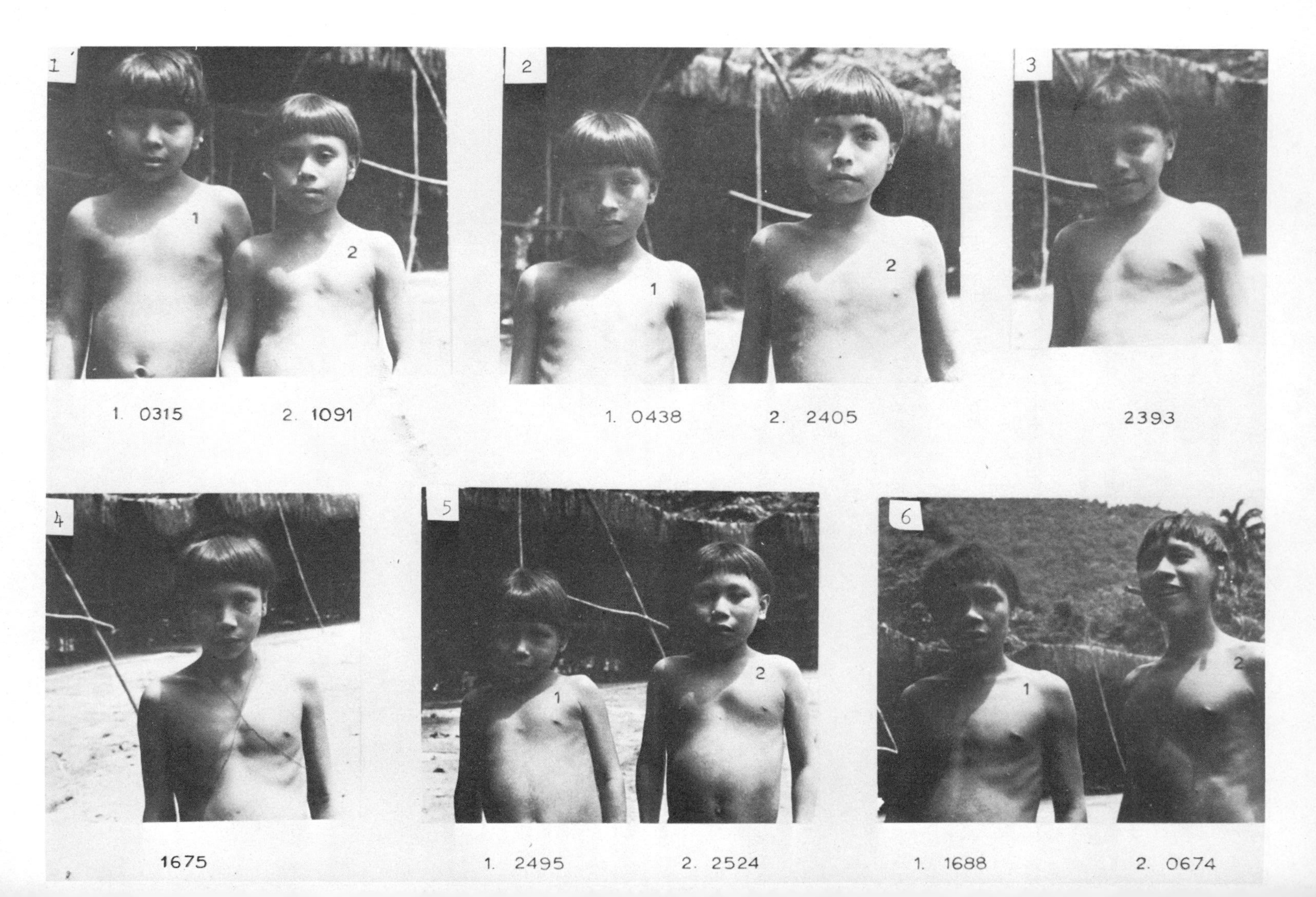
1
1. 0315
2. 1091
2
1. 0438
2. 2405
3
2393
4
1675
5
1. 2495
2. 2524
6
1. 1688
2. 0674

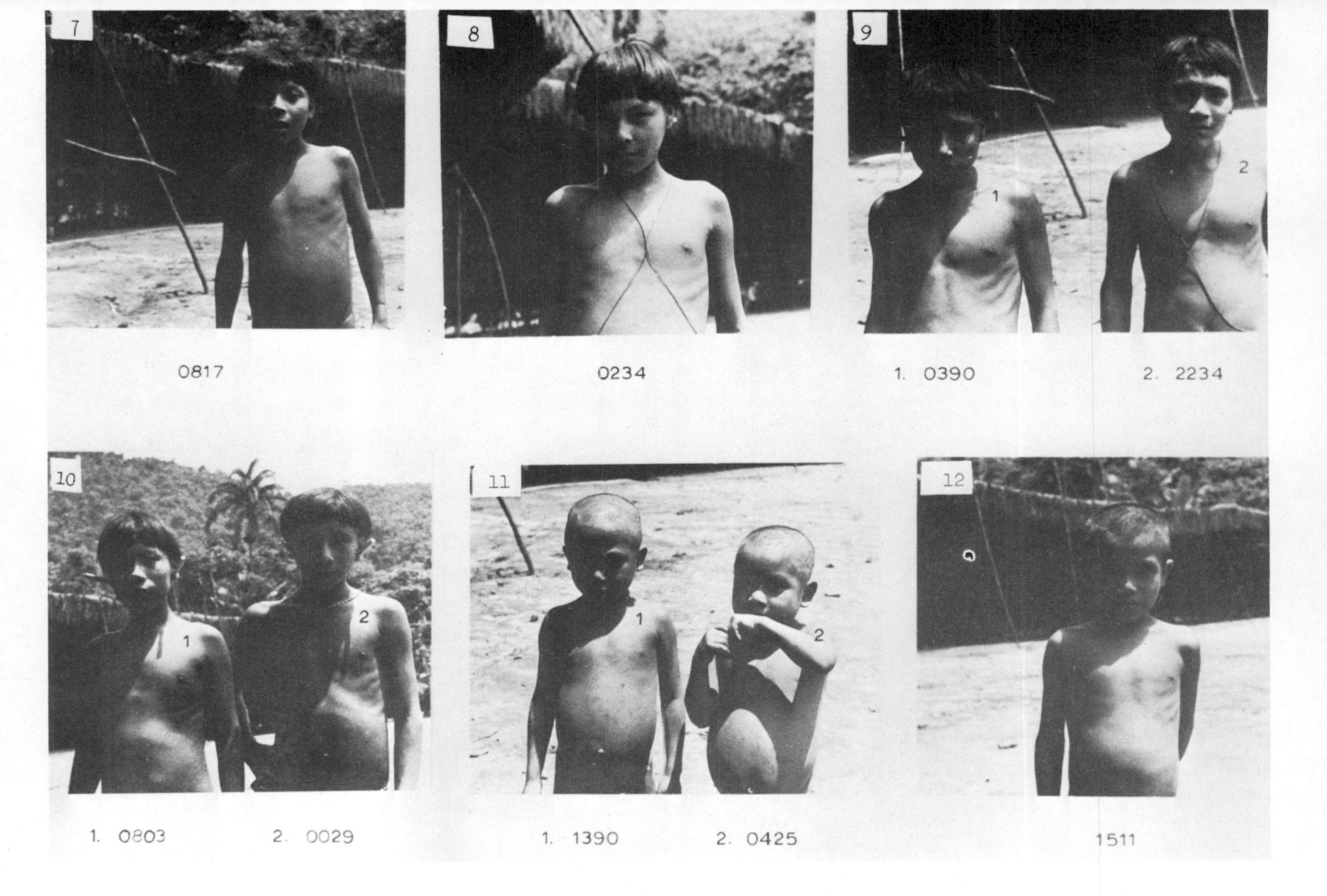
7
0817
8
0234
9
1. 0390
2. 2234
10
1. 0803
2. 0029
11
1. 1390
2. 0425
12
1511

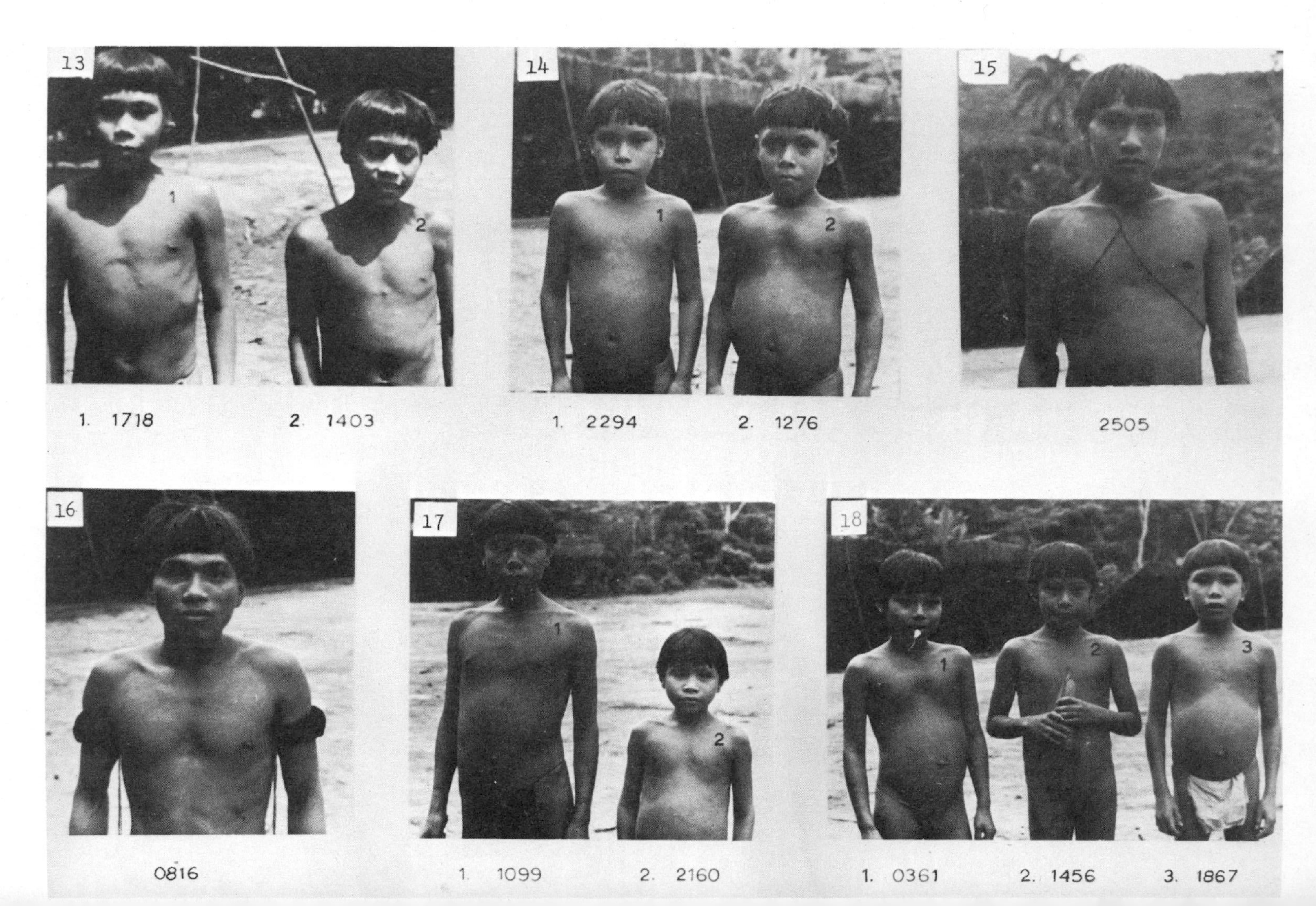

13
14
15
1. 1718
2. 1403
1. 2294
2. 1276
2505
16
17
18
0816
1. 1099
2. 2160
1. 0361
2. 1456
3. 1867

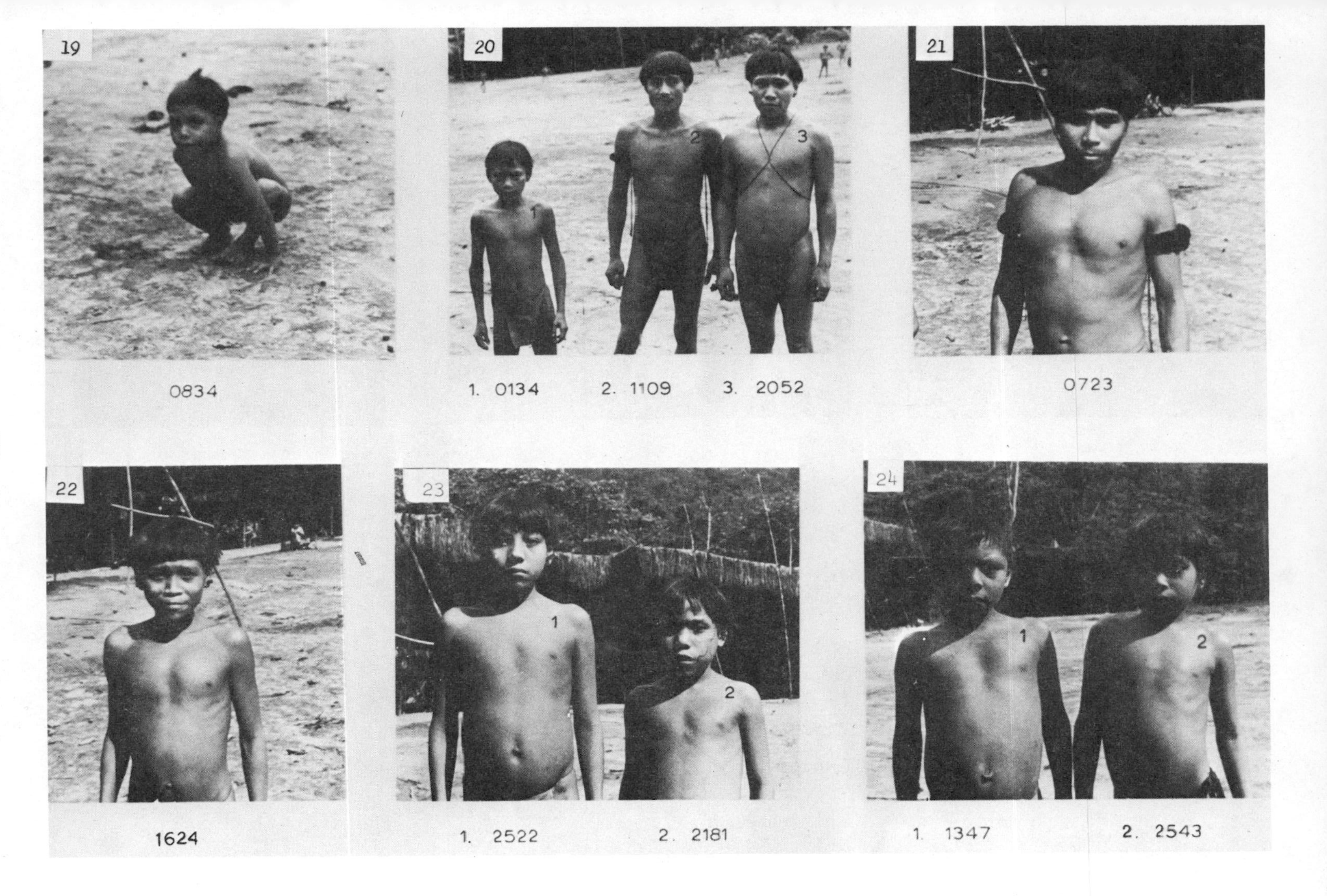
19
0834
20
1
2
3
1. 0134
2. 1109
3. 2052
21
0723
22
1624
23
1
2
1. 2522
2. 2181
24
1
2
1. 1347
2. 2543

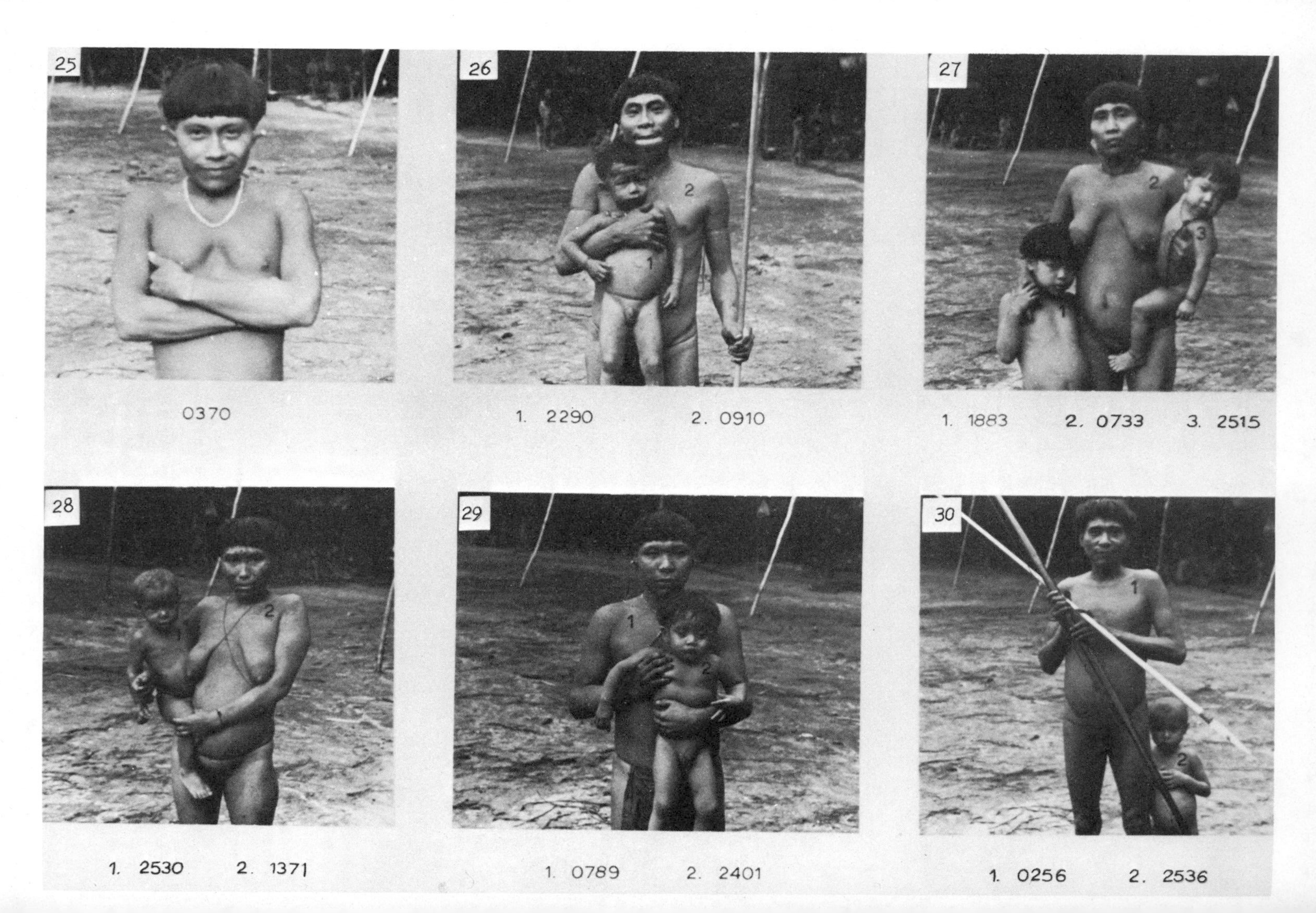
25
0370
26
1. 2290
2. 0910
27
1. 1883
2. 0733
3. 2515
28
1. 2530
2. 1371
29
1. 0789
2. 2401
30
1. 0256
2. 2536

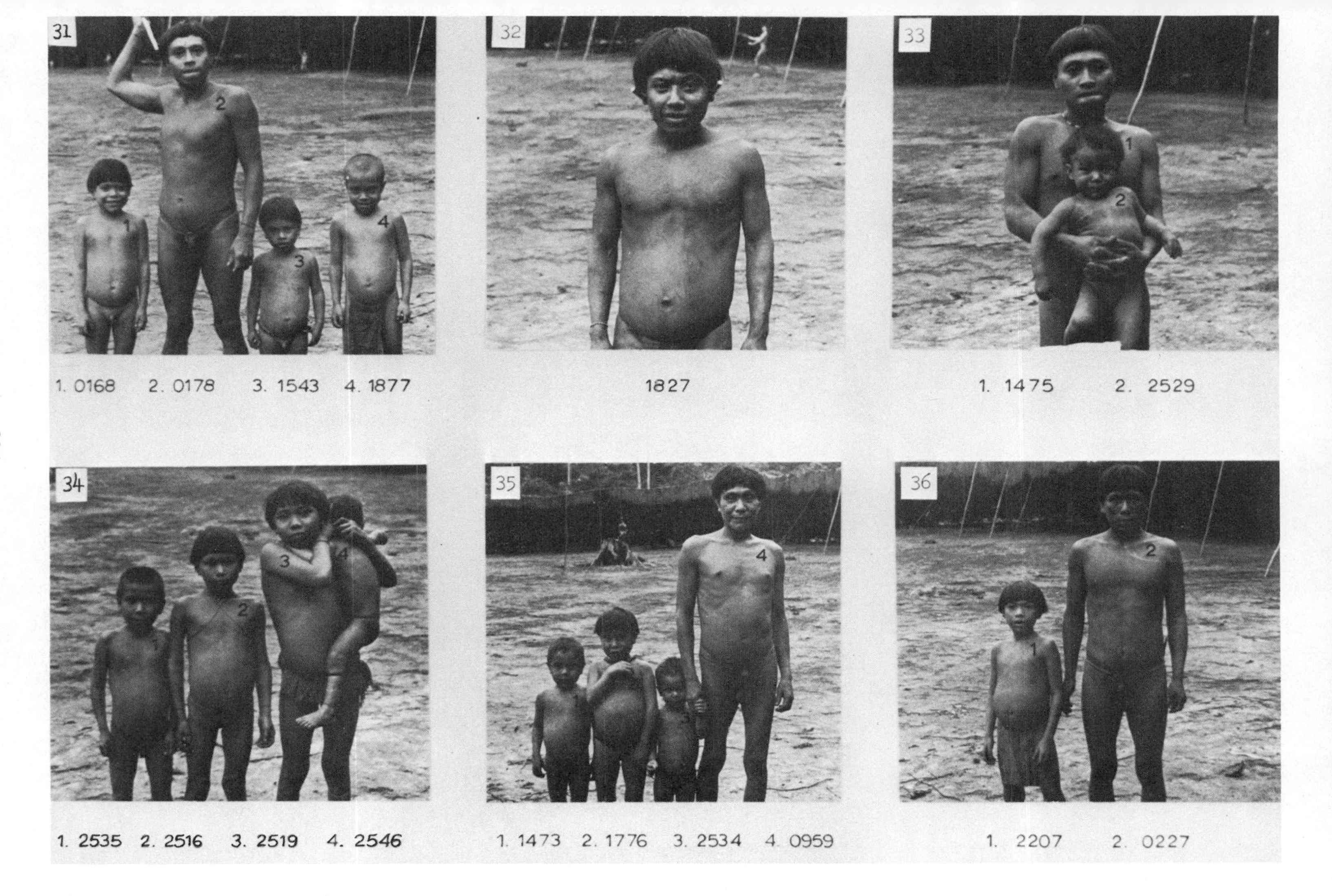

1. 0168 2. 0178 3. 1543 4. 1877

1827

1. 1475 2. 2529

1. 2535 2. 2516 3. 2519 4. 2546

1. 1473 2. 1776 3. 2534 4. 0959

1. 2207 2. 0227

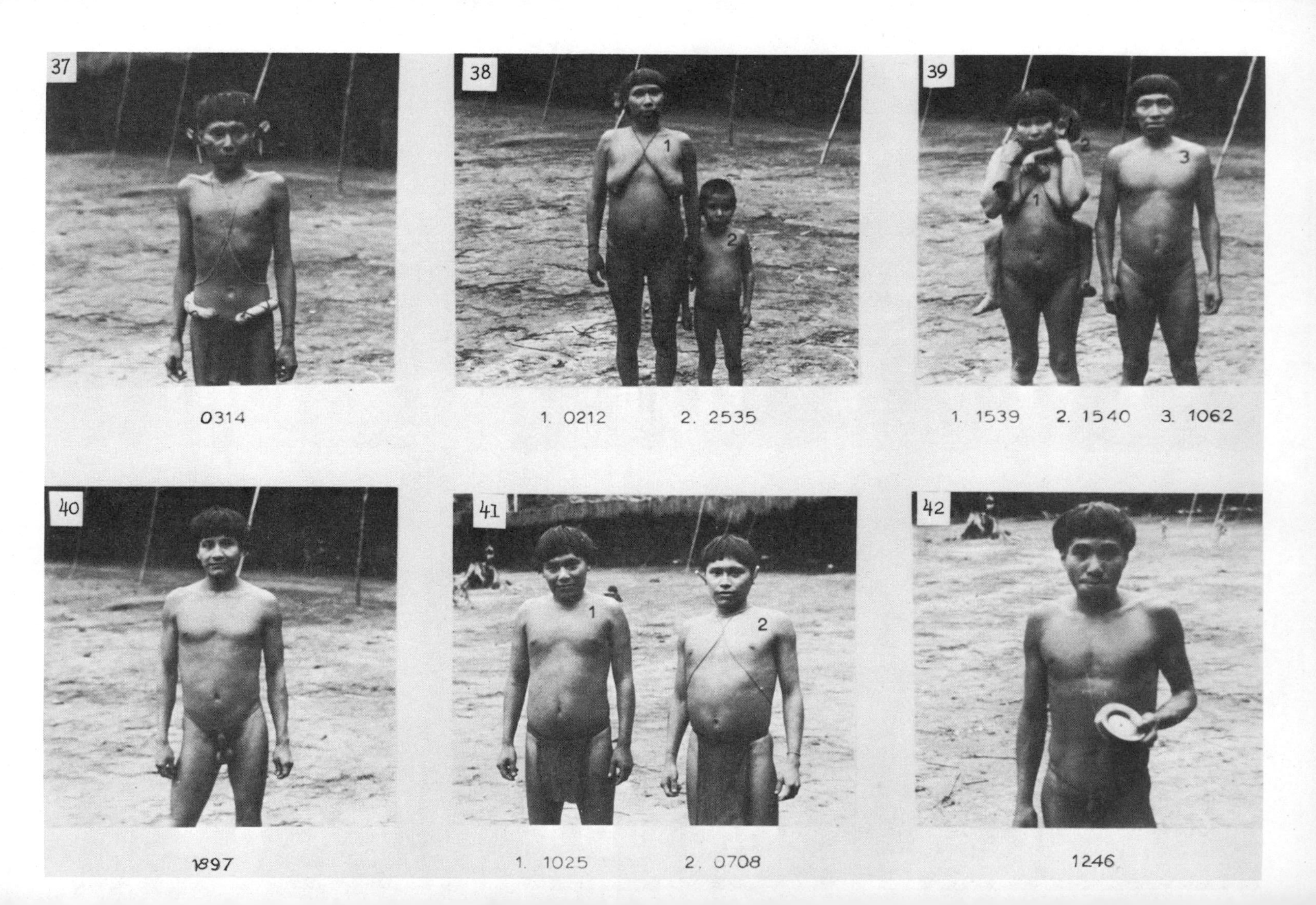
37
0314
38
1. 0212 2. 2535
39
1. 1539 2. 1540 3. 1062
40
1897
41
1. 1025 2. 0708
42
1246

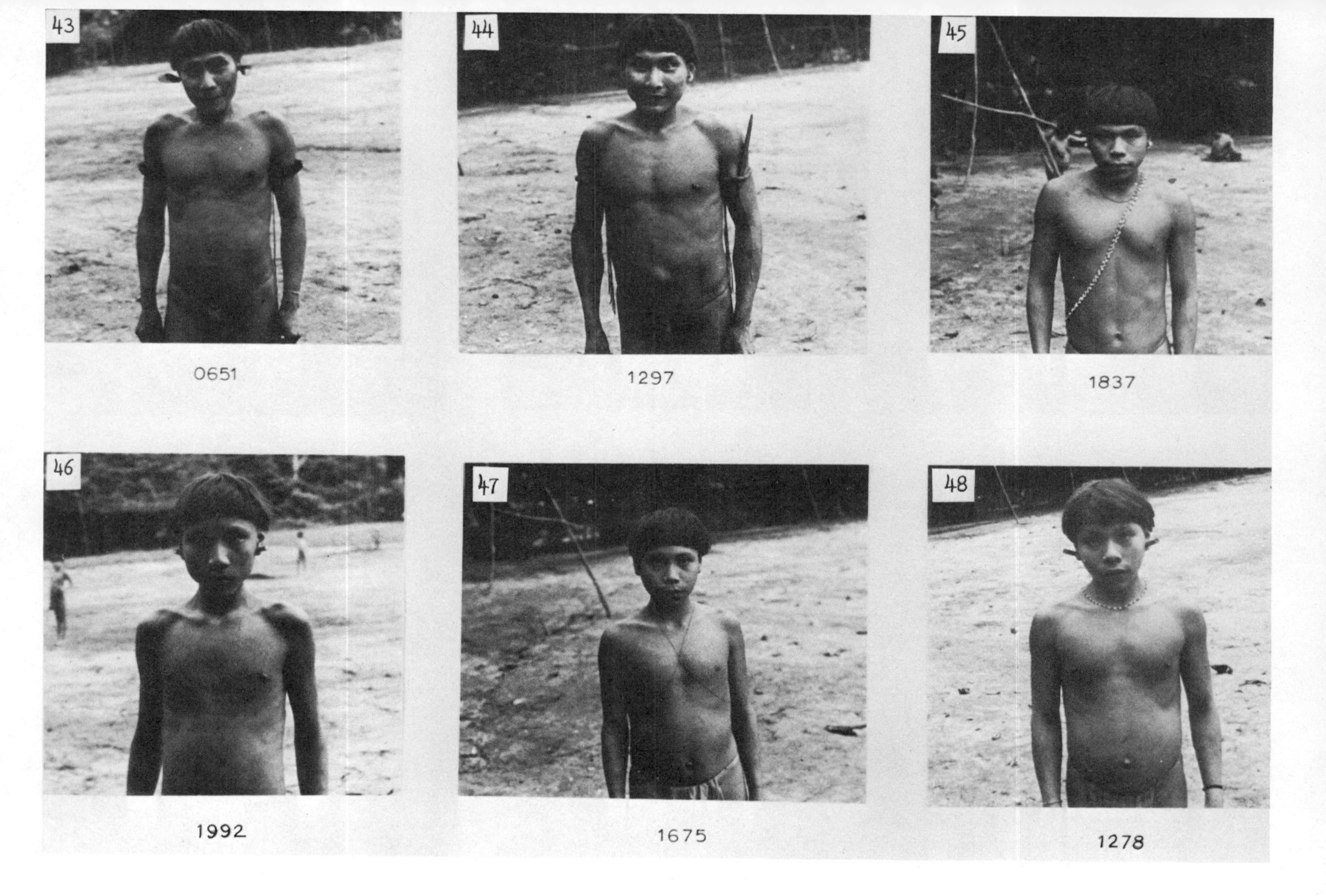
43
0651
44
1297
45
1837
46
1992
47
1675
48
1278

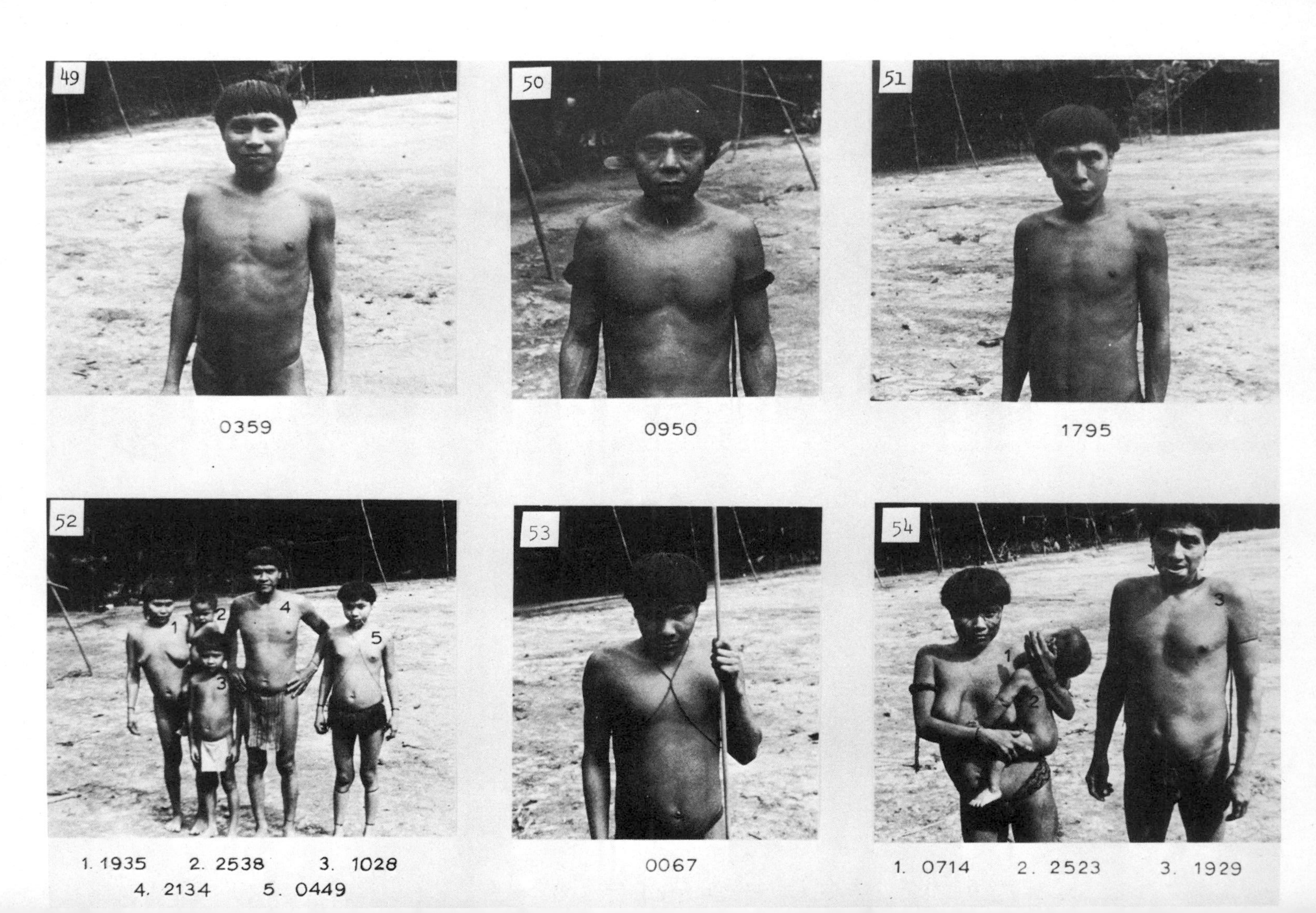

0359

0950

1795

1. 1935 2. 2538 3. 1028
4. 2134 5. 0449

0067

1. 0714 2. 2523 3. 1929

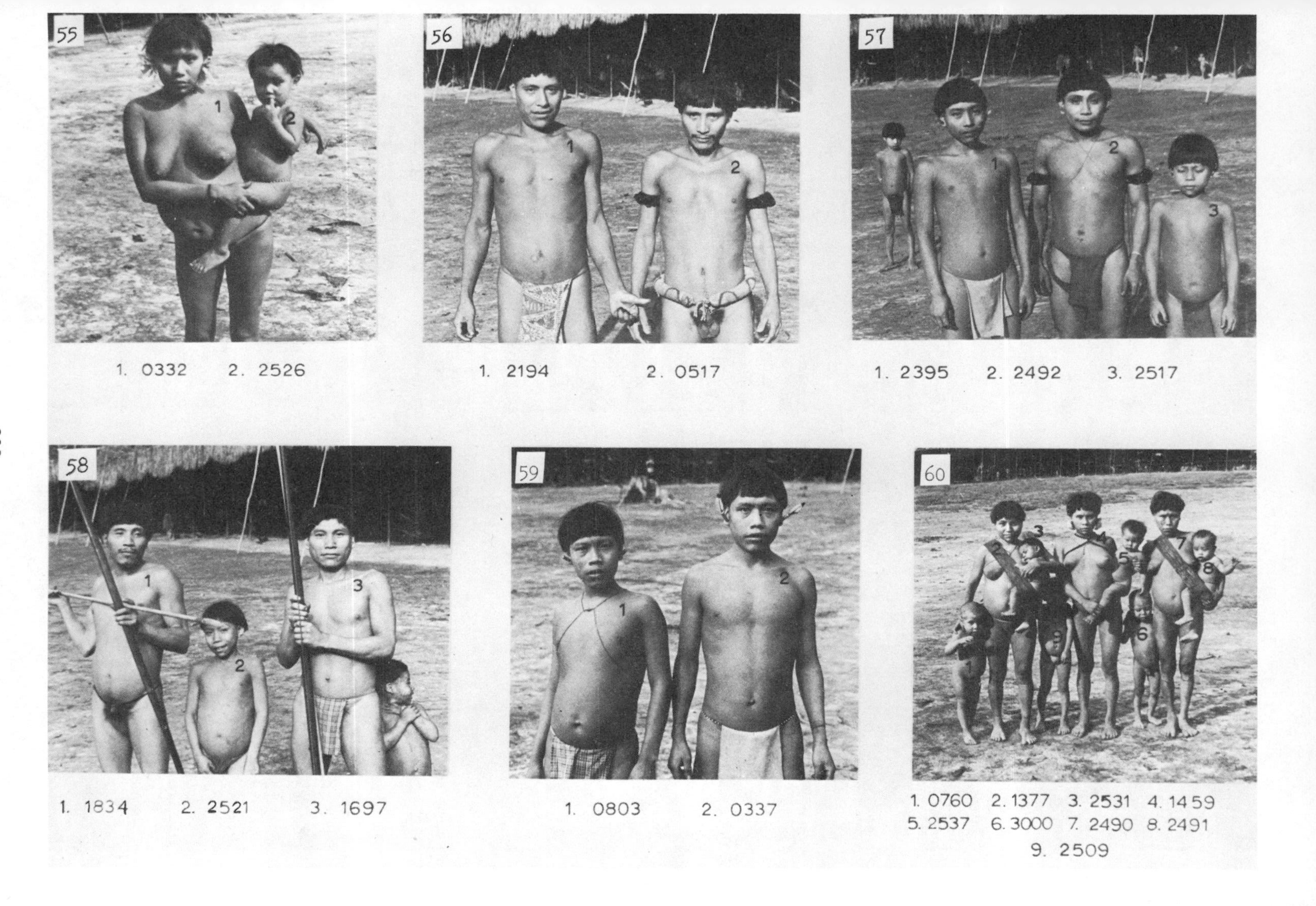

1. 0332 2. 2526

1. 2194 2. 0517

1. 2395 2. 2492 3. 2517

1. 1834 2. 2521 3. 1697

1. 0803 2. 0337

1. 0760 2. 1377 3. 2531 4. 1459
5. 2537 6. 3000 7. 2490 8. 2491
9. 2509

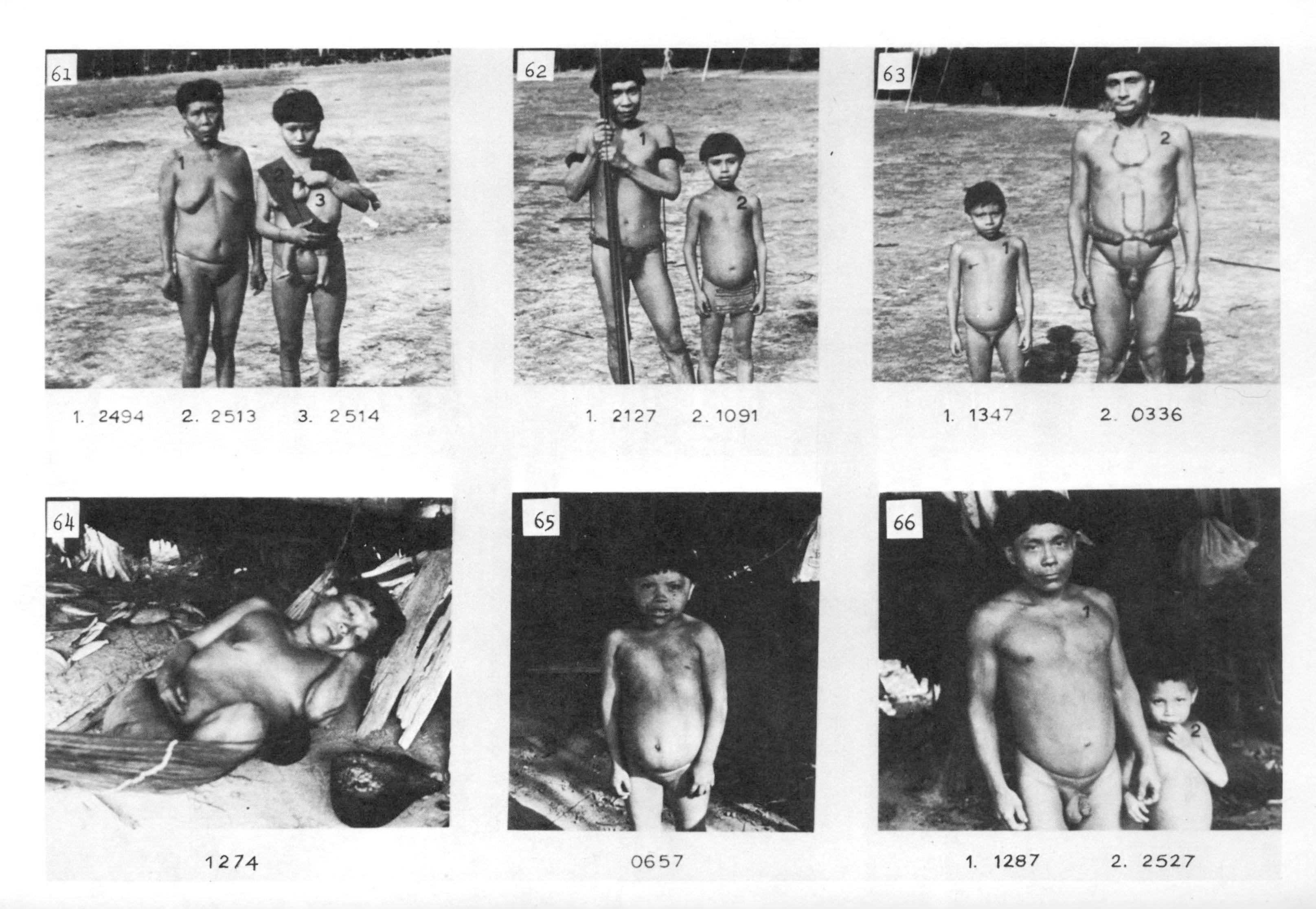

61: 1. 2494 2. 2513 3. 2514

62: 1. 2127 2. 1091

63: 1. 1347 2. 0336

64: 1274

65: 0657

66: 1. 1287 2. 2527

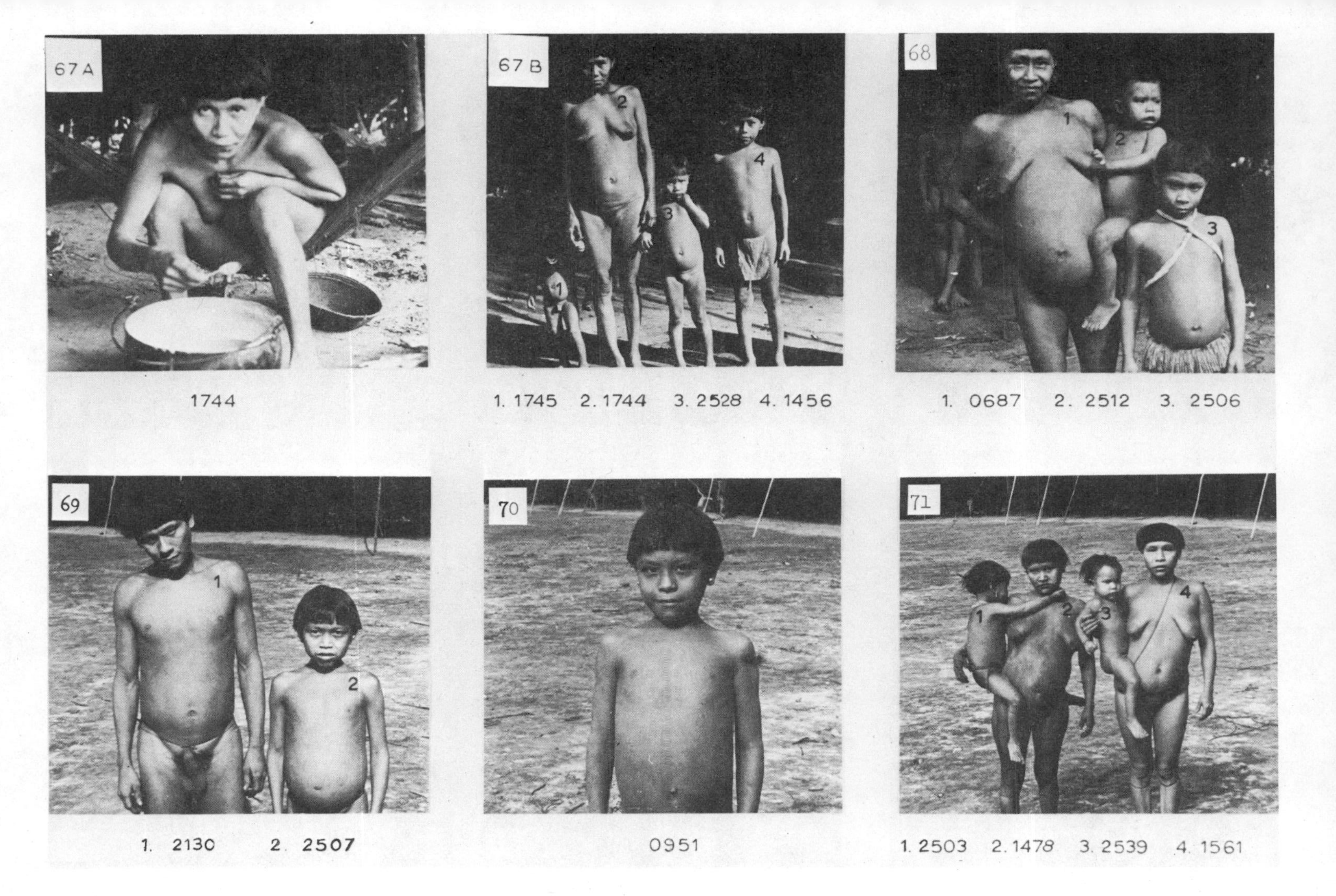

67 A — 1744

67 B — 1. 1745 2. 1744 3. 2528 4. 1456

68 — 1. 0687 2. 2512 3. 2506

69 — 1. 2130 2. 2507

70 — 0951

71 — 1. 2503 2. 1478 3. 2539 4. 1561

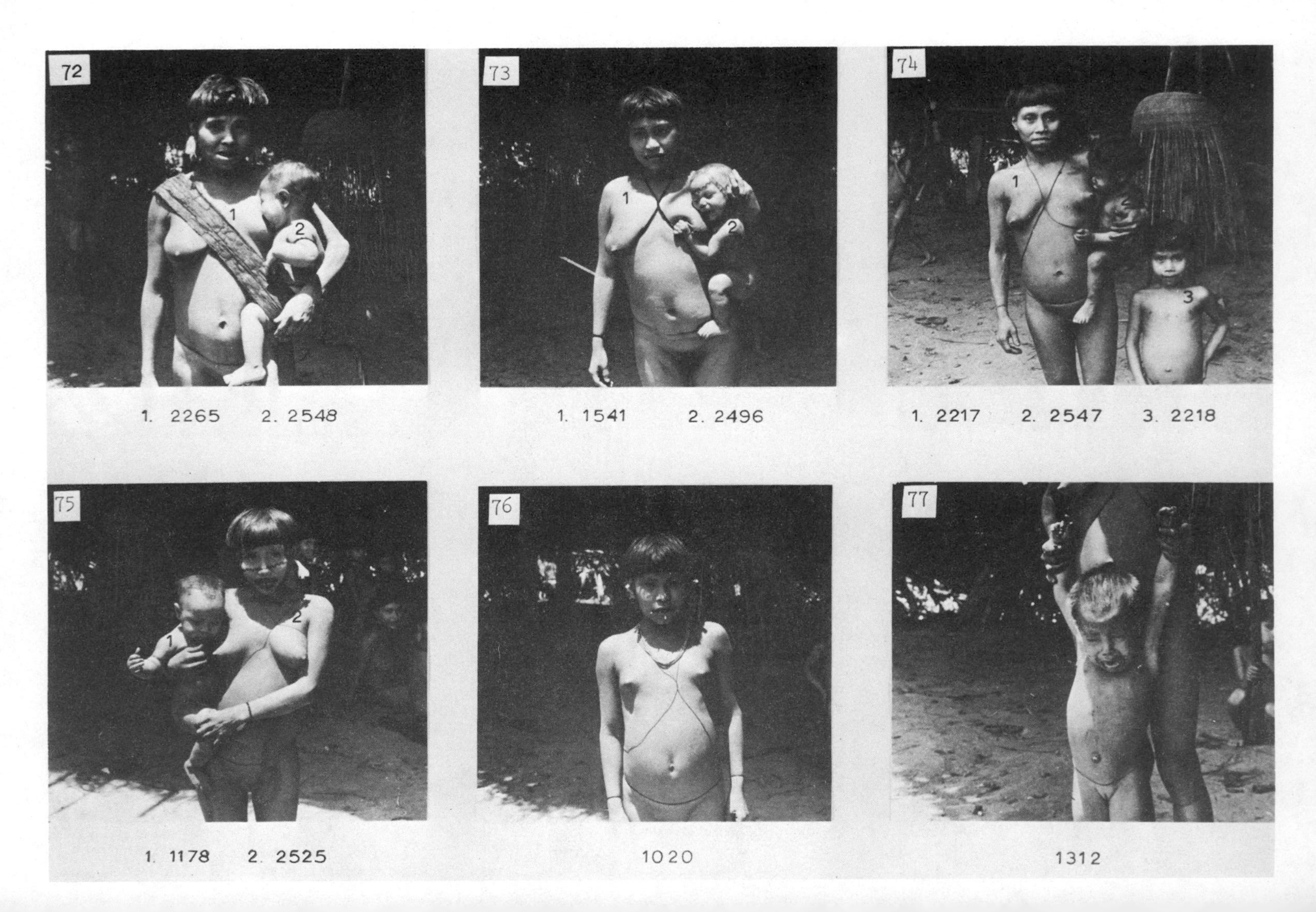

1. 2265 2. 2548

1. 1541 2. 2496

1. 2217 2. 2547 3. 2218

1. 1178 2. 2525

1020

1312

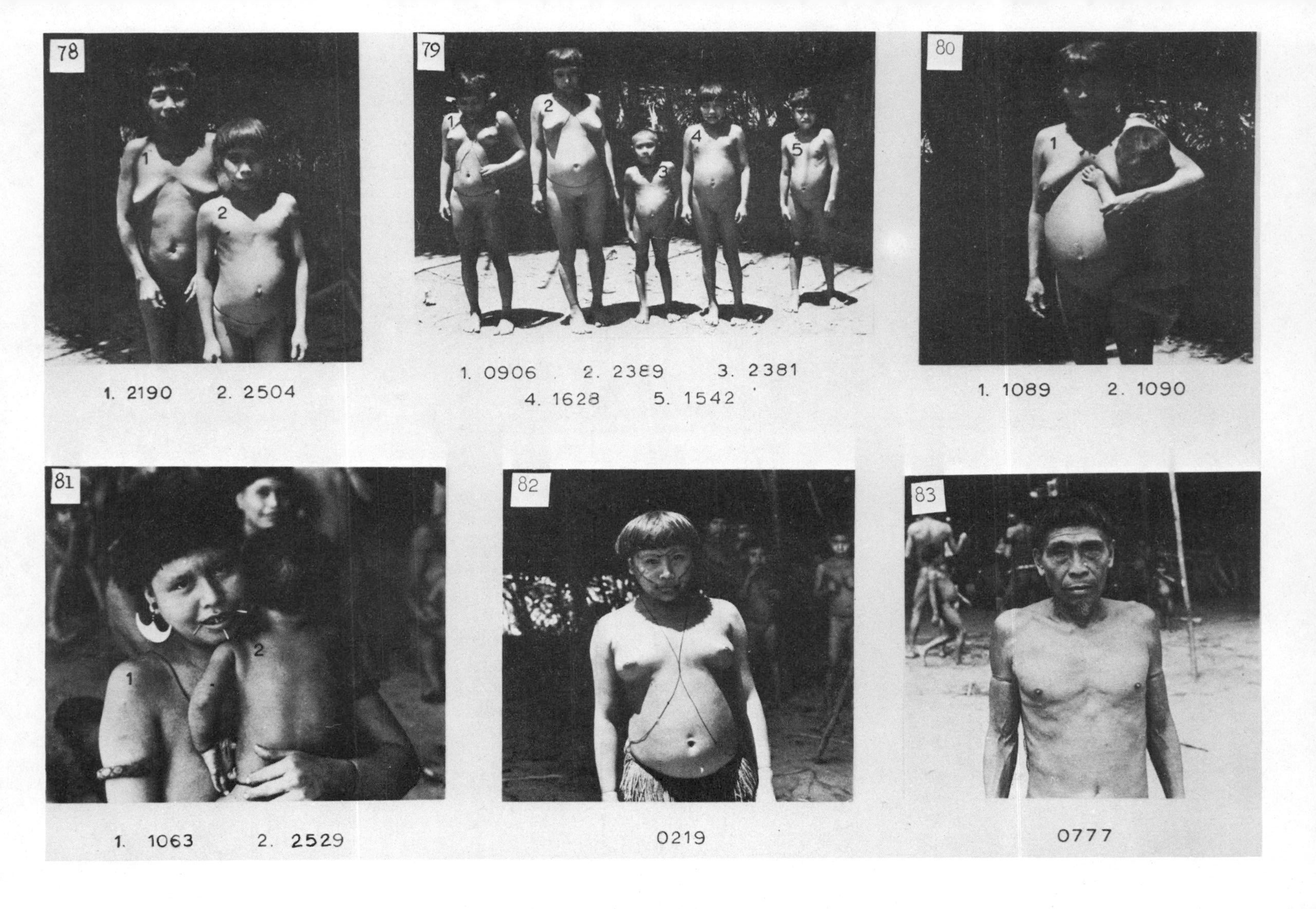
78
1. 2190 2. 2504
79
1. 0906 2. 2389 3. 2381
4. 1628 5. 1542
80
1. 1089 2. 1090
81
1. 1063 2. 2529
82
0219
83
0777

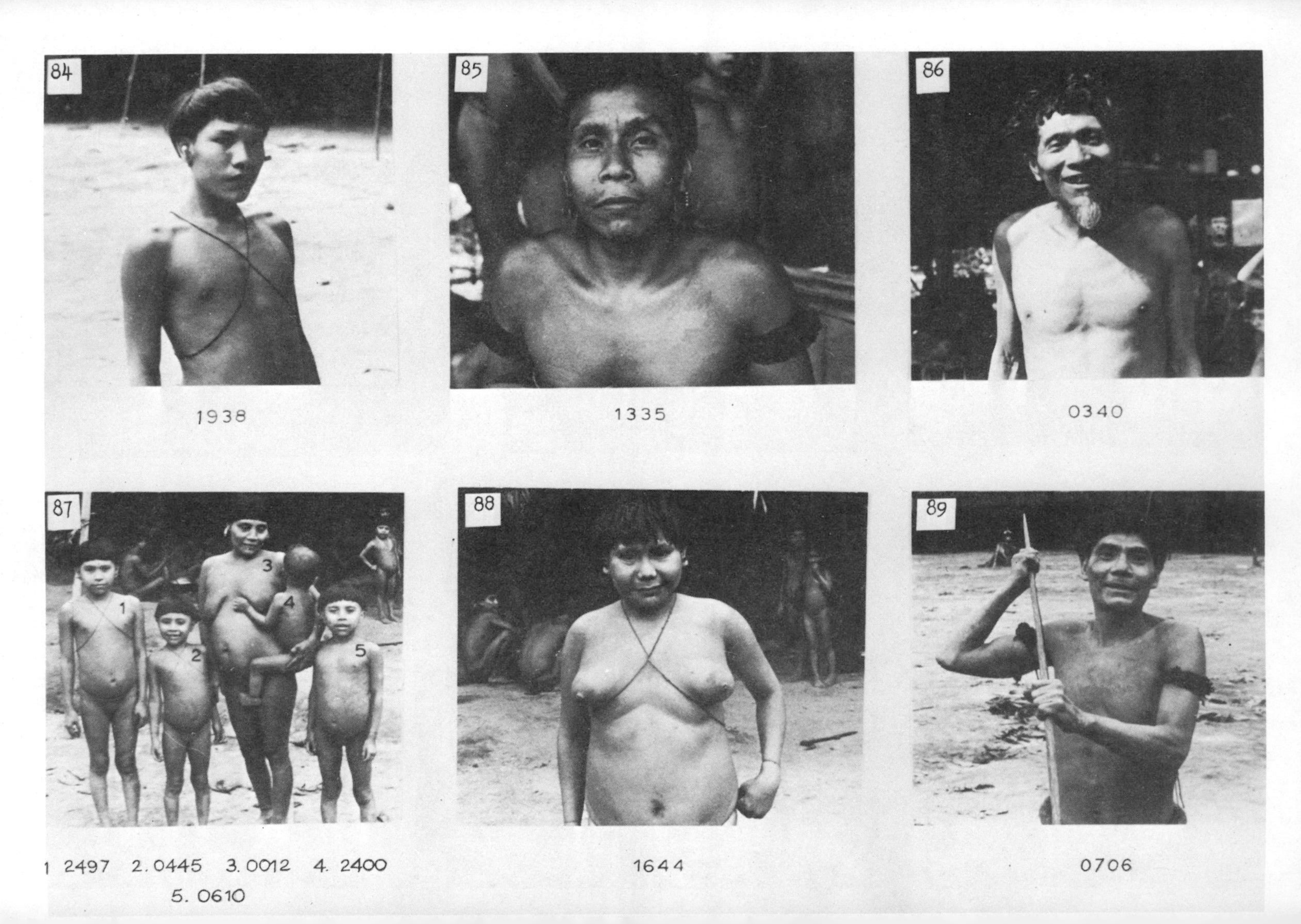
84
85
86
1938
1335
0340
87
1
2
3
4
5
1 2497 2. 0445 3. 0012 4. 2400
5. 0610
88
1644
89
0706

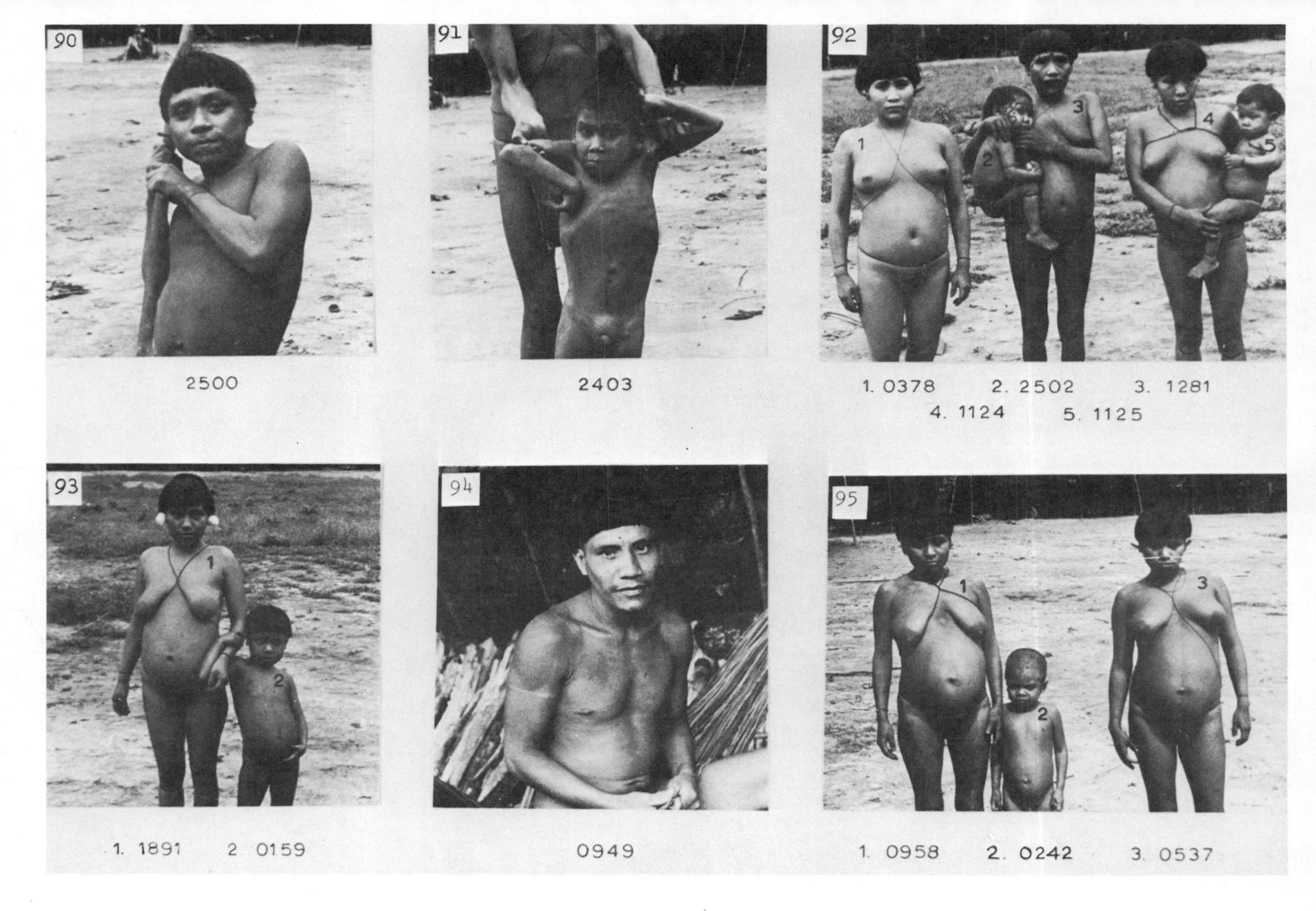
90
2500
91
2403
92
1. 0378 2. 2502 3. 1281
4. 1124 5. 1125
93
1. 1891 2 0159
94
0949
95
1. 0958 2. 0242 3. 0537

1. 1339 2. 1059 3. 2493

1. 2488 2. 2209

1. 0833 2. 2545

1. 0833 2. 2545

1126

1014

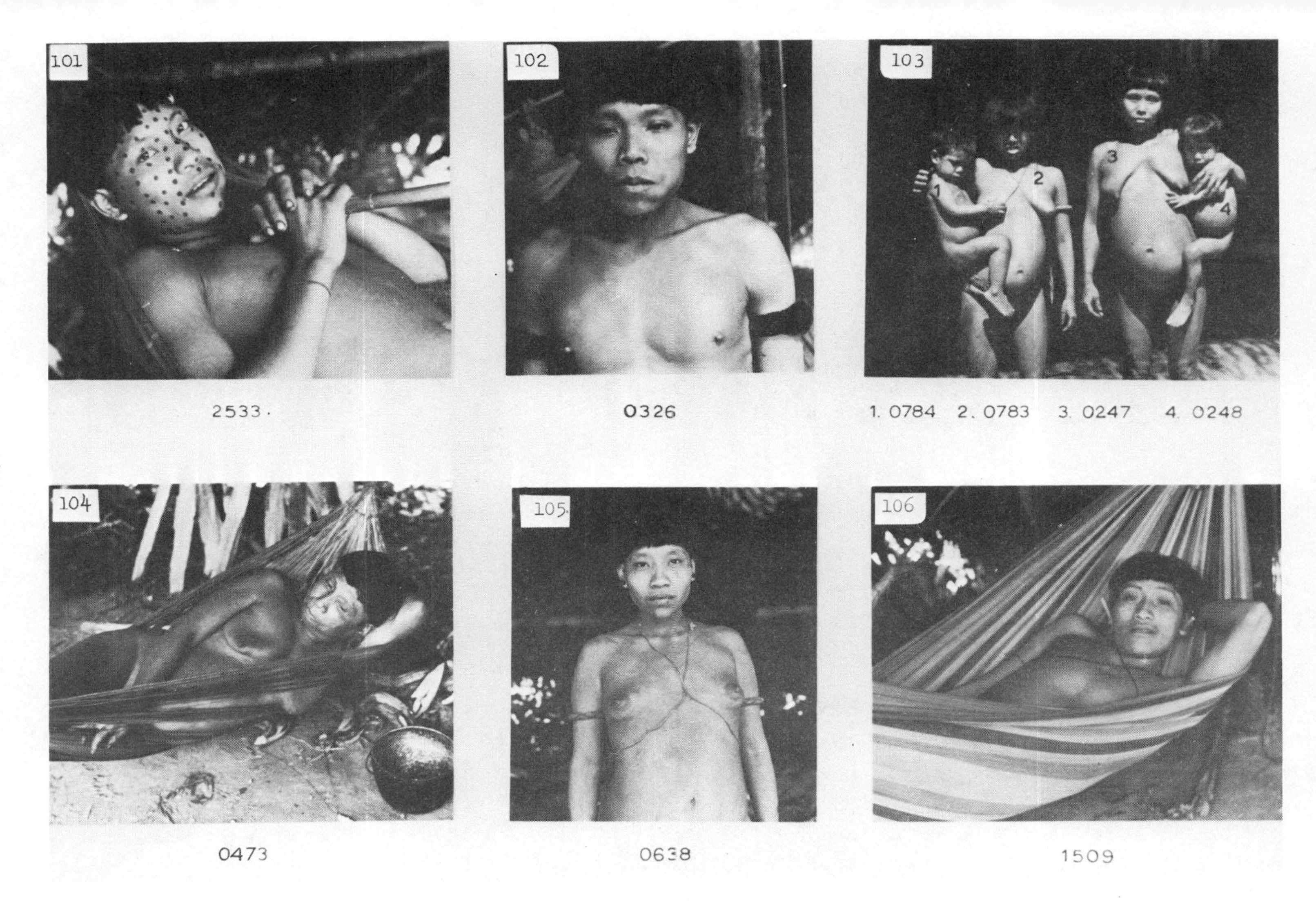

2533.

0326

1. 0784 2. 0783 3. 0247 4. 0248

0473

0638

1509

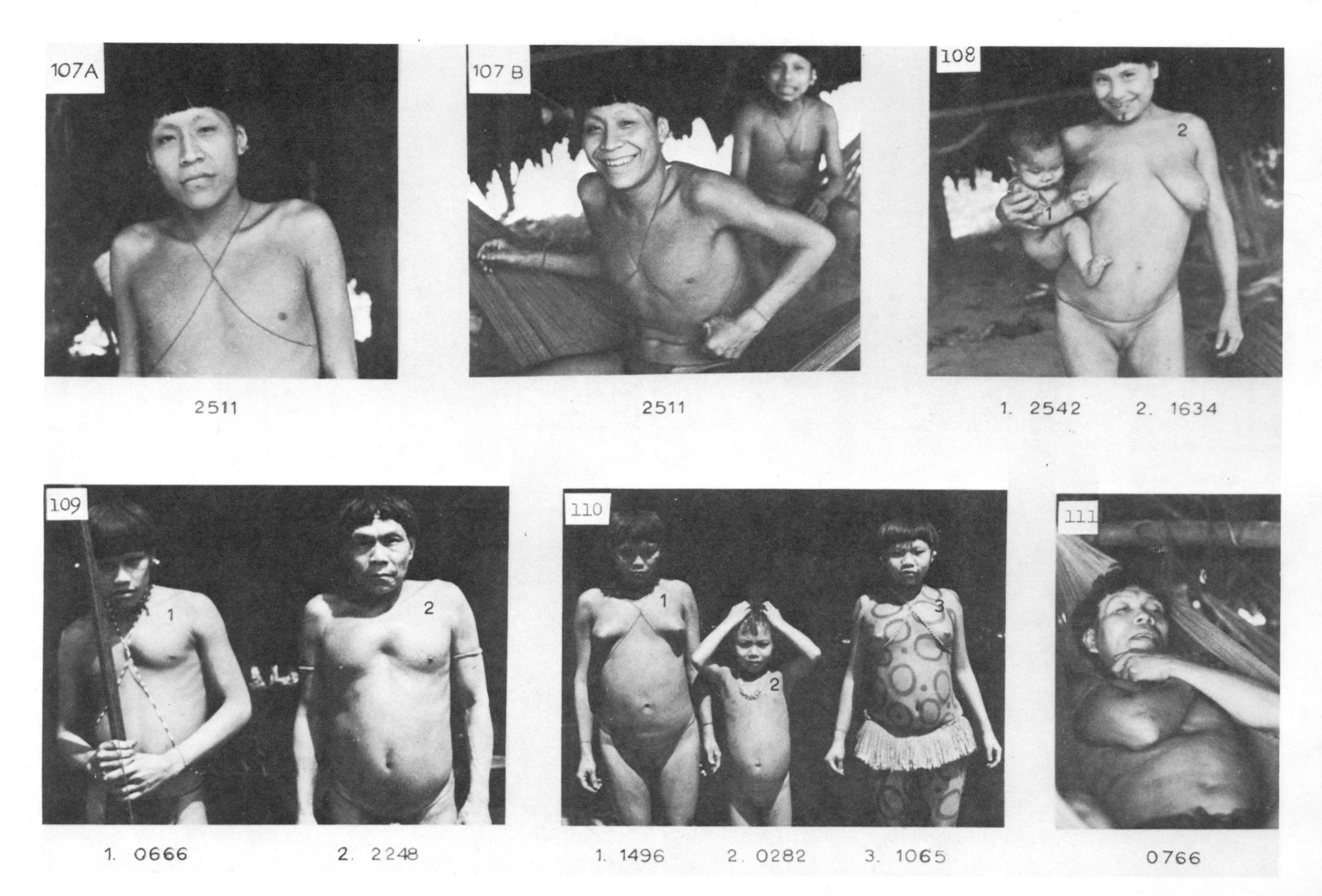

107A
2511
107 B
2511
108
1. 2542 2. 1634
109
1. 0666 2. 2248
110
1. 1496 2. 0282 3. 1065
111
0766

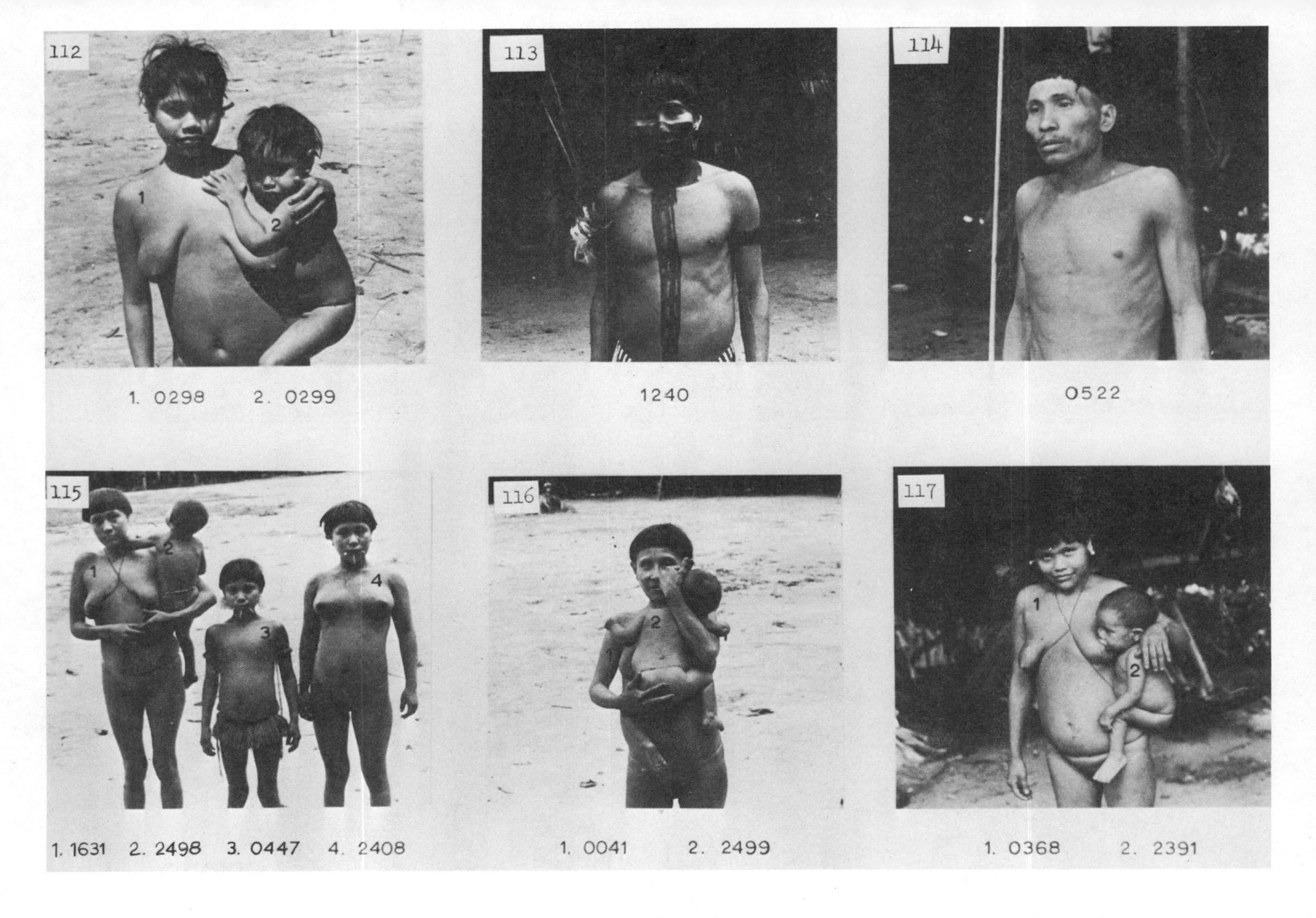
112
1. 0298 2. 0299
113
1240
114
0522
115
1. 1631 2. 2498 3. 0447 4. 2408
116
1. 0041 2. 2499
117
1. 0368 2. 2391

118
2256
119 A
1. 1861 2. 2398
119 B
1. 1861 2. 2398
120
.1706
121
1. 1206 2. 2518
122
0202

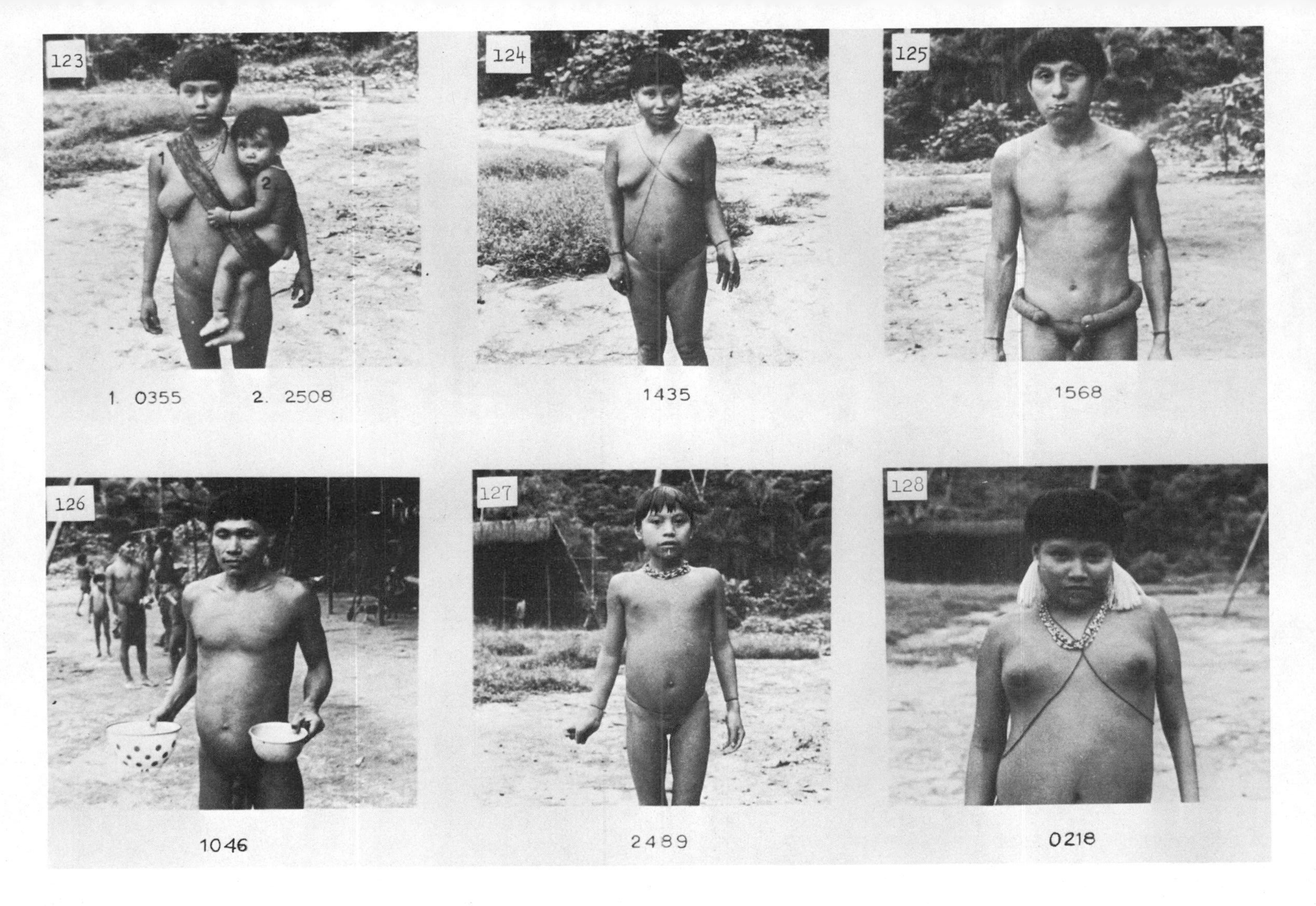
123
1
2
1. 0355 2. 2508
124
1435
125
1568
126
1046
127
2489
128
0218

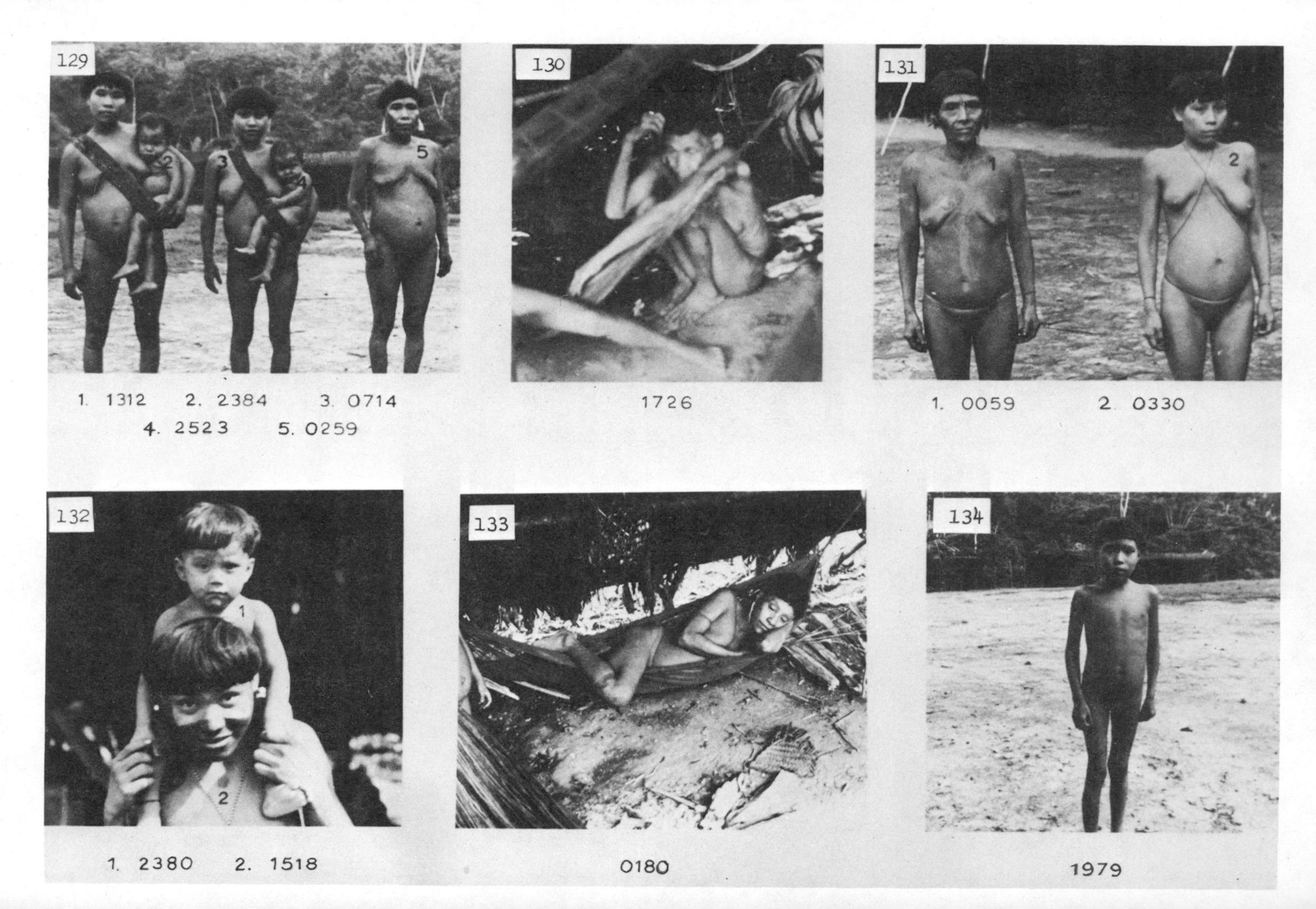

129
1. 1312 2. 2384 3. 0714
4. 2523 5. 0259

130
1726

131
1. 0059 2. 0330

132
1. 2380 2. 1518

133
0180

134
1979

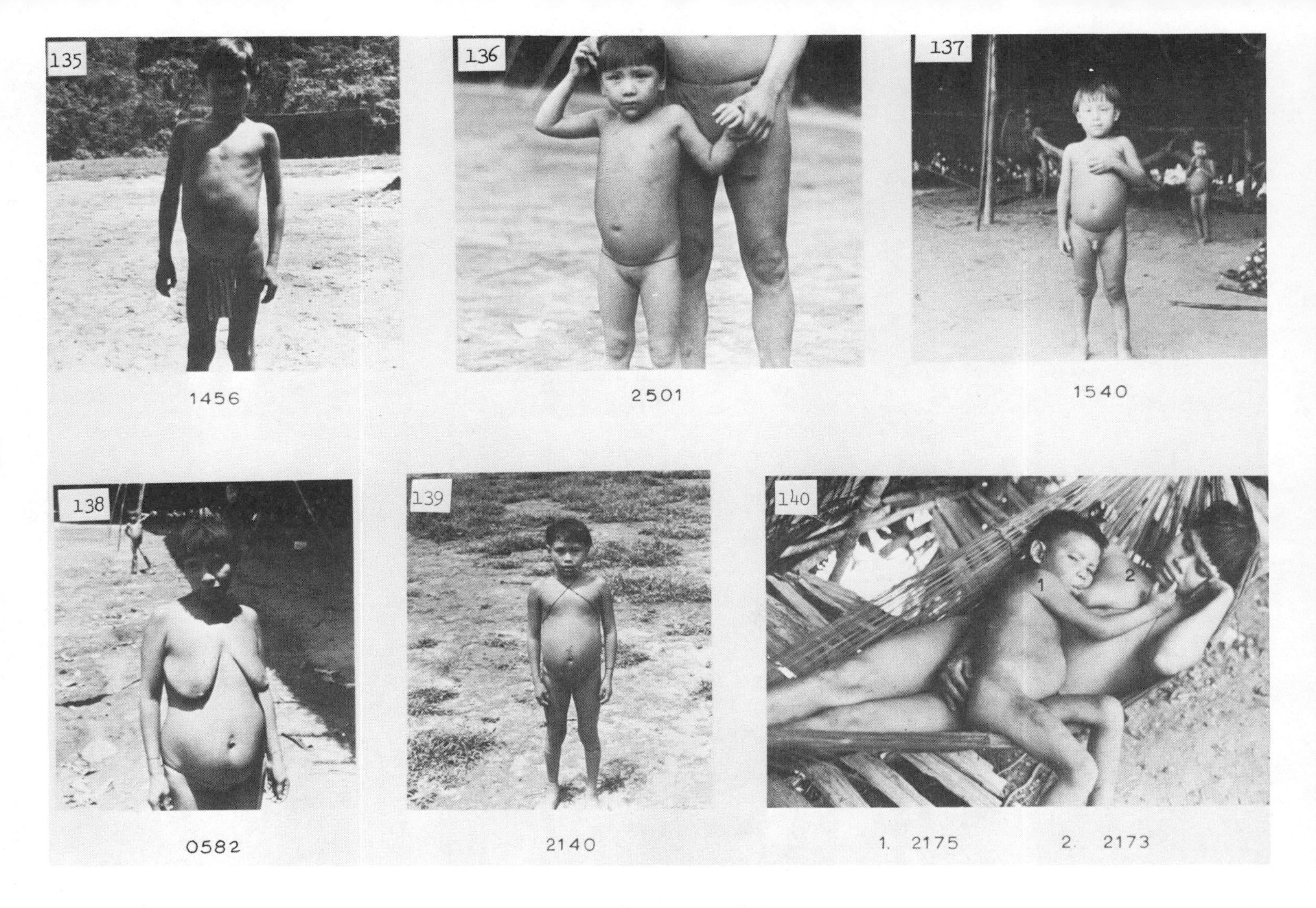

135
1456
136
2501
137
1540
138
0582
139
2140
140
1
2
1. 2175
2. 2173

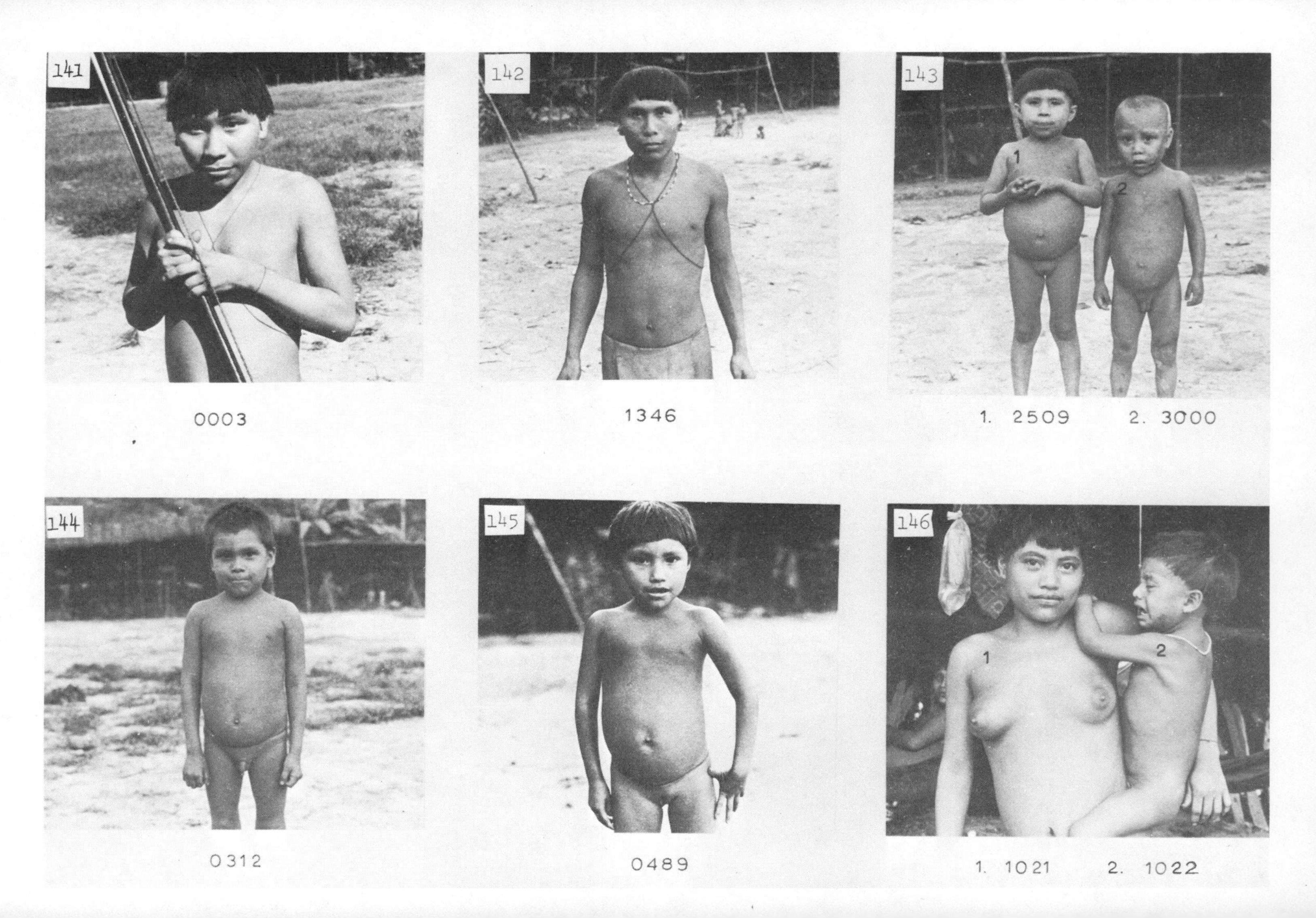
141
0003
142
1346
143
1
2
1. 2509 2. 3000
144
0312
145
0489
146
1
2
1. 1021 2. 1022

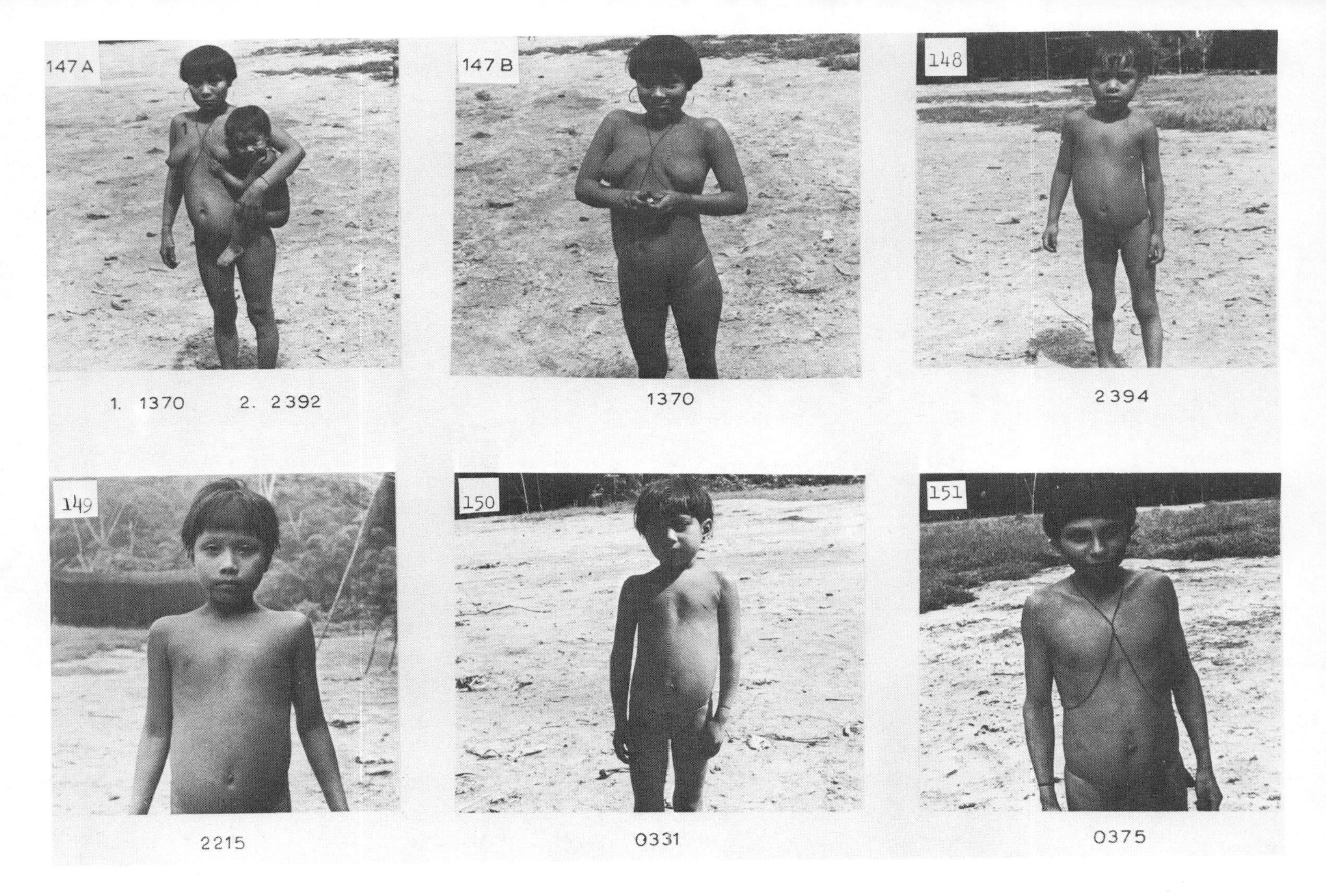
147 A
1. 1370 2. 2392
147 B
1370
148
2394
149
2215
150
0331
151
0375

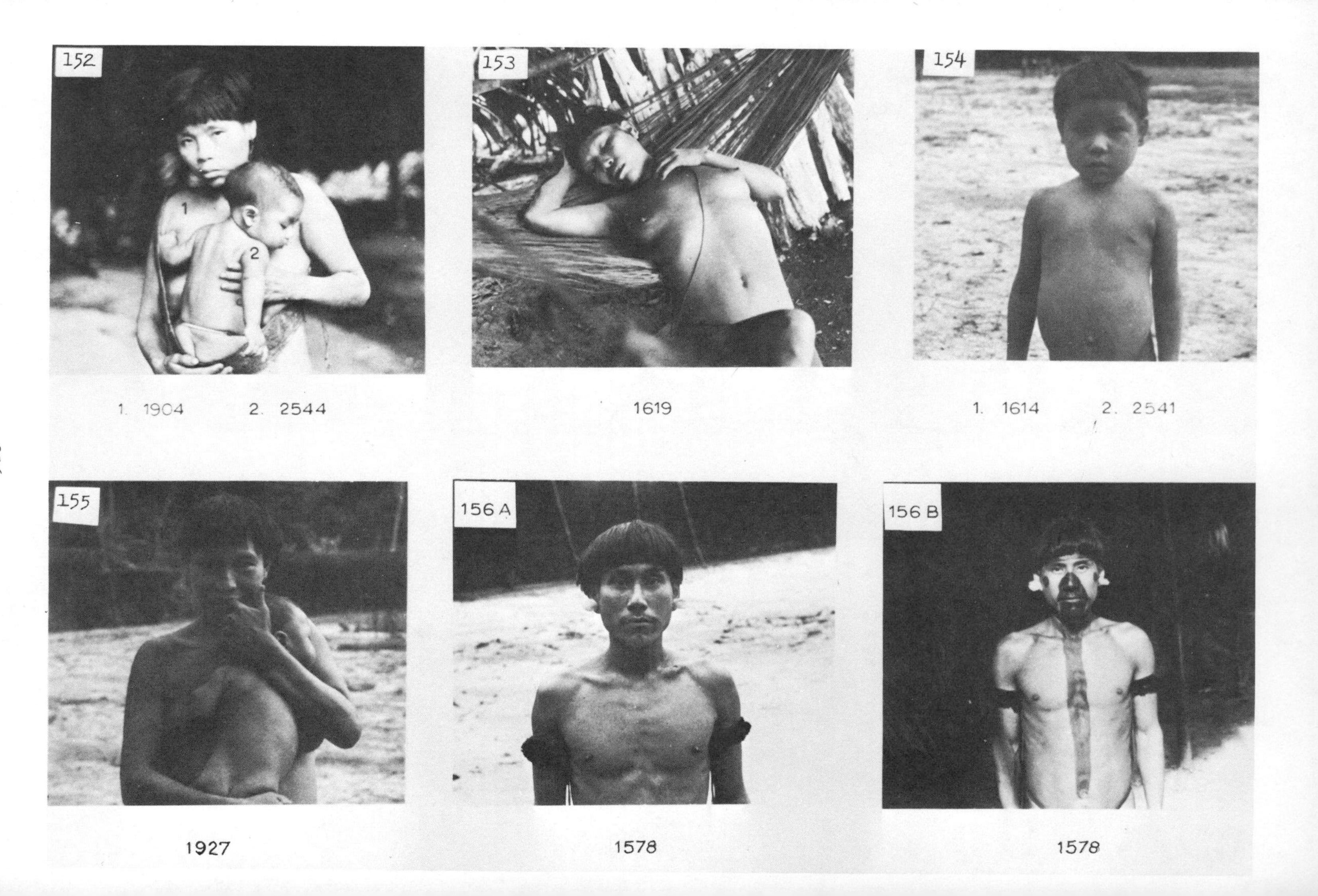

1. 1904 2. 2544

1619

1. 1614 2. 2541

1927

1578

1578

APPENDIX F

Scale diagram of Mishimishimaböwei-teri

PLAN, PROFILE, AND PHOTOGRAPHIC COMPOSITE

Column 8 of Appendix A gives the "Residence" of all the Mishimishimaböwei-teri. This refers to the actual place within the village where they sleep.

The photograph (pp. 258-259) is a composite of four photographs taken with a 35mm wide-angle lens, the camera being located halfway between Sections B and C of the village (see plan view, p. 259). While appearing as a "horseshoe" in shape from this angle, the village is actually circular: the 35mm lens has distorted the perspective somewhat. In 1971 the village had no palisade, although its members had active wars with several of its neighbors. The palisade had been gradually dismantled and used as firewood.

The plan view is drawn to scale. Each section's front posts are numbered clockwise, beginning with "1" in each section. The data given in Column 8 of Appendix A refers to these post numbers. The trail that leads to the village bathing area and water supply—Mishimishimaböwei-u—passes between Sections D and E.*

The profile view, and accompanying table, provides the dimensions of the several sections of the village. Depending on the height of the roof above ground level at dimension D, each section has one or more support poles to hold the weight of the roof. These are not drawn in either the plan or the profile views because they are ripped out so frequently for fighting or threats to fights that they change in location very rapidly. A few of them can be seen in the composite photograph.

DIMENSIONS OF MISHIMISHIMABÖWEI-TERI

Dimension	*Section A*	*Section B*	*Section C*	*Section D*	*Section E*	*Section F*
A	1′ 3″	1′ 10″	0′ 0″	1′ 0″	1′ 0″	0′ 0″
B	3′ 0″	4′ 3″	3′ 8″	2′ 4″	3′ 0″	3′ 4″
C	9′ 8″	10′ 3″	11′ 0″	6′ 10″	9′ 2″	9′ 4″
D	14′ 6″	15′ 6″	19′ 7″	11′ 6″	18′ 0″	15′ 2″
E	2′ 0″	6′ 7″	2′ 0″	3′ 0″	3′ 0″	3′ 6″
F	7′ 10″	6′ 2″	7′ 0″	7′ 6″	6′ 10″	6′ 6″
G	10′ 9″	9′ 0″	17′ 6″	8′ 0″	8′ 8″	8′ 8″

* A series of 35mm photographs (taken with a 50mm lens) was also shot from the "survey center" (shown in the plan view) to document the details of construction in each segment of the village. These will be published elsewhere.

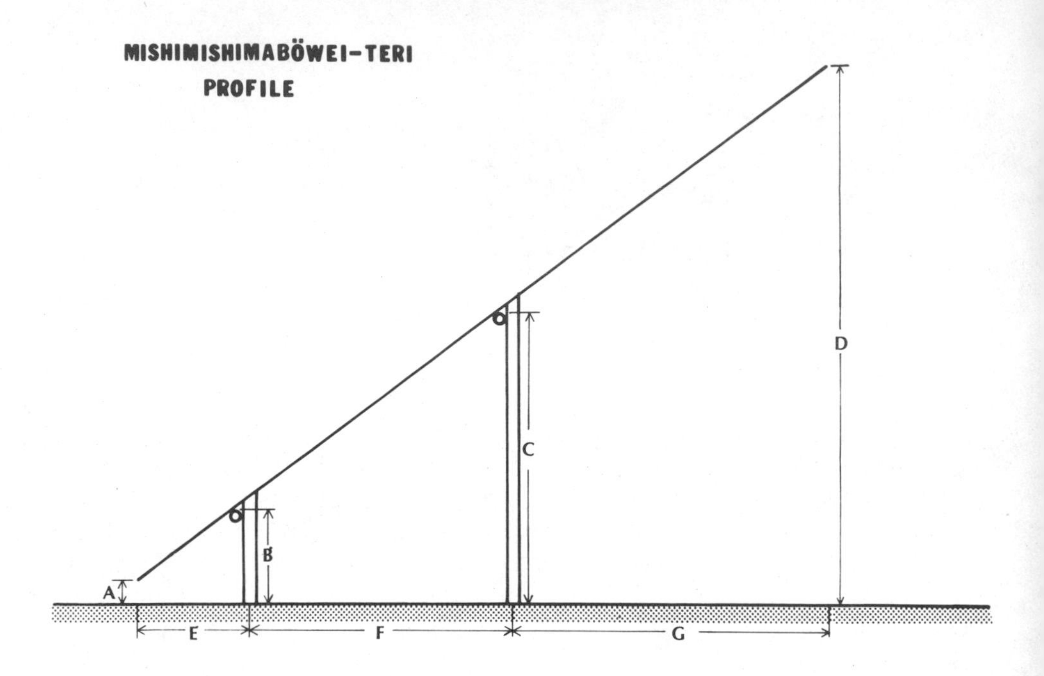

This appendix has several major uses. First, all of the ethnographic films will be referred to by the specific location within this village where they were shot, along with the position of the camera at the time of shooting. Second, the composition of the village and the relationship by kinship group, genealogy, and sleeping place of all individuals can be analyzed in meticulous detail using Appendices A and F (Chagnon and Levin, ms. The complete genealogical relationships are not given in this book). Finally, a scale model of the village can be constructed from these data; a number of architects and public school teachers have indicated an interest in doing this.

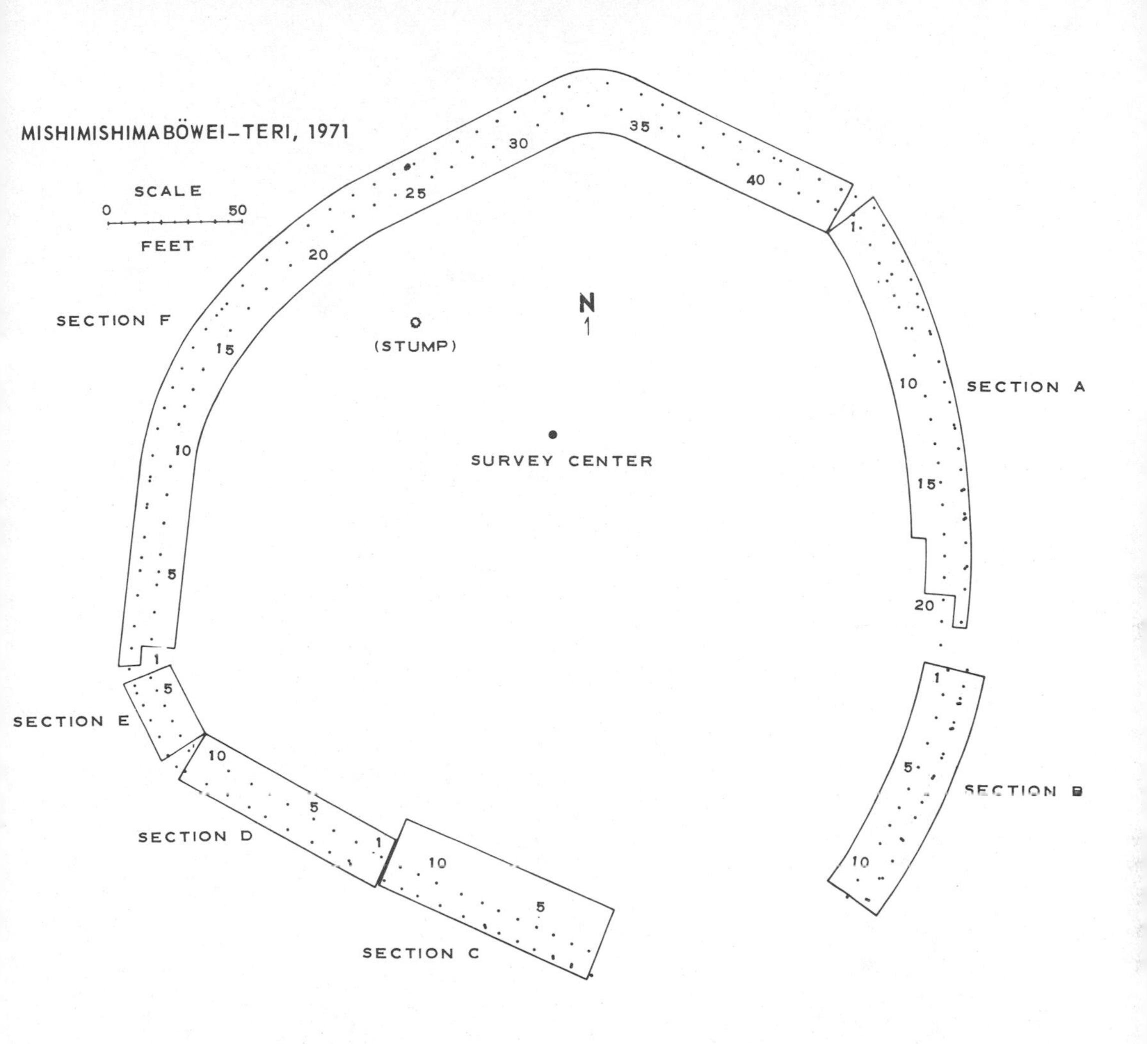

MISHIMISHIMABÖWEI–TERI, 1971
SCALE
0
50
FEET
N
(STUMP)
SURVEY CENTER
SECTION A
SECTION B
SECTION C
SECTION D
SECTION E
SECTION F

APPENDIX G

Ethnographic films on the Yąnomamö

BACKGROUND TO THE FILMS

In 1964, during my first field trip, I realized the importance of taking film on selected aspects of Yąnomamö culture and borrowed a 16mm Bolex camera from the Photographic Department of Instituto Venezolano de Investigaciones Científicas (I.V.I.C.), the institution that served as my host during all my work in Venezuela. I had no training or experience in motion picture filming, but was fairly adept at 35mm still photography. My initial efforts at filming were crude and undisciplined, but some of the resulting footage proved to be useful and of moderately good quality (see the ethnographic portions of the film *Yanomama: A Multidisciplinary Study*, listed below). Although my skill at taking motion picture improved with practice, I realized that I could not, by myself, do justice to the subject and perform effectively as an ethnographer as well. The demands of conventional ethnography were, at many points, incompatible with attempts to obtain a comprehensive film document of important aspects of Yąnomamö culture. I felt that the ethnographic films were of sufficient importance to my overall study that a more ambitious, professional attempt should be made to do the task properly.

Accordingly, I contacted Timothy Asch of Brandeis University in 1967. His philosophy of filming and training in anthropology were such that a collaborative attempt could be worked out. He was aware of the demands of the field because of his previous work in Japan and Africa, and I was, by then, familiar enough with the problems of filmmaking that I could appreciate the difficulties he, as filmmaker, would face.

As a pilot attempt to develop our mutual filming and ethnographic interests, Asch joined me in 1968 to film a Yąnomamö feast and to document aspects of multidisciplinary field studies (See *The Feast and Yanomama: A Multidisciplinary Study*). I selected the feast as the subject to film for several reasons. First, it was a predictable event and I was certain that we would be able to get the film during the course of the field trip. Second, it was a single, specific event that could be put into a larger sociocultural context of village history, politics, and economics. Thus, in addition to providing an excellent subject to illustrate Asch's filmmaking methodology (Asch, 1972; in press), it would result in an ethnographically significant film of considerable use to teachers and researchers alike. Finally, the feast illustrated a number of classic themes in theoretical anthropology —the nature of reciprocity and the historical dimension of alliance formation— and these themes had already been discussed in my written publications. Thus, the film would complement the written material.

We both learned a great deal from the 1968 collaboration and agreed to extend it further on another field trip. Meanwhile, I continued to take a Bolex camera with me on my annual field trips and filmed particular incidents that, when put into a larger, more professionally conceived body of film, would have an ethnographic and pedagogic utility they would have otherwise not had. One such event I filmed was the two-day shamanistic drama given in the film *Magical Death*, which I shot in 1970 while living in Mishimishimaböwei-teri. Taken by itself, this event would be a somewhat bizarre happening. But, when put into the context of all the films Asch and I later shot, and viewed against the written materials, *Magical Death* acquires a different and more comprehensive quality. For example, when seen with the several films on the *Myth of Naro* (described below) and with the several films on the daily life of Dedeheiwä, the shaman whose activities are described in *Magical Death*, it becomes a much more useful film for teaching students about politics, religion, and ritual. The ethnographic facts have not changed, but the context against which they should be viewed has become widely expanded. It is unlikely that written materials alone could have provided the necessary context to make a film like *Magical Death* comprehensible to viewers in introductory anthropology courses.

RECENT FILMING

In 1971 Asch and I again worked together in the field. One important lesson we learned on our 1968 trip was that we had to have a sound man in order to film efficiently. I had been the sound man in 1968, but because I was holding the microphone and the Nagra tape recorder, I was unable to direct Asch's attention to significant events that were outside the field of his vision as he was shooting a particular sequence: every time I opened my mouth, my statements were indelibly recorded on the sound track. We therefore invited Craig Johnson to join us for the 1971 filming and to take all sound. Johnson had been working with me editing the film *Magical Death*.

Before leaving for the field, however, Asch and I drew up a list of significant ethnographic items or events we hoped to film, and we had settled on the village of Mishimishimaböwei-teri, a village whose history, residents, and current political relationships I had previously pieced together from information I had collected during the previous five years. I knew, therefore, who the important people were in the village and how they fitted into the larger social life of the group, and how their village was articulated in trade and political ties to all the villages in that large region. We planned from the outset to concentrate our filming efforts on these individuals and their families, hoping to illustrate the nature of Yąnomamö social life by reference to a small number of concrete examples, filming the same individuals or groups in a wide variety of contexts. The 80,000 feet of film we shot in Mishimishimaböwei-teri in 1971, therefore, constitutes an extension of my long-term study of that village and reflects what both Asch and I feel to be a scientifically and pedagogically sound way to make ethnographic films. The same footage shot by someone else in the same village would be of only marginal educational or scientific value without the other ethnographic information to give the film meaning and context. By the same token, our footage is only of marginal value unless the ethnographic facts that lie behind it are considered as an inseparable matrix against which the interpretation of the film is constantly checked.

PRODUCTION OBJECTIVES

At the present time we have approximately 110,000 feet of film on the Yąnomamö, the great bulk of which was shot in the village of Mishimishimaböwei-teri. Our plans and objectives for producing and distributing the films grow out of our philosophy of ethnographic filming and the several educational and scientific objectives we had in mind when we shot the original footage.

First, the film was shot with definite documentary goals in mind: we will be producing a very large number of short films, approximately thirty-five to forty-five, on special ethnographic topics. This will enable us and our colleagues to select from a wide variety of films for particular courses in anthropology and emphasize very specific and interrelatable ethnographic topics. That is, the teacher/researcher has maximum flexibility in picking films that are relatable to his own interests. Most of these films will be distributed with a minimum amount of interpretation imposed on the soundtrack or in subtitles, but the films will be accompanied by supplementary study guides giving specific details about the events and the individuals who were filmed. A number of these films lend themselves to theoretical or methodological problems in anthropology, and will be treated from those perspectives, both in the films and in the study guides.

Second, we intend to utilize the footage in some of the smaller films to make more general ethnographic films. Thus, we may produce a short, special film about the pattern of meat distribution and later use the same footage in a more general film on social organization, the latter including material about fighting, endocannibalism, feasting, daily activities, headmanship, *and* the social organization of meat sharing. These general films can be used in classes where the instructor wishes to devote more of his course to lectures and readings, but would like to supplement these with a single film that covers a broader range of topics. By extension, excerpts from the several general films could be combined to provide the widest possible coverage of ethnographically significant topics in a single, but perhaps lengthy, film. This is still in the planning stage, and has a very low priority at the moment.

Third, we are developing the film resource in conjunction with John Marshall's similar efforts with his !Kung Bushmen film and will produce a film-based curriculum for use in public school systems. Some of these films will, of course, have great relevance to topics taught at the college level and will be used there as well. Thus, it will be possible, for example, to compare the social organization of meat sharing in both !Kung Bushmen and Yąnomamö society—or any of a wide variety of topics, ranging from ecological adaptation to shamanism and curing.

Fourth, we intend to place a complete, unedited copy of all our footage in a national film archive when such an archive is funded, and the entire body of film will be available to responsible, trained researchers. It will not be long before some of the events shown in the films will become a component of "memory culture" to the Yąnomamö, and the footage will be an extremely valuable and accurate record.

Fifth, the films convey an important dimension of Yąnomamö culture that cannot be adequately captured with the written word. Many of the films focus on individuals and their families in a wide variety of social contexts, and through these films one can gain a more comprehensive and qualitatively unique appreciation of both the individuals and their culture than could be obtained through conventional ethnography. I feel that these films will prove to be useful in communicating to students of anthropology a sense of reality that will encourage them to learn more about other cultures and appreciate them in their own terms.

AVAILABILITY OF THE FILMS

At the present only two of the films are available for purchase or rental. These are:

	Purchase Price
(A) *The Feast*	$75.00
(B) *Yanomama: A Multidisciplinary Study*	$156.00

Both films are sold through the National Audiovisual Center (NAC) in Washington, D.C., and are rented through a large number of university film libraries and other, government film libraries, both in the United States and abroad.

Most of our films are not yet in distribution and will be coming out over the course of the next year or two. Since we do not yet know who the distributors of these new films will be, we invite our colleagues to write to us for a current list of available films and where they can be either purchased or rented:

Film Distribution
Documentary Educational Resources (DER)
24 Dane St.
Somerville, Mass. 02143

LECTURE SLIDES

A number of our colleagues have expressed interest in obtaining a standard set of 35mm transparencies for use in their lectures. We plan to produce a set of slides that will include conventional ethnographic topics such as gardening activities, ceremonial, technology, aggression, shamanism, geography, and daily activities as well as slides that show, by graphs and diagrams, marriage patterns, social organization principles, and demographic characteristics. The slides will be accompanied by a printed list that describes the content of each transparency.

LIST OF FILMS*

1. *The Feast* (1971) (29 min). Currently available. Winner of numerous film awards, including Cine 1970 and First Prize in the 1972 American Film Festival (educational films). This film focuses on alliance practices and how feasting and trading create and maintain political alliances between once-hostile

* The numbers given next to each film title refer to our assigned laboratory number; note that *not all of our titles are listed.*

villages. It illustrates the material presented in Chapter 4 of *The Fierce People* and is widely used in conjunction with that book. See review by Kenneth Kensinger, 1971.

2. *Yanomama: A Multidisciplinary Study.* (1971) (43 min). Currently available. Winner of numerous film awards, including Cine 1971 and Second Prize in the 1972 American Film Festival (educational films), competing in the latter against *The Feast.* This film describes the nature of the multidisciplinary fieldwork conducted by me and my American and Venezuelan colleagues on our 1968 expedition to the Yąnomamö area. The relationship between demography, human genetics, serology, epidemiology, linguistics, physical anthropology, cultural anthropology, and other medical disciplines is graphically shown through the efforts of specialists in these fields as they collect blood specimens, make dental examinations, and participate in other ways in the fieldwork. The film also includes a brief, but comprehensive, description of Yąnomamö culture. It is extremely useful in introductory courses in anthropology where the relationship between physical anthropology, cultural anthropology, and linguistics is given in the classroom. See reviews by Paul Baker (1972) and Michael Hannah (1972).
3. *Magical Death.* Tentatively available in late 1973. This film focuses on the role of the shamam, Dedeheiwä in this case, in curing his co-villagers and sending sickness to enemy villages. The use of hallucinogenic snuff is shown in its daily context. More important, this film illustrates how religion serves political ends and how shamans can manipulate the spirit world to demonstrate their allegiance to allies. Like *The Feast*, this film focuses on one specific event and describes its development in terms of the history of political relationships between two villages, Bisaasi-teri and Mishimishimaböwei-teri, that are entering into a new alliance. It is a very powerful, dramatic film and should be used in conjunction with lectures and/or with one of the mythology films described below (*Myth of Naro*). See review by Eric Wolf, 1972.
4. *The Yąnomamö Myth of Naro as Told by Kąobawä* (17 min). Kąobawä, headman of Bisaasi-teri, relates the same myth, a version that differs slightly from the one told by Dedeheiwä. (No. 29, below). Equally enchanting and humorous, it provides the basis for a comparative examination of two versions of the same myth told by knowledgeable men from different villages.
5. *Ocamo Is my Town* (23 min). This film describes fourteen years of activity by a Salesian priest in an attempt to acculturate a village of Yąnomamö on the Ocamo River. The difference in approach, attitude, and philosophy of this missionary contrasts in many ways with similar approaches made by the members of the New Tribes Mission.
6. *Tug-of-War* (7 min). A group of approximately twenty Mishimishimaböwei-teri villagers play tug-of-war in a rainstorm.
7. *Children in the Rain* (10 min). Approximately sixty children play in the rain to amuse themselves.
8. *Arrows* (9 min). A large group of boys engage in an arrow fight in the village clearing, shooting blunt arrows at each other to learn how to dodge arrows as well as to shoot accurately. The game ends when one of the boys, Möawä's son, is injured and falls to the ground with a minor wound on his cheek. His father breaks up the game by brusquely threatening to "revenge" his son.
9. *The Axe Fight* (10 min). A powerful film about a fight that erupted in Mishimishimaböwei-teri between the members of several different lineages. They attack each other with axes, clubs, and machetes, delivering a number of well-aimed but constrained blows with the blunt ends of their weapons. The remarkable feature of this film is that the organization of the village by lineage composition and marriage alliances is clearly revealed in the

contest: the fighters fall into three groups—lineal descent groups—and align themselves according to marriage bonds between the groups. Ideally suited to discuss the general principles of marriage, descent, and alliance in Yąnomamö society. A detailed description of the genealogical relationship between all significant participants in the fight will be published in an accompanying study guide.

10. *Dedeheiwä Weeds His Garden* (23 min). This is a quiet, sensitive film about one aspect of Dedeheiwä's daily life. He cleans the weeds out of his maturing manioc garden and rests while his wife tenderly delouses him. About a dozen children, most of them his own, crawl over him in their play activities.
11. *New Tribes* (15 min). This film shows dedicated members of the New Tribes Mission attempting to teach the children of Bisaasi-teri their way of life. They describe their philosophy and methods for acculturating the Yąnomamö to Western ways and Christianity.
12. *Dedeheiwä Washes His Children* (15 min). Dedeheiwä takes a number of his young children to the river and washes them carefully and patiently while his sick wife remains in the village.
14. *Children at Reahumou Play* (6 min). A group of children roast meat in a make-believe house in the village clearing and share it with each other in a "distribution" (*reahumou*).
15. *Chopping Wood* (10 min). The irksomeness of daily wood collecting is revealed as a woman patiently and strenuously chops a large log into kindling for her hearth.
16. *Möawä Making a Hammock* (12 min). The village headman, Möawä, patiently works on a hammock while his wife looks on and fondles his leg periodically.
17. *Children's Magical Death* (7 min). A group of young boys, ranging in age from five to ten years, emulate their fathers by pretending to be shamans. They blow large quantities of make-believe drugs (ashes from the hearth) into each others' nostrils and become *shiwariyo* ("intoxicated") from the make-believe drug. They prance as shamans and fall "unconscious" from their efforts.
19. *Grooming before Dedeheiwä's House* (5 min). Dedeheiwä, being a patient and gentle man, is respected but not feared by the village children. A group of them rest in front of his house and delouse each other.
21. *Möawä Burns Felled Timber* (13 min). Möawä and his wife work in the garden gathering up brush and burning it in preparation for planting crops.
24. *Collecting Rasha Fruit* (9 min). A young man patiently and carefully ascends a thorny *rasha* tree to harvest the fruit. He ascends the prickly tree with an ingenious device, a pair of climbing scaffolds.
25. *The River Mishimishimaböwei* (25 min). An in-depth study of the use of the village water supply for bathing and drinking.
26. *Children Making a Hammock* (10 min). A small group of boys learn the techniques of hammock manufacture as they attempt to make a small hammock of spun cotton.
27. *Morning Flowers* (25 min). A quiet, in-depth portrait of the daily activities in Dedeheiwä's and Möawä's section of the village. The women and children quietly make decorations from brilliant yellow blossoms. The kinship and marriage ties between these two families will be described and analyzed in the context of their daily activities.
29. *The Yąnomamö Myth of Naro as Told by Dedeheiwä* (25 min). This film gives the intellectual and spiritual background of Yąnomamö beliefs about the *hekura* spirits and their creation when one of the Ancestors, Naro (Opossum), initiated the use of harmful magic and killed his brother in a fit of passionate jealousy over the later's two beautiful wives. The soundtrack

contains a voice-over simultaneous English translation of the myth as Dedeheiwä tells it in Yąnomamö. It is a delightful, amusing film because the teller "acts out" the roles of the various characters in the myth as he relates the incredible and fabulous deeds they perform.

30. *Kąobawä Trades with the Reyaboböwei-teri* (8 min). Kąobawä and some of his co-villagers make a long trip to the village of Reyaboböwei-teri to feast with them, but by the time they arrive, the meat has been eaten by the hosts. A trade follows, but without much enthusiasm because both hosts and guests are annoyed that the feast could not be held for lack of meat.
31. *Hunting Crickets* (12 min). A group of children perfect their archery by hunting and shooting crickets in the roof thatch with tiny bows and arrows.
32. *Doing Anthropological Fieldwork in Mishimishimaböwei-teri* (50 min). Many of the field methods I describe in this book were filmed in 1971. This film, in addition to illustrating the methods, also brings out the nature of the field situation and how the ethnographer—me—relates to the members of the village in a wide range of circumstances.
33. *Bride Service* (10 min). One of Dedeheiwä's sons returns to the village with a large bird he bagged with his arrow, and a basketful of wild fruits. Dedeheiwä conspicuously shouts across the village for the boy's father-in-law to come and claim the food. The man sends his youngest wife, a girl of some ten years of age, to fetch the items. They are so heavy that she cannot handle them, and she collapses to the ground amid roars of laughter from the others.
34. *Reahumou* (15 min). Möawä killed a tapir and presented it to his brothers-in-law, who comprise an important political bloc in the village. They cook the meat, dismember it, and distribute it to the rest of the village. The women move in after the meat has been distributed, and share out the bones and scraps of skin and fat. Then the dogs arrive after the women are through and pick among the scant leftovers. A detailed examination of the kinship relationships between givers and receivers is provided in the study guide that will accompany the film.
36. *Moon Blood* (10 min). Dedeheiwä recites the myth of the origin of Man from the blood of Moon. Voice-over English translation.
38. *Dedeheiwä's Sons Gardening* (20 min). Two of Dedeheiwä's adult sons plant their newly cleared gardens with plantain, manioc, and other root crops.
39. *Death of a Prominent Man* (15 min). One of Möawä's important agnates from Ironasi-teri died after a visit to a distant village in 1971. Word of his death is passionately and tearfully chanted to the man's brothers-in-law. A year later the brothers-in-law hold a mortuary ceremony for him and mix some of his remains (ashes) in a gourd of plantain soup and consume it.
40. *The Twin Cycle Myths* (25 min). Daramasiwä, a prominent man in Mishimishimaböwei-teri, tells the myth of the Twin Heroes, Omawä and Yoasiwä (Yoawä), and their adventures with Jaguar. Voice-over English translation. [This may be divided into two parts in the final production phase.]

This is only a partial list of films to provide an idea of the resource and its scope. At least two dozen other films are either nearly complete or roughed out in preliminary editing forms. These include ten films on specific myths, five films on technology and cultivation, numerous films on children's activities, and several films on social activities of various kinds, such as wife beating, raiders preparing to depart, gardening activities, and shamanism.

Finally, none of the planned general films have been described. The films will draw on footage from those listed here and other footage not described here.

Glossary

AFFINES: Relatives by marriage. These can also include blood relatives when, for example, a man marries his mother's brother's daughter. The word "cognate" is used to describe those blood relatives who are related by marriage. Cognates also include kinsmen who have a common ancestor.

AGNATES: Persons who trace their relationships to each other through males. This is distinct from cognatic kinship, where the relationship may be traced through either males or females.

BIFURCATING MERGING: A term used to describe the widespread type of kinship system in which an individual's paternal relatives are distinguished (bifurcated) from maternal relatives in the terminology. Furthermore, a single term is used in reference to, for example, father and father's brother; that is, they are merged terminologically into the same kinship category. The Yąnomamö have the most commonly found variant of this type, the Iroquois system. See Iroquois kinship terms.

BILATERAL CROSS-COUSINS: In practical terms, an individual's mother's brother's children together with his father's sister's children. Unilateral cross-cousins are mother's brother's children or father's sister's children, but not both. These two terms are frequently used in discussions of types of marriage rules found in primitive societies. Mother's brother's daughter is a unilateral cross-cousin; properly speaking, she is a matrilateral cross-cousin. In Yąnomamö (Iroquois) kinship this person is simultaneously father's sister's daughter. Some societies have rules forbidding marriage with the latter type of cousin, that is, they have a unilateral cross-cousin marriage rule. See Cross-cousins.

COGNATES: Individuals who are related to each other through either males or females. See Affines, Agnates.

CORPORATION: A group of people sharing some estate, having definite rights with respect to each other and to the estate, and able to demonstrate their membership to that group by citing a recognized rule concerning recruitment.

CROSS-COUSINS: The children of a man and his sister are cross-cousins to each other. The children of a man and his brother are parallel cousins to each other. Similarly, the children of a woman and her sister are parallel cousins.

DEMOGRAPHY: The study of populations with the intention of gathering certain kinds of vital statistics, such as birth rate, death rate, and family size.

DEMONSTRATED KINSHIP: Tracing relationships to kinsmen by citing the putative biological links. See Lineage.

IROQUOIS KINSHIP TERMS: Classifying both kinds of cross-cousins (matrilateral and patrilateral) into the same kinship category and distinguishing them from brothers and sisters and parallel cousins. In most Iroquois systems the parallel cousins are called by the same terms that are used for brothers and sisters.

LEVIRATE: A rule enjoining a man to marry the widow of his dead brother.

LINEAGE: A kinship group comprised of people who trace relationships to each other through either males or females, but not both. If the relationship is traced through males, as among the Yanomamö, the group so defined is a patrilineage. The distinctive feature of the lineage is that the relationships are demonstrated by citing genealogical links. In a clan, relationships are merely stipulated by citing the fact that the two individuals in question belong to the same named kinship group. In short, a clan is a named lineage the members of which do not remember or do not care how they are related to each other biologically. See Demonstrated kinship.

LOCAL DESCENT GROUP: Among the Yanomamö, a group of people who are related to each other patrilineally, who live in the same village, and one of whose major functions is to arrange marriages for the younger members of the group. It is usually the older males of the group who arrange the marriages.

MATRILATERAL: Tracing relationships on the mother's side, such as mother's brother.

PATRILATERAL: Tracing relationships on the father's side, such as father's sister.

REPRODUCTIVE PERFORMANCE: The total number of children sired by a man or born to a woman.

SIBLINGS: One's brothers and sisters.

SORORAL POLYGYNY: A type of marriage in which a man marries two or more women who are related to each other as sisters.

TEKNONYMY: The practice of addressing an individual by the name of one of his children rather than by his own personal name. A kinship term is used in combination with the child's name, such as father of so-and-so.

References cited

Asch, Timothy, 1972, "Making Ethnographic Film for Teaching and Research," *Program in Ethnographic Film (PIEF) Newsletter*, Vol. 3, No. 2, Washington, D.C.: American Anthropological Association.

Asch, Timothy, 1974, "New Methods for Making and Using Ethnographic Film," in *Education and Cultural Process*, George D. Spindler, ed., New York: Holt, Rinehart and Winston, Inc.

Baker, Paul, 1972, Review of 16mm film *Yanomama: A Multidisciplinary Study, American Anthropologist*, 74:195–196.

Carneiro, Robert L., 1961, "Slash-and-Burn Cultivation among the Kuikuru and Its Implications for Cultural Development in the Amazon Basin," in *The Evolution of Horticultural Systems in Native South America: Causes and Consequences. A Symposium*, Johannes Wilbert, ed. Caracas: *Antropológica*, pp. 47–67.

Carneiro, Robert L., 1970, "A Theory of the Origin of the State," *Science*, 169: 733–738.

Carneiro, Robert L., (ms), "Village Fissioning as a Function of Population Size."

Chagnon, Napoleon A., 1966, *Yąnomamö Warfare, Social Organization and Marriage Alliances*, doctoral dissertation, University of Michigan, Ann Arbor: University Microfilms.

Chagnon, Napoleon A., 1968a, *Yąnomamö: The Fierce People.* New York: Holt, Rinehart and Winston, Inc.

Chagnon, Napoleon A., 1968b, "Yąnomamö Social Organization and Warfare," *War: The Anthropology of Armed Conflict and Aggression*, Morton Fried, Marvin Harris, and Robert Murphy, eds. Garden City, N.Y.: Natural History Press, pp. 109–159.

Chagnon, Napoleon A., 1968c, "The Culture-Ecology of Shifting (Pioneering) Cultivation among the Yąnomamö Indians," *Proceedings of the VIII International Congress of Anthropological and Ethnological Sciences*, 3:249–255. (Reprinted in D. Gross, ed., [in press], *Peoples and Cultures of Native South America.* Garden City, N.Y.: Doubleday & Company, Inc.)

Chagnon, Napoleon A., 1971, "The Five-Day Itch," *Michigan Alumnus*, 78 (3): 6–10.

Chagnon, Napoleon A., 1972, "Tribal Social Organization and Genetic Microdifferentiation," in *The Structure of Human Populations*, G. A. Harrison and A. J. Boyce, eds., Oxford: Clarendon Press, pp. 252–282.

Chagnon, Napoleon A., 1973, "Yąnomamö," in *Primitive Worlds*, Washington, D.C.: National Geographic Society, Special Publications Series, pp. 141–183.

Chagnon, Napoleon A., 1973, *Magical Death*, 16mm film.

Chagnon, Napoleon A., and Michael J. Levin, (ms), "Computer methods for analyzing marriage types and marriage frequencies among the Yąnomamö Indians."

Chagnon, Napoleon A., and Michel J. Levin, (ms), "Genealogical, Social and Kinship Distances in a Yąnomamö Village."

Evans-Pritchard, E. E., 1940, *The Nuer.* Oxford: Clarendon Press.

Fried, Morton H., 1967, *The Evolution of Political Society: An Essay in Political Anthropology.* New York: Random House, Inc.

Hajnal, J., 1963, "Concepts of Random Mating and the Frequency of Consanguineous Marriages," *Proceedings of the Royal Society*, 159:125–177.

Hannah, Joel M., 1972, review of *Yanomama: A Multidisciplinary Study, American Journal of Physical Anthropology*, 36:453–454.

Hiorns, R. W., G. A. Harrison, A. J. Boyce, and C. F. Kushemann, 1969, "A Mathematical Analysis of the Effects of Movement on the Relatedness between Populations," *Annals of Human Genetics*, 32:237–250.

Harris, Marvin, 1968, *The Rise of Anthropological Theory.* New York: Thomas Y. Crowell Company.

Kensinger, Kenneth, 1971, review of *The Feast*, *American Anthropologist*, 73: 500–502.

Lathrap, Donald W., 1970, *The Upper Amazon.* New York: Praeger Publishers, Inc.

Lévi-Strauss, Claude, 1963, "The Concept of Archaism in Anthropology," in *Structural Anthropology*, by Claude Levi-Strauss, Chapter VI, New York: Basic Books, Inc., pp. 101–119.

Levin, Michael J., and Napoleon A. Chagnon, (ms), "Computer methods for Anthropologists."

Lewontin, R. C., 1965, "Selection in and of Populations," in *Ideas in Modern Biology*, John A. Moore, ed. *XVI International Congress of Zoology, Proceedings*, Garden City, N.Y.: Natural History Press, pp. 297–311.

Lizot, Jacques, 1970, "Compte rendu de mission chez les Indiens Yanõmam," Paris: *L'Homme*, X(2):116–121.

Lizot, Jacques, 1971a, "Aspects économiques et sociaux du changement culturel chez les Yanõmam, Paris: *L'Homme,* XI(1):32–51.

Lizot, Jacques, 1971b, "Remarques sur le vocabulaire de parente Yanõmam," Paris: *L'Homme*, XI(2):25–38.

MacCluer, J., J. Neel, and N. Chagnon, 1971, "Demographic Structure of a Primitive Population: A Simulation," *American Journal of Physical Anthropology*, 35:193–207.

Morton, N. E., Y. Imaizumi, and D. E. Harris, 1971, "Clans as Genetic Barriers," *American Anthropologist*, 73:1005–1010.

Needham, Rodney, 1962, *Structure and Sentiment.* Chicago: University of Chicago Press.

Neel, James V., 1970, "Lessons from a 'Primitive' People," *Science*, 170:815–822.

Neel, J. V., W. R. Centerwall, N. A. Chagnon, and H. L. Casey, 1970, "Notes on the Effect of Measles and Measles Vaccine in a Virgin-Soil Population of South American Indians," *American Journal of Epidemiology*, 91:418–429.

Neel, J. V., T. Asch, and N. A. Chagnon, 1971, *Yanomama: A Multidisciplinary Study*, (16mm film), Washington, D.C.: The National Audiovisual Center.

Neel, J., T. Arends, C. Brewer, N. Chagnon, H. Gershowitz, M. Layrisse, Z. Layrisse, J. MacCluer, E. Migliazza, W. Oliver, F. Salzano, R. Spielman, R. Ward, and L. Weitkamp, 1971, "Studies on the Yanomama Indians," *Proceedings of the Fourth International Congress of Human Genetics. Human Genetics*, September 1971, pp. 96–111.

Neel, James V. and Richard H. Ward, 1970, "Village and Tribal Genetic Distances among American Indians, and the Possible Implications for Human Evolution," *Proceedings of the National Academy of Sciences*, 65 (2): 323–330.

Nimuendaju, Gurt, 1939, *The Apinaye.* Washington, D.C.: Anthropological Series, Catholic University of America, Vol. VIII.

Nimuendaju, Curt, 1942, *The Šerente.* Los Angeles: Publications of the Frederick Webb Hodge, Anniversary Publications Fund, Vol. IV.

Nimuendaju, Curt, 1946, *The Eastern Timbira.* Berkeley: University of California Publications in American Archaeology and Ethnology, Vol. XLI.

Rose, F. G. G., 1960, *Classification of Kin, Age Structure, and Marriage: A Study in Method and A Theory of Australian Kinship.* Wissenschaften zu Berlin, Völkerkundliche Forschungen 3, Berlin: Akademic Verlag.

Sahlins, Marshall D., 1961, "The Segmentary Lineage: An Organization of Predatory Expansion," *American Anthropologist*, 63:322–345.

Sahlins, Marshall D., 1963, "Remarks on Social Structure in Southeast Asia," *Journal of the Polynesian Society*, 72 (1): 39–50.

Sahlins, Marshall D., 1965, "On the Ideology and Composition of Descent Groups," *Man*, Art. 97, pp. 104–107.

Sahlins, Marshall D., 1968, *Tribesmen.* Englewood Cliffs, N.J.: Prentice-Hall, Inc.

Service, Elman R., 1962, *Primitive Social Organization.* New York: Random House, Inc.

Vayda, Andrew P., 1961, "Expansion and Warfare Among Swidden Agriculturalists," *American Anthropologist*, 63: 346–358.

Ward, Richard H., 1970, *Micro-Differentiation and Genetic Relationships of Yanomama Villages*, doctoral dissertation, University of Michigan, Ann Arbor: University Microfilms.

Ward, Richard H., 1972, "The Genetic Structure of a Tribal Population: The Yanomama Indians. V. Comparison of a Series of Networks," *Annals of Human Genetics.*

Wolf, Eric, 1972, Review of 16mm film *Magical Death, American Anthropologist*, 74:196–198.

Wright, Sewall, 1922, "Coefficients of Inbreeding and Relationship," *American Naturalist*, 56:330–338.